EPHESIANS

EPHESIANS

A Theological Commentary for Preachers

Abraham Kuruvilla

CASCADE *Books* · Eugene, Oregon

EPHESIANS
A Theological Commentary for Preachers

Cascade Books
An Imprint of Wipf and Stock Publishers
199 W. 8th Ave., Suite 3
Eugene, OR 97401

www.wipfandstock.com

ISBN 13: 978-1-4982-0304-3

Cataloging-in-Publication data:

Kuruvilla, Abraham

    Ephesians : a theological commentary for preachers / Abraham Kuruvilla.

    xii + 254 p. ; 26 cm. —Includes bibliographical references and index(es).

    ISBN 13: 978-1-4982-0304-3

    1. Bible. Ephesians—Commentaries. 2. Bible. Ephesians—Homiletical use. I. Title.

BS2695.4 K85 2015

Manufactured in the U.S.A.

04/20/2015

അങ്ങയ്ക്കായ് ദൈവത്തെ സ്തുതിയ്ക്കുന്നു!

To my father
who exemplified for me
the fatherhood
named after
the Father in heaven

സകല പിതൃത്വത്തിനും പേർ വരുവാൻ കാരണമായ

പിതാവിന്റെ സന്നിധിയിൽ ഞാൻ മുട്ടുകുത്തുന്നു.

Ephesians 3:14–15

CONTENTS

ACKNOWLEDGMENTS

The first two commentaries in this series were on two narrative books of the Bible, Mark and Genesis. So it was with the delightful anticipation of a change that I welcomed the current project on the Letter to the Ephesians.

In this venture, my gratitude goes to writers of a number of exegetical commentaries on Ephesians that made my task considerably easier. Many thanks to the scholars who have pored over this letter, thought deeply and carefully about it, and produced tomes of impressive caliber. I am privileged to be standing on some great shoulders.

Students in their first preaching class at Dallas Seminary tackle portions of Ephesians in one of their sermons for that course. Hearing the whole book preached each semester has been particularly stimulating, and my love for the magnificent letter has only grown with time. Its scope is vast and its reach broad, yet it touches the heart: the abundant grace of God, the inexhaustible love of Christ, and the enriching filling by the Spirit, create within believers an unshakeable hope in the grand and glorious plan of God to consummate all things in Christ, one day, soon and very soon!

> Now to Him who is able to do superlatively, beyond all that we ask or think, according to the power that works in us, to Him [be] the glory in the church and in Christ Jesus to all generations, forever and ever. Amen!

Ephesians 3:20–21

Abraham Kuruvilla
Dallas, TX
Feast of the Transfiguration 2014

ABBREVIATIONS

1–2 En.	*1–2 Enoch*
1–4 Macc	1–4 Maccabees
1QM	*War Scroll*
1QS	*Rule of the Community*
'Abot R. Nat.	*'Abot de Rabbi Nathan*
b.	Babylonian Talmud
BDAG	*Greek-English Lexicon of the New Testament and Other Early Christian Literature* (Bauer, Danker, Arndt, Gingrich)
BDF	*A Greek Grammar of the New Testament and Other Early Christian Literature* (Blass, Debrunner, Funk)
Ber.	*Berakot*
Esd	Esdras
Exod. Rab.	*Exodus Rabbah*
Jdt	Judith
Jub.	*Jubilees*
PGM	*Papyri graecae magicae: Die griechischen Zauberpapyri* (Preisendanz)
Pss. Sol.	*Psalms of Solomon*
Qidd.	*Qiddušin*
Sib. Or.	*Sibylline Oracles*
Sir	Sirach/Ecclesiasticus
T. Asher	*Testament of Asher*
T. Benj.	*Testament of Benjamin*
T. Dan	*Testament of Dan*
T. Job	*Testament of Job*
T. Jud.	*Testament of Judah*
T. Naph.	*Testament of Naphtali*
T. Reub.	*Testament of Reuben*
T. Sol.	*Testament of Solomon*
T. Zeb.	*Testament of Zebulun*

Tg. Ps.	*Targum* on the Psalms
Tg. Ps.-J.	*Targum Pseudo-Jonathan*
Tob	Tobit
Wis	Wisdom of Solomon
Yebam.	*Yebamot*

INTRODUCTION

Theology, Goals, Prolegomena

"He made known to us the mystery of His will . . .
the consummation of all things in Christ
—the things in the heavens and the things on the earth."

Ephesians 1:9–10

The goal of preaching is to bring to bear divine guidelines for life from the biblical text upon the situations of the congregation, to align the community of God to the will of God for the glory of God. In other words, the ancient text is to be applied to the modern audience.[1] This is the preacher's burden—the translation from the *then* of the text to the *now* of listeners, with authority and relevance. This commentary is part of a larger endeavor to help the preacher make this move from text to praxis.

Particularly pertinent is how this translation from text to praxis may be conducted with respect to the "bite-sized" portion or quantum of the scriptural text that is employed weekly in the corporate gathering of the body of Christ—the pericope.[2] The pericope is the basic textual unit of Scripture handled in such assemblies, the foundational element of the weekly address from the word of God, and the primary way in which the people of God come into contact with their Scriptures. What in this slice of the sacred text is intended to be carried over into the life of the Christian? What exactly is the author of the text saying that needs to be heard by the listeners of the sermon?[3]

---

1. For more on this concept of preaching, see Kuruvilla, *Privilege the Text!* and *A Vision for Preaching.*

2. While acknowledging its more common connotation of a portion of the Gospels, "pericope" is employed here to demarcate a segment of Scripture, irrespective of genre or length, that forms the textual basis for an individual sermon.

3. For the purposes of this commentary no particular distinction will be made between the divine

THEOLOGY

Elsewhere it was proposed that the critical component of the ancient text to be borne into the lives of the modern audience was the *theology of the pericope,* or what the author is *doing* with what he is saying in the text. This is what moves the people of God to valid application, for pericopal theology is the ideological vehicle through which divine precepts, priorities, and practices are propounded for appropriation by readers.[4] A biblical pericope is therefore a literary instrument inviting men and women to organize their lives in congruence with the theology revealed in that pericope. The goal of any homiletical transaction, thus, is the gradual alignment of the church, week by week, to the theology of the biblical pericopes preached. It is pericope by pericope that the various aspects of Christian life, individual as well as corporate, are progressively brought into accord with God's design for his creation—this is the goal of preaching: faith nourished, hope animated, confidence made steadfast, good habits confirmed, dispositions created, character molded, Christlikeness established.[5]

All such discrete units of pericopal theology together compose a holistic understanding of God and his relationship to his people, and each individual quantum of pericopal theology forms the weekly ground of life transformation by calling for alignment to the requirements of God, resulting in the assimilation of Christlikeness. I call this a *christiconic* hermeneutic.[6] In brief, if each pericope depicts a facet of the ideal world that God would have, each pericope then projects an aspect of divine demand: the precepts, priorities, and practices of God's ideal world, or how that world is to run. Since the only one to comprehensively and perfectly fulfill the requirement of every pericope in Scripture is Jesus Christ, the perfect Man, every pericope is, in essence, projecting what it means to be more like Christ, i.e., a facet of Christlikeness, with the whole canon portraying a plenary image of Christ. After all, it is God's ultimate design to conform his children into the "image" (εἰκών, *eikōn*) of his Son, Christ (Rom 8:29). In a sense, this week-by-week and sermon-by-sermon alignment to the divine demand in each pericope is an imitation of Christ, a movement of the children of God towards increasing Christlikeness. This is at the core of the *theological* hermeneutic followed in this commentary: a hermeneutic specifically geared for preaching. Because children of God are called to conform to the image of Christ, preachers everywhere are, in turn, called to discern the theology of the pericope—i.e., the facet of Christlikeness depicted therein—and apply it to the widely diverse situations of believers across the globe, across millennia, and across cultures, to enable them to imitate the perfect Man, their divine Master.[7] In other words, while pericopal theology tells us *what* Christ looks

and human authors of the biblical text.

4. See Kuruvilla, *Text to Praxis,* 142–90; and "Pericopal Theology," 265–83.

5. Adapted from Tertullian, *Apology* 39.

6. See Kuruvilla, *Privilege the Text!* 238–68.

7. This, of course, is not to deny the fullness of the *deity* of Jesus Christ. But it must be remembered that it is into the likeness of his perfect *humanity* that God's people are being transformed.

like, application in sermons directs us to *how* we can look more like him, in our own particular circumstances.

Indeed, this notion seems to be specifically reflected in Ephesians. In Eph 4:20–21, where expressions unique to the NT occur—"learning Christ" and the idea of "truth in Jesus"—"Paul is referring to Jesus' life as the master performance of the truth and the church's task of studying Jesus' life—his words, his actions, his way with people."[8] And in imitating Christ (or following him), God's people are gradually being conformed to his image, and are progressively inhabiting God's ideal world, abiding by its precepts, priorities, and practices.

In general, most Bible scholars and theologians have not been coming to the text of Scripture with the eyes and heart of preachers; therefore the pericope has been neglected as a textual unit of theological value, and the goal of life transformation— usually a pastoral concern—has tended to be subjugated to other academic interests. The standard interpretive operation adapted by non-preachers is to look *through* the text, employing the text merely as a plain-glass window to glimpse those elements *behind* it: the chronology, history, and cultural elements of the events the text talks about. Rather, I claim that since the text is a *version* of events—and an inspired version at that—what interpreters must do is to consider the text as a stained-glass window depicting the author's agenda in the text itself (i.e., what the author was *doing* with what he was saying). In other words, rather than look *through* the text, the preacher must look *at* the text, for it is the text, not the events behind it, that is inspired and "profitable for teaching, for reproof, for correction, for training in righteousness; that the man of God may be complete, equipped for every good work" (2 Tim 3:16–17). And therefore, to catch the author's agenda—the theology of the pericope—preachers must privilege and attend to the text.[9]

In this regard, Gombis calls for a "narrative approach" rather than a "scientific approach" to this letter.

> Conceiving of Ephesians as a collection of theological artifacts that need to be excavated by interpretive archaeologists digging around for nuggets of truth and arranging them in a doctrinal catalog ends up blinding us to the powerful dynamic of what Paul is *doing* in this letter. Thinking in terms of a drama allows the letter to unfold in all its richness and complexity. A narrative framework includes movement and action. . . . [F]acts might work nicely in a textbook or an encyclopedia, but they do not ignite a compelling vision of living as the people of God in the new world created by the resurrection power of the Spirit. Reading Ephesians as a drama opens up a more robust understanding of what Paul is *doing* in this letter.[10]

Unfortunately, the importance of the pericope and its theology—what the author is *doing* with what he is saying—and its employment in sermons for the edification of

---

8. Gombis, *The Drama of Ephesians*, 16.

9. For more on this, see Kuruvilla, *Privilege the Text!* 90–135.

10. Gombis, *The Drama of Ephesians*, 15 (italics added).

God's people, have generally been neglected by Bible scholars. This work seeks to correct that misdirection.

GOALS

I come to the book of Ephesians, and indeed to all of Scripture, with a reading bias that is Protestant and evangelical. I take it that a biblical author writes purposefully, creating a text with intention, each part of it contributing to the overall theological agenda of the book. This commentary also assumes that every pericope in the canonical Scriptures may be employed for application by the church universal.[11] The divine discourse that the canon is, renders it efficacious for the transformation of the individual and community into the will of God, and it asserts the right of every one of its constituent parts to be heard. Thus, no pericope of Ephesians may be disregarded for the purpose of preaching. And application is, of course, the culmination of the preacher's endeavors.[12] The employment of the Bible as the foundation of the existence, beliefs, and activities of the church assumes that its interpretation *will* culminate in application—life change for the glory of God. Divine discourse always demands a response.

The goal of this commentary, part of a long-term endeavor to rectify the neglect of the pericope and its theology, is essentially this: to develop the theology of each pericope of Ephesians for preachers so that they may be able to proceed from this crucial intermediary to a sermon that provides valid application, i.e., application that is both authoritative and relevant. There is, thus, a twofold aspect to the homiletical transaction: the exposition of the theology of the pericope, and the delineation of how the latter may be applied in real life.

Text **Theology** **Application**

The first move, from text to (pericopal) theology, draws meaning *from* the biblical text with authority; the second, from theology to praxis, directs meaning *to* the situations of listeners with relevance. The advantage of employing pericopal theology as the

11. See Kuruvilla, *Privilege the Text!* 65–86, for a set of "Rules for Reading" that respect the special nature and hermeneutics of the biblical text.

12. Classical rhetoric knows of three directions of audience responses sought by a rhetor: a *judicial* assessment of past events, a *deliberative* resolve with regard to future actions of the audience, or an *epideictic* appreciation of particular beliefs or values in the present. See Quintilian, *Institutio oratoria* 3.7–9; Anaximenes, *Rhetorica ad Alexandrum* 1421b; Aristotle, *Rhetoric* 1.3.1. Sermonic application, in parallel to this three-fold shape of rhetorical purpose, may also be considered broadly as responses culminating in a change of mind (a response of cognition), a change of action (a response of volition), or a change of feeling (a response of emotion). For reasons of clarity and utility, applications in sermons are best conveyed as imperatives (as are the examples in the preaching outlines of this commentary). Such imperatives may, of course, depending on the preacher, be explicit or implicit in the actual sermon.

intermediary between text and praxis is that its specificity for the chosen text makes possible a weekly movement from pericope to pericope, without the tedium of repetition of theological themes, but with a clear progression and development of distinct theological ideas as one preaches through a book. In sum, the theology of the pericope (a crystallization of which is labeled "Theological Focus" in this commentary) functions as the bridge between text and praxis, between the circumstances of the text and those of the reading community, enabling the move from the *then* to the *now*, from text to application. The resulting transformation of lives reflects a gradual and increasing alignment to the values of God's kingdom (or a gradual and increasing approximation of Christlikeness), as pericopes are sequentially preached. Thus, a pericope, as a quantum of the biblical text, is more than *informing*; it is *transforming*, for as the people of God adopt its theological values, they are becoming rightly oriented to God's will, and more closely reflecting Christlikeness.

Such a conception of preaching should not cause one to construe divine demand as merely a litany of dos and don'ts that a capricious God burdens his people with. Not at all! In fact, there is no compulsion to obey, although there are strong incentives to do so, both positive and negative. Instead, God's call to be aligned with his demand is a gracious invitation to inhabit his ideal world, and to enjoy its fullness of blessing, in the presence of God. It is a divine offer that should capture our imaginations and set afire our affections for God's ideal world, for "our action emerges from how we *imagine* the world."[13] This vision of the good life captivates us not with propositions and points but with "a picture of what it looks like for us to flourish and live well" in every facet of our existence—a vision cast by the preacher from the word of God: pericopal theology.[14] This is the vision of a *world in front of the text,* God's ideal world, painted by Scripture, and portrayed in preaching—a glimpse of the divine kingdom. And as this world is gradually unveiled by faithful preaching,

> [t]he goods and aspects of human flourishing painted by these alluring pictures of the good life begin to seep into the fiber of our . . . being (i.e., our hearts) and thus govern and shape our decisions, actions, and habits. . . . Attracted by it and moved toward it, we begin to live into this vision of the good life and start to look like citizens who inhabit the world that we picture as the good life. We become little microcosms of that envisioned world as we try to embody it in the here and now.[15]

It is the biblical canon, preached by the leader of the people of God in the context of their worship of God, that portrays what this divine world and kingdom looks like, how it functions, and how the community is to inhabit it. Pericope by pericope, the theological picture of the world is unveiled. This is the world God would have; and this is the kind of people God would have us be.

---

13. Smith, *Imagining the Kingdom*, 31–32.

14. Smith, *Desiring the Kingdom*, 53.

15. Ibid., 54.

This work does not intend to lead preachers all the way to a fully developed sermon on each pericope; rather, it seeks to take them through first move from text to (pericopal) theology: the *hermeneutical* aspect of sermon preparation. Though that is the primary focus, the commentary does provide two "Possible Preaching Outlines" for each pericope, to advance preachers a few more steps closer to a sermon. However, preachers are left to work out this second move from theology to sermon/application (the *rhetorical* aspect of sermon preparation) on their own, providing appropriate moves-to-relevance, specific application, illustrations, etc., all of which can be done only by the shepherd who knows the flock well. Beyond a few general guidelines, it is impossible for a third party to determine what exactly specific application looks like for a particular audience. That task is between the preacher, the Holy Spirit, and the congregation. Therefore, this is not a "preaching" commentary, in the usual sense. Rather it is a "theology-for-preaching" commentary, i.e., a work that seeks to undertake an extremely focused interpretation of the text, one that moves the preacher from pericope to theology, en route to a sermon. In that sense, this is a "theological" commentary, with theology defined as *pericopal theology* (see "Theological Focus of the Pericope" throughout this commentary).

This commentary is primarily geared for those interested in preaching through Ephesians. While there might be many types of sermons possible from Ephesians, this work will seek to help the preacher proceed pericope by pericope, by isolating the theology of the pericope and discerning the momentum and development of the themes pericope by pericope. Ephesians is broken down into twelve pericopes, best preached in back-to-back sermons, so that the thrust and momentum of the whole book might be respected.[16]

Commentaries were described by Ernest Best as "the backbone of all serious studies of scripture."[17] Therefore, it is hoped that not only preachers, but all interested laypersons, Sunday school teachers, and others who teach Scripture will find this commentary—a small vertebra in that spinal column—helpful. For that matter, if application is the ultimate goal of Bible study of any kind and at any level, a work such as this promises to be useful even for those working their own way through Ephesians devotionally. To help students along, the entire text has been translated, with particular attention to the word plays, structural elements, and other linguistic clues to the theology of each pericope. The result is a bit more wooden than other English translations, but I believe that for the purposes of engaging the *doings* of the author in the text, a

---

16. The essence of the hermeneutic employed in this work is essentially the same as that used for my earlier commentaries on Mark and Genesis (see Kuruvilla, *Mark* and *Genesis*). While the genre of Ephesians is, of course, different, for the purposes of a preaching commentary, the hermeneutic applied is similar to the ones in the series preceding this. In any genre, by this theological hermeneutic, a synthetic approach is adopted with a view to discerning what the author is *doing* with what he is saying. Rather than leave the reader/preacher at the level of analysis (the common terminus of most critical commentaries), I have sought to go further integrating the products of analysis in order to catch the thrust (theology) of the text, pericope by pericope. In this, the study of letter is not very different from that of story.

17. Best, "The Reading and Writing of Commentaries," 358.

translation that is close to the original text as much as possible is invaluable. Which brings me to another point: while a working knowledge of Greek will be very handy for the reader, Greek terms and phrases, wherever referred to in the commentary, have been both transliterated and translated, in order to enable those not as facile with the original language to use this work efficiently.

Needless to say, in all sermonic enterprises, quality and depth and intensity of the preaching go only so far towards achieving the spiritual formation of listeners. Augustine (*De doctrina christiana* 4.27.59) noted wisely: "But whatever may be the majesty of the style [of the preaching], the life of the speaker will count for more in securing the hearer's compliance," not to mention the divine work of the Spirit in the hearts of listeners. Therefore, this commentary is submitted with the prayer that preachers, the leaders of God's people, will pay attention to their own lives first and foremost, as they work through Ephesians, seeking to align themselves to God's demand in each pericope of the book, thus becoming, in the power of the Spirit, more Christlike.

PROLEGOMENA

With the goal of maximizing the benefit-to-size ratio, this commentary will not repeat matters discussed extensively in standard works on Ephesians—historical criticism, redaction criticism, and textual criticism—unless they are immediately relevant to the theological interpretation of the pericope at hand. Neither will this work dwell unduly upon the authorship, date, and postulated sources of Ephesians, abundant information on which may be unearthed from standard commentaries on the book.[18] With Stephen Fowl, I heartily agree: "I have to some extent risked a lesser degree of attention to scholarly disputes around aspects of Ephesians in favor of keeping my attention focused more closely on displaying the argument of Ephesians."[19] However, at the very beginning of the letter to the Ephesians, one encounters a major text-critical problem, in 1:1. Since it deals with authorship and provenance, I will address it here in the prolegomena.

Destination

For Eph 1:1, most manuscripts have τοῖς ἁγίοις τοῖς οὖσιν ἐν Ἐφέσῳ καὶ πιστοῖς ἐν Χριστῷ Ἰησοῦ (*tois hagiois tois ousin en Ephesō kai pistois en Christō Iēsou*, "to the saints who are in Ephesus and believers in Christ Jesus"). But major witnesses like 𝔓46 (third century—the earliest manuscript of Ephesians), and ℵ* and B* (both fourth century), among others, omit ἐν Ἐφέσῳ, leaving an awkward syntax: "to the saints who are [. . .] and/also believers in Christ Jesus." The reason for the omission is inexplicable. To be sure, the letter might have been a circular, directed to different churches, with the name of the city to be filled in, but there is no extant copy with the

---

18. See, for instance: Hoehner, *Ephesians*; O'Brien, *Ephesians*; Lincoln, *Ephesians*; Thielman, *Ephesians*; Best, *Ephesians*; Snodgrass, *Ephesians*; Barth, *Ephesians*.

19. Fowl, *Ephesians*, 2.

name of another city tacked on.[20] Moreover, traditional readings of the text unanimously accept the inclusion of ἐν Ἐφέσω. According to John Chrysostom (*Homilies on Ephesians,* Argument), Paul was the author and the Ephesians were the recipients, to whom Paul "entrusted . . . his profoundest concepts." Harold Hoehner concludes that it is improbable to exclude the Ephesian address from 1:1 on the basis of just three ancient manuscripts.[21]

Chrysostom also was full of praise for the letter, "full of sublime thoughts and doctrines" (*Homilies on Ephesians,* Argument). Modern commentators are not far behind him, though author and recipients continue to be debated over. Hoehner called Ephesians "one of the most influential documents in the Christian church," while O'Brien saw it as "one of the most significant documents ever written." "The divinest composition of man," declared the poet Coleridge. The "quintessence of Paulinism," was Bruce's assessment, while Snodgrass pronounced it "[a] bombshell."[22]

Ephesians consistently attempts to keep readers' focus on the cosmic scope of its drama, particularly, the consummation by God of all things in Christ (1:10).

> [We] desperately need a heavenly vision of reality so that we will not be hood-winked into thinking that life is all about maintaining social status and accumulating stuff. Our default behavior is to interpret the world and our lives according to our own earthly vision of reality, taking into account only that which we can see and account for in natural terms. Simply by living in this world and going through our day-to-day patterns of life the conviction is subtly reinforced to us that this is all there is. We come to think and live as if everything that happens in our lives has only earthly causes, as if the real entities running the world and ordering our lives are national powers, corporate entities or the companies for which we work. It is supremely difficult, as many of us have come to see, or at least we can say that it is not natural, to envision our lives from the conviction that Christ is cosmic ruler of all things.[23]

In a sense, then, Ephesians seeks to disabuse us of the notion that everything in the universe is centered around our own needs and devices. Rather, God is at the center of it all, the universe is his stage, and his plans for the cosmos are being fulfilled. In this grand and glorious plan, however, God has deigned to include humans, and how we are to align ourselves with this great divine design is the thrust of the letter to the Ephesians.

---

20. See 1 Pet 1:1; Rev 1:4 for circular epistles. See Hoehner, *Ephesians,* 144–48, for an excursus on the textual problem in Eph 1:1. He observes that the omission is limited to the Alexandrian text-type, rendering the lacuna suspect; there is wide geographical support for the inclusion of the phrase (ibid., 146).

21. Ibid.

22. Ibid., 1; O'Brien, *Ephesians,* 1; Coleridge, *Specimens of the Table Talk,* 82; Bruce, "St. Paul in Rome. 4," 303; Snodgrass, *Ephesians,* 17.

23. Gombis, *Ephesians,* 23.

Style

Surprisingly enough for a letter, Ephesians lacks the typical epistolary form: there are no personal greetings, and only general topics are addressed, rather than any immediate issue dealing with the Ephesian congregation. The overall style appears to be quite liturgical, with repetitions and parallelisms (synonymous words and notions linked with "and," 1:8; 2:1; 6:14–16; or linked with genitives—for instance, when dealing with power, 1:19; 3:7; 6:10; with God's will, 1:5, 11; or with peace, 2:14, 15, 17; etc.), and long drawn-out sentences, with multiple relative clauses and participial phrases giving the whole document a sense of convolutedness (1:3–14; 1:15–23; 2:1–7; 3:1–7; 4:11–16; 6:14–20); often it is hard to decipher the precise relationship between subordinate clauses. As well, one can spy rhetorical figures such as paronomasia and alliteration, and numerous prepositional phrases with ἐν (*en*, "in/with").[24] However, considering the grandness of the subject matter, its doxological and prayerful tone, these stylistic idiosyncrasies do not seem at all out of place: it has a liturgical, often worshipful tone. In any case, Ephesians is a magnificent work: "The clear structure and beautiful unity of the epistle, the force with which decisive points are made, and the warmth of devotion and concern, above all the grandeur of the praise given to God on the ground of the love he has demonstrated to enemies and strangers—these elements reveal the hand of a genius and master."[25]

Authorship

The letter itself claims to have been written by Paul: 1:1 and 3:1 mention him by name. The author appears to know his audience: he has heard of their faith and love (1:15; also see 3:2—*they* have heard of Paul's stewardship of the gospel), he gives thanks and intercedes for them, and asks for their prayers in return (1:16; 6:19–20), and seems familiar with how they have been taught in days past (4:21). Of course, the fact that he has only *heard* of the Ephesians' spiritual state could indicate his distance from them, but this is best explained by the fact that, if the letter were written by Paul, it was composed at least seven years after the apostle had last been in that city (see Acts 24:27; 27:9; 28:11, 30). During that gap, there might well have been significant changes in the house churches in Ephesus, as well as new converts, new leaders, new issues. Ancient attestation has consistently been part of the external evidence pointing to Pauline authorship. The Muratorian Canon, several church fathers, and also third-century Gnostic texts from Nag Hammadi cite it as a Pauline letter.[26]

In the last three centuries, however, this traditional view been challenged.[27] Among the arguments made against Pauline authorship are: less personal presence;

---

24. See Lincoln, *Ephesians,* xlv–xlvi.

25. Barth, *Ephesians,* 50.

26. See Tertullian, *Monogamy* 5, and *De praescriptione haereticorum* 36; Origen, *Against Celsus* 3.20; Basil the Great, *Adversus Eunomium* 2.10. Polycarp, *To the Philippians* 12.1, labels Eph 4:26, along with Ps 4:5, as "Scripture"—the first NT book to be so labeled by the early church fathers.

27. Hoehner, *Ephesians,* has sixty-one pages on the debate about authorship (ibid., 1–61)!

differing theological emphases (there is less in Ephesians on the death of Christ and on dying with Christ, but more on resurrection and exaltation; more on a realized eschatology that sees the future as almost in place; less on the local church, more on the universal body of Christ: Eph 1:22; 3:10, 21; 4:4; 5:23–25, 27, 29, 32); a language and style dissimilar to that of the undisputed letters (many *hapax legomena*; vocabulary more similar to that of post-apostolic literature; etc.); and the close relationship of Ephesians to Colossians, suggesting that one was copied from the other by a non-Pauline scribe.[28] But these issues are all eminently resolvable.

The impersonal nature of the letter might be explained, as noted, by Paul's long absence from Ephesians.[29] There are no personal greetings at the end of 2 Corinthians, Galatians, the Thessalonian letters, and Philippians, either. But on the other hand, neither does Paul ask his readers to pray for him in 1 and 2 Corinthians, Galatians, or Philippians; he does in Eph 6:19–20. Perhaps Paul did expect the letter to gain a wider hearing beyond those located in Ephesus (see Col 4:16 for example). His prayers, in any case, seem to indicate at least some familiarity with the church there (Eph 1:16; 6:19–20). To a great extent, the content of this letter explains the difference in language and style, as well as emphases, from other Pauline missives.

Ephesians has 2,429 words, demonstrating a vocabulary of 530, of which forty-one words are unique to Ephesians in the NT; eighty-four are found only in Ephesians and nowhere else in Paul, though present elsewhere in the NT. In comparison, Galatians has 2,220 words, displaying a vocabulary of 526, of which thirty-one are unique to this book; eighty are not found elsewhere in Paul, though they show up in the NT. That makes Ephesians and Galatians quite comparable in terms of language and vocabulary, but Galatians is accepted as being Pauline.[30] In any case, statistics can be misleading. As was mentioned, special contexts and special concepts (and special moods and special relationships with readers) require special words, especially when you have a specially gifted writer doing the composing. For instance, the dermatology-related words—of particular interest to me as a practicing skin physician—"spot" and "wrinkle" found in 5:27 are unique: the first is found only here and in 2 Pet 2:13; the second only in Ephesians in the NT. As well, the martial context in Eph 6:11–17 demanded the deployment of some rarely used words: "armor," "schemes," "world-forces," "shoeing," "preparation," "shield," "arrows," "helmet," etc. After all, "[a]uthors are not machines that duplicate vocabulary and style."[31]

> To suggest that he could not have written in this vein is really to question Paul's resourcefulness. These sentences are not out of character with his other letters. Perhaps in a more reflective mood, when there were no major or pressing pastoral problems, the apostle deliberately used exalted liturgical language (some of

---

28. Lincoln, *Ephesians*, lxii–lxvi.

29. Though, it must be admitted that, in the letter to the Romans, whom he had never met, there is an extensive list of personal greetings in its conclusion.

30. Hoehner, *Ephesians*, 40.

31. Ibid., 61.

which may have been borrowed from early Christian worship) as he praised God . . . and edified his predominantly Gentile readers.[32]

The differing emphases between Ephesians and other Pauline letters also simply reflect the differences in content and in the exigencies of the situations he was writing to. In addition, there is the striking uniqueness of the extended blessing of Eph 1:3–14, quite appropriate for the theological thrust of the letter. This paean of praise stands out, with no parallel in Paul's other writings. It is highly doubtful that an imitator wanting to pass off Ephesians as a Pauline composition would make his copied letter commence in a fashion unlike that of any other epistle of Paul.[33]

One of the strongest arguments against Pauline authorship is the relationship of Ephesians to Colossians; apparently the former depends heavily upon the latter in verbiage and structure. Of course, there is nothing to rule out the possibility that the same author wrote both, and for fairly similar audiences. In any case, the closest parallel is between Eph 6:21–22 and Col 4:7–8, which are virtually identical in twenty-nine consecutive words. Elsewhere there are only three locations where the parallel extends to seven words, and only two where five words correspond.[34] And out of a total of 2,429 and 1,574 words for Ephesians and Colossians, respectively, only 246 words are shared between the two, most of them conjunctions, pronouns, prepositions, and proper nouns.[35] All of this does not lend much credence to the theory of duplication of Colossians by a non-Pauline copier to produce the Ephesian letter. Similarity of content is sufficient to explain the similarity of vocabulary.

The fact is that in the first few centuries of the early church, apocryphal and pseudepigraphical apostolic letters were quite rare.[36] If Ephesians were pseudonymous, it would be impossible for its author to write in such splendid fashion, à la Paul, without his being well known in the early church. "[E]arly Christians knew how

---

32. O'Brien, *Ephesians*, 7–8.

33. Long sentences elsewhere in Paul are found in Rom 3:21–26; 5:12–18; 11:33–39; 1 Cor 1:4–8; Phil 1:3–7; 2 Thess 1:3–10.

34. Also see Eph 1:1–2 and Col 1:1–2; Eph 1:7 and Col 1:14; Eph 2:5 and Col 2:13; Eph 3:2 and Col 1:25; Eph 3:9 and Col 1:26; Eph 4:16 and Col 2:19; Eph 4:32 and Col 3:13; Eph 5:5–6 and Col 3:5–6; Eph 5:19–20 and Col 3:16–17; Eph 6:1–4 and Col 3:20–21; Eph 6:5–9 and Col 3:22—4:1. O'Brien, *Ephesians*, 8–9.

35. Hoehner, *Ephesians*, 31. Also, to compare the two letters further, there are thirty-eight words unique to Colossians and not found elsewhere in the NT; sixty-three words in Colossians not found elsewhere in Paul, but do occur in the NT (forty-one and eighty-four for these categories, respectively, in Ephesians). Considering Ephesians and Colossians together, of the 246 words they share, eleven are unique to these two books (not occurring elsewhere in the NT) and twenty-one are not found elsewhere in Paul, but present in other books of the NT (ibid.). These low numbers make it unlikely that one book was cribbed from the other.

36. Bauckham, "Pseudo-Apostolic Letters," 487. Most known pseudepigraphical works were composed centuries after the lives of those who are its protagonists; many works are apocalyptic. And none of them were taken seriously by Judaism (*Enoch, Testament of the Twelve Patriarchs,* etc.) or by the early church (*Letter of Aristeas, Epistle of Jeremiah, Epistle to the Laodiceans,* etc.). Tertullian, *Baptism* 17, rejects *The Acts of Paul* for being "falsely so named." Even as late as the Second Council of Nicaea (787 CE), it was thought best to proscribe "a forged Epistle to the Laodiceans . . . which our fathers rejected as being alien." See *Sacred Councils: Book 8,* 6.5 (1125–26).

to pass on the teachings of an authority figure without using the literary device of pseudonymity."[37] And they also knew the dangers of falsifying authorship: 2 Thess 2:1–2 has Paul warning of "a message or a letter as if from us." In 2 Thess 3:17 he draws attention to the greeting in his own handwriting, perhaps as a sign of authenticity. And for one recommending the need for truthfulness in Ephesians (Eph 4:15, 24–25; 5:9; 6:14), it would hardly be in character to promote a letter purporting to have come from another.[38]

Internally, the vocabulary, style, themes present, and the use of OT citations, seem to lean in the direction of Paul's authorship. In any case, the argument for authorship is, for preaching purposes, somewhat moot. "[I]t is not immediately evident that there are actual instances in Ephesians where one would interpret a word or phrase differently based on the judgment that Paul did or did not write Ephesians."[39] While there is certainly something to be said for authorial motives as one interprets a text, such motives are not to be brought in from the outside, even if one can access such motives accurately. Rather assessments about motive must be made from the text itself, from its semantics and its pragmatics. Besides grammatical, linguistic, and rhetorical conventions operating in the culture, and identification of historical and geographical referents, recourse to external information is not essential, certainly not an author's external motive for writing the text.[40] In any case, whether it was Paul who wrote the letter or one of his disciples, the background data would not change significantly. "Ephesians plays the role it does in the life and worship of Christians because it is

37. O'Brien, *Ephesians*, 42–43.

38. Ancient cultures did not look too kindly upon forgeries of this kind. Herodotus, *Histories* 7.6, reports on Onomacritos who was exiled for having interpolated an oracle in the works of a pre-Homeric poet, Musaeus. Suetonius, *Divus Claudius* 9.2 and 15.2, calls for severe punishment for forgers; the latter text describes a punishment by amputation. The late second century bishop of Antioch, Serapion, prohibited the *Gospel of Peter* from being read in a local church, declaring that while receiving Peter and the other apostles as Christ himself, "those writings which falsely go under their name . . . we reject"—he called such works *pseudepigrapha*, "false writings" (Eusebius, *Historia ecclesiastica* 6.12.2–3). Origen rejected a treatise entitled the *Doctrine of Peter,* for it was "not composed by Peter or by any other person inspired by the Spirit of God" (*First Principles* Preface 8). All of this shows that the early church leaders were not gullible or credulous about these matters. And if they were inclined to copy material, ancient writers seem to have been comfortable with acknowledging the fact. The author of 2 Macc 2:23 admits that he is condensing the five-volume work of Jason of Cyrene into a single book. It appears that the ancient perspective on authentic writings was not very different contemporary ideas of "literary proprietorship" (Hoehner, *Ephesians*, 47–48).

39. Fowl, *Ephesians*, 11.

40. Semantics essentially deals with the language and structure of the text; pragmatics with what the author *does* with the semantic elements. For the latter, pertaining to hermeneutics for homiletics, see Kuruvilla, *Privilege the Text!* 31–54. The author's internal or *proximal* motive, i.e., what an author *does* with what he says is part of the pragmatics of the text. This is critical to determine, of course, but *from the text itself.* On the other hand, the motive external to the text, the *distal* motive for writing any text—"fame and fortune, or failing that, tenure," as Fowl wryly puts it (*Ephesians*, 13)—is, for the most part, irrelevant to textual interpretation. I accept the veracity and integrity of the human authors of Scripture and do not expect to be deceived by them in their writings that have been accepted as part of the Christian canon: their external motives, whatever they might be, are honest and trustworthy.

part of the canon, not because it is written by Paul or not written by Paul. The text is canonical, Paul is not."[41]

Barth sums up the controversy well: "In view of the insufficient linguistic and historical arguments, and of the prejudicial character of the theological reasons exhibited against Ephesians, it is advisable for the time being to still consider Paul its author."[42] So, in conclusion, there seems to be adequate evidence to construe Ephesians as having originated from the pen of Paul. One can at least defer to the inspired author's desire to imply that Paul is the writer and respect that intent. In any case, for preaching purposes, it does not make a difference.

Purpose

The letter was likely written by Paul during his Roman imprisonment, while awaiting trial, in ca. 61–62 CE, and at the same time as Colossians and Philemon (Acts 24:27; 25:6–28:31; Eph 3:1; 4:1; 6:20–21). He had made a first trip to Ephesus in 52 CE (Acts 16:6; 18:18–21), and a second in 53 CE; he remained there for two and a half years, till 56 CE (Acts 18:18–21; 19:1–20:12; 1 Cor 16:8). In 57 CE he visited with the leaders of Ephesian church at Miletus on his way to Jerusalem from Corinth (Acts 19:21; 20:3–38). It is quite possible that there were only Jewish Christians when that church was established (Acts 18:19–21, 27). This letter, though, is to Gentiles (Eph 2:11; 3:1; 4:17); obviously written later, it appears to be addressed to a congregation much changed from Paul's earlier visits, though they certainly knew of him (1:1; 3:1, 2, 7, 8, 13; 4:1; 6:20–22).

O'Brien notes that "[o]f all the letters in the Pauline corpus, Ephesians is the one that appears to be the most general and least situational. No particular problem appears to be addressed in the epistle, and it does not have the same sense of urgency or response to a crisis as do Paul's other letters."[43] This has produced a number of ideas about the purpose of the letter.

Arnold explains the purpose of Ephesians as having to with the pervasive influence of magic, astrology, and mystery religions in the environs of the Ephesian Christians, living under the perceived influence of the city's patron goddess, Artemis.[44] Likely, many who came to Christ entered the church ferrying such ideas in, creating the temptation of syncretism and the conflation of Christian faith and magical beliefs. That might explain why there is more on these "powers" in the letter to the Ephesians than in other Pauline epistles (though see Rom 8:38; 1 Cor 2:6–8; 10:19–21; 15:24–26; Gal 4:3, 9; Phil 2:10). Though these powers are exerting their forces for evil against hu-

---

41. Fowl, *Ephesians*, 9.

42. Barth, *Ephesians*, 49.

43. O'Brien, *Ephesians*, 49.

44. Arnold, *Ephesians*, 123. "Of all ancient Graeco-Roman cities, Ephesus, the third largest city in the Empire, was by far the most hospitable to magicians, sorcerers, and charlatans of all sorts" (Metzger, "St. Paul and the Magicians," 27). In Acts 19:18–19, under the influence of Paul's preaching, local Ephesian practitioners of the black arts burned their books, which were valued at 50,000 pieces of silver, about 50,000 days' worth of wages!

manity (Eph 2:1–3), Ephesians teaches that God's power is superior and Christ is supreme, and that access to this power is possible for the child of God (1:19–23; 4:8–10; 6:10–20). All other "powers"—forces of evil—had been subjected to the authority of Christ, and therefore the believer could withstand their virulent opposition.[45] Besides, these inimical powers are controlled by God and their final overthrow has already been announced (Rev 20:3).

Others consider unity as the theme of Ephesians; "unity," ἑνότης (*henotēs*), occurs in the NT only in Eph 4:3, 13; "one" occurs fourteen times: in 2:14, 15, 16, 18; 4:4 (×3), 5 (×3), 6, 7, 16; 5:33. Moreover, there are the συν- (*syn-*) words that also show up fourteen times, bespeaking a sense of unity with the use of that preposition ("with"). Most of them deal with union with Christ. No surprise then, that "in Christ" or synonymous expressions are found thirty-six times in Ephesians to indicate the sphere in which such unity is to be accomplished. And "church" is used nine times: 1:22; 3:10, 21; 5:23, 24, 25, 27, 29, 32. In addition, there are a number of metaphors employed for this community of God's people: biological (1:22, 23; 2:16; 4:4, 12, 16; 5:23, 30), architectural (2:20–22; 4:12, 16), and sociological (5:21–33). It is in this body that humanity is united.

The emphasis on the church and its unity might explain the fact that "love" appears to be a major theme in this letter, the ground of unity within the church. As a noun and as a verb it occurs twenty times. Ten of the twenty-four instances of the verb in all of Paul (including the Pastoral Epistles) are found in Ephesians; and ten of the seventy-five occurrences of the noun in Paul's writings show up here (second only to the fourteen times in 1 Corinthians). Hoehner calculates that for every thousand words of Ephesians, the noun or verb shows up 8.23 times, compared to the 3.31 times per thousand words in all the other letters of Paul: Ephesians talks of love with more than twice the frequency than do the rest of Paul's writings.[46] "Unity without love is possible, but love without unity is not."[47]

All of these notions—power, unity, and love—may be integrated into a central message that is magnificent in design and cosmic in scope. Cosmic reconciliation of all things is the theme of this letter, established early on in 1:9–10—the goal is clearly stated there: *the consummation of all things in Christ—the things in the heavens and the things on the earth in him.* The integral relation between the heavens and the earth should not be missed. Not only does God's plan encompass the entirety of the cosmos, what happens in one of those spheres impacts what happens in the other; there is a close connection between the two domains, as Ephesians often implies. And, perhaps no less important is the fact that God's people are part of a larger drama than they can even imagine. Human history, particularly of the people of God, is the arena for vast battle—one that has *already* been won . . . but *not yet.* If the children God ever felt their

45. Arnold, *Ephesians*, 167–72.

46. Hoehner, *Ephesians*, 104. The breakdown is as follows—God's love: 1:6; 2:4 (×2); 3:17; 6:23; Christ's love: 3:19; 5:2, 25; believers' love for one another: 1:4, 5; 4:2, 15, 16; 5:2, 25, 28 (×3), 33; and believers' love for Christ: 6:24.

47. Ibid., 105.

lives were insignificant, they need to take note of Ephesians: their lives are the vehicles for the manifestation of divine victory in the cosmos; indeed, in some ways, their own victories in spiritual battles redound to God's own victory and his glory.

Caragounis sees this divine action of consummation in Christ as bipartite: dealing with the inimical "powers" ("the things in heaven") and the church ("the things on earth"). These are the two entities that are objects of the divine summing up. However, this consummation means one thing for those enemies of God and another thing for the people of God.[48] In fact, I would say they are two sides of the same coin. The church on earth experiences God's resurrection power and is exalted with Christ (1:19–23; 2:6–7), and the hostile forces in heaven are defeated by the same divine power and subjected under Christ. O'Brien observes that Eph 3:9–10 brings both parts of this consummation into juxtaposition: the people of God and the powers against God. Key terms, "make known," "administration," and "mystery" are employed both here and in 1:9–10. In the earlier passage, the consummation of all things in Christ is stated as the final goal of divine action. In 3:9–10, the unity of all (believing) humankind (2:13–16; 3:3–6) is offered as evidence to those "powers" of God's manifold wisdom. The church proves that the authority of the inimical powers, that formerly kept humankind enslaved (2:1–3), has been incontrovertibly broken and that their final defeat is just a formality. The decisive work of God is well under way and inexorably moving to its predetermined conclusion: the glory of God. Indeed the co-opting of the church into the battle against the powers (6:10–20) means that "[t]he church is not only the pattern but also the means God is using to show that his purposes are moving triumphantly to their climax."[49] Both positive and negative faces of the single coin of the consummation, pertaining respectively to those in heaven and those on earth, are "already" being manifest, though the final stage of each is "not yet."

And, in this grand and glorious scheme of God, the church is not only exalted, but it is being filled with the very fullness of God (1:23; 2:21–22; 3:17, 21; 4:6, 10, 15; 5:18–20)—divine glory that glorifies the church as well. The children of God are instructed to grow into Christ and to become the divine dwelling of God in Christ by the Spirit.

This makes the canvas of Ephesians as vast as the cosmos, upon which is being painted the grand masterpiece of divine action. As Gombis labels it, the letter to the Ephesians is "a drama in which Paul portrays the powerful, reality-altering, cosmos-transforming acts of God in Christ."[50] In light of this vastness, limited only by the boundaries of the universe, it is surprising how many have thought that the Bible is narrow in its scope. Here is how Nobel-prize winning physicist, Richard P. Feynman, saw it:

> It doesn't fit together. It seems to me that the ideas of conventional religion—like in the Bible and so forth—are very limited. They didn't realize the tremendous

---

48. *The Ephesian* Mysterion, 144–46.

49. O'Brien, *Ephesians*, 63.

50. Gombis, *The Drama of Ephesians*, 15.

extent of the world, or the length of time in which things have been going on. It seems to me impossible, in a certain sense, that so much attention could be paid to man as is advertised in the usual religion and so little attention paid to the rest of the world. It doesn't seem to me that this fantastically marvelous universe, this tremendous range of time and space and different kinds of animals, and all the different plants, and all these atoms with all their motions and so on, all this complicated thing can merely be a stage so that God can watch human beings struggle for good and evil—which is the view that religion has. The stage is too big for the drama.[51]

Feynman may be right in declaring that religionists did not comprehend the vastness of the universe. But he is certainly mistaken in thinking that "[t]he stage is too big for the drama." Hardly! The drama is as vast as, if not more than, the stage. And the action is nothing but dangerous, requiring the immense power of God for victory. As Annie Dillard famously said:

On the whole, I do not find Christians, outside the catacombs, sufficiently sensible of conditions. Does anyone have the foggiest idea what sort of power we so blithely invoke? Or, as I suspect, does no one believe a word of it? The churches are children playing on the floor with their chemistry sets, mixing up a batch of TNT to kill a Sunday morning. It is madness to wear ladies' straw hats and velvet hats to church; we should all be wearing crash helmets. Ushers should issue life preservers and signal flares; they should lash us to our pews.[52]

This illimitable of power of God is working to accomplish his grand and glorious plan to consummate all things—heavenly and earthly—*in Christ*, noted emphatically in Eph 1:10 by repeating the phrase "in Him."

Christ is the one *in whom* God chooses to sum up the cosmos, the one in whom he restores harmony to the universe. He is the focal point—not simply the means, the instrument, or the functionary through whom all this occurs. . . . The emphasis is now on a universe that is centred and reunited in Christ. The mystery which God has graciously made known refers to the summing up and bringing together of the fragmented and alienated elements of the universe in Christ as the focal point. All things are to be summed up in God's anointed one and presented as a coherent totality in him.[53]

The "Drama" of Ephesians

Gombis's idea of Ephesians as a "drama" resonates well with the theological hermeneutic I espouse. In fact, I would claim that this sense of drama pervades every text of Scripture in every genre; what authors are *doing* with what they are saying is projecting a *world in front of the text*. Such world-projections, such depictions of the ideal world as God would have it, should capture our imaginations and enthrall us with this divine vision. "If we see the outworking of God's salvation in the world as a powerful, divinely

51. Feynman, "Appendix I," 426.
52. Dillard, *Teaching a Stone to Talk*, 52.
53. O'Brien, *Ephesians*, 59.

driven story that is unfolding by the power of the Spirit, overtaking and enveloping all of creation, we can begin to gain a vision for how we can play our role in this great, surprising and invigorating narrative." Into this ideal world, we are graciously invited by God himself, who beckons us to inhabit this world and to live by its precepts, priorities, and practices. Thus information is not the goal of the Bible; rather, it is *transformation*. "[God] wants to shape our imaginations and our life trajectories, our vision of the world and our conception of ourselves and others."[54] And this transformation plays a key role in God's grand and glorious plan to consummate all things in Christ. That he has deigned to include human beings in this cosmic endeavor as active participants is a wondrous and incomprehensible truth. His people aid and abet the plan of God by abiding by the precepts, priorities, and practices of the ideal new world that he graciously invites his people to inhabit.

It is because the universe is fractured and comminuted as a result of sin that a consummation of all things in Christ becomes a necessary plan of God: a creation in which Jesus Christ is the singular head over all, and in whom, all things are filled with the divine fulness by the Spirit. With this as God's goal, one can see why Ephesians is written to address many of these earthly disunions and to bring humankind back into a heavenly unity in Christ—all (believing) humanity, participants in marriage, parents and children, workers and employees, etc. In a world where disunity pervades—in racism, individualism, "genderism," and so on, no doubt provoked and propagated by hostile forces—the consummation of all things in Christ is good news, indeed. Here, then, is the "drama" of Ephesians in my conception, presented in twelve "scenes" (pericopes).

The first pericope raises the curtain on God's grand and glorious plan for the cosmos—the consummation of all things in Christ. Into this grand and glorious plan, all (believing) humans have been recruited, God's scheme for them extending from eternity past to eternity future. A blessed God blesses his people in his Son, with grace, love, and delight (Eph 1:1–14)!

In co-opting them into his grand scheme, believers are assured not only of the steadfast hope of God's calling and that they are God's own glorious inheritance in the future, but also that divine power—involved in the raising and exaltation of Christ over death and every inimical power in the universe—is working on their behalf, for them who are the fullness of Christ and the expression of divine rule in the cosmos (Eph 1:15–23).

A "natural history" of the incorporation of humankind into the grand and glorious plan of God is now detailed in the next two pericopes (2:1–10 and 2:11–22). Once lost in sin, influenced for the worse by the world, by evil powers, and by their own flesh, and deserving only of the wrath of God, Christians have now been saved by grace through faith. They now share their Savior's exaltation, proclaiming to the universe the mercy, love, grace, and kindness of God, by their very salvation and their sanctification in good works (Eph 2:1–10).

---

54. Gombis, *Ephesians*, 17.

The "natural history" continues: they who were once unbelievers and far from God, have been brought near into the community of God's people as believers. Now God's people comprises all humanity—all those who have believed in Christ, the personification and producer of peace. Christ removed the condemnation of humankind for sin and makes possible its access to God, as he builds believers together into a holy temple, a dwelling of God in the Spirit (Eph 2:11–22).

Paul's own divinely empowered role in God's administration of the hitherto unknown mystery of the universality of the church was to serve the co-opting of all (believing) humanity into the community of God's people. This grand role of the apostle—howbeit paradoxical, for he was only a prisoner, and one who was "less than the least of all the saints"—becomes the paradigm for the ministry of all believers, as God accomplishes his eternal and glorious plan through them (Eph 3:1–13).

The accomplishment of God's plan through believers involves their being strengthened by the Spirit and thereby being conformed, more and more, to Christ by faith. Not only as individuals, but corporately as well, God's plan is being worked out as believers in community comprehend the magnitude of Christ's love for them. This enables them to become filled to the fullness of God, i.e., God glorified in the church and dwelling in it—the church increasingly becoming the holy temple of God (Eph 3:14–21).

This business of being conformed to Christ's image, strengthened by the Spirit, receives practical attention in the remainder of Ephesians. Christians are called to selfless love that leads to unity in the body reflecting the unity of the Godhead, and called to the exercise of the grace-gifts given by Christ. These grace-gifts, appropriately granted to every believer and to church leaders, enable the latter to facilitate the ministry of the former, so that the church may be built up in unity to the full and mature stature of its head, Christ (Eph 4:1–16).

Believers, no longer living licentiously, ignorant and devoid of divine life, have learned Christ and are being divinely renewed in the likeness of God. Now they are to manifest that divine character as they maintain unity and engage in activities that build one another and are conducive to the development of community: eschewing anger, sharing resources, speaking grace, controlling temper, and forgiving divinely (Eph 4:17–32).

This brings us to the imitation of God and of Christ's selfless love, that call for the abandonment of illicit "love," i.e., sexual immorality in word and in deed, that elicits the wrath of God. Rather, believers are to adopt a lifestyle that is wise and worshipful, being filled by the Spirit and with the divine fullness of God in Christ, that invites the pleasure of God (Eph 5:1–20).

Such wise living involves a number of proper household relationships, outlined in the next two pericopes (5:21–33 and 6:1–9), all conditioned by the filling by the Spirit of the divine fullness of God in Christ. This fullness of God in the church is manifested in the mutual submission of believers in the fear of Christ, and in the modeling of the relationship of husband and wife after the relationship between Christ and the church—sacrificial love on the part of the husband and submission to authority on the part of the wife (Eph 5:21–33).

The divine demand for proper household relationships that are conducive to unity continues in this pericope. Such relationships among believers in households involves children being obedient to parents, and parents gently instructing their children. In addition, slaves and masters treat one another with sincerity of heart, doing God's will and serving him, the divine Master of all humankind. This brings them reward in the future on the day of reckoning (Eph 6:1–9).

Finally, the book closes with a return to issues of the transcendent. Victory against supernatural foes, who are always arrayed against God and the people of God, can be achieved only by divine empowerment. Such empowerment is granted to the believer in the form of God's own armor—relating to the attributes (belt-truth, breastplate-righteousness), deeds (shoe-peace, shield-faith, helmet-salvation), and utterances of God (sword-word). This comprehensive view of life as a battle fought with divine enablement calls for utter dependence of the believer upon God for everything, expressed in constant, alert, Spirit-driven prayer (Eph 6:10–24).

So the broad theological thrust of Ephesians may be summarized this way: *A blessed God blesses his people graciously and lovingly in his beloved Son, redeeming them as his own possession to undertake divinely empowered good works, so that they may manifest his power and glory as a united body of all (believing) humanity, exercising grace-gifts for edification to Christlikeness, with selfless love abandoning all activities not conducive to community, adopting a wise and worshipful lifestyle pleasing to God—filled by the Spirit with the divine fullness of God in Christ, submitting to one another, modeling marital relationships after the Christ-church relationship, maintaining household structures in accordance with God's plan—and gaining victory over supernatural foes by divine empowerment—all of this an integral part of God's grand and glorious plan to consummate all things in the cosmos in Christ.*

As Gombis concludes:

> Ephesians, then, functions to radically alter and reorient our vision of reality in the most comprehensive sense. Paul wants us to inhabit a new story, to take on a new and renewed set of practices, to see ourselves as part of a radically different and outrageously life-giving story of God redeeming the world in Jesus Christ. In order to participate in this, we need a radical reorientation of our vision of the world. This is what Ephesians aims to do for us, and in that sense it provides a heavenly vision of reality—a conception of reality that we can gain in no other way than by letting the drama of Ephesians become the dominant interpretive framework through which we view God, ourselves, others and the world.[55]

And by that altered conception of reality, by the transformation of the lives of the Christian and the church in the power of the Spirit, God is glorified and his grand and glorious plan to consummate all things in Christ is furthered. This is the goal of preaching, and of preaching the letter to the Ephesians in particular. What a noble task!

55. Ibid., 23.

PERICOPE 1

A Blessed God Blesses

Ephesians 1:1–14

[Blessor Blessed: God's Grand and Glorious Plan]

SUMMARY, PREVIEW

Summary of Pericope 1: The first pericope of the letter, 1:1–14, proclaims why God who is so free with blessing is worthy of being blessed himself. His glorious plan to consummate all things in Christ finds its expression in this text, and also how he co-opts man into this grand cosmic scheme of his. Chosen before time to be holy, God predestined humans to be his children, redeeming them in Christ, appointing them as his own inheritance, and pledging by the Holy Spirit to give them, in turn, an inheritance—all for the praise and glory of God. He is surely worthy of blessing!

Preview of Pericope 2: The next pericope (1:15–23) comprises Paul's prayer for his readers. He intercedes for their enlightenment by the Spirit that they may know God: that is, the hope of his calling, the magnificence of their status as God's inheritance and, above all, the greatness of God's incomparable power manifest in them, as the raised and exalted Christ, the authority above all other cosmic authorities, becomes their head, and they his body and his fullness.

1.   Ephesians 1:1–14

THEOLOGICAL FOCUS OF PERICOPE 1

1   **A God who blesses his people with every blessing in his beloved Son, graciously, lovingly, and delightedly redeeming them for his glory as his own Spirit-sealed possession and to obtain a Spirit-guaranteed inheritance—an integral part of the divine plan to consummate all things in the universe in Christ—is worthy of blessing (1:1–14).**

   1.1   A God who blesses his people with every blessing in his Son is worthy of blessing (1:1–3).

   1.2   God's gracious choice of believers as his children, as he redeems them through his beloved Son, is accomplished in love and with delight, for his glory (1:4–8a).

   1.3   God's delighted announcement of his will establishes that all things in the universe will be consummated in Christ (1:8b–10).

   1.4   The summit of God's plan involves his people's destiny as his Spirit-sealed possession, and their obtaining a Spirit-guaranteed inheritance, that they may live for God's glory (1:11–14).

OVERVIEW

The bulk of this pericope is formed by the blessing in 1:3–14, the longest sentence in the NT, composed of 202 words. The closest a single sentence in the NT comes to this one is the forty-four words of 2 Cor 1:3–4, and the fifty-three words of 1 Pet 1:3–5. Barth calls it an "infinitely long, heavy, and clumsy sentence." O'Brien agrees that it is "marked by an accumulation of relative clauses and phrases whose relation to one another is often difficult to determine."[1] Another characterized it as "the most monstrous sentence conglomeration" he had ever run across in Greek![2] This "clumsy" and "monstrous" sentence is full of redundancy and amplifications, with relative clauses: 1:6b, 7, 8, 9c, 11, 13 (×2), 14; participial phrases: 1:3, 5, 9, 13; infinitival constructions: 1:4, 10, 12; numerous prepositional expressions, fifteen of them employing ἐν (*en*, "in"); and several genitival structures. This seems to fit Aristotle's "continuous" style that is "arrhythmic" and not compact: "By 'continuous' I mean that style which has no end in itself, unless its subject matter run out" (*Rhetoric* 3.9–10). Paul seems to have gone non-stop here, till he exhausted himself in 1:14![3] "[E]ach thought builds on the previous one, sometimes explaining, sometimes elaborating, sometimes supplementing, sometimes contributing something new, and sometimes picking up again what has already been said."[4]

   The style is redolent of liturgy and formal speech, its repetitive nature giving the utterance rhythm and motion, and altogether emphasizing the theological thrust of

---

1. Barth, *Ephesians*, 77; O'Brien, *Ephesians*, 90.

2. I.e., *das monströseste Satzkonglomerat*. See Norden, *Agnostos Theos*, 253n1.

3. See Fowler, "Aristotle on the Period," 89–99; The "continuous" style is opposed to one that is "periodic," that "has a beginning and end in itself and a magnitude that can easily be grasped" (Aristotle, *Rhetoric* 3.9.3).

4. Lincoln, *Ephesians*, 18.

the text.[5] And "the succession of long syllables in a number of places periodically slows down the flow of words so that a chant-like effect is produced as the eulogy is spoken."[6] Such a blessing of God reflects the tone and style of the Jewish בְּרָכָה (*brakah*, "blessing"), the benediction upon God by his people, as for instance in 2 Sam 22:47–49 (= Ps 18:46–48) and 1 Kgs 8:56–61. Ephesians is acknowledged to have been written in a Greek style that sparkles with Semitic, OT influences, also seen in the liturgical language of Qumran literature, with "long-drawn-out, loosely connected tape-worm sentences."[7] Such expressions were therefore part of sacred jargon, being uttered as thanksgivings for a variety of divine blessings (Gen 24:27; Ruth 4:14; 1 Sam 25:32, 39; 1 Kgs 1:48; 5:7, 21; Ezra 7:27–28; Pss 28:6; 124:6; Luke 1: 68–75). Both in rabbinic literature (e.g., the Eighteen Benedictions, see *b. Ber.* 4–5), and that of Qumran (e.g., 1QS 11:15), such blessings are common. Jesus himself gave thanks in this fashion: Matt 14:19; 26:26; Mark 6:41; 14:22; Luke 9:16. In the NT, the adjective εὐλογητὸς (*eulogētos*, "blessed," Eph 1:3) is used only of God: Mark 14:61; Luke 1:68; Rom 1:25; 9:5; 2 Cor 1:3; 11:31; Eph 1:3; 1 Pet 1:3. All of this marks out Eph 1:3–14 as elevated language. "In one sense the language is exalted and extravagant and yet, in another, the very repetition of phrases reveals its poverty and inadequacy to do justice to its subject"—what God has done, is doing, and will do "on the grandest scale and broadest canvas."[8]

Structure

The complications of outlining such a complex sentence are obvious; Hoehner lists over forty attempts to structure Eph 1:3–14![9] A number of alternatives are possible: based on the three main verbs—"He chose" (1:4), "He engraced" (1:6), and "He lavished" (1:8); based on three aorist active participles—"blessed" (1:3), "predestined" (1:5), and "made known" (1:9); based on the three expressions of the divine will (1:5, 9, 11); based on the trifold work of the persons of the Godhead—the Father (1:3–6), the Son (1:7–12), and the Spirit (1:13–14)—with each of these three sections concluding with a repetition of "to the praise of the/His glory" (1:6, 12, 14)[10]; based on the status of being "in Christ" (1:3, 10, 12), "in whom" (1:7, 11, 13), and "in Him" (1:4, 9, 10); or based upon a triadic scheme related to time: past (the election of God, 1:3–6), the present (the redemption by God, 1:4–9), and the future (the hope in God, 1:10–14).

The absence of a clearly definable structure does not mean the blessing is an unplanned outpouring of words. The work of each person of the Trinity is carefully developed and then concluded with a refrain of praise. *God the Father* blesses (1:3),

---

5. There are eight lengthy sentences in Ephesians: 1:3–14, 15–23; 2:1–7; 3:2–13, 14–19; 4:1–6, 11–16; 6:14–20; at least three, 1:3–14, 15–23; and 3:14–19, are liturgical or doxological.

6. Ibid., 12.

7. Kuhn, "The Epistle to the Ephesians," 116, 120.

8. Lincoln, *Ephesians*, 43.

9. Hoehner, *Ephesians*, 154–61.

10. Trinitarian elements in Ephesians are also found in: 1:17, 2:18, 22; 3:1–5, 14–17; 4:4–6; 5:18–20.

chooses (1:4), predestines his people as children (1:5, 11), engraces (1:6), lavishes his grace on believers (1:8), makes known his grand plan (1:9–10), purposes for his good pleasure (1:9), and works all things according to his will (1:11), "for the praise of the glory of His grace" (1:6). There is clearly an emphasis on God's "purpose" and "will" as he acts: pointed mentions are made of God's good pleasure and his will (1:5, 7, 9, 11), his grace (1:7), his purpose (1:11), and his counsel (1:11).

God the Son is the sphere in which every divine blessing is offered and received (1:1, 3, 4, 5, 6, 7, 9, 10 [×2], 11, 12, 13 [×2]). In 1:1–14, "Christ," its equivalent, or the appropriate pronoun referring to him, occurs fifteen times; and "in Christ/whom/Him," twelve times. The resounding of "in Christ" indicates that the work of God is accomplished in/through Jesus Christ. If from 3:13 we assume that Paul's readers were downhearted because of his tribulations for their cause, he might have penned this opening section of the letter to encourage them about the glorious work of God being accomplished on their behalf "in Christ." Indeed, God's ultimate goal is to sum up everything "in Christ" (1:10), all "for the praise of His glory" (1:12).

God the Spirit shows up at the beginning and end of the blessing: every blessing God's people receive is "spiritual" (1:3), and it is this Person who is the mark of God's ownership of his people and the guarantee of the fulfillment of the divine purpose (1:13–14), "for the praise of His glory" (1:14).[11]

The impelling force of God's action is his divine purpose, its agency is his Son, and its goal is his glory. The pericope is theocentric through and through. But the many first person plural pronouns (1:3, 4, 5, 6, 7, 8, 9, 11, 12, 14) and verbs (1:7, 11, 13) also demonstrate that the work of God is directed towards his people, the ones that Paul will later call the "church" (1:22). There is clear progress from praise to God (1:3), to description of his grand plan (1:4–12), to its application to believers (1:13–14). So this blessing is hardly an abstraction far removed from the real world; rather, the divine work described here fully encompasses the people of God. In fact, Lincoln sees "God as the origin and goal of salvation, Christ as its mediator, and believers as its recipients" giving the passage another threefold division: theological, christological, and ecclesiological.[12]

Purpose

Heil's structuring of 1:3–14 is helpful to glimpse the overarching thrust of the pericope (the corresponding phrases in each element are shown in italics below)[13]:

---

11. O'Brien, *Ephesians*, 91–92.

12. Lincoln, *Ephesians*, 43.

13. Heil, *Ephesians*, 17–18.

A		*our* Lord Jesus Christ; *spiritual* blessing; *holy* and blameless;
		to the praise of the glory of *his* grace; **in the Beloved** (1:3–6)
	B	*in whom* we have redemption; mystery *of His will*;
		pleasure which he *purposed* **in Him** (1:7–9)
	C	all *the things* **in Christ** (1:10a)
	C'	*the things* in the heavens and *the things* on earth **in Him** (1:10b)
	B'	*in whom* also we have obtained an inheritance;
		purpose of the one who works; *counsel of His will*; **in Christ** (1:11–12)
A'		*Holy Spirit*; *our* inheritance;
		to the praise of His glory (1:13–14)

The first five elements (*A, B, C, C',* and *B'*) end with the preposition "in" (ἐν, *en*) and a reference to Christ (in bold, above); the last (*A'*), disrupting this pattern, concludes with a climactic recurrence of "to the praise of His glory."

> This leaves the audience with the lasting impression that the point of we believers being extremely blessed with the love of God "in Christ" (1:3), within the realm of our being "in love" (1:4b), in which God has graced us "in the Beloved" (1:6), having made known to us the mystery, according to his pleasure that he purposed "in him" (1:9), to unite under one head all things "in the Christ" (1:10b), the things in heaven and the things on earth "in him" (1:10c), "in the Christ" (1:12) in whom the first believers hoped, is that we might respond to this extravagant divine love by exuberantly praising God's glory—that we might be "to the praise of his glory [1:6, 12, 14]!"[14]

Having chosen believers *in love* (1:4), God graced them *in the Beloved* (1:6); this bespeaks an underlying theme of this section—God's overwhelming love. "Our loving response as believers who have been gifted with the love of God is to praise the glory that God has manifested in loving us who have been incorporated into Christ, *the Beloved*."[15]

In sum, whatever its outline, the theological endpoint is clear: "[A]s Paul begins his general letter to Christians in Asia Minor, he meditates on God's gracious purposes in Christ, and praise to God wells up within him. His desire is that this adoration might overflow to his readers, so that they will be stimulated to respond as he does and give glory to God for all the gracious blessings to them."[16] What Paul/the Holy Spirit intends readers and listeners to do is to engage in praise, particularly in light of God's grand plan to consummate all things in Christ and to co-opt his people into this glorious scheme.

14. Ibid., 73.
15. Ibid., 69.
16. O'Brien, *Ephesians*, 92–93.

1.1 Ephesians 1:1–3

THEOLOGICAL FOCUS OF PERICOPE 1.1

1.1   A God who blesses his people with every blessing in his Son is worthy of blessing (1:1–3).

TRANSLATION 1.1

1:1   *Paul, an apostle of Christ Jesus, by the will of God, to the saints who are in Ephesus and believers in Christ Jesus.*

1:2   *Grace to you and peace from God our Father and the Lord Jesus Christ.*

1:3   *Blessed [be] the God and Father of our Lord Jesus Christ, who has blessed us with every spiritual blessing, in the heavenlies, in Christ,*

NOTES 1.1

1.1   A God who blesses his people with every blessing in his Son is worthy of blessing.

The prologue, 1:1–2, follows the standard Pauline pattern with name of sender, recipients, and greetings. Attending to the greetings of letters tells the reader much about the sender's philosophy of life. Lucian of Samosata, the second-century Greek rhetorician and satirist, reports that Plato dispensed with the then-standard greeting, "Joy!" opting for "Prosper!" instead. He thought the former to be not serious, and the latter to be the satisfactory condition of body and soul. Pythagoras disagreed. He employed "Good health!" which he considered the greatest need of humans. So also Epicurus—health was the chief blessing one could hope for (*Pro lapsu inter salutandum* 3–6). But Paul wishes his readers "Grace and peace!" likely a holdover from the priestly benediction in Num 6:24–26, which also has "grace" and "peace."[17] Unlike the usual liturgical benedictions, this one is not only from God the Father, but also from God the Son (Eph 1:2). The rest of the letter goes on to explicate this unusual opening—how God, through his Son, gives his people grace and peace.

Paul establishes his credentials at the outset—this is an official apostolic missive. "Apostle" simply means "sent one" or "messenger," as in John 13:16; Rom 16:7; 2 Cor 8:23; Phil 2:25.[18] Paul, as one called and sent by Jesus, is numbered among this group of leaders (Rom 1:1; 1 Cor 1:1; 2 Cor 1:1; Col 1:1; 1 Thess 2:6; 1 Tim 1:1; 2 Tim 1:1; Titus 1:1).[19] And this ministry of his was a result of the "will of God," a notion that echoes in this pericope (Eph 1:1, 5, 9, 11).

17. Grace (Eph 1:2, 6, 7; 2:5, 7, 8; 3:2, 7, 8; 4:7, 29; 6:24) and peace (2:14, 15, 17; 4:3; 6:15, 23) echo throughout this letter. The former is the cause and the latter is the result: divine grace yields peace from God in every sphere of life.

18. Though "apostle" primarily refers to the Twelve called and sent by Jesus (Matt 10:2–4; Mark 3:16–19; Luke 6:13–16; Acts 1:13, 22–23; 4:33), others also bear the title: Barnabas (1 Cor 9:5–7; Acts 14:4, 14), James (1 Cor 15:7; Gal 1:19), Apollos (1 Cor 4:6, 9), and Matthias (Acts 1:26).

19. In Ephesians, the apostles (with the prophets) are the foundation of the church (2:20), leaders gifted by God to the church (4:11), who play important roles in the growth of the church into maturity,

"Saints" are those who have been set apart for God and for his service, "a people for God's own possession" (1 Pet 2:9).[20] These "saints" in Eph 1:1 are also the "believers" (see 1:13); both descriptors are likely encompassed by the article, "the," before "saints"; and the "and" linking the two is likely explanatory (an epexegetical καί, *kai*)— "the saints, i.e., the believers."[21]

Ephesians 1:1–2 can be organized this way[22]:

> **A**   Paul, an apostle of *Christ Jesus* (1:1a)
> **B**   by the will of *God* (1:1b)
> **C**   to the saints who are *in* Ephesus (1:1c).
> **C'**   and believers *in* Christ Jesus (1:1d)
> **B'**   Grace to you and peace from *God* our Father (1:2a)
> **A'**   and the Lord *Jesus Christ* (1:2b)

The center of the structure denotes the dual locations of the saints: *in* Ephesus, and *in* Christ Jesus (1:1cd). "In Paul's mind, just as these Christians actually live in the region near Ephesus, they also live in Christ. The terrain, location, climate, values, and history of the place where people grow up and live help define who they are. Just as "in Ephesus" defines Paul's readers in this fashion, so also "in Christ" defines who believers actually are. In light of the many occurrences of "in Christ" (and its equivalents) in this pericope, and the parallel with "in Ephesus," the phrase "in Christ" in 1:1 indicates the sphere in which saints/believers exist, rather than denoting the object of the belief of the saints.[23]

In Romans (1:8), 1 Corinthians (1:4–9), Philippians (1:3–8), Colossians (1:3–8), 1 Thessalonians (1:2—3:13); 2 Thessalonians (1:3–12), 2 Timothy (1:3), and Philemon (4–5), a thanksgiving for God's work in his readers follows Paul's greetings. In Ephesians, rather than a thanksgiving, the apostle breaks out into a blessing—the thanksgiving follows later, in 1:15–23.[24]

There are three forms of the word "bless" in Eph 1:3: adjective, εὐλογητὸς (*eulogētos*, "blessed"), verb, εὐλογέω (*eulogeō*, "bless"), and noun εὐλογία (*eulogia*, "blessing"). The One who is *blessed blesses* his people with every *blessing*. Three ἐν-clauses—"*with* every spiritual blessing, *in* the heavenlies, *in* Christ"—describe in crisp terms that these blessings are of a supernatural source: they are of the Spirit, from the heavens, and in Christ.

---

into Christ (2:21; 4:13).

20. God's people are always set apart and consecrated unto him and his service as holy: Exod 19:5–6; Lev 11:44–45; often, divine demand for holiness is given the rationale "for I, Yahweh, your God am holy" (or words to that effect, in Lev 19:2; 20:7; 21:8; 22:32; etc.).

21. Interestingly, it is Christ who "made holy" (5:26); but it is believers who are responsible to "be holy" (1:4).

22. Heil, *Ephesians*, 16–17. Similar items in each element are italicized.

23. Snodgrass, *Ephesians*, 40.

24. Second Corinthians opens the same way: a blessing follows the greeting (1:3–4).

The entire scope of divine blessing upon humankind is encompassed in "every spiritual blessing," with "spiritual" indicating that which pertains to or belongs to the Holy Spirit, i.e., having a supernatural source (as also do the gifts and fruit of the Spirit). "These gracious gifts are not simply future benefits but are a present reality for us, since they have already been won for us by God's saving action in Christ."[25] God has already blessed believers in this fashion, and such blessings are experienced even in this age.

"Heavenlies" (ἐπουράνοις, *epouranois*) occurs seventeen times in the NT, of which five are in Ephesians (1:3, 20; 2:6; 3:10; 6:12). In this letter, it is consistently employed to denote a location, whether of God, of Christ (1:3, 20; 2:6), or of evil powers (3:10; 6:12). The divine location appears to be "above" and the demonic one below, related to the "air" (1:20–21; 2:2).[26] The other NT instances always deal with God in contrast to what is earthly, insignificant, and transient (John 3:12; 1 Cor 15:40, 48–49; Phil 2:10; 2 Tim 4:18; Heb 3:1; 6:4; 8:5; 11:16; 12:22). Thus, here in 1:3, "in the heavenlies" likely refers to another description of the source of the divine blessings—not only from the Spirit, but also from the heavenlies. "The sense [of 'in the heavenlies'] is local, but the phrase serves also to reinforce the divine origin of the blessings."[27] Yet another specification of where the blessings are found is in the closing phrase "in Christ" (1:3). Though not a physical location, "in Christ," is the realm or sphere for the experience of divine blessings—"the believer incorporated in Christ, gives the best sense in this context."[28]

Thus the beginning of the blessing is a remarkable statement of how the *blessed* God *blesses* his people with every *blessing*: these blessings are of the Spirit, from the very presence of God, and experienced in the "realm" of Jesus Christ. What exactly those blessings are is explained in the remainder of the pericope.

1.2   Ephesians 1:4–8a

THEOLOGICAL FOCUS OF PERICOPE 1.2

1.2   God's gracious choice of believers as his children, as he redeems them through his beloved Son, is accomplished in love and with delight, for his glory (1:4–8a).

TRANSLATION 1.2

1:4   *because He chose us in Him before the foundation of the world, that we may be holy and blameless before Him; in love*

---

25. O'Brien, *Ephesians*, 97.

26. In classical Greek, "heavenlies" indicated the abode of the gods (Homer, *Iliad* 6.129; *Odysseus* 17.484), or, as a substantive, the one who dwells in that location, i.e., a god (Theocritus, *Idyll* 25.5).

27. Best, *Ephesians*, 114.

28. Hoehner, *Ephesians*, 172. "In Christ" or its equivalent occurs thirty-six times in Ephesians and twelve times in this pericope (1:1, 3, 4, 7, 9, 10 [×2], 11, 12, 13 [×2]; 1:6 has "in the Beloved").

1:5 *He predestined us for adoption as sons, through Jesus Christ, unto Himself, according to the good pleasure of His will,*

1:6 *for the praise of the glory of His grace [with] which He engraced us in the Beloved.*

1:7 *in whom we have redemption through His blood, the forgiveness of our trespasses, according to the riches of His grace*

1:8a *which He lavished on us;*

NOTES 1.2

1.2 God's gracious choice of believers as his children, as he redeems them through his beloved Son, is accomplished in love and with delight, for his glory.

The conjunction, καθώς (*kathōs*, "just as," 1:4), is best seen as causative, a common pattern in a blessing that gives a reason thereof (as, for e.g., in Luke 1:68–79): God is blessed, *because* (or, *inasmuch as*) he chose us. The idea of being chosen "in Christ" (Eph 1:4) includes the idea of the Son of God being the representative for all believers, i.e., believers are those incorporated into Christ, the proxy, if you will, for humankind. Such an election in eternity past, preceding creation, is also reflected in Rom 8:29 and 2 Tim 1:9, all of this emphasizing that God's choice was one of sovereign love and grace, independent of any human merit or temporal exigency.[29]

God's choice of believers, we are told, was made "before" (πρὸ, *pro*) the foundation of the world (Eph 1:4), and they are said to be "predestined/destined before" (προορίζω, *proorizō*, 1:5, a word exclusively used of God in the NT). Both "choice/election" and "predestination" were intended to be seen synonymously, and without connoting any temporal distinction between the occurrences of each. Both point to a sovereign choice on the part of God; the redundancy is not an unusual way of expressing things in a liturgical blessing; this is especially true in Ephesians. Predestination is therefore simply another way to describe God's setting apart of those chosen, that they may be holy and blameless.[30]

> Paul's use of language in Ephesians generally, and in this benediction particularly, moreover, is as lavish in its own way as the grace of God, which he praises. Redundancy, then, is not a valid objection to understanding προορίσας ἡμᾶς [*proorisas hēmas*, "He predestined us"] as a restatement of ἐξελέξατο ἡμᾶς [*exelexato hēmas*, "He chose us"]. Paul simply turns the jewel slightly and views it from a different angle, now describing God's primordial action on behalf of his people not as his choice but as his predetermination of them.[31]

And, importantly, this choice and predestination was not a whimsical operation on God's part, but one begun and carried out "in love" (1:4). "In love" in Ephesians occurs six times: excluding 1:4, four times they are used of human love (4:2, 15, 16;

---

29. Ibid., 175, remarks that "chose" is the only verb in the blessing of 1:3–14 that is not subordinate to another element. In syntax, too, God's choice is totally independent!

30. Fowl, *Ephesians*, 14.

31. Thielman, *Ephesians*, 51.

5:2), and once of divine love (3:17; divine love is also found in 2:4; 3:19; 5:2, 25). "Love" is rarely, if ever, linked to the moral purity implied by the preceding phrase "holy and blameless."[32] Connecting "in love" with the following phrase, dealing with divine predestination makes better sense: a personal filial relationship—"sonship"—is appropriately described as having been established "in love." So, accomplished in love, this is a relationship that brings God delight—"the good pleasure of his will" (1:5). God is not a "grim Lord," but a "smiling Father," who "in love" predestined for his own "pleasure."[33] Adoption by human fathers, permitted under Roman law, occurred out of the need to continue the family line; adoption by the divine Father, on the other hand, is simply because he loves those he adopts; and he delights in the adopting.

This notion of God choosing his people in love is also found in the OT (Deut 7:7–8; 10:15; also see 1 Thess 1:4).[34] But the fact that divine election is always dependent only upon divine love, and not upon human action, does not preclude the chosen ones' responsibility for a way of life, as a consequence of the relationship now established between God and his people. They are chosen *to be* "holy and blameless," i.e., to be conformed to the image of Christ (Rom 8:29). In light of Eph 5:27, that uses the same words "holy and blameless" in the context of being "presented to Himself," the phrase "before Him," here in 1:4 might be referring to the same eschatological presentation of the church on the day of the Lord Jesus Christ (1 Cor 1:8; Heb 12:14). This makes the span of God's choice of his people in Eph 1:4 extend from eternity past to the last things—a grand plan, indeed!

No wonder this draws praise from God's people (Eph 1:6). This God is blessed and worthy of praise because of his sovereign, loving, and joyful action bringing believers into relationship with him, he as Father and they as his children. We find in 1:6a the first of a string of genitives in Ephesians—the "praise of the glory of His grace" (the others are in 1:18b, 19b; 2:2b; 3:7; 4:13a, 13b). This is typical of the author's style, perhaps being employed to emphasize the grandeur of the concepts he was scripting.[35] Here it indicates the end-point of God's election and predestination: that his glorious grace, demonstrated by his sovereign choice that was made in love and executed with delight, may be praised. This election and appointment by God was the "grace" (χάρις, *charis*) with which his children were "engraced" (χαριτόω, *charitoō*)—"ingratiated with grace."[36] As with election ("in Christ," 1:4) and predestination ("through Jesus Christ," 1:5), this engracing was accomplished "in the Beloved" (1:6). In other words,

---

32. Hoehner, *Ephesians*, 184, argues that "love" is elsewhere linked to holiness and blamelessness, in 4:1–2/4:15 (but the concepts are too distant from each other) and in 5:25, 28, 33/5:27 (but here the ones who love are husbands and Christ, and the ones made holy and blameless are wives and the church).

33. Barth, *Ephesians*, 81. As Paul makes clear, prior to this adoption, believers were "sons of disobedience" and "children of wrath" (2:2, 3).

34. In the OT, Israel was seen as the "firstborn" of Yahweh (Exod 4:22; Deut 14:1; Isa 1:2; 30:9; Jer 31:9; Hosea 11:1; also see Rom 9:4). The phrase implies a personal, intimate relationship with God—"unto Himself"—achieved "through Jesus Christ" (Eph 1:5), i.e., because of their union with him. See Fowl, *Ephesians*, 42.

35. Thielman, *Ephesians*, 53.

36. Hoehner, *Ephesians*, 203.

God's action "in love" (ἐν ἀγάπῃ, *en agapē*, 1:4) is achieved "in the Beloved" (ἐν τῷ ἠγαπημένῳ, *en tō ēgapēmenō*, 1:6).[37]

How exactly the benefits of election and predestination were actualized "in Christ" (1:4), "through Christ" (1:5), and "in the Beloved" (1:6) is explained in 1:7–8a. The redemption of God's people *in Christ* is in view here (1:7 begins with "in whom")—the work of Christ: it was "through His blood" that "the forgiveness of our trespasses" was achieved (1:7).[38] Note that this redemption and forgiveness in 1:7ab is bounded on either side by mentions of God's grace (1:6 and 1:7c–8a).

> "His grace [with] which He engraced us" (1:6)
> **Redemption/Forgiveness** (1:7ab)
> "His grace which he lavished upon us" (1:7c–8a)

Indeed, God was not only gracious in his predestination (1:6), he was lavishly so in his redemption (1:8)—"according to *the riches of* His grace" (1:7), i.e., by the measure of the wealth of his grace. Rather than an accidental facet of his redemptive work, grace is integral to God's rescue mission of his people. In other words, for the Christian, it is divine grace through and through.

1.3   Ephesians 1:8b–10

> **THEOLOGICAL FOCUS OF PERICOPE 1.3**
>
> 1.3   God's delighted announcement of his will establishes that all things in the universe will be consummated in Christ (1:8b–10).

TRANSLATION 1.3

1:8b   *with all wisdom and insight*

1:9   *He made known to us the mystery of His will, according to His good pleasure that He purposed in Him*

1:10   *for the administration of the fullness of times, the consummation of all things in Christ—the things in the heavens and the things on the earth in Him;*

---

37. "Beloved" was a title for Christ in the early church; see Ignatius, *To the Smyrnaeans* (in the greeting); *Barnabas* 3:6; 4:3, 8. Incidentally, "beloved" and "good pleasure" show up together at the baptism of Jesus: Matt 3:17/Mark 1:11/Luke 3:22.

38. A future aspect of this redemption is referred to in 1:14 (and 4:30). The word ἀπολύτρωσις (*apolytrōsis*, "redemption") was the price for freeing a captive or a slave (*Letter of Aristeas* 12, 33; Philo, *Good Person* 114).

NOTES 1.3

*1.3   God's delighted announcement of his will establishes that all things in the
universe will be consummated in Christ.*

"Wisdom and insight" (1:8) is likely a hendiadys that, with the adjective "all" qualifying the pair of terms together, indicates the broad scope of God's cognition.[39] In all
likelihood, it goes with the verb that follows, "making known" (1:9)—i.e., how God
made known the mystery of his will was with his incomparable "wisdom and insight."
Later on, Paul will pray for "wisdom" that is linked to "knowledge" (1:17); "wisdom"
is also connected to "making known" in 3:10; and "insight" and "making known" are
linked in 3:4. Also, the pattern of opening a section with an ἐν-clause, seen in 1:4d ("in
love") and 1:7a ("in whom"), is used here in 1:8b ("with [ἐν] all wisdom and insight";
also see 1:11a, 13a, which also open with "in whom").

Not only did God lavish his grace upon believers in the sovereign and joyous
choice of his children, he was equally delighted to make the fact known to them: this
matter of "making known" was also, like God's predestination (1:5), "according to his
good pleasure" (1:9). God's delight is in not just in accomplishing his work, but also
in letting his people know what he has done. And this "good pleasure" is "purposed in
Him [Christ]" (1:9), i.e., it was in and through Christ that God's purpose to achieve his
"good pleasure" was realized.[40] One is struck by how much joy all of his work on behalf
of his children is bringing to God—the repeated "good pleasure" (1:5, 9) is poignant.

And what was God's delighted announcement, the content of what was "made
known," the "mystery of his will"(1:9)? That announcement comes in 1:10, and with
the revelation of its content, the blessing of 1:3–14 achieves its climax, (see chiastic
structure above). "Mystery" indicates a previously hidden secret (3:9) that has now
been revealed (Rom 16:25–26; Eph 3:3, 5; Col 1:25–27). In Ephesians, it points to
God's broad scheme of salvation through Jesus Christ that is to be consummated in the
last days: Eph 1:9; 3:3, 4, 9; 5:32; 6:19. Here, too, the divine will was "for the administration of the fullness of the times," i.e., for the management of the last days that have
already begun—God's grand plan for the final outcome for the entire universe.[41] What
is administered or managed in the fullness of times is revealed as "the consummation

---

39. "Wisdom" and "insight" are found together in Prov 1:2; 3:13, 19; 7:4; 8:1; 10:23; 16:16 (LXX).
Pairing of words in synonymous fashion, linked by "and," is common in this letter: Eph 1:4, 8; 2:1, 4, 19;
3:17; 4:14, 16, 17, 24; 5:2, 27; 6:5, 18.

40. And with that we get another word that begins with προ: προέθετο (*proetheto*, "purposed," 1:9).
The temporal connotations of the preposition πρό echoes throughout the blessing: πρό (*pro*, "before,"
1:4); προορίσας (*proorisas*, "He predestined," 1:5); προορισθέντες (*prooristhentes*, "having been predestined," 1:11); and προηλπικότας (*proēlpikotas,* "who hoped beforehand," 1:12). It is likely that such an
emphasis operates in 1:9 as well for God's purposing—*prior* purposing—as well as in 1:11, for πρόθεσιν
(*prothesin,* "purpose"). This echo of προ inclines readers to attribute to these words a "before-time" sense,
in keeping with the origination of the divine plan in eternity past. See Thielman, *Ephesians,* 63.

41. "Administration," οἰκονομία (*oikonomia,* 1:10) is used of the management of households, cities,
states, and here, of the universe. It has the sense of ordering, arranging, or even implementing God's will.

[or 'summing up'] of all things in Christ"—this is the content of the mystery. This is the direction, the trajectory of the history of creation.[42]

Other references in Ephesians to "mystery" usually deal with present realities (3:3–6, 9, 10; 5:32; 6:19; also see Col 1:26, 27; 2:2; 4:3). This simply indicates that the grand plan of "consummation of all things in Christ" mentioned in Eph 1:10 has already begun (see 1:22, 23)—a "realized eschatology." But it is to be completed and fulfilled in the day of Christ, when "every knee will bow . . . and every tongue confess that Jesus Christ is Lord to the glory of God the Father" (Phil 2:10–11). So from the vantage point of "now," the end has already begun and God's "administration of the fullness of times" is under way!

So in Eph 1:10, "the consummation of all things in Christ" is the synopsis of everything, "a restoration of harmony with Christ as the point of reintegration"—he is the unifying and single end of the cosmos ("all things" indicates "all creation": 3:9), and everything is coming together in him.[43] And this takes place in "the fullness of time," the eschatological age of the rule of Christ. "God is in the process of organizing the entire universe, both its heavenly dimension and its earthly dimension, around Christ. The historical course of the universe finds its organizational principle in him."[44] Thus Christ is not just the agent or means by which God sums up all things; he is himself the one who is the focal point of this consummation.[45]

The instances of "in Christ" earlier in the blessing pointed to the Second Person of the Trinity *in whom* believers have been chosen, predestined, engraced, and redeemed. But in 1:9–10, the scope of the divine blessing in Christ broadens to encompass the entirety of created order, a universe centered and focused upon the Lord Jesus Christ. While "things in the heavenlies and the things on the earth" are meant to indicate all of creation, there is more to it than just that. The "heavens" and the "earth" represent two contrasting domains, realms, or spheres: in the former are supernatural powers (both of good and of evil) and in the latter is the church. The defeat of evil in the heavenlies and the unification of all (believing) humankind on earth, a unity adumbrated in the reference to those two spheres, is a significant part of the "consummation of all things in Christ."[46] In other words, this universe-wide consummation includes the conquering of all evil powers and their being placed in subjection at Christ's feet (1:20–22a), the appointing of Christ in headship over the church (1:22b–23; 4:15; 5:23), and the

---

42. The infinitive, ἀνακεφαλαιώσασθαι (*anakephalaiōsasthai*, 1:10), is a rhetorical term indicating the summing up of an argument of an orator (Dionysius of Halicarnassus, *Antiqutates romanae* 1.90.2; Quintilian, *Institutio oratoria* 6.1.1), likely derived from κεφάλαιον (*kephalaion*), "brief statement concerning some topic or subject, main thing, main point" ("κεφάλαιον," BDAG 541 [italics removed]). It is used only one other time in the NT, in Rom 13:9, with the same sense of a summation—of a portion of the Decalogue. Here in 1:10 there might be a sense of recapitulation or renewal in the ἀνα- (*ana-*) prefix of the word that hints at the restoration of what was lost in the fall.

43. Lincoln, *Ephesians*, 33.

44. Thielman, *Ephesians*, 68.

45. O'Brien, *Ephesians*, 111–12.

46. Ibid., 112–13. "In Him" (end of 1:10) and "in whom" (beginning of 1:11) appear back to back: Paul, overcome with awed wonder has apparently lost track of his syntax!

unifying of humankind into the single body of Christ (2:11–22). "To be in Christ, therefore, is to be part of a program which is as broad as the universe, a movement which is rolling on toward a renewed cosmos where all is in harmony. . . . [T]he effect of this part of the blessing is to produce confidence in the God whose gracious decision embraces everything in heaven and on earth, and to inspire those who echo it to play their part in God's administration of the fullness of the times in Christ."[47] In Christ, all things are coming together, all things united under the headship of one Lord, Jesus Christ. In Christ, all things are being set right, all things harmonized under the rulership of one Lord, Jesus Christ. In Christ, all things are being made whole, all things transformed by divine purpose in one Lord, Jesus Christ. And in Christ, all things are achieving their divinely intended end, all things consummated under the preeminence of one Lord, Jesus Christ. A powerful encouragement, indeed!

1.4 Ephesians 1:11–14

> **THEOLOGICAL FOCUS OF PERICOPE 1.4**
>
> 1.4 The summit of God's plan involves his people's destiny as his Spirit-sealed possession, and their obtaining a Spirit-guaranteed inheritance, that they may live for God's glory (1:11–14).

TRANSLATION 1.4

1:11 *in whom also we have been claimed [by God] as an inheritance, having been predestined according to the purpose of Him who works all things according to the counsel of His will,*

1:12 *that we, who hoped beforehand in Christ, may be for the praise of His glory;*

1:13 *in whom also you, hearing the word of truth, the gospel of your salvation—in whom also believing, you were sealed with the Holy Spirit of promise*

1:14 *(who is the pledge of our inheritance) until the redemption of [God's own] possession, for the praise of His glory.*

NOTES 1.4

1.4 *The summit of God's plan involves his people's destiny as his Spirit-sealed possession, and their obtaining a Spirit-guaranteed inheritance, that they may live for God's glory.*

In 1:11, there is an advance in thought from the earlier portions of the blessing: the privilege of being God's children (1:5) has now become the honor of being God's inheritance[48]: "predestined" as children to being "predestined" as inheritance. That this

---

47. Lincoln, *Ephesians*, 44.

48. The word, ἐκληρώθημεν (*eklērōthēmen*, 1:11, only here in the NT) is an aorist passive first-person plural, from κληρόω (*klēroō*), "to appoint by lot," an OT concept: 1 Sam 14:41; Isa 17:11 (LXX). Thus the sense in Eph 1:11 would be "we were appointed as a portion by lot" ("κληρόω," BDAG 548). That the portion is God's is implicit in the passage and consonant with the same idea in the OT of God's people being his inheritance: Deut 4:20; 7:6; 9:26, 29; 14:2; 32:9; Ps 33:12 (LXX); etc. "[T]he image of the inheritance

is a deliberate action on God's part is clear from the synonymous concepts piled up—"predestined," "purpose," "counsel," and "will" (1:11)—making believers an especially privileged lot (pun intended). In the grand plan of God to consummate all things in Christ, his chosen children maintain an exalted status—as God's own inheritance (1:11) and possession (1:14). "He carefully planned to make his people his heirs before he did it. This action was neither haphazard nor dependent on anything they would do to earn it."[49] This was no "divine roll of the dice," but a preconceived, purposeful, thought-out resolution on the part of God, who "works all things" (1:11).[50] No divine whim, fancy, or caprice here. Earlier, in 1:5, 9, the emphasis was on God's joyful plan as he worked on behalf of his people. Then, in 1:9–10, it was on God's delightful announcement of his magnificent scheme to unite all things in Christ. Here, in 1:11–12, the emphasis is on the intentional, weighed, and considered decision of God as he made believers his inheritance. "All things"—in heaven and on earth—may be consummated in Christ (1:10), but believers remain at the summit of the divine plan: they are the very inheritance and possession of God himself, who works "all things" according to his will (1:11). The repeat of "all things" (1:10, 11) makes it clear that this same God who executes his grand plan to consummate *all things* in Christ (1:10), he it is—the one who accomplishes *all things* by his will (1:11)—he it is who inherits and possesses believers. Surely then, this exalted position of the children of God as a divine possession is the zenith, the summit of God's magnificent purposes for humanity in Christ. One also notices that on either side of God's plan of consummation (*C–C'*, in the structure shown earlier and partly reproduced below) is the triumphant note of what he has done for believers (*B* and *B'*):

> **B** *in whom* we have redemption; mystery *of His will*;
> pleasure which he *purposed* **in Him** (1:7–9)
>   **C** all *the things* **in Christ** (1:10a)
>   **C'** *the things* in the heavens and *the things* on earth **in Him** (1:10b)
> **B'** *in whom* also we have obtained an inheritance;
> *purpose* of the one who works; counsel *of His will*; **in Christ** (1:11–12)

What a glorious privilege!

That this exceedingly high standing of believers is established, confirmed, and guaranteed is underscored in 1:13–14.[51] There are several words in 1:13 that are integral to the Christian mission: "heard," "word," "truth," "gospel," "salvation," and "believed."[52] Paul appears to be relating events that occurred with the Ephesians' placing their trust

---

of God seems to covey the idea that God's true possession has become alienated from God and awaits restoration" (Fowl, *Ephesians*, 59). As Paul will describe in Eph 2, sin was the ultimate alienator.

49. Thielman, *Ephesians*, 74.

50. Fowl, *Ephesians*, 49.

51. As he finally runs out of breath in 1:13–14, Paul seems to have lost his place, creating an anacoluthon, an example of broken syntax, not uncommon in Paul: Rom 2:17–22; 5:6; 2 Cor 4:6; Gal 2:4, 6; 1 Tim 1:3–4.

52. Best, *Ephesians*, 148.

in Jesus Christ as Savior. The word they heard was the truth, the gospel of their salvation (1:13; Jas 1:18). And having heard and believed this word, they were sealed with the "Holy Spirit of promise"—i.e., the "promised Holy Spirit," adumbrated in the OT (Isa 32:15; 44:3; Ezek 11:19; 36:26–27; 37:14; Joel 2:28–29; also Acts 2:33; Gal 3:14). Seals in the ancient Near East guaranteed the authenticity (1 Kgs 21:8; John 3:33; 6:27; 1 Cor 9:2) or ownership and protection (Deut 32:34; Matt 27:66; Rev 7:3–8; 9:4; 20:3) of the sealed object. Here in Eph 1:13, perhaps all of these concepts operate: those sealed with the Holy Spirit are authenticated as possessors of the blessings of God, for they are owned by him, protected by him, and kept by him until the "fullness of times" and the "consummation of all things in Christ" (also see 2 Cor 1:22; Eph 4:30). The unique status of God's children as his inheritance and possession is vouchsafed by his seal—the Holy Spirit.

The Holy Spirit, is himself the seal; in addition, he is also a "pledge," a down payment guaranteeing subsequent delivery of goods and services—those relating to believers' "inheritance" (Eph 1:14; 2 Cor 1:22; 5:5)—"until the redemption of [God's own] possession." In a clever turn of phrase, the children of God—his "inheritance" (Eph 1:11)—are guaranteed an "inheritance" of their own (1:14), when they experience the fullness of "redemption," involving, no doubt, the experience also of the comprehensive scope of "every spiritual blessing" (1:3).[53] It is at the consummation of redemption in the eschaton that the full delivery of divine promises and blessings to believers ("inheritance") will be experienced—that is their ultimate end in Christ, to fully experience "every spiritual blessing" (1:3). A number of financial terms are employed in this pericope, providing a graphic image of a divine Buyer who purchases his people out of bondage ("redemption," 1:7, 14), pays with blood (1:7), seals what is now his (1:13, 14), and offers a down payment until the final delivery date (1:14). Here then is further confirmation of God's grace towards his people, entirely based upon God's own sovereignty, faithfulness, and love.

And the goal of such a prestigious divine appointment of believers as God's inheritance/possession, and their guarantee of a rich inheritance—all noted to be part of God's grand consummating plan for the universe—is that "we who hoped beforehand in Christ may be [exist] for the praise of His glory" (1:12). "Hoped beforehand" translates the perfect participle προηλπικότας (*proēlpikotas,* 1:12; only here in the NT). "Beforehand" (note the prefix προ-/*pro-*) does not indicate the past, but the present, in relation to (i.e., *before*) the future when the "consummation of all things in Christ" will occur. Until then, Christians are those who have "hoped beforehand" (unlike unbelievers without hope, 2:12). This hope is "in Christ," of course, the one who made it all possible. Thus the idea of a future consummation (1:10) is, in 1:12, hoped for by all believers[54], and indeed by all creation (Rom 8:19–22, with "hope" there as well):

53. The return to this theme of *spiritual* blessing (from πνευματικός, *pneumatikos,* 1:3) is evidenced by the mention of the *Spirit* (πνεῦμα, *pneuma,* 1:13).

54. Some scholars consider the movement from "we" in Eph 1:11–12 to "you" in 1:13 indicating a change of addressees: from all believers to Gentile believers (e.g., O'Brien, *Ephesians,* 115). However, there has been nothing in the blessing this far to suggest such a divided group of readers/listeners. First- and second-person shifts also occur in the blessings in 2 Cor 1:3–7 and 1 Pet 1:3–5 without change in addressees. There is no reason to suspect that the "we" in Eph 1:11 is any different from the "we" employed earlier: ἐν ᾧ καὶ ἐκληρώθημεν (*en hō kai eklērōthēmen,* "in whom also we have been claimed

> Christ is the very person in whom all Christians exist, and therefore the participation of all believers in this summing up of all things is assured. Now, however, before all that happens, believers live in hope that it will happen, a hope that is not some fragile expectation that may or may not come to pass, but a hope whose basis is Christ himself. God has made his people heirs so that even now "we who hope beforehand"—before the full summation of all things in Christ—will exist for "the praise of his glory."[55]

Consummation of all things in Christ, possession by God, inheritance guaranteed by the Spirit—what a hope!

SERMON FOCUS AND OUTLINES

> **THEOLOGICAL FOCUS OF PERICOPE 1**[A]
>
> **1   The God who abundantly blesses his people, graciously redeeming them as part of his plan to consummate all things in the universe in Christ, is worthy of being blessed (1:1–14).**

A. In the view of preaching espoused in this commentary, the exposition of the theology of the pericope (represented by the "Theological Focus"), with all the power and potency of the text, is the critical task of the homiletician. Needless to say, the preacher must also provide the congregation with specifics on how the theological thrust of each pericope may be put into practice so that lives are changed for the glory of God.

This is the first pericope of Ephesians, and as such it sets the stage for the rest of the book. The key verse of Ephesians, 1:9–10, is also located here, and tells us of the grand and glorious plan of God to consummate all things in Christ. And under this plan all other elements are subsumed, and in the recording of this plan all other facets of the letter find their place.

A considerable portion of the Notes was given to substantiating the theology of the pericope, the biblical author's *doing* with what he was *saying*. Of course, most of that validation need not (should not!) show up in the sermon, but only what the preacher deems necessary for a particular audience.

Possible Preaching Outlines for Pericope 1[56]

I.   God's Grand Plan

---

as an inheritance," 1:11) is structurally identical to ἐν ᾧ ἔχομεν (*en hō echomen*, "in whom we have," 1:7). Besides, earlier themes recur in 1:11–12—predestination (1:5 and 11), divine will (1:1, 5, 9 and 11), praise (1:6 and 12), and divine purpose (1:9 and 11)—indicating similarities in idea and audience. Thus, the introduction of the second person plural, "you" in 1:13, is simply an emphatic exhortation to consider the benefit of being in Christ as theirs personally—the privilege of being "sealed" by the Holy Spirit. "In whom also" from 1:11 is repeated in 1:13, further reinforcing the greatness of this privilege.

55. Thielman, *Ephesians,* 72.

56. One must see the points in these outlines as "moves," rather than static chunks of information dumped on the unwary listener. See Kuruvilla, *A Vision for Preaching.* The outlines provided are deliberately skimpy; they are intended merely to be suggestions for further thought—rough-hewn stones to be polished by the preacher. It is nigh impossible to prescribe an outline without knowing the particular audience it is to be used for, and therefore this commentary will refrain from micromanaging homiletics for the preacher. Some equally abbreviated suggestions for development are provided below each main

> God blesses his people in Christ with every blessing (1:1–3)
> God chooses and redeems his people (1:4–8a)
> God's grand plan for the cosmos (1:8b–10)

II. Man's Glorious Place

> Man deliberately chosen (1:4–8a): before time, in love, with grace, to be holy[57]
> Man told of God's plan (1:8b–10)
> Man, God's inheritance and heir of a divine inheritance—a Spirit-certified standing (1:11–14)

III. *Bless the Lord!*[58]

> How we fail to bless/praise God adequately for his grand and glorious plan
> How this failure may be remedied[59]

Another option is given below, with minor variations:

I. The Work of God

> Blessing with every blessing (1:1–3)
> Redemption through Christ (1:4–8a)
> Consummating all things (1:8b–10)
> Sealing by the Spirit (1:11–14)

II. The Role of Man

> To be holy (1:4)
> To be for the praise of God's glory (1:6, 12, 14)

III. *Bless the Lord!*

> How we fail to bless/praise God adequately for his grand and glorious plan
> How this failure may be remedied

---

point.

57. The notion of being holy will be developed in subsequent pericopes of Ephesians. Focusing on praise in this first pericope would be the most expedient way to preach it.

58. Outlines in this commentary will have an imperative of some sort as a major outline point—the application. The specificity and direction of that imperative is between the Holy Spirit, the preacher, and the audience.

59. Perhaps a corporate activity that blesses the Lord vocally, intentionally, and actively could be organized either within or separate from the worship gathering. Perhaps calling for individuals to bless the Lord in their own devotions is also appropriate.

PERICOPE 2

Christ's Power and Christ's Body

Ephesians 1:15–23

[Paul's Prayer; God's Power; Church's Position]

REVIEW, SUMMARY, PREVIEW

Review of Pericope 1: In Eph 1:1–14, Paul proclaims why the God who blesses is worthy of being blessed himself. His glorious plan to consummate all things in Christ, and his co-opting of humankind into this grand cosmic scheme finds its expression in this text: chosen to be holy, predestined to be God's children, redeemed in Christ, appointed as God's inheritance, and guaranteed an inheritance by the Spirit—all for the glory of God.

Summary of Pericope 2: The second pericope of Ephesians (1:15–23) comprises Paul's prayer for his readers. After thanking God for their faith and their love, he proceeds to intercede for their enlightenment by the Spirit that they may know God, i.e., the hope of his calling and the magnificence of their status as God's inheritance. The bulk of this pericope is formed by Paul's prayer that they would comprehend the greatness of God's incomparable power manifest in them, as the raised and exalted Christ—the authority above all other cosmic authorities—becomes their head, and they his body and his fullness.

Preview of Pericope 3: The next pericope, Eph 2:1–10 portrays the state of unbelievers. Controlled by evil powers, the world, and their own fleshly appetites, they are deserving of the wrath of God. But God, in

38

his mercy and love, saves them by grace through faith, co-exalting them with their Savior! All this displays to the cosmos God's mercy, love, grace, and kindness, as these transformed believers do the good works already prepared by God for them to do.

2. *Ephesians 1:15–23*

> **THEOLOGICAL FOCUS OF PERICOPE 2**
>
> **2   The church is intimately acquainted with God's incomparable power, and manifests that power as the fullness of Christ and as the expression of divine rule in this age (1:15–23).**
>
> 2.1   Believers are intimately acquainted not only with the hope of God's calling and his glorious inheritance that they are, but also with his great power working for them (1:15–18).
>
> 2.2   The church is the manifestation of God's incomparable power, for, as the fullness of Christ, the church is the expression of divine rule in this age, one that is over every other conceivable authority (1:19–23).

OVERVIEW

After the long sentence of Eph 1:3–14, we have yet another in 1:15–23 (169 words) that makes up Pericope 2. This pericope makes a clear transition from the previous one by introducing first person singular pronouns, "I" (1:15) and "my" (1:16), and the first person verb, "[I] do not cease" (1:16). From the blessing of the first pericope (1:3–14), we now move to a thanksgiving (1:15) followed by a prayer (1:16–19) that ends in praise (1:20–23). In the prayer, Paul asks that believers—blessed with every spiritual blessing, chosen, predestined, engraced, redeemed, forgiven, possessed as divine inheritance, and sealed for the reception of their own inheritance (1:3–14)—may have a deeper relationship with this God and a greater experience of his blessings and, especially, of his power. While the first pericope was more theocentric, this one is more ecclesial, focusing upon the body of Christ, though both pericopes mention all three Persons of the Trinity.

Connections with the first pericope are evident: "for this reason" (1:15) points back to the blessing of 1:3–14; "saints" (1:15, 16 and 1:1); "God" and "Father" (1:17 and 1:3); "glory" (1:17, 18 and 1:6, 12, 14); "faith [πίστις, *pistis*] in the Lord Jesus" (1:15) and "believers [πιστοῖς, *pistois*] in Christ Jesus" (1:3; also see 1:13); "wisdom" (1:17 and 1:8); "riches" (1:18 and 1:7); "inheritance" (1:18 and 1:14; also see 1:11); "hope" (1:18; see 1:12). Thus, Pericope 2 is closely connected to the previous one: Christ, the one in whom God will consummate "all things" (1:10) is the one under whose feet God has placed "all things" in subjection (1:22) and placed as head over "all things" (1:22), the one who fills "all things in all ways" (1:23): the repeats of "all things" are hard to miss. *Everything* necessary for that final consummation is provided for, in Christ, by God.

Several themes to be sounded in the remainder of the letter are also foreshadowed in this pericope: victory in the battle over spiritual powers (1:20–22 and 2:2, 6; 4:8; 6:10–17); the metaphor of the body for the church (1:23 and 2:16; 3:6; 4:4, 11–16; 5:22–33); the church as the fullness of Christ who is the fullness of God (1:23 and 2:21–22; 3:17, 19); "wisdom" and "revelation" (1:17 and 3:3, 10); and divine work accomplishing the consummation of all things (1:19–23 and 3:20).[1]

As with the previous pericope, a number of outlining schemes have sought to organize 1:15–23: besides the opening section in 1:15–16, one can see here the past (what God has done, 1:20), present (God's power on behalf of believers, 1:17–19), and future (the hope and the glory, 1:18). Or there might be a Trinitarian theme, again after the introduction of 1:15–16—theological (the work of God in Christ, 1:18–21), christological (the work of Christ as the head of the church and over all things, 1:22–23), and pneumatological (the work of the Spirit in revelation, 1:17). In any case, there is a clear ecclesial focus in this pericope: thanksgiving and prayer for the saints (1:15–18), God's power working for them (1:19–23), and God's Son ruling over all things for the benefit of the church that he heads (1:22–23). This section thus places the church right in the middle of God's grand and glorious purposes for all of creation, particularly as the recipient of God's power that works on its behalf. Functionally, this pericope is a prayer that God's people may understand their place in this magnificent scheme orchestrated by God.

Paul's prayer is tripartite, dealing with hope, glory, and power; the third element takes most of the space in 1:15–23 (1:19–23). "The intercession is a prayer for the realization of the blessings of the eulogy in the lives of the readers," essentially that those lavishly blessed by God (Pericope 1) may comprehend hope, glory, and power (1:18–19)—"the hope to which God has called them, the rich inheritance which he possesses in them, and the mighty power by which he energizes them."[2] Of the three facets of his request, the first two—that believers might grasp "the hope of His calling" and "the riches of the glory of His inheritance in the saints" (1:17)—hark back to the blessing of Pericope 1: divine choice and predestination (i.e., calling) were mentioned in 1:4, 5, 11; hope in 1:12; and God's inheritance and possession in 1:11, 14. The third facet of Paul's prayer, that the saints may be enlightened about divine power (1:19–23), is the longest of the three; with its relative clauses and extensions that wind down only at the end of the chapter, it is doubtless the apostle's main request. Thus, in this pericope, there is an ecclesial focus linked to God's might—the church as the recipient of divine power.

The important privilege of God's people detailed in 1:3–14 is reasserted in 1:15–23 with significant expansion. Not only are the saints chosen, predestined, engraced, redeemed, informed, and possessed by God, it is on their behalf that God exerts his incomparable power. And God works this power for his people by resurrecting, enthroning, and exalting Jesus Christ over all things. How does this benefit the church?

1. Thielman, *Ephesians*, 90.

2. O'Brien, *Ephesians*, 125–26.

This preeminent Christ, "far above all rule and authority and power and dominion," who, as head over "all things," subjects "all things" under his feet, is actually *given to the church*, which is his body and which he fills (1:21–23). In other words, this possession of God, the church (1:11, 14), itself possesses Christ, who fills it and heads his body (1:22–23). With the church and its experience of divine power as the focus of this passage, Pericope 2 (1:15–23) may be organized this way[3]:

> **A** love for *all* the saints (God's people); God *may give* the Spirit (1:15–18)
> 　　**B** the *surpassing* (ὑπερβάλλω, hyper*ballō*) greatness of His power (1:19)
> 　　　　**C** worked *in* [ἐν, *en*] Christ, *at* [ἐν] God's right, *in* [ἐν] the heavenlies (1:20)
> 　　**B'** *far above* (ὑπεράνω, hyper*anō*) all hostile agencies (1:21)
> **A'** *all* (×4); and *gave* Christ to the church (God's people) (1:22–23)

This structure emphasizes the centrality of Christ (*C*, 1:20) but also explains the greatness of divine power (*B* and *B'*, 1:19, 21), working on behalf of the church (mentioned in *A* and *A'*, 1:15–18, 22–23).

2.1   Ephesians 1:15–18

THEOLOGICAL FOCUS OF PERICOPE 2.1

2.1　Believers are intimately acquainted not only with the hope of God's calling and his glorious inheritance that they are, but also with his great power working for them (1:15–18).

TRANSLATION 2.1

1:15 *For this reason, I, in particular, having heard about your faith in the Lord Jesus and your love for all the saints,*

1:16 *do not cease giving thanks for you, while making mention [of you] in my prayers:*

1:17 *that the God of our Lord Jesus Christ, the Father of glory, may give you the Spirit of wisdom and of revelation in the knowledge of Him—*

1:18 *having had the eyes of [your] heart enlightened—so that you may know what is the hope of His calling, what [are] the riches of the glory of His inheritance in the saints,*

NOTES 2.1

2.1　*Believers are intimately acquainted not only with the hope of God's calling and his glorious inheritance that they are, but also with his great power working for them.*

"For this reason" (Eph 1:15) points back to blessing of Pericope 1 (1:1–14). Paul has just reminded the saints that their choice by God and his redemption and possession of them, as well as their sealing by the Spirit for their own inheritance, was for the

---

3. Modified from Heil, *Ephesians*, 19–20. Similar items in each element are italicized.

praise of the glory of God (1:6, 12, 14). The apostle is now thankful, having heard that they were doing exactly that—living for God's glory by demonstrating their "faith in the Lord Jesus" and their "love for all the saints" (1:15). These two elements balance each other well: "Faith in Christ apart from love for the saints is dead or incomplete; love for the saints apart from faith in Christ reduces the church to just another social service provider."[4] As in 1:1, which had "believers *in* [ἐν, *en*] Christ Jesus," here, "faith *in* [ἐν] Jesus Christ" is likely to indicate more than just the object of faith or belief. Thielman notes that faith terminology with an ἐν clause in Pauline writings "most often describes the sphere in which faith operates" (i.e., *in* Jesus Christ; see Gal 5:6; 1 Tim 1:14; 3:13; 2 Tim 1:13; 3:15)—"we should be careful not to make the separation between sphere and object too watertight."[5] Faith in Christ as the object tends to deal mostly with salvific faith exercised at the point of conversion (justification); faith in Christ as sphere is the ongoing faith exercised as one continues the Christian life in the realm of Christ (sanctification). In any case, Paul is commending the Ephesians for their vertical orientation (faith in Christ: object and/or sphere) as well as for their horizontal one (love for the saints).[6] Then Paul launches into his prayer for his readers (1:16b–23). "Petitionary prayer is an essential weapon in his apostolic armoury. Paul knows that he is engaged in a deadly spiritual warfare and needs to make use of the whole armour of God; he heeds his own advice [given in 6:18]."[7]

The content of Paul's intercession is described in 1:17–19: that the "Father of glory"[8] would give them the Holy Spirit,[9] the one who gives "wisdom" and "revelation" (likely another hendiadys typical of this letter, that makes the terms synonymous, thus characterizing the Spirit), so that they may grow in the knowledge of God.[10] Believers already have the indwelling Spirit (1:13), so this prayer in 1:17 is for a special manifestation of the Holy Spirit, that God's people may grow in the knowledge of the divine, with a more intimate understanding of God. Earlier, Paul had stated that God, in his "wisdom [σοφία, *sophia*] and insight," "made known [γνωρίζω, *gnōrizō*]" his will to his people (1:8–9). Now Paul prays that God's people will be given, by the Spirit, "wisdom

4. Fowl, *Ephesians*, 55.

5. Thielman, *Ephesians*, 94. Even if the faith were in the object/person of Jesus Christ, the equation of faith with love in 1:15 makes it clear that the faith would not just be justifying faith, but an ongoing, continuing (sanctifying) faith that governs the entirety of the Christian life (2 Cor 5:7).

6. There is a shorter manuscript reading of 1:15 that omits "love"; this shorter reading is superior on external grounds of having older witnesses. But the omission makes it a harder and somewhat unclear reading: "faith in the Lord Jesus and that for/toward all the saints." Though it is difficult to be certain, the longer reading is, on internal grounds of clarity, to be preferred.

7. O'Brien, *Ephesians*, 129.

8. "Father of glory," likely means "all-glorious Father" (seeing the genitive as adjectival), as in the terms "God of glory" (Acts 7:2; Ps 28:3), "Lord of glory" (Num 24:11; 1 Cor 2:8), and "king of glory" (Ps 24:7, 8, 9, 10). See Barth, *Ephesians*, 148.

9. Though without an article, πνεῦμα (*pneuma,* "spirit") still indicates the Holy Spirit (as in Matt 12:28; Mark 1:18; Luke 1:15, 35, 41, 67; Rom 1:4; 8:4, 5, 9, 13, 14; Gal 5:5, 16; 1 Pet 1:2). Thus one finds a Trinitarian reference in Eph 1:17 with all three persons of the Godhead mentioned.

10. The Holy Spirit as revealer is also seen in Eph 3:4–5; and he is described as the "spirit of wisdom" in Isa 11:2 (also see 1 Cor 2:6–16).

[σοφία]" and "revelation in the knowledge [ἐπίγνωσις, *epignōsis*]" of God (1:17). In other words, Paul is praying that believers, through the work of the Holy Spirit, would grow in the knowledge of God. Believers already have had their hearts enlightened (1:18).[11] Because their heart-eyes have been opened to see light, *therefore* God can give them, by the Spirit of wisdom and of revelation, knowledge of him.

What will they specifically know about God as a result? The answer to this is introduced in a petition that has three clauses, beginning, respectively, with τίς, τίς, and τί (*tis, tis,* and *ti,* "what"): "*what* is the hope of His calling, *what* [are] the riches of the glory of His inheritance in the saints, and *what* [is] the surpassing greatness of His power towards us who believe" (1:18–19). In other words, Paul desires that they know the hope to which God has called them, the glorious inheritance[12] that God possesses in them, and the great power of God working for them.[13]

Each of these three clauses becomes more elaborate than the one preceding it.[14] The first two deal with elements already noted in Pericope 1 (1:1–14): "hope," "calling" (i.e., election and predestination), and God's "inheritance." It is quite likely that the "hope of His calling" is linked to the "riches of the glory of His inheritance in the saints." These were part of a continuum that began with election and predestination in eternity past (1:4–5, 11; 1:12 also mentions those who have "hoped beforehand"), that continued with redemption in the present (1:7), and that will arrive at the summit with the "consummation of all things in Christ" in the future (1:10), on a day when God will completely possess his inheritance (1:11–14). This "[h]ope for believers is not the world's wishful thinking, but the absolute certainty that God will make true what he has promised," a conviction grounded upon the trustworthiness and faithfulness of God.[15] Paul is praying that believers will have hope in the magnificent purposes of God's call and the extraordinary value with which he sees them—his rich "glorious inheritance." "This part of the writer's petition, then, is that the readers might appreciate the wonder, the glory of what God has done in entering into possession of this people,

---

11. Again, Paul is getting carried away here: the verb, πεφωτισμένους (*pephōtismenous,* "having had . . . [your] heart enlightened," 1:18), is in the accusative, and does not agree with its subject, ὑμῖν (*hymin,* "you," 1:17), which is in the dative. The reason is probably that the subject "you" is several words away from πεφωτισμένους. Consequently, the verb has been attracted to the "you" that *follows* it, which is in the accusative (ὑμᾶς, *hymas,* 1:18). The perfect passive participle πεφωτισμένους is best read as being causal, thus: "having had . . . [your] hearts enlightened" (see Wallace, *Greek Grammar,* 631n47). That believers' hearts (i.e., the eyes thereof) are enlightened is substantiated in that, in this letter, unbelievers are said to be in darkness (4:18; 5:8). The "heart" in its Semitic conception is the center of the life of an individual (but not in contrast to the mind).

12. "Glory of His inheritance," i.e., "His glorious inheritance."

13. O'Brien, *Ephesians,* 133.

14. The first is a simple clause with a genitival construct; the second has two genitives and adds on a prepositional phrase ("in the saints"); the third has two prepositional phrases ("towards us who believe," and "according to the working of the strength of his might") and is a complex clause with a cascade of genitives.

15. Hoehner, *Ephesians,* 265. Those separated from Christ, on the other hand, are without hope (2:12). The hope of God's calling is also mentioned in 4:4.

the Church . . . and the immense privilege it is to be among these saints."[16] The relative brevity of the first two clauses of Paul's prayer reflects the fact that it summarizes what has already been covered in 1:3–14.

In sum, this knowledge, that Paul prays God would grant the Ephesians, will be threefold: of the hope of the divine calling—God's choice and predestination of believers (1:4–5, 11); of the riches of the glory of God's inheritance and possession that they are (1:11, 14); and of the greatness of God's power exercised on their behalf (1:19–21). It is this third clause, in 1:19, separated from the first two with "and," that stands out. There is also a shift in 1:19 to a first person plural pronoun; 1:15–18 dealt in second person plural pronouns (and the less frequent first person singular pronouns and one first person singular verb: "I . . . do not cease"). This shift to a first person plural in 1:19 indicates that *all* believers, including Paul himself, benefit from the working of God's incredible power. So 1:19 commences a new theme in the letter; the incredible power of God that is working on behalf of believers is explained in 1:19–23.

2.2   Ephesians 1:19–23

THEOLOGICAL FOCUS OF PERICOPE 2.2

2.2   The church is the manifestation of God's incomparable power, for, as the fullness of Christ, the church is the expression of divine rule in this age, one that is over every other conceivable authority (1:19–23).

TRANSLATION 2.2

1:19 *and what [is] the surpassing greatness of His power towards us who believe—according to the working of His mighty strength—*

1:20 *which [power] He worked in Christ, raising Him from the dead and seating [Him] at His right hand in the heavenlies,*

1:21 *far above every rule and authority and power and dominion and every name that is named, not only in this age but also in the one to come;*

1:22 *and He put all things in subjection under His feet, and gave Him as head over all things to the church,*

1:23 *which is His body, the fullness of Him who fills all things in all ways.*

NOTES 2.2

2.2   *The church is the manifestation of God's incomparable power, for, as the fullness of Christ, it is the expression of divine rule in this age, one that is over every other conceivable authority.*

Several of the words that indicate "power" in the NT show up in 1:19, δύναμις, ἐνέργεια, κράτος, ἰσχύς (*dynamis, energeia, kratos, ischys,* "power," "working," "strength," and

---

16. Lincoln, *Ephesians,* 60.

"might," respectively).[17] This accumulation of synonyms lends solemnity and seriousness to the descriptions. It is perhaps only fair to authorial intent for interpreters to "resist the temptation to parse the logic of the phrase and the meaning of its terms precisely."[18] It is highly unlikely that any delicate nuance is being indicated in the employment of different terms for power(s) here. Rather this piling on of synonyms effectively emphasizes the incomparability of divine power. "The important thing for the Ephesians to understand, the eyes of their heart having been enlightened, is that this power has been deployed on their behalf and on behalf of all who believe."[19] The magnitude of this operation of God, wrought for church, is thus driven home. The potency of Paul's description is evident in his use in 1:19 of the participle of ὑπερβάλλω (*hyperballō*, "surpassing"; it is used only five times in the NT, always by Paul: 2 Cor 3:10; 9:14; Eph 1:19; 2:7; 3:19) and the noun μέγεθος (*megesthos*, "greatness," employed only here, in the NT). Both these rare terms are found in the magical papyri and in inscriptions from Ephesus, a collection of materials dating from the second century BCE to the fifth century CE, with spells, incantations, and the like.[20] These early Christians in Ephesus "lived in a milieu characterized by flourishing magical practices, the renowned Artemis cult, and a variety of other Phrygian mysteries and astrological beliefs." Such powers, they believed, influenced every facet of their lives. Therefore they existed in a state of perpetual fear of inimical supernatural powers, as they strove to manipulate them in ways that would guarantee positive results.[21] Set against this background, Paul's declaration is a strong word of comfort as it emphasizes the supremacy of God's power over every other. Ephesians 1:21 labels four entities of hostile powers, balancing the four synonyms of divine power in 1:19: ἀρχή, ἐξουσία, δύναμις, κυριότης (*archē, exousia, dynamis, kyriotēs*, "rule," "authority," "power," and "dominion," respectively; "every name" is a more exhaustive summary phrase, including beings both natural and supernatural). Each set of four, in 1:19 and 1:21, contains the term δύναμις. Thus the listing of four hostile powers in 1:21 is likely intended to be a contrast to the four specifications of divine power in 1:19.

The decisive demonstration of divine power, Paul declares in 1:20, was the resurrection of Christ and his exaltation in heaven, thereby subjecting every other power under Christ's feet and giving him as head to the church (1:20–22). Interestingly, the

---

17. All of the uses of words for power in Ephesians "represents a substantially higher concentration of power terminology than in any other epistle attributed to Paul," with the exception of 1 Corinthians which is thrice that of the size of Ephesians. This letter has highest percentage of such terminology for an NT book (Arnold, *Ephesians*, 1). In other NT texts where any of the terms in 1:19 are found together, there are never more than two in a given instance; here there are four (Hoehner, *Ephesians*, 271)!

18. Thielman, *Ephesians*, 101.

19. Fowl, *Ephesians*, 59. "Power towards us who believe" (1:19) is equivalent to "power that works in us" (3:20).

20. Arnold, *Ephesians*, 73. He notes that three of the terms—δύναμις, ἰσχύς, and κράτος, occur together in the magical papyrus, *PGM* 35.15–23, in a recipe employed for conjuring angels (ibid., 74–75).

21. Arnold, *Ephesians*, 167. Also see Introduction. "[O]ne should also recognize that in the ancient world there was no hard-and-fast boundary between spiritual forces and social and material forces." Supernatural, hostile forces in the heavenlies can manifest in a variety human structures in the 'earthlies' (see Dan 7–8, 10; Rev 13; 1 Cor 10)" (Fowl, *Ephesians*, 61).

atonement does not figure here; it is all about the power of God exercised in the resurrection and exaltation of Jesus Christ. His seating at the Father's right—a position of great honor equivalent to a sharing of the divine throne "in the heavenlies" (see Ps 110:1; Rev 3:21)—denotes the fulfillment of his mission on earth (which included the atonement, of course). In Ephesians, evil powers also occupy the heavenlies (3:10; 6:12), so Paul goes on to further specify the scope of Christ's exalted reign over all powers. In terms of time, the eternal scope of Christ's reign is denoted in the phrase "not only in this age but also in the one to come." In terms of space, the imagery in 1:20–21 is striking: Christ is seated "at His [God's] right hand," "in the heavenlies," and "far above" every other conceivable power. In this unprecedented location and for unending time, Jesus Christ reigns supreme (Phil 2:9) as the Messianic ruler. Thus both space and time are encompassed in this depiction, and divine power in Christ overrides them all as he subjects every other existing power in the universe under his feet forever. It is God vs. all other powers in every place and in every time, and Paul has no doubt who the victor is. "All things" have been subjected by God "under His [Christ's] feet" (Eph 1:22; citing Ps 8:6), for Christ is "far above" them all (1:21). The organization of the statements that describe Christ's station in 1:22 is notable for its chiastic structure:

```
A    all things
   B    under
      C    His feet,
      C'   head
   B'   over
A'   all things
```

Christ is in complete control! While it is not completely manifest yet, Christ's control is incontrovertible, and his power is unconquerable and illimitable. It will come to full light one day, at the "consummation of all things" (1:10). That Christ is head over all things also implies that he is head over the church: both cosmos and church are under his headship. Thus, until the day of consummation, the church, "which is His body" (1:23), is a manifestation of divine control. The significance of this for the daily lives of Christians cannot be understated: the community of God's people, headed by God's Son, is playing an active and crucial role in the spiritual battle of the universe—their lives form an arena for this warfare. In and through them, God is demonstrating his control and his Son's headship, as well as the magnificent plan to consummate all things in Christ.

In just the same way as Paul linked the "consummation of all things in Christ" (1:10) to the privileged status of believers (1:11–14), so also the rulership and headship of Christ (1:20–22a) is linked to the church, to whom this ruler/head is given (1:22b–23). The magnificent consummation of all things in Christ noted in Pericope 1 had its end point in God's possession of the church; the glorious headship of Christ here in Pericope 2 has its telos in his headship of the church—his body—to which he was given. Both these ideas are probably synonymous. It is quite likely that divine possession of the church is accomplished by Christ heading and filling the church. "In this way the Church is seen to have a special role in God's purposes for the cosmos."[22]

But the significant point here is that this same incredible power that God "worked in Christ" (1:20) is at work for believers—"for us who believe" (1:19). Though all of this exercise of God's might may seem rather distant from the earthly sojourn of his people, Paul is at pains to link the supernatural overpowering and subjection of hostile entities with the existential realities of the people of God: this enthroned Christ, far above every power, is the one who has been given as head over all things *to the church* (1:22), his body. Thereby, every antagonistic power is subject not only to Christ but also to his body, the church—another facet of the saints' marvelously privileged position! "All the rule and authority God has given to Christ can be used on behalf of the Church, since God has also given this exalted Christ to the Church. In Christ, who is head over all, the Church has one who is greater than all the powers ranged against it."[23] In this sense, the church is more powerful (in Christ) than every other anti-God power.

The pericope closes, as it began, with a focus on the community of God's people ("saints," in 1:15–16; "church," in 1:22–23). After a thrilling statement about divine power, its manifestation in the exaltation of Christ, and the comprehensive scope of Christ's authority (1:20–22a), we have a return to earth, as it were, in the mention of the church (1:22b–23). And a striking utterance is made: This exalted Christ, superior to all powers, and to whom all powers are subject, was given as Head-over-all-things to the church ("to the church" comes at the end of the clause for emphasis, 1:22).That is, in his capacity as head over all things, Christ serves for the benefit of the church.[24]

Almost every part of the final verse, 1:23, is dense; only a reasonable estimation of its sense can be made, and that without too much certainty. The words in τὸ πλήρωμα τοῦ τὰ πάντα ἐν πᾶσιν πληρουμένου (*to plērōma tou ta panta en pasin plēroumenou,* "the fullness of Him who fills all things in all ways") are obviously alliterated, and they carry the combination of a cognate noun and its related verb (πλήρωμα and πληρόω, *plērōma* and *plēroō,* "fullness" and "to fill," respectively).[25] Thielman agrees: "[Paul] may have been more concerned with the majestic rhetorical effect that he created with the phrase," than with any fine nuancing of fullness or filling.[26] Besides, the two phrases in 1:23 appear to be parallel:

---

22. Lincoln, *Ephesians,* 70.

23. Ibid., 79.

24. Besides Eph 1:22–23, Christ as "head"—the expression of his ruling authority—and the church as "body" is found in 4:4, 15; 5:23.

25. Ibid., 72. In fact, Paul seems to have liked this paronomasia well enough to deploy it in again in Eph 3:19: ἵνα πληρωθῆτε εἰς πᾶν τὸ πλήρωμα τοῦ θεοῦ (*hina plērōthēte eis pan to plērōma tou theou,* "that you might be filled to all the fullness of God").

26. Thielman, *Ephesians,* 116. See Witherington, *The Letters to Philemon, the Colossians, and the Ephesians,* 245–46.

Noun	Genitive modifier
τὸ σῶμα (*to sōma* "body	αὐτοῦ *autou*) His"
τὸ πλήρωμα (*to plērōma* "the fullness	τοῦ ... πληρουμένου *tou ... plēroumenou*) ... of Him who fills"

This rhetorical play may solve some of the difficulties of this verse: clearly "body" and "fullness" are being rendered equivalently. Thus the church (the "body" of Christ) is his "fullness." Moreover, the thrust of 1:22b is upon "the church" (which ends the clause) and it would seem appropriate to consider 1:23 as dealing with the same subject as well. Thus we have two definitions of the church in 1:23: it is the "body" of Christ, *and* the "fullness" of Christ.[27] What exactly is this "fullness" (πλήρωμα)?

It is very likely that the idea of πλήρωμα in Ephesians refracts the OT concept of divine presence, akin to God's *Shekinah* glory.[28] Though the noun πλήρωμα never occurs in the LXX, the related verb πληρόω and its cognate noun πλήρης (*plērēs*, "filling") show up often with this sense in Isa 6:1; Jer 23:24; Ezek 43:5; 44:5 (LXX); etc. Psalm 71:19 (LXX) explicitly utters a wish that God may "fill" all the earth with his glory.[29] Such a notion of πλήρωμα fits Eph 3:19 and 4:13 ("fullness of God/Christ"; also see Col 1:19; 2:9). As in the OT, where it referred to divine presence, so also in Eph 1:23 the church is seen as the locus of divine presence in this dispensation. In this pericope, 1:15–23, the association between deity and called humanity is inescapable: God's inheritance and possession in the saints is one of glory (1:18; and 1:11–12, 14), his divine power is directed "toward us who believe" (1:19), and the saints are closely identified with Christ and his work (1:20 with 2:6) as his body (1:22–23). It is in this context that Paul asserts that the church is therefore "the fullness of Him" (1:23; 2:22; 3:19; 4:13). This "fullness," then is the presence and power of God. In the OT he filled the sanctuary, now in Christ, he fills the church that thereby partakes of the divine fullness. If the church is a "holy temple in the Lord" and "a dwelling of God in the Spirit" (2:21–22), it makes sense to see the church as the divine fullness—i.e., its state of being

27. Barth, *Ephesians*, 158.

28. שכינה, *shknh*, "dwelling," comes from the root שכן, *shkn*, "to dwell," and refers to the dwelling presence of God, particularly in the sanctuary (משכן, *mshkn*, "tabernacle," comes from the same root). While the word does not show up in the OT, in rabbinical thought *Shekinah* constantly denoted divine presence and has traditionally been linked to biblical manifestations of God's glory (Isa 6:1; Ezek 8:4; Jer 14:21; 17:12; etc.). See *Tg. Ps.-J.* that translates Exod 25:8 with שכינה; *'Abot R. Nat.* 18b–19a that comments on "glory" in Ezek 43:2 as being the *Shekinah*; and *Exod. Rab.* 32:4 and *b. Ber.* 17a on Exod 34:29–35; etc.

29. So also in Philo: see *Allegorical Interpretation* 3.4 ("God has filled everything and spread to every thing"); *Dreams* 2.221 ("I am there and everywhere, *filling all places* [πεπληρωκὼς τὰ πάντα, *peplērōkōs ta panta*]"); also *Questions and Answers on Genesis* 4.130.

filled by God in Christ.[30] Elsewhere in Ephesians, only God (Christ and the Spirit, to be specific) is seen to do any filling (4:10; 5:18; also see Col 2:10).

Thus, here in Eph 1:23, the church is already said to be sharing in the divine "fullness," though, later in 3:19, Paul's prayer is that readers "might be filled to all the fullness of God." "Thus, the two sides of Pauline eschatology are precisely balanced, the 'already' and the 'not yet.' In the immediate context, however, where the apostle's concern is to assure the readers of the wealth of their resources in Christ, the stress is on the 'already.'"[31] In sum, the church, Christ's body, is filled by Christ (it is the "fullness of Him"), who fills "all things in all ways."

That the church does not exhaustively or exclusively contain the "fullness" of Christ is also clear from 1:23, for he fills "*all things* in all ways"—Christ fills other things besides the church. This is quite congruent to the OT concept of divine "fullness": though God filled the limited space of the sanctuary, he also filled the entire universe (Ps 71:19; Jer 23:24). In this sense, the cosmos itself becomes a "sanctuary" of sorts: Isa 66:1–2; Ps 78:69; etc.[32] Thus both the church and "all things" are filled with Christ, though in qualitatively different fashion, of course. "All things" includes both humanity and the angelic realm, even the hostile powers of Eph 1:21. In the case of the church, the filling includes an impartation of grace and power and all that that implies. In the case of "all things," the filling denotes Christ's overwhelming rulership.[33] In other words, the church is differently characterized here from all the other recipients of divine filling. "[O]nly the church is his [Christ's] body, and he rules it, that is, he fills it in a special way with his Spirit, grace, and gifts: it is his fulness. By speaking of the church as Christ's 'body' and 'fulness,' he [Paul] emphatically underlines its significance within God's purposes."[34] And so ecclesiological and cosmological perspectives are juxtaposed in 1:22–23 to emphasize the greatness of Christ's rule, *and*

---

30. Lincoln, *Ephesians*, 75. Thus πλήρωμα is best considered in the passive sense: church is filled by Christ, rather than Christ being filled by the church (πλήρωμα in the active sense). The question of how πληρουμένου should be read is also a tricky one. It is probably best considered being in the middle voice, but with an active sense, i.e., Christ is the one doing the "filling," rather than the one being "filled" (1:23b). See Lincoln, *Ephesians*, 77; also see Arnold, *Ephesians*, 82–85. In Koine, the middle form of verbs can often be active in sense (BDF §316). Though the middle voice of this verb never occurs elsewhere in the NT, and only rarely in period literature with an active sense (Dawes, *The Body in Question*, 241), reading it so makes the best sense of τὰ πάντα ἐν πᾶσιν (*ta panta en pasin*): "all things in all ways." If πληρουμένου were to be read as a passive verb—presumably with God filling Christ—τὰ πάντα ἐν πᾶσιν would need to be read adverbially, "entirely/in all ways" (see Hoehner, *Ephesians*, 294, 299–301). This is unusual for the NT (see 1 Cor 12:6; 15:28; Col 3:11) and rather unclear in its thrust. On the other hand, reading τὰ πάντα ἐν πᾶσιν as "all things in all ways," maintains the rhetorical link with τὰ πάντα ("all things") in Eph 1:10, 11 and 22 (×2).

31. O'Brien, *Ephesians*, 151.

32. See Kuruvilla, *Genesis*, 39–49, for the idea of the created universe as a divine temple; also see Gombis, "Being the Fullness of God," 260–62.

33. See Arnold, *Ephesians*, 83–85.

34. O'Brien, *Ephesians*, 152.

to underscore the significance of the church, which in this age is the "the focus for and medium of Christ's presence and rule in the cosmos."[35]

In sum, in this pericope and in the rest of the letter, "the combination of 'fullness' and 'Spirit' language refers to *the abiding presence of God in Christ with, in, and among his people.* While Christ 'fills' all things in that his rule as Lord is cosmic in scope, his presence (and his glory) resides uniquely in the church (1:23; 4:10–13). God has created the church to be his new temple, the place on earth where he dwells 'by the Spirit' (2:22)."[36] All this to say, great is the power of God in Christ that is at work on behalf of the church.

> The brief characterization of the Church at the end of the thanksgiving period reinforces that it is constantly to be seen in its relation to Christ. It is his body, the community of believers as an organic whole, which belongs to him and over which he rules. It is his fullness, the community which he fills supremely with his presence and dynamic rule. This depiction of the Church is in the context of the cosmic extent of Christ's activity. Yet such a context only serves to set in sharper relief the significance of the Church's role. For, yes, Christ is the head over all things, but as head over all he has been given to the Church, and only the Church *is* his body. And yes, Christ is filing all things in terms of his sovereign rule, but he fills the Church in a special sense with his Spirit, grace, and gifts (cf. 4:7–11), so that only the Church *is* his fullness.[37]

God has given Christ to the church as Head-over-all-things—to the church that is the body of Christ, and is filled by Christ who fills all things in all ways. And the church, the fullness of Christ, is the manifestation of divine power and rule in this dispensation. If one thought being the inheritance of God and his possession was a tremendous privilege (Pericope 1), consider what is described in Pericope 2. Astounding!

SERMON FOCUS AND OUTLINES

THEOLOGICAL FOCUS OF PERICOPE 2

2 The church manifests God's incomparable power for, as the fullness of Christ, it expresses his divine rule in this age (1:15–23).

In this second pericope, Paul's intercession is for believers to be enlightened by the Holy Spirit regarding the hope of their calling and the magnificence of God's inheritance of them as his own possession—both elements of divine blessing that were noted in Pericope 1. Therefore these get only brief mention in Pericope 2. The thrust of this pericope is the third item that Paul wishes his readers to be enlightened about: the incomparable power of God working on behalf of believers. A sermon on this pericope would work best if focused on this facet of Paul's prayer.

The power of God works on behalf of the church and is manifested by the church in that the resurrected Christ was exalted as the head of church—which is Christ's

---

35. Lincoln, *Ephesians*, 77.

36. Gombis, "Being the Fullness of God," 262.

37. Lincoln, *Ephesians*, 80.

fullness, his body. This resurrected and exalted Christ, now head of his body, is far above every other power, authority, dominion, and rule in the cosmos. And by virtue of Christ's intimate association with the church, believers share in that exalted status. No more need they be troubled by the hostile powers of the universe.

I have chosen to draw from Paul's commendation of the Ephesians (1:15–16) for application: "powerful faith" and "powerful love." Powerful faith trumps the fear of every other so-called authority in the universe vying for power and dominion. The spiritual beings antagonistic to God and his people need have no sway over the Christian whose faith is in a powerful God who resurrected and exalted a powerful Christ as the powerful Head over the church that he fills, and over "all things" in the cosmos. And powerful love liberates the believer from the results of that same fear of inimical forces—those insecurities and apprehensions that keep one from demonstrating self-sacrificial love for the saints. As was mentioned with the outlines for Pericope 1, these general applications must be made far more specific and concrete, applicable to the particular audience the preacher addresses.

Possible Preaching Outlines for Pericope 2

I. Paul's Prayer
    Spirit's enlightenment that believers might know God (1:17)
    Knowing God by understanding the hope of his calling (1:18a)
    Knowing God by understanding the magnificent inheritance of God they are (1:18b)
    [Transition: Knowing God by understanding his power working for them (1:19)]
II. God's Power
    Manifest in the resurrection and exaltation of Christ (1:20)
    The absolute authority of the exalted Christ (1:21–22a)
III. Church's Position
    The church with this powerful Christ as its Head (1:22b)
    The church as the body of its Head, the powerful Christ (1:23a)
    The church as Christ's fullness (1:23b)
IV. *Live powerfully!*
    Failure of individuals and churches to live powerfully
    How specifically to have powerful/fearless faith (1:15–16)
    How specifically to show powerful/fearless love (1:15–16)

A Problem–Solution–Application outline is given below[38]:

I. PROBLEM: Our Fearfulness
    Inadequate faith (1:15–16)
    Inadequate love (1:15–16)
II. SOLUTION: God's Powerfulness
    The church has powerful Christ as its Head (1:20–22b)
    The church is the body of its Head, the powerful Christ (1:23a)
    The church is this powerful Christ's fullness (1:23b)
III. APPLICATION: *Live powerfully!*
    Have powerful/fearless faith
    Show powerful/fearless love

---

38. This age-old rhetorical scheme is easy to organize and manipulate; perhaps the reason is because we tend to think that way. There might very well be a hard-wiring in our brains for a problem-solution-application sequence.

PERICOPE 3

Church: Demonstration of Divine Grace

Ephesians 2:1–10

[Gentiles' Former and Present Situation; Good Works Displaying God]

REVIEW, SUMMARY, PREVIEW

Review of Pericope 2: In Eph 1:15–23, Paul thanks God for his readers' faith and love, and he prays that they may know God, i.e., the hope of their calling and the magnificence of their status as God's inheritance. As well, he prays that they would comprehend God's great power manifest in them, as the exalted Christ, above all other cosmic powers, is installed the head of the church, and the church is made his body and fullness.

Summary of Pericope 3: The third pericope of Ephesians (2:1–10) paints a dire picture: the state of unbelievers. Their lives are controlled by evil powers, by the dictates of the world, and by their own fleshly appetites. Unbelievers are marked by disobedience, and are deserving of the wrath of God. But God, in his mercy and love, saves them by grace through faith, co-enlivening, co-raising, and co-seating them with Christ in the heavenlies: co-exalted with their Savior! And all this for the purpose of displaying to the cosmos the attributes of God—his rich mercy, great love, and surpassingly rich grace and kindness—by believers doing the good works already prepared by God for them to do.

Preview of Pericope 4: The next pericope, Eph 2:11–22, depicts unbelievers being brought from the outside to inside the community of

God's people, by the work of Christ. The barrier of the condemnation of sin was removed by Christ's atonement, thus unifying all (believing) humanity in peace into a single body to God, one that is now being grown into the very dwelling of God.

3. Ephesians 2:1–10

THEOLOGICAL FOCUS OF PERICOPE 3

3   **Believers, once lost in sin, influenced by the world, evil powers, and their own flesh, and deserving of divine wrath, who were saved by grace through faith, now share in Christ's exaltation, demonstrating to the universe God's mercy, love, grace, and kindness, as they undertake good works (2:1–10).**

   3.1   The lifestyle of believers prior to salvation—lost in sin, influenced by the world, evil powers, and their own flesh—is deserving of divine wrath (2:1–3).

   3.2   Believers in Christ, saved by grace through faith, share in the privileges of Christ's exaltation, and demonstrate to the universe God's initiative in extending mercy, love, grace, and kindness (2:4–7).

   3.3   God's initiative operating in the whole process of salvation is for the eternal, cosmic demonstration of the greatness of his grace as believers undertake good works (2:8–10).

OVERVIEW

According to Best, the next few pericopes are a sort of narrative, telling the story of the move of Gentile unbelievers to Christianity (Eph 2:1–10), their assimilation with the people of God (2:11–22), and how God plans to use them, specifically to make known his grand and glorious plan of consummating all things in Christ (3:1–13).[1] While the first two pericopes described the privileged status of believers in the plan of God, this pericope (2:1–10) and the next (2:11–22) remind the believers of the Ephesian church of their state prior to obtaining God's gracious blessing. Pericope 3 (2:1–10) portrays their past condition of death, sinfulness, and fleshly evil, in contrast to their current experience of divine mercy, grace, and love that saved and exalted them. Pericope 4 (2:11–22), likewise, depicts their prior status of separation from the community of God, in contrast to their present state of membership in a new body, the church, the product of God's reconciling work.[2] Pericope 5 (3:1–13), using the paradigm of the apostle himself, will demonstrate how believers are co-opted into playing a key role in furthering God's grand consummation program.

There are strong echoes here of Pericope 2 (1:15–23): resurrection and exaltation/session (1:20; 2:5–6); "heavenlies" (1:20; 2:6); evil influences ("age/course," "rule/ruler," and "authority," occur in 1:21 and 2:2); "working" (of God in 1:19–20; of the evil spirit in 2:2); the age to come (1:21; 2:7); "surpassing" ("greatness of His power,"

---

1. Best, *Ephesians*, 198.

2. Lincoln, *Ephesians*, 85.

1:19; "riches of His grace," 2:7). Similarities between this pericope and Pericope 1 (1:1–14) include the mentions of "riches" (1:7 and 2:4, 7); "grace" (1:6, 7 and 2:5, 8); and "Beloved"/"love" and "loved" (1:6 and 2:4). As well, there are contrasts between Pericope 3 and Pericope 1: "sons of disobedience" (2:2) and "children of wrath" (2:3) vs. sonship (1:5); "desires/will" of the flesh (2:3) vs. "will" of God (1:1, 5, 9, 11).

A number of contrasts are visible within this pericope, 2:1–10, itself, that develops its thrust: "dead" in sin (2:1, 5) vs. "co-enlivened"[3] (2:5); following the "course of this world" and the dictates of the "the ruler of the authority of the air, [the ruler] of the spirit that is now working the sons of disobedience" (2:2) vs. being related intimately to Christ and exalted with him in the heavenlies (2:5–6); God's wrath (2:3) vs. God's mercy, love, grace, and kindness (2:4, 5, 7); and finally, the contrast in lifestyles between those who once "walked" in the evil way, according to the bidding of evil powers that are now in subjection to Christ (2:1–2), and those who are now to "walk" in God's way (2:10).

Gombis sees a pattern in the structure of the larger swathe of text, 1:20—2:22. In ancient Near Eastern mythology, warfare between deities concluded with the victor being proclaimed preeminent in the pantheon of gods. Subsequently, a temple or palace was erected for the triumphant one where his/her devotees engaged in celebrating the honors of the triumph and the deity's ascendancy. This ideological pattern of divine warfare included these elements: conflict, victory, kingship, house-/temple-building, and celebration—a typical framework in the ancient world to account for the supremacy of a particular god. This stylistic layout also appears to be followed in 1:20—2:22.[4]

Ephesians 1:20–2:22	Elements of Victorious Warfare
1:20–23	Lordship
2:1–16	Conflict–victory
2:17	Victory shout
2:18	Celebration
2:19–22	House-/temple-building

The bold claim of 1:20–23, that Jesus Christ had been exalted to the position of cosmic lordship, is defended in 2:1–16, with the vindication of his credentials as triumphant over all other powers. These hostile forces that held humanity bondage (2:1–3) were defeated by Christ, and their captives were freed from death, raised, and exalted, demonstrating divine victory to conquered foes (2:4–7)—a triumph accomplished entirely by this strong one's initiative and power (2:8–10). With this victory, a new humanity of believers that transcended racial and national divides and that overcame these schisms was created—the conqueror's subjects unified as one citizenry (2:11–16). A victory

---

3. Or "made us alive together with." Throughout, I have translated Greek words beginning with συν- (*syn*, the preposition "with") rather woodenly, by prefixing the corresponding English words with "co-" to reflect the structure of the original word.

4. Gombis, "Ephesians 2," 405–8. He notes as examples, the Ugaritic Baal Cycles, and the *Enuma Elish*, as well as Exod 15; Pss 24, 46; and Rev 12, besides Eph 1:20—2:22.

shout proclaimed the peace so brought about (2:17), followed by the celebration of access to this God (2:18). Thereupon, the construction of a new temple began—the church, the locus where God in Christ dwells by his Spirit (2:19–22).[5]

The current pericope (Pericope 3, 2:1–10), with two sentences, 1:1–7 and 1:8–10, is bounded on either side by περιπατεῖν, *peripatein,* "to walk" (in 2:2 and 2:10).[6] As well, "dead in transgressions and sins" is found in 2:1 and 2:5, and "by grace you have been saved" in 2:5 and 2:8, tying it all together as a cohesive unit. In terms of development, 2:1–3 details the Ephesian believers' earlier sin-ridden status; 2:4–5, their salvation (and God's mercy, love, and grace); 2:6, their exalted status in Christ; 2:7, God's purpose in this exaltation; and 2:8–10, the gracious working of God in their lives.[7] The emphatic focus upon the work of God in every facet of the Christian's life is impossible to miss here.

3.1 Ephesians 2:1–3

> **THEOLOGICAL FOCUS OF PERICOPE 3.1**
>
> 3.1 The lifestyle of believer prior to salvation—lost in sin, influenced by the world, evil powers, and their own flesh—is deserving of divine wrath (2:1–3).

TRANSLATION 3.1

2:1 *And while you were dead in your transgressions and sins,*

2:2 *in which you formerly walked according to the course of this world, according to the ruler of the authority of the air, [the ruler] of the spirit that is now working in the sons of disobedience,*

2:3 *among whom we all also formerly lived in the lusts of our flesh, performing the desires of the flesh and of the mind, and were by nature children of wrath, as also [were] the rest;*

NOTES 3.1

3.1 *The lifestyle of believer prior to salvation—lost in sin, influenced by the world, evil powers, and their own flesh—is deserving of divine wrath.*

One important observation to start with: the first person plural "you," in 2:1, and the second person plural "we," in 2:3, do not designate Gentiles and Jews, respectively. There has been no reason, thus far, to suspect any such ethnic discrimination on Paul's

---

5. Gombis, "Ephesians 3:2–13," 315.

6. "To walk" is a Semitism that means "to live," primarily in a moral and ethical fashion: Gen 17:1; Ps 1:1; Isa 33:16; Micah 6:8; etc. (using הלך, *hlk,* "to walk"); so also in the NT, employing περιπατέω (*peripateō,* "to walk"): Eph 2:2, 10; 4:1, 17 (×2); 5:2, 8, 15; Col 1:10; 2:6; 3:7; 4:5; etc.

7. Though Pericope 2 is quite logical in layout, Thielman confesses that its ideas are "expressed in a syntactically disjointed way, probably betraying the occasional and oral nature of the letter's origin" (*Ephesians,* 119). No doubt, this somewhat ad hoc feel compounds the emotive power of the content.

part. In fact, there is a back and forth shift between first and second person plural nouns in this pericope.

2:1–2	Second person plural
	2:3–7 First person plural
2:8–9	Second person plural
	2:10 First person plural

Moreover 2:1 is repeated in 2:5 with the only difference being the pronoun, suggesting the general equivalence of these pronouns and the persons so indicated. Thus the first person plural simply denotes Paul including himself among those who were once in sin—the plight of every believer in times past (notice the emphasized "we *all*" in 2:3)—but are now in Christ.

The opening "and" followed by a participle (giving a temporal sense: "while you were dead," 2:1), and the succession of clauses in 2:2–3, leave 2:1–3 as a dangling, incomplete sentence. In fact, 2:1 is repeated in 2:5 to clarify where Paul was going with that derailed train of thought, and to get it back on track. Nonetheless, the incompleteness achieves a suspenseful tension that is resolved only with the disjunctive "but" in 2:4 and the three main verbs in 2:5–6.

The life of non-Christians is characterized in this pericope as one of death—death to God, i.e., a lack of response to God or anything related to God: they were dead in their "transgressions and sins."[8] There are four ἐν-clauses in 2:2–3: "in which [i.e., in transgressions and sins] you formerly walked," "in the sons of disobedience," "in/among whom [i.e., in/among the sons of disobedience] we also formerly lived," and "in the lusts of our flesh." The flesh is that ethical entity in humans that opposes God and is irredeemable and incorrigible, constantly battling the indwelling Spirit (in believers) to have its way (Rom 8:5–8; Gal 3:3; 5:16–17). Being "in the flesh" is to be in a sphere of existence in which one is unable to please God (Rom 8:8). In Gal 5:16–24, the "lusts of the flesh" are contrasted with the "fruit of the Spirit." "All humankind has chosen willfully and thoughtfully to live among the sons of disobedience and to act on their rebellious cravings, desires, and thoughts."[9]

This is the only occurrence of θέλημα (*thelēma*, "desire/will," Eph 2:3) in this letter that stands for the desire of humanity, specifically that of the flesh and of the mind; elsewhere it indicates the "will" of God (1:1, 5, 9, 11; 5:17; 6:6).[10] Thus, "desires of the flesh and of the mind" emphasizes the anti-God stance and activities of the "sons of disobedience" and the "children of wrath" (2:2–3). And, in light of Paul's later concern that believers do not lapse into the sexually immoral conduct characteristic of the

---

8. The phrase "transgressions and sins" is characteristic of the redundant style in Ephesians (already seen in 1:4, 8, 17, etc.).

9. Ibid., 127.

10. The combination of "flesh" and "mind" in 2:3 is another of the typical redundancies in this letter. "Rather than making fine anthropological distinctions, this language reinforces the comprehensive picture of alienation from God outside of Christ" (Fowl, *Ephesians*, 71).

"sons of disobedience" (5:3–6), it is possible that the "desires" here also point to some inappropriate sexual behavior.[11]

All of this paints the hopeless predicament of unbelievers, mired as they are in the depths of degrading evil. And, prior to regeneration, the entire sphere of the Ephesians' life was governed by evil that affected their environment (they lived "according to the course of this world," 2:2) and their inclinations ("the desires of the flesh and of the mind," 2:3), and by the evil influences of a nefarious foe ("the ruler of the power of the air, [the ruler] of the spirit that is now working," 2:2).[12] The *ruler of the authority of the air*" (2:2) employs words (and cognates of words) that had shown up in 1:21 to describe hostile powers. There, however, it was God's power "working" to overcome these forces (1:20); here, in the pre-Christ "age," it is the evil powers that are in ascendancy, "working" in unbelievers (2:2). So powerful are the influences of these evil beings that their victims are referred to as "sons of disobedience," people characterized by disobedient lives, "rebels against the authority of God who prefer to answer the promptings of the archenemy."[13] Fowl observes wryly that the "sons of disobedience" are quite obedient—just not obedient to *God*. "The picture painted in 2:2 is of people who are in the thrall of forces opposed to God. Satan has captivated them; they are under Satan's dominion."[14] And the result—divine punishment: the "sons of disobedience" are also "children of wrath" (2:3).

In sum, the sphere of unbelievers' existence was that of "transgressions and sin" (2:1), "in which" they used to walk, the ethical realm to which they belonged (2:2). And implicated in this mess are the "world" and the "[evil] ruler" (external influences; 2:2), and the "flesh/mind" (internal influence; 2:3)—a total pervasiveness of sin in every aspect of their lives. This was a dire situation, indeed! That this was true of such people "by nature" (2:3) indicates that humanity is *born* dead to God.[15] The inherent sinfulness of humankind is indicated in that expression (Rom 5:12, 19; Job 14:1–4; 15:14; Pss 51:5; 58:3; Jer 3:25; 2 Esd 7:68, 118); born with the "flesh," humans are born sinful. "Unbelievers are 'dead,' not because of a succession of sins which brought death,

---

11. Thielman, *Ephesians*, 126.

12. O'Brien, *Ephesians*, 155–56. Likely the mention of a "ruler" indicates a hierarchical ordering of entities in the dark realm under some authority. The word translated "course" in Eph 2:2 is αἰών, *aiōn*, that also means "age." The word had already been employed in 1:21 and will show up again in 2:7; 3:9, 11, 21. More than a chronological era, it means "course" or "mode of existence," one that is anti-God and alien to his standards. The "air" in which this evil power operates (2:2) is that intermediate space between heaven and earth, ostensibly the theater of evil spirits. Plutarch, *Moralia* 274b ("Roman Questions," 40), noted that the "open air" is "full of gods and spirits"; likewise, Philo, *De gigantibus* 1.6, who observed that demons hover in the "air." But Christ is located "far above" this arena (Eph 1:21; 4:10), and all of those evil powers are located under his feet (1:22).

13. O'Brien, *Ephesians*, 161. This labeling of a person as a "son of *X*" is a Hebraism that denotes one's "dominant characteristic or affiliation . . . a fundamental disposition" (see Acts 4:36, where Barnabas is named the "son of encouragement"; Fowl, *Ephesians*, 69–70). So also "children of wrath" in Eph 2:3. "Wrath" and "sons of disobedience" are also found together in 5:6.

14. *Ephesians*, 70.

15. Death as penalty for sin is oft noted in the Bible: Gen 2:16–17; 3:3–4; Lev 18:5; Deut 30:19; Rom 1:32; 5:12–14, 18–21; 6:23; 7:9–11; 8:2, 13; 1 Cor 15:56; Col 2:13; Rev 3:11.

but because they have never come alive as believers. . . . 'Children of wrath by nature' thus describes 'a permanent condition' in the relation of unbelievers to God."[16]

3.2 Ephesians 2:4–7

> **THEOLOGICAL FOCUS OF PERICOPE 3.2**
>
> 3.2 Believers in Christ, saved by grace through faith, share in the privileges of Christ's exaltation, and demonstrate to the universe God's initiative in extending mercy, love, grace, and kindness (2:4–7).

TRANSLATION 3.2

2:4 *but God, being rich in mercy, because of His great love with which He loved us,*

2:5 *even while we were dead in transgressions, co-enlivened [us] with Christ—by grace you have been saved—*

2:6 *and co-raised and co-seated [us] in the heavenlies in Christ Jesus,*

2:7 *in order that in the coming ages He might demonstrate the surpassing riches of His grace in kindness toward us in Christ Jesus;*

NOTES 3.2

3.2 *Believers in Christ, saved by grace through faith, share in the privileges of Christ's exaltation, and demonstrate to the universe God's initiative in extending mercy, love, grace, and kindness.*

Finally, in 2:4–6 we come to the three main verbs of the single sentence that comprises 2:1–7, describing three divine operations, each prefixed with συν- (*syn-*, the preposition "with," translated as the prefix "co-"): συνεζωοποίησεν, συνήγειρεν, συνεκάθισεν (*synezōpoiēsen, synēgeiren, sunekathisen,* "co-enlivened," "co-raised," "co-seated"; 2:5, 6). All three indicate identification with Jesus Christ with whom believers were enlivened (or made alive), raised, and seated—all of these happened also to Christ in 1:20. Thus these actions of God may be considered further expressions of divine power, continuing the theme from Pericope 2 (1:19–20).[17]

Paul's goal in this pericope is to mark a contrast between the past ("dead," 2:1) and the present ("alive," 2:5): twice he uses "formerly" (2:2, 3). Once walking according to world, controlled by evil forces, and indulging in fleshly lusts, by nature doomed for wrath (2:1–3), they are now loved and engraced so as to be made alive with Christ, raised with Christ, seated with Christ, in the heavenlies in Christ (2:4–6; below). The old "course" is of the world and in sin (2:2); but soon comes a new age that is of Christ and in the "heavenlies" (2:6). Notice also the contrast between "by nature" (2:3) and "by grace" (2:5, 8). The destinations of the two groups are diametrically opposite—one

---

16. Best, *Ephesians*, 211. Of its thirty-six instances in the NT, only in five does ὀργή (*orgē*, "wrath") refer to human wrath; the rest indicate God's (Hoehner, *Ephesians*, 323).

17. The three συν-compounded words are found only here and in Luke 22:55; Col 2:12, 13; 3:1 in the NT; they are rare in classical Greek literature and even in the LXX.

is doomed for divine wrath (2:3), the other is the recipient of God's mercy, love, grace, and kindness (2:4, 5, 7, 8). Believers have moved from one to another. One gets the sense that there has been a change of lineage: from doomed "by nature" to exalted "in Christ." The extensive recounting of "[t]he gravity of their previous condition [2:1–3] . . . serves to magnify the wonder of God's mercy."[18]

"You were dead" (2:1), *but God* "made us alive" (2:4). "Children of wrath" (2:3) have now become God's children, saved by grace through faith. Indeed, to underscore the plight of unbelievers prior to this divine intervention, the wording of 2:1 is repeated: "even while we were dead in your trespasses." The first person plural ensures that Paul himself is counted amongst those now receiving God's mercy, love, grace, and kindness. The magnitude of divine mercy is described as "rich" (πλούσιος, *plousios,* 2:4); God's kindness is described likewise (πλοῦτος, *ploutos,* "riches," 2:7).[19] This was no miserly donation out of pity, but a lavish gift of grace made in love.

What a shared destiny—what is true of Christ, is now also true of believers! Indeed, it is only because of their identification in Christ that believers in him are enlivened, raised, and seated with him. Even though the compound συν-verbs indicate the co-experience with Christ, the point is reinforced by the addition of the phrases "with Christ" and "in Christ" in 2:5, 6, denoting the sphere in which this divine enlivening, raising, and seating of believers occurs. The similarities of the raising up and seating of Christ and that of believers are striking (1:20; 2:6). While "power" is not mentioned here in Pericope 3, there can be no doubt that these parallels signal that the same divine might that worked in Christ (1:19–20a) is also working in believers. The identification of believers with Christ is extensive, including the sharing of his destiny. With Christ in the heavenlies, with him "far above" every inimical power— all subjected under his feet (1:21–22)—believers, too, are in a position of superiority over these hostile forces. Thus, their bondage to the world, the evil ruler, and the flesh (2:2–3) has been broken in this identification with Christ. No longer does the child of God have to succumb to these influences of evil. Of the co-seating with Christ, Arnold notes that "there is no other theological construct which could so effectively and vividly communicate to the readers their access to the authority and power of the risen Lord."[20] Yet the battle continues (and equipment for this conflict is provided in Ephesians 6) as long as the flesh remains—i.e., it is lifelong. Thus, victory is *already* achieved, *but not yet.*

---

18. O'Brien, *Ephesians,* 158.

19. God as gracious and compassionate and merciful echoes as a theme in the OT and Jewish literature: Exod 34:6; Num 14:18; Neh 9:17; Pss 86:5, 15; 103:8; 145:8; Joel 2:13; Jonah 4:2; Sir 2:11; etc. These are reiterations of what is almost a confessional formula, first articulated by Yahweh himself in Exod 34:6.

20. Arnold, *Ephesians,* 148. It is to be noted that the seating of believers in the heavenlies is not at God's right hand as it was for Christ (1:20): that is obviously a seat reserved for a special person. There is another difference between what has happened to the saved and the Savior: believers' experience of being enlivened, raised, and seated is a positional status (at least for now, in this age); Christ's was an actual resurrection and exaltation.

This salvation by grace (2:5; also 2:8) includes the enlivening, raising, and seating of believers with Christ, as well as rescue from bondage to sin and from divine wrath.[21] The unique perfect periphrastic structure (verb of being + anarthrous participle) to describe salvation, ἐστὲ σεσῳσμένοι (*este sesōmenoi*, "you have been saved," 2:5), emphasizes salvation with its continuing state and ongoing benefits. God's grace not only saves (justifies), but also continues to sanctify believers (and will one day glorify them, as well). And of course, it is a *divine* passive—God is the one doing all the saving.[22] While aorist verbs are used to describe the making alive, raising up, and seating with Christ, salvation employs a perfect verb, indicating the special nature of this endeavor. With its clear past indication, the perfect pulls the aorists ("co-enlivened," "co-raised," and "co-seated") into the past as well—these are being considered as already accomplished divine undertakings.[23] In any case, by these stunning actions undertaken by God, believers have already become partners with Christ in the events of redemptive history.

> For [Paul], Christ's death was a death to the old order, to the powers of this age, including sin, and his resurrection was a coming alive to a new order, in which he functioned as Lord with the power of God. Christ's death and resurrection changed the power structures in history. For believers to have died and been raised with Christ was the equivalent of having been transferred from the old dominion to the new, because in God's sight they had been included in what had happened to Christ. The fact of temporal distance created no major problem for Paul because he did not think of individuals as isolated from the power sphere in which they existed, but rather viewed present existence as continuing to be determined by the events on which it was founded. He saw the new dominion as a whole as participating in those events of Christ's death and resurrection through its representative head.[24]

This is incredible: "sons of disobedience" and "children of wrath," who were fraternizing with the enemies of God (2:1–3), are now, in Christ Jesus, afforded all the benefits and privileges that appertain to God's Son!

One striking element in this account of salvation is the absence of any mention of the cross or Christ's atoning work, unlike in Rom 5:6–11 or even Col 2:11–15, which is otherwise quite similar to Eph 2:5–6 and its surrounding context. Moreover, in the seven undisputed Pauline letters, there is significant attention paid to believ-

21. "Grace" is a major theme of this letter, occurring in 1:2, 6, 7; 2:5, 8; 3:2, 7, 8; 4:7, 29; 6:24. It means unmerited or undeserved favor—"favour towards men contrary to their desert" (Burton, *Galatians*, 424).

22. In all of these divine transactions described in 2:4–10, God's initiative resounds throughout. As Best rightly noted, "[w]e can arrange neither to be born nor to be reborn" (*Ephesians*, 215).

23. A future actual resurrection for believers waits: Rom 8:23, 29; 11:15; 1 Cor 15:12–58; 2 Cor 4:16—5:10; Phil 3:21; 1 Thess 4:16; 2 Tim 2:11, 18. The co-seating with Christ likely indicates the future co-reign of the believer with him: Matt 13:43; Rom 8:17, 30; 1 Cor 6:2; 2 Tim 2:12; 1 Pet 2:9; Rev 3:21; 5:10; 20:4; 22:5. Thus Eph 2:6 is another example of a realized eschatology—a future event considered as having been actualized in the past. Unlike the undisputed Pauline letters, "Ephesians clearly emphasizes the realized aspect of the tension" (Thielman, *Ephesians*, 137).

24. Lincoln, *Ephesians*, 108.

ers dying or suffering with Christ (Rom 6:5–6; 1 Cor 1:18–2:5; 4:8–17; 5:7–8; 6:7; 9:19–23; 10:31—11:1; 2 Cor 4:7–12; 8:8–9; Gal 2:19; Phil 3:10; 1 Thess 2:14–15; Phlm 1). However in Ephesians, such an emphasis is lacking, and that might explain the absence of any statement about the cross (though see 1:7: "redemption through His blood"; and 3:1, 13; 6:20, for Paul's suffering for the cause of Christ; but there are no συν- words that indicate believers co-suffering or co-dying with Christ, as there are in Rom 6:3, 4, 6; 8:17). The emphasis in this pericope, and in the one before, on evil powers and their incapacitation fits the focus here on resurrection and exaltation, rather than on death and suffering.[25]

3.3 Ephesians 2:8–10

> **THEOLOGICAL FOCUS OF PERICOPE 3.3**
>
> 3.3 God's initiative operating in the whole process of salvation is for the eternal, cosmic demonstration of the greatness of his grace as believers undertake good works (2:8–10).

TRANSLATION 3.3

2:8 *for by grace you have been saved through faith; and this not of yourselves, [but] the gift of God;*

2:9 *not of works, so that no one may boast,*

2:10 *for we are His workmanship, having been created in Christ Jesus for good works that God prepared beforehand, so that we may walk in them.*

NOTES 3.3

3.3 *God's initiative operating in the whole process of salvation is for the eternal, cosmic demonstration of the greatness of his grace as believers undertake good works.*

This salvation wrought by God was no private act done under cover, but a public demonstration, even proof (the verb, ἐνδείχνυμι, *endeichnymi,* "to show" can also mean "to prove") of divine grace and kindness—a display for all eternity on a cosmic scale.[26] This was the goal of God's co-enlivening, co-raising, and co-seating of believers with Christ. "It can be said that if the raising of Christ from death to sit in the heavenly realms was the supreme demonstration of God's surpassing [ὑπερβάλλον, *hyperballon,* 1:19] power, then the raising of believers from spiritual death to sit with Christ in the heavenly realms is the supreme demonstration of God's surpassing [ὑπερβάλλον,

---

25. See Thielman, *Ephesians,* 136–37.

26. Three ἐν (*en,* "in") phrases again show up in 2:7: "*in* the coming ages," "*in* kindness," and "*in* Christ Jesus," all modifying the verb "demonstrate" (three other ἐν phrases also occurred in 2:2–3; see above). The plural "ages" in 2:7 indicates "one age supervening upon another like successive waves of the sea, as far into the future as thought can reach," so that "[t]hroughout time and in eternity the church, this society of pardoned rebels, is designed by God to be the masterpiece of his goodness" (Bruce, *The Epistles to the Colossians, to Philemon, and to the Ephesians,* 288).

2:7] grace."[27] Thus, God's concern is not just individuals or even the community of his people; it involves the whole of creation, the entire universe to which his grace is put on display. According to Lincoln, there are three implications of divinely wrought salvation: a future is assured, for the new order that has commenced; God is continuing to work in believers, displaying his grace for all eternity; and the magnificence of what God has done becomes clearer as time marches on, its fullness to be revealed in the eschaton.[28] All of this is part of the consummation of all things in Christ, for the glory of God (1:6, 12, 14), the ultimate goal.

In structure, 2:8a makes an assertion, followed by 2:8b and 2:9a, each a negative statement, but with some extra information added: "this not of yourselves, [but] the gift of God" (2:8b), and "[this] not of works, so that no one may boast" (2:9a). The referent of "this" in 2:8 (and of "this" implied in 2:9) is best taken as referring to the entire process of God's saving work.[29] God's glorious salvation is, all of it, a gift from God. Paul pointedly makes it clear by a deviation from normal word order: 2:8c literally has "of God the gift," thus juxtaposing "of yourselves" with "of God"—making 2:8bc literally read "and this not of yourselves, *of God* the gift."[30]

There is no doubt at all about the universality of both the predicament of sin and the provision of God's salvific grace to *all* who believe, "by faith" (2:8). While the salvation graciously offered is universal in its provision, it is not universal in its application, for the instrument of that salvation is faith on the part of the believer.[31] "Although it is tempting to think of salvation on the model of some transaction between God and believers, there is nothing humans can do to evoke God's salvation or to earn it. In the societies of late capitalism, where almost every encounter can be reduced to a set of transactions between autonomous agents, this is a hard notion to accept."[32] But salvation is neither initiated by human effort (2:8), nor is it a reward for human good deeds (2:9).[33] How could it be, when humans are "dead," controlled by the world, evil pow-

27. Lincoln, *Ephesians*, 110.

28. From ibid., 111.

29. The antecedent of the neuter τοῦτο (*touto*, "this," 2:8) is likely not πίστεως (*pisteōs*, "faith") or χάριτι (*chariti*, "grace"), both of which are feminine. Neither can "this" refer to ἐστε σεσῳσμένοι (*este sesōsmenoi*, "you are saved"), which employs a masculine participle. Also notice that οὐκ ἐξ ἔργων (*ouk ex ergōn*, "not of works") in 2:9 is parallel to οὐκ ἐξ ὑμῶν (*ouk ex hymōn*, "not of yourselves") in 2:8. If the latter qualifies τοῦτο, then so does the former, by parallelism. In that case, if τοῦτο referred to faith in 2:8, to say in 2:9 that "*faith* is not of works" is tautological. It would make better sense to say that *salvation*—the whole package—is "not of works," making "this" in 2:8 also refer to salvation (Thielman, *Ephesians*, 143n2). It might well be that Paul could also have been thinking of the neuter τὸ σωτήριον (*to sōtērion*, "salvation," as used in 6:17). Hoehner observes that τοῦτο frequently points backwards, not forwards in this letter: 1:15 referring to 1:3–14; 3:1 referring to 2:11–22; and 3:14 referring to 3:1–13. So, "[r]ather than any particular word it is best to conclude that τοῦτο refers back to the preceding section," 2:4–8a, and especially 2:8a, salvation-by-grace-through-faith (*Ephesians*, 343).

30. Interestingly enough, "gift" does not occur anywhere else in the Pauline letters.

31. Ibid., 341. Also coming into play in all this is divine choice and predestination (1:5, 11).

32. Fowl, *Ephesians*, 79.

33. For salvation "not of works," also see 2 Tim 1:9; Titus 3:5. For works as opposed to faith, see Rom 3:20, 28; 4:1–5; 9:32; Gal 2:16; 3:2–5, 7, 9.

ers, and the flesh, and headed to suffer divine wrath (2:1–3)?[34] Anglican Archbishop William Temple once said: "All is of God: the only thing of my very own which I can contribute to redemption is the sin from which I need to be redeemed."[35]

As was noted, this pericope begins with how these saved ones *once* used to "walk" (2:2); it ends with how they *now* should "walk" (2:10). Thus "good works" in 2:10 is the diametric opposite of "trespasses and sins" in 2:1. Notice the parallels:

2:1–2	τοῖς παραπτώμασιν καὶ ταῖς ἁμαρτίαις (*tois paraptōmasin kai tais hamartiais* "in transgressions and sins	… ἐν αἷς … *en hais* … in which	ποτε περιεπατήσατε *pote periepatēsate*) you formerly walked"
2:10	ἐπὶ ἔργοις ἀγαθοῖς (*epi ergois agathois* "for good works	… ἐν αὐτοῖς … *en autois* … in them	περιπατήσωμεν *peripatēsōmen*) we may walk"

Thus, though salvation is not "of works" (2:9), the outcome is *for* works (2:10). Works are not the ground of salvation, but the goal thereof—salvation's fruit, not its root.[36] Thus all of salvation—justification *and* sanctification[37]—is a divine operation of grace, for God it is who has "prepared beforehand" those good works for them to perform (2:10).[38] That grace is involved in both facets of salvation (justification, 2:8–9; sanctification, 2:10) is also clear from the syntax of 2:8–10. Two γὰρ (*gar,* "for") statements (2:8–9 and 2:10), each including a ἵνα (*hina,* "so that") clause, expand 2:7 and explain why God's grace is demonstrated. Firstly, "*for* by grace" those who believe—i.e., those who have faith—are saved, "*so that* no one may boast" (2:8–9). Secondly, divine grace was also offered "*for* good works," "*so that*" believers might "walk in them" (2:10). In both cases, justification and sanctification, God's initiative of grace stands firm and unshakeable.[39]

---

34. O'Brien, *Ephesians,* 176.

35. Temple, *Nature, Man, and God,* 401.

36. This is a concept found often in the NT: see Rom 4:5; 1 Cor 1:24; 2 Cor 8:7; 9:8; Gal 5:6; 1 Thess 1:3; 2 Thess 1:11; Jas 2:14–26; Rev 1:19; etc. Good deeds are commended in Rom 2:7, 10; 13:3; Acts 9:36; Gal 6:10; 1 Tim 2:10; 5:10; 6:18; and using another formulation, in 1 Tim 5:25; Titus 2:7, 14; 3:8, 14; Heb 10:24. On the concept of good works as "obedience of faith" (Rom 1:5) see Kuruvilla, *Privilege the Text!* 195–207, and ibid., 252–58, for the value of such obedience in the Christian life.

37. Believers' glorification, too, is of God's grace as well, as Eph 2:6–7 indicates (also see 1 Cor 1:3–6; 1 Pet 1:10, 13).

38. Adding to the πρό- (*pro-*) words that have been encountered thus far (1:4, 5, 9, 11, 12; see Pericope 1) is yet another in 2:10: προετοιμάζω (*proetoimazō,* "prepare beforehand"). In line with the others, this indicates that God's preparation of good works for his children to perform has also been planned "before the foundation of the world" (1:4). One might carp that this eliminates human freedom, but are humans *absolutely* free in the first place? "We are always acting under the influence, constraint, and encouragement of things, processes, circumstances, and people outside of ourselves. Sometimes we recognize these influences; often we are unaware of their effects on us. . . . The notion of freedom as freedom from all constraint is simply unintelligible," not to mention unbiblical (Fowl, *Ephesians,* 81).

39. It is quite likely that Paul intends both justification and sanctification in the saving work of God mentioned in 2:5 and 2:8, without making a temporal distinction between the two. Both are gracious acts of God and both are actualized by the believer's faith: even the walking in good works is predicated

This formulation [in 2:10] is an emphatic way of underlining the ethical dimension already present in the assertion of 1:4 that God chose believers before the foundation of the world, in order that they might be holy and blameless before him in love. To say that God has prepared the good works in advance in his sovereign purpose is also to stress in the strongest possible way that believers' good deeds cannot be chalked up to their own resolve, but are due solely to divine grace. It is grace all the way. Even the living out of salvation in good works is completely by grace. But this is not a total determinism. God has prepared the good works in advance "in order that we might live in them." The human activity of "walking" is still necessary; the actual living out of God's purpose in the world has to take place.[40]

In sum, "we are His *workmanship*"—ποίημα (*poiēma*, 2:10), which is used elsewhere by Paul in Rom 1:20, for the creation of the universe. Here, then, is a *second* creation, of sorts, in Eph 2:10. In fact, the verb used here, κτίζω (*ktizō*, "create"), is employed in Ephesians only of the first creation of the universe and for this *second* creation of a new peoples (see 3:9 for the former; 2:10, 15; 4:24 for the latter). In any case, in the NT κτίζω is always used to describe a work of God.[41] The construction in 2:10 is quite emphatic that this is God's doing: literally, "For his workmanship, we are." That marks the critical significance of what is happening in salvation. God is certainly doing an amazing thing, a part of his grand scheme to "consummate all things *in Christ*." Likewise, even here, this "workmanship" of God—believers—are created *in Christ Jesus*.[42] In other words, the role of believers is nothing less than a participation in God's magnificent scheme for the cosmos in Christ.

SERMON FOCUS AND OUTLINES

THEOLOGICAL FOCUS OF PERICOPE 3

3 Believers, sharing Christ's exaltation, demonstrate to the universe God's mercy, love, grace, and kindness as they undertake good works (2:1–10).

The third pericope of Ephesians contrasts the past and present states of believers. Before salvation in Christ, they were "dead" in sins, controlled by evil powers and by the influences of the world and their own flesh, and destined for divine wrath. But God co-enlivened them with Christ, co-raised them with Christ, and co-seated them with Christ in the heavenlies, for this purpose: that they may display the abundance of divine mercy and love, his grace and kindness, through the good works God has already prepared for them to undertake.

---

and grounded upon faith (the "obedience of faith"). For good works, performed in the power and equipping of God, see: 2 Cor 9:8; Col 1:9–12; 2 Thess 2:16–17; Heb 13:20–21.

40. Lincoln, *Ephesians*, 115–16.

41. Besides those verses in Ephesians, see Matt 19:4; Mark 13:19; Rom 1:25; Col 1:16; 3:10; 1 Tim 4:3; Rev 4:11 (×2); 10:6.

42. Here, as in most occurrences of the phrase, the sense of "in Christ Jesus" is of the sphere into which believers have been introduced. As a result, all of these magnificent benefits accrue to them.

Possible Preaching Outlines for Pericope 3

I.   PAST: The Status of Unbelievers
      "Dead" in sin (2:1)
      Controlled by evil entities (2:2b)
      Influenced by the flesh and world (2:2a, 3a)
      Fate: Deserving of divine wrath (2:3b)
II. PRESENT: The Station of Believers
      Co-enlivened, co-raised, and co-seated with Christ in the heavenlies (2:4–6)
      Cause: God's rich mercy, great love, surpassingly rich grace and kindness (2:4–7)
III. FUTURE: The Service of Christians
      Saved by grace through faith as a gift from God (2:8)
      No grounds for boasting (2:9)
      Entirely God's workmanship created in Christ (2:10a)
      For good works that God himself has already prepared (2:10b)
IV. *Show off God: do good works!*
      [For possible unsaved listeners:] Trust in Christ as only God and Savior[43]
      [For saved listeners, the church:] Specifics on doing good works[44]

Adjusting the placement of ideas yields another outline that emphasizes the contrast between the state of unbelievers and that of believers:

I.   Ruinous State of Unbelievers
      "Dead" in sin (2:1)
      Controlled by evil entities (2:2b)
      Influenced by the flesh and world (2:2a, 3a)
      Consequence: God's wrath (2:3b)
II. Rich State of Believers
      Co-enlivened, co-raised, and co-seated with Christ in the heavenlies (2:4–7)
      Cause: God's rich mercy, great love, surpassingly rich grace and kindness (2:4–9)
      Consequence: God's pleasure in doing the good works he already prepared (2:10b)
III. *Reveal God: do good works!*
      [For possible unsaved listeners:] Trust in Christ as only God and Savior
      [For saved listeners, the church:] Specifics on doing good works

43. Most biblical pericopes do not have a hermeneutical constraint directing the preacher to present the gospel of salvation, but surely this pericope calls for it. Having tracts available, counselors to talk to/with, organizing evangelistic campaigns, etc., would work well as specific application.

44. On the other hand, most biblical pericopes—if not all—*do* have a hermeneutical constraint: their thrusts are directed towards believers—how those already in relationship to God may undertake their divinely mandated responsibility to live lives in a manner pleasing to God. In the context of the demonstration of God's mercy, love, grace, and kindness, the preacher might give specifics regarding good works that manifest these specific attributes of God.

PERICOPE 4

From Far to Near

Ephesians 2:11–22

[Unbelievers' Former and Present Condition; Growing God's Temple]

REVIEW, SUMMARY, PREVIEW

Review of Pericope 3: In Eph 2:1–10 unbelievers are portrayed as controlled by evil powers, the world, and their own fleshly appetites, and as deserving of the wrath of God. But God, in his mercy and love, saves them by grace through faith, co-exalting them with their Savior! And all this to display to the cosmos God's mercy, love, grace, and kindness, as believers do the good works already prepared by God for them to do.

Summary of Pericope 4: The fourth pericope of Ephesians (2:11–22) continues the theme of contrasting former and present situations of unbelievers. They have been brought from the outside to inside the fold of God's people, from "far" to "near," by the work of Christ, thus creating a new body, marked by peace. The barrier of the condemnation of sin was removed by Christ in his atoning work, unifying outsiders and insiders into a single body of believing humanity peacefully reconciled to God. This integrated body is now being transformed in Christ into the very dwelling of God in the Spirit. That, too, is a significant aspect of God's consummation of all things in Christ.

Preview of Pericope 5: The next pericope, Eph 3:1–13, has Paul, a prisoner and "less than the least of all the saints," proclaiming what God has done through him. Thus the church is encouraged: every saint is vital

66

to God's purpose, and it is through the church and through each individual making up the church that God is made known to the cosmos, thus furthering his grand and glorious plan to consummate all things in Christ.

4.   *Ephesians 2:11–22*

THEOLOGICAL FOCUS OF PERICOPE 4

4   **Believers, formerly far from God as unbelievers, have now been brought near, into the community of God's people—all humanity united in one body by the work of Christ who removed the condemnation of the law and won for it access to God—and are now being grown together into the dwelling of God in the Spirit (2:11–22).**

    4.1   Believers, formerly in a dire situation far from God as unbelievers, have now been brought near, into the community of God's people, by the work of Christ (2:11–13).

    4.2   The removal by Christ of the condemnation of the law, the enmity, rendered it possible for all (believing) humanity to be united in one body, reconciled to God in peace, and thus to gain access to God, through Christ, in the Spirit (2:14–18).

    4.3   The grand hope of believers, as all things are being consummated in Christ, is that they are being grown together into a temple, a dwelling of God, in Christ, and in the Spirit (2:19–22).

OVERVIEW

As with Pericope 3, salvation benefits are uppermost in this pericope. But here there is a strong affirmation of the unity of the body of Christ, without distinction of ethnic background. Traditionally 2:11–22 has been interpreted as underscoring primarily a Jew-Gentile unity in Christ and their reconciliation with each other.[1] While that is of course a pertinent issue—as Paul writes to a mainly Gentile audience that has now been introduced to the church, which was until then constituted by Jewish believers[2]—the text is putting more emphasis upon the oneness of the new body ("one new person" and "one body," 2:15, 16) achieved by Christ's reconciling work on the cross that opened up the boundaries of the community of God to *all* (believing) humanity. As will be described further, this pericope portrays another facet of God's magnificent purpose to consummate all things in Christ (1:10)—the uniting of humanity into one new body reconciled to God.

Heil structures the pericope this way[3]:

---

1. For instance, Best, *Ephesians*, 325, asserts that in this pericope, "the cosmic framework sinks into the background and the idea is expounded exclusively in terms of the Jew–Gentile distinction."

2. Considering the rather unfruitful evangelistic enterprise of Paul in the synagogue at Ephesus (Acts 19:8–9) and his productive engagement with Gentiles in that city (19:19–20), it is likely the Ephesian church had a Gentile majority.

3. Modified from Heil, *Ephesians*, 22–24. Similar elements are italicized.

> **A**   *you; in the flesh* (×2); *strangers; without God* (2:11–12)
>   **B**   *you* who were once *far ... near; our* peace (2:13–15a)
>   **C**   that he might create *in Himself* (2:15b)
>   **D**   into *one* new person (2:15c)
>   **D'**   both in *one* body (2:16a)
>   **C'**   killing the enmity *in Himself* (2:16b)
>   **B'**   peace *to you; far ... near; we have* access (2:17–18)
> **A'**   *strangers; of God; you;* dwelling *of God; in the Spirit* (2:19–22)

The central focus on the oneness of humanity ("one new person") as it is reconciled to God "in one body" is central to this pericope (*D, D'*); peace between God and the "one new person," the church, has been made (*B, B'*) by Christ "in Himself" (*C, C'*). The far have been brought near and access to God through Christ and in the Spirit has been achieved (*B, B'*).[4] The remarkable outcome of this is that all believers, irrespective of ethnicity or genetic constitution, are co-citizens in the community of God and members of the divine household. Once strangers without God, they are now no longer godless strangers but a divine temple, a dwelling of God in Christ and in the Spirit (*A, A'*).

Generally, this pericope follows the "formerly-now" schema of the previous pericope: description of plight (2:11–12 and 2:1–4); divine response to plight (2:13–18 and 2:5–9); and implications of that divine response for present existence (2:19–22 and 2:10). Of course, all of Eph 2 follows from Paul's intercession in 1:15–23, where he prays for his readers' enlightenment, particularly regarding God's great power acting on their behalf. Pericopes 3 and 4 are portrayals of this divine might transforming them from what they were "formerly" to what they are "now." Thus, this structure "is more than a rhetorical device"; it is a "testimony to the fact that God had been mightily at work in their lives," as both Pericopes 1 and 2 affirmed.[5]

There is, no doubt, a difference in orientation between Pericope 3 (2:1–10) and Pericope 4 (2:11–22), reflected in the way each pericope employs the συν-prefixed words. In the former, a relationship of the individual to God is in view[6]; in the latter, it is still a relationship to God that is in view, but humankind is showcased as united in one body, without regard to ethnic background, and it is the relationship of this *united body* to God that is in view in 2:11–22.[7]

---

4. The only two first person plural references in this pericope are in 2:14 and 2:18 (in *B* and *B'*).

5. O'Brien, *Ephesians*, 183.

6. While a group is being addressed in 2:1–10, the focus is on individual sins and individual faith, by which one comes to Christ by grace.

7. Table below is from Thielman, *Ephesians*, 149.

Ephesians 2:1–10 (With Christ)	Ephesians 2:11–22 (With the body of Christ)
As *individuals* reconciled to God	As *one body* reconciled to God
συνεζωποίησεν, *synezōpoiēsen* "co-enlivened" (2:5)	συμπολῖται, *sympolitai* "co-citizens" with the saints (2:19)
συνήγειρεν, *synēgeiren,* "co-raised" (2:6)	συναρμολογουμένη, *synarmologoumenē* "co-fitted" (2:21)
συνεκάθισεν, *synekathisen* "co-seated" (2:6)	συνοικοδομεῖσθε, *synoikodomeisthe* "co-built" (2:22)

In this pericope the incorporation of all humans into one new body reconciled to God, i.e., the church, is in focus. This differs from the traditional interpretation of this passage as dealing exclusively and specifically with a union of Jews and Gentiles. In my reading, 2:11–22 does not neglect the union of humanity into "one new person" and "one body" (2:15, 16). But the emphasis is on this united body being brought together, as one, *to God*: the "bringing near" in Pericope 4 moves humankind proximal *to God* (2:13); reconciliation is *to God* (2:16); access of humankind is *to God* (2:18); and the household, temple, and dwelling is that *of God* (2:19, 21, 22). So all of this continues the grand and glorious plan of God to consummate all things in Christ (1:10), the theological thrust of the letter as a whole.

There is a shift from the second person plural "you" in 2:11–13 to the first person plural "our" in 2:14.[8] Though the "you," is specifically noted to be Gentiles (2:11), that does not necessarily make the subsequent "our" refer to Jews alone. Rather the first person plural functions the same way as it did in 2:3–7, 10—standing for *all* believers, irrespective of ethnicity or genetics. Here, Gentiles are now incorporated into a new body in which there is no discrimination between peoples. "[T]he new community of which these Gentiles have become a part is not simply a development out of Israel. It is a new creation," a new united body.[9] So it is not simply a horizontal reconciliation between two feuding ethnicities that has taken place; rather, a new "body," a new "person," has been "created" (2:15, 16) and reconciled to God. Doubtless, this implies interethnic unity, for the people of God, in OT days and even into the time of the NT church, were essentially Jewish. Therefore, this pericope teaches that all the various divisions of humankind have now, in Christ, been reduced to nothing, as far as entering into a relationship with God is concerned. And to describe the privileges of this new creation, Paul undertakes here "a comparison between these particular Gentile readers' pre-Christian past in its relation to Israel's privileges [2:11–12] and to their Christian present in the church [2:13–22]. . . . The mention of Israel, then, only functions as part of this comparison and serves the purpose of brining home to the readers the greatness of their salvation."[10] This was a major accomplishment in

---

8. There is also a second person plural pronoun in 2:17 in the OT citation there.

9. O'Brien, *Ephesians*, 184.

10. Lincoln, "The Church and Israel," 609.

God's consummation of all things in Christ—all (believing) humanity united as one in Christ, by the Spirit, for God.

4.1   Ephesians 2:11–13

THEOLOGICAL FOCUS OF PERICOPE 4.1

4.1   Believers, formerly in a dire situation far from God as unbelievers, have now been brought near, into the community of God's people, by the work of Christ (2:11–13).

TRANSLATION 4.1

2:11 *Therefore remember that formerly you, Gentiles in the flesh, the ones called "uncircumcision" by the ones called "circumcision" in the flesh, hand-done—*

2:12 *[remember] that you were at that time without Christ, excluded from the citizenship of Israel, and strangers to the covenants of promise, having no hope, and godless in the world.*

2:13 *But now in Christ Jesus you who formerly were far have been brought near by the blood of Christ.*

NOTES 4.1

4.1   *Believers, formerly in a dire situation far from God as unbelievers, have now been brought near, into the community of God's people, by the work of Christ.*

To further underscore God's gracious action (2:8–10), believers—here, the Gentiles— must "remember" their past state and their current position: notice "formerly" (2:11, 13) and "at that time" (2:12), as opposed to "now" (2:13). What the Gentiles were, prior to salvation, i.e., "in the flesh" (2:11), is contrasted with their being "in Christ" afterwards (2:13). But it is not only the Gentiles who get a pejorative label in 2:11 ("the ones called 'uncircumcision'"); so do the Jews ("the ones called 'circumcision'"). And it is not only the former that are "in the flesh"; so are the latter.[11] The parallel vocabulary in each case makes this obvious:

> **A**   "remember that formerly you, Gentiles
> **B**   in the flesh,
> **C**   the ones called 'uncircumcision'
> **C'**   by the ones called 'circumcision'
> **B'**   in the flesh, hand-done—
> **A'**   [remember] that you were at that time ...."

---

11. The phrase "in the flesh" may be characterizing the actual ritual of circumcision—both its absence and its presence being visible in the "flesh" (= body). Another option would be to see it as referring to a state *not* "in Christ," i.e., that of unbelievers, both Gentiles and Jews.

Notice, however, the extra descriptor tacked on for the Jews: "hand-done." That is clearly deprecatory; the term χειροποίητος (*cheiropoiētos*) frequently characterizes what is merely human and necessarily evil—often denoting idols in the OT—in contrast to what is divine and spiritual (Mark 14:58; Acts 7:48; 17:24; Col 2:11; Heb 9:11, 24; see Lev 26:1, 30; Isa 2:18; 10:11; 16:12; 19:1; 31:7; 46:6; Dan 5:4 LXX; also see Ps 115:4). It is not just Gentiles before salvation who are being regarded negatively, so are the Jews (ostensibly pre-salvation).[12] The powerful "equation" of the two peoples in the structuring of 2:11–12 was noted above.

There can be no doubt that both Gentiles and Jews are mentioned in rather disparaging terms in 2:11; the latter do not, at least in this letter and for Paul's purposes in it, seem to have any advantage over the former.

The former status of the Gentiles as unbelievers is described as being "without Christ" (2:12), in stark contrast to their current status "in Christ Jesus" (2:13)—this phrase forms the heading of a list of related descriptors that follow.[13] Therefore, being once "excluded from the citizenship of Israel" (2:12) before conversion must imply a current inclusion within "Israel" as those who are in Christ post-conversion: this would entail a spiritual reading of "Israel" as "the people of God," the community of God's people, rather than as an ethnic and genetically distinct people group of which the Gentiles never become part. And so, since Gentiles never join ethnic/genetic Israel but become part of spiritual "Israel," the word πολιτεία (*politeia*, "citizenship") is also best taken as the citizenship of these Gentiles in the community of God's people. Gentiles, before being in Christ, were excluded from citizenship in this community of the people of God (spiritual "Israel"). Indeed, the fact that 2:19 asserts that believing Gentiles are now συμπολίτης (*sympolitēs*, "co-citizens"—a cognate of πολιτεία) with the *saints* and *members of God's household* indicates that their citizenship is with the people of God and not with an ethnic/genetic grouping as 2:12 might suggest on the surface. Likewise, in its other uses in the NT, ἀπαλλοτριόω (*apallotrioō*, "exclude," 2:12) indicates alienation from God, not from ethnic Israel or its unique polity: Eph 4:18 and Col 1:21. Thus the same sense must operate in Eph 2:12; the primary focus is upon the relationship between humanity and God and not upon that between one race and another.

Moreover, these Gentiles, in their earlier days "separate from Christ," were also at that time "strangers to the covenants of promise" (Eph 2:12), similarly implying that now, "in Christ," they are "no longer strangers" (2:19) to these "covenants of promise." This clearly cannot be saying that the Gentiles are *now*, after salvation (i.e., "in Christ"), possessors of the specific promises and covenants belonging to Israel. The "covenants of promise," then, must be referring specifically to the Abrahamic covenant that promised blessings for *all nations* (Gen 12:2–3; 17:6,16; 18:18; 22:18; Acts 3:25; Gal 3:8,

---

12. In Eph 2:11, at least, both the Gentiles and Jews appear to be unbelievers. A similar anti-circumcision sentiment is found in Rom 2:28–29; Gal 6:15–16; Phil 3:3; Col 2:11.

13. "*Without* Christ" is also perhaps in contrast to the συν- (*syn-*) words (the preposition means "with") encountered in 2:5–6: "co-enlivened," "co-raised," and "co-seated," i.e., *with* Christ.

14[14]) and, perhaps, to the New Covenant (Jer 31:31–34), in which the church participates by virtue of being "in Christ" (Matt 26:28/Mark 14:24/Luke 22:20; Acts 2:32–33,
38–39; 1 Cor 11:25; 2 Cor 3:6; Heb 8:6–13; 9:15; 10:16–17; 12:24). That Gentiles are
later described as being "co-partakers of the *promise in Christ Jesus through the gospel*"
(Eph 3:6), also seems to indicate that these "covenants of promise" (2:12) relate not to
any particular feature of Israel or Jewishness, but to the privilege of being in Christ.[15]

The last two descriptors in Eph 2:12 denote the direness of the Gentiles' past situation: "having no hope and godless in the world"—hopeless and godless. The hope is
what was set forth in Christ (1:12), and that which is related to the divine call (1:19):
it is the hope for the future when all things will be consummated in Christ (1:10) and
believers will be finally possessed by God as his inheritance and they receive theirs
(1:14). Of course, without any relationship to Christ, the Gentiles before salvation
were effectively also "godless," for access to God was only through Jesus Christ (as 2:18
will make clear).[16]

There is one more descriptor of the Gentiles that has to be dealt with: they were
once "far" (2:13). Like the disjunctive "but God . . ." in 2:4, here we have "but now . . ."
(2:13), contrasting former and current situations of the Gentiles. Those who were once
"far" have now been made "near" (2:13). That this nearness has been accomplished "by
the blood of Christ" indicates that nearness refers to a relationship with God, and that
those who are near are the community of God's people, believers in Christ. Of course,
for the most part, in those days the church as a whole had a majority of Jews, so those
"near" were primarily Jewish. But here in Eph 2:13 the statement that the Gentiles were
"brought near *by the blood of Christ*" denotes that this nearness is their current saved
state, and "farness" was their former unsaved state.[17] In other words it is the distance
from God that distinguishes the respective labels here in Eph 2.

Following right after the description of the "godlessness" of the Gentiles in times
past (2:12), this depiction of their being "near" in 2:13 points to proximity to God and
inclusion within the community of God, irrespective of ethnicity or genetics. Besides,
the reconciliation language of 2:16 and the affirmation of access to God in 2:18 would

14. See also the blessings to Isaac, Gen 26:4, and to Jacob, 28:14; also see Ps 117:1; Isa 2:2–4; 11:10;
49:6; 60:3; etc., for other OT evidence of divine blessing for Gentiles.

15. Elsewhere in the OT the New Covenant is also described simply as a "covenant" (Isa 49:8; Hos
2:18), as "My covenant" (Isa 59:21), as an "everlasting covenant" (Isa 24:5; 55:3; 61:8; Jer 32:38–40; 50:5;
Ezek 16:60; 37:26), or as a "covenant of peace" (Isa 54:10; Ezek 34:25). Also see Ezek 11:19–20; 18:31;
36:23–36; 37:15–28.

16. The word, ἄθεος, *atheos,* effectively meant "atheist," and is used as such in Josephus, *Against
Apion* 2.146; Justin Martyr, *First Apology* 6.1; 13.1; 46.3; etc.

17. In the OT, the "near/far" antithesis described the Jew/Gentile distinction, essentially based upon
ethnicity and genetics; see Isa 57:19 (which is cited in Eph 2:17), and also Ps 148:14 (for Jews as "near")
and Deut 28:49; 2 Chr 6:32; Jer 5:15; Act 2:39; 22:21; etc. (for Gentiles as "far"). "Coming near" appears to have designated Jewish proselytes in the LXX (see Deut 10:18; 12:18; etc.). Indeed, "proselyte,"
προσήλυτος, *prosēlutos,* is from the Greek προσελεύσεται, *proseleusetai,* "he will come near." Therefore,
while "near" in the OT indicated ethnic/genetic Jews, here the term "near" must indicate not an ethni-
cally or genetically distinct people, but simply those who were "near" to God—i.e., the community of
God's people, "brought near by the blood of Christ."

also argue that the bringing "near" of all (believing) humanity is towards *God* (see below for the interpretation of 2:14–15 that also substantiates this reading).[18] In sum, Gentile unbelievers (those "far") were incorporated into the church—"brought *near* by the blood of Christ" (2:13). "[I]t does not mean that these Gentile Christians, like proselytes, have now become members of the commonwealth of Israel, but rather that they have become members of a newly created community whose privileges transcend those of Israel," as the rest of this pericope demonstrates.[19] What Christ accomplished was the inclusion of all (believing) humanity within the boundaries of the community of God. In an earlier dispensation, one had to be a proselyte or a Jew to be "near." Not so now. *All* who desired to be "near" could come to God by faith in Christ, an initiative of divine grace, as Pericope 3 affirmed.

Ethnic and genetic division—and, for that matter, every other kind of division among humanity—is thereby rendered null and void for the purpose of entering into a relationship with God in Christ. In other words, 2:13 is outlining the fulfillment of the Abrahamic covenant and the blessing of God upon *all* nations as *one* people, part of God's grand scheme of consummating all things/people in Christ.[20]

4.2 Ephesians 2:14–18

> **THEOLOGICAL FOCUS OF PERICOPE 4.2**
>
> 4.2 The removal by Christ of the condemnation of the law, the enmity, rendered it possible for all (believing) humanity to be united in one body, reconciled to God in peace, and thus to gain access to God, through Christ, in the Spirit (2:14–18).

TRANSLATION 4.2

2:14 *For He Himself is our peace, who who made both one and who destroyed the middle wall of partition—the enmity—in His flesh,*

2:15 *by nullifying the law of commandments in decrees,[21] so that He, in Himself,*

18. Also see 2:19, where the Gentiles have now become part of the "saints" and of "God's household."

19. Lincoln, *Ephesians*, 139.

20. Regarding this magnificent consummation in Christ of all things, in heaven and on earth, O'Brien notes that one particular "obstacle" that needed to be overcome to achieve this consummation was the resolution of the relationship of Jews and Gentiles, which he equates with "the things on the earth," in 1:10; the subjection of the hostile powers, O'Brien claims, was the consummation of "things in the heavens" (*Ephesians*, 182–83). That the specific relationship of two insular peoples in the first century was a major "obstacle" to the consummation of all things in the cosmos in Christ is unconvincing. Rather, the unity of humankind in the new "body," the divine household/temple/dwelling, was the critical issue that needed management on earth—the bringing of all (believing) humanity that was *far from God*, irrespective of ethnicity, to a station *near to God*, within the community of God's people.

21. There are three aorist participles in 2:14–15: ποιήσας (*poiēsas*, "made," 2:14), λύσας (*lysas*, "destroyed," 2:14), and καταργήσας (*katargēsas*, "nullifying," 2:15). The fact that only the first two participles are linked by "and" indicates that only those two are in parallel, with the third, "nullifying," being a participle of means, explaining how Christ made both one and destroyed the barrier: "by nullifying." See Hoehner, *Ephesians*, 375; Wallace, *Greek Grammar*, 630.

> might create the two into one new person, making peace,
>
> 2:16 and that He might reconcile both in one body to God through the cross, killing the enmity in Himself.
>
> 2:17 And He came and proclaimed peace to you, the ones far, and peace to the ones near;
>
> 2:18 for through Him we both have access in one Spirit to the Father.

NOTES 4.2

4.2   *The removal by Christ of the condemnation of the law, the enmity, rendered it possible for all (believing) humanity to be united in one body, reconciled to God in peace, and thus to gain access to God, through Christ, in the Spirit.*

This section, Eph 2:14–18, reverts to the first person plural pronouns; they begin and end 2:14–18. Apart from 2:17 that has a second person plural as it cites Isa 57:19, second person plurals are found only in Eph 2:11–13 and 2:19–22, referring to the Gentiles who were once "far," but are now "near" and part of the community of God's people. Here, in 2:14–18, the subjects are no longer Gentiles, but *all* believers, including Paul himself (thus the first person plurals)—the united body, the new person, created by Christ.

The "for" that commences 2:14 shows that this verse explains the bringing near of the Gentiles "in Christ Jesus" and "by the blood of Christ" (2:13)—i.e., into the community of God. "Peace" takes plenty of space in this pericope—2:14, 15, 17 (×2), and there is "reconciliation" in 2:16 as well. Christ is shown as *being* peace (2:14), *making* peace (2:15), and *proclaiming* peace (2:17).[22] Christ who is peace appears to be making peace between "both" (2:14, 16, 18) and "two" (2:15), unifying them into "one"/"one new person"/"one body" enabling access "in one Spirit to the Father" (2:14, 15, 16, 18).[23] What are the two entities that were made "one" and between whom Christ made peace? The nearest antecedents to the first instance of "both" (2:14) are those who were "far" (i.e., unbelievers), and those who are "near" (i.e., believers; 2:13). The fact that Gentiles become "co-citizens with the saints" and "members of God's household" (2:19) also suggests that the "two" parties were these Gentile unbelievers prior to their salvation and the "saints," believers making up God's community. However, 2:14–18 have been seen by most commentators as dealing exclusively with an inter-ethnic, inter-racial bringing together of Jews and Gentiles and the peace effected between them. This reading implies that "both" in 2:14 refers back to these two people groups in 2:11; however the closest referents of "both" are the "far" and the "near" (2:13). So

---

22. Also see Isa 9:5; Micah 5:5. Indeed, the Christian gospel is itself good news characterized by "peace" (Eph 6:15).

23. There is a gender shift for ἀμφότερα, *amphotera*, "both": it is neuter in 2:14, and masculine in 2:16, 18. In 2:14, "both" refers generically in the neuter to two parties or classes (believers and unbelievers), whereas in 2:16 and 2:18, concrete personhood is in view. "Both" in 2:16 follows "person" (ἄνθρωπος, *anthrōpos*, literally "man") in 2:15, perhaps attracting the masculine gender as a result. Notice also the masculine τοὺς δύο (*tous duo*, "the two") in 2:15, likely also exerting pressure on the gender of "both."

the primary thrust of 2:14–18 appears to be that the union accomplished by Christ ("our peace," 2:14) is of those who were once unbelievers (the "far") and those already believers (the "near"). Of course, it cannot be denied that in Paul's day the "far" were mostly Gentile, and the "near" mostly Jewish. In any case, Christ, "our peace," has "made both one." In other words, it is the inclusion of Gentiles in God's community (once mostly Jewish) that is in view: thus *all* (believing) humanity has been brought near to God, unified. How did Christ do this?

Jesus Christ made "both"/"two" into "one" by "destroying the middle wall of partition" (2:14) and "nullifying the law of commandments in decrees" (2:15). Whatever these barriers might be, they are labeled as "the *enmity*" (2:14). Later, in 2:16, Christ is said to have reconciled "both" to God by "killing the *enmity*." These instances of "enmity" are abrogated by Christ, "in His flesh" (2:14), "in Himself" (2:15, 16), and "through the cross" (2:16); indeed one might add "in Christ Jesus" and "by the blood of Christ" in 2:13 to this list of how Christ removed the "enmity" and established peace. All this suggests that this barrier, the "enmity," is a single entity, standing between the "far" and the "near" (2:14–16) *and* between man and God (2:16–18), which Christ removed, thus bringing peace between the various parties.

Now we are in a better position to identify what the barrier was between unsaved and saved, and between humankind and God, and what exactly was "destroyed" and "nullified" (2:14b–15a). Commentators have generally thought that it was the Mosaic Law that was abolished, for apparently this entity "separated Jews from Gentiles both religiously and sociologically, and caused deep-seated hostility."[24] But none of the terms used in 2:14–15 to describe the object of destruction and nullification—"middle wall of partition," and "law of commandments in decrees"—are found in contemporary Jewish literature to refer to the Mosaic Law. Of the two parties referred to as "both"/"two" (2:14, 15, 16, 18), one was primarily Gentile (those "far") and the other primarily Jewish (those "near," the church in Paul's day). Therefore it is, of course, possible that the Mosaic Law created division and hostility between them.[25] But in this case one would have to posit a different "enmity" that separated man from God—sin. The Mosaic Law, given to man by God himself, could hardly have been the cause of separation between man and God.

And there is yet another potential problem: If it were the Mosaic Law that made up the partition, Paul seems to be labeling it as something outdated, oppressive, and hostile—"enmity"—that is to be "destroyed," "nullified," and "killed" (2:14, 15, 16). But this is hardly how the law is viewed elsewhere in the NT, often by Paul himself. It is said to have been written for all believers (1 Cor 9:8–10) and, frequently, demands of the

---

24. O'Brien, *Ephesians*, 196.

25. There is a second-century BCE work, *Letter of Aristeas*, that observes: "Our Lawgiver [Moses] . . . *fenced us around* [from περιφράσσω, *periphrassō*; its cognate, περίφραγμα, *periphragma*, "surrounding fence," corresponds to φράγμος, *phragmos*, "partition," in Eph 2:14] with impenetrable ramparts and walls of iron so that in no way should we mingled mingle with any of the other nations . . ." (139; also ibid., 142). Though this is a tenuous link, it is conceivable that the descriptions in Eph 2:14–15 point to the Mosaic Law as a metaphorical fence that kept Jews distinct from Gentiles, particularly in the days of the early church, the "far" separated from the "near."

Christian made in the NT are grounded upon those same OT laws, even in this very letter: Eph 6:2 (as also in Rom 13:9; Gal 5:14; 1 Tim 5:18; Jas 2:8–11; 1 Pet 1:15–16).[26] After all, *all* Scripture is profitable (2 Tim 3:16). Indeed, the laws of the OT are God's laws (Rom 7:22, 25; 8:7; 1 Cor 7:19), and they are declared to be good, holy, righteous, and spiritual (Rom 7:12–14, 16; 1 Tim 1:8). So much so, Paul can "joyfully concur" with this law of God (Rom 7:22) and "establish" it (3:31). There is no hint in Pauline discussions in the NT that any of God's laws have been nullified.[27] Jesus' assertion in Matt 5:17, that he came not to abolish the Law or the Prophets, but to fulfill it, should not be taken to indicate he fulfilled *and thus abrogated it*. His explicit statement goes against that assumption, as also does 5:19, where he declares that annulling even "one of the least of these commandments" renders one "least in the kingdom of heaven." Rather the child of God is to keep and teach the commandments, upon which greatness in the kingdom is predicated.

What, then, might be the thrust of Paul's statements in Eph 2:14–15? How can we put the various observations on this text together, to explain the data coherently? I submit that what keeps people from being part of the community of God (the separation between believers and unbelievers—the "near" and the "far") is the law's condemnation of sin—the sentence pronounced in/by divine law. And this is the *same* barrier that keeps man from God, too. Historically, what God demanded of his people was enshrined in the Mosaic Law; later such divine demand included every one of the laws of Scripture, in both Testaments.[28] It is this *condemnation* of the law for sin that has been removed by the blood of Christ, i.e., by his atoning work. It is not that God's demands/laws have been removed en masse, but only the condemnation of the law pronounced upon the sinner, for the price of sin has now been paid. Thus, "law of commandments in decrees," here in 2:15, serves as a convenient shorthand for the condemnation that it lays upon sinners. But "in Christ" there is no longer any condemnation for sin

---

26. And see Matt 5:17–20; John 7:19; Rom 3:31; 1 Cor 14:34.

27. Others have recognized this ambiguity between how Eph 2:14–15 is read and how the rest of the NT treats the Law. "[T]aking the dividing law in this way [as a barrier] could lead one to think that the law had been destroyed by Christ. This would directly contradict the Gospels, Romans, and Galatians. It could also feed a theology that has God making everlasting covenants with Israel only to break those promises in favor of promises to Christians" (Fowl, *Ephesians*, 91). Cranfield describes the common understanding of the law as being abrogated as a "modern version of Marcionism" that regards the biblical history as "an unsuccessful first attempt on God's part at dealing with man's unhappy state, which had to be followed later by a second (more successful) attempt (a view which is theologically grotesque, for the God of the unsuccessful first attempt is hardly a God to be taken seriously)" (*Romans*, 2:862). Usually, those who explain that the "nullification" of the law in Eph 2:15 denotes its abolition, subsequently attempt to attenuate the force of this cancellation to make portions of the law applicable in the current dispensation: its "moral" aspects. Others, like Hoehner, *Ephesians*, 376, assert that "[o]nly those [laws] that have been reiterated in the NT" are binding upon believers today. But such a piecemeal approach to divine demand just does not work: it has to be all or none (Jas 2:10).

28. "Divine demand" encompasses *all* of God's law—pre-Mosaic commands, Mosaic Law, law of Christ, laws of his millennial reign, etc. And, by divine demand, I do not mean to exclude non-imperatives in Scripture; every pericope in every genre depicts a view of how God's ideal world should run—its precepts, priorities, and practices. In that sense, every biblical pericope makes a divine demand upon humankind.

that affects the standing of believers with God for eternal life (Rom 8:1). Those who trusted Jesus Christ as their only God and Savior from sin are finally and forever freed from eternal condemnation for breakage of God's demand/law. All that to say, divine demand/law is not rendered inoperative for those in Christ—all of it is still valid; it is only *the condemnation for not abiding by the law* that has been removed.[29] Divine demand/law, in its theological sense, is always valid, for all humanity.[30]

Notice the seeming inconsistency when Eph 2:15 (that says the law is "nullified," from καταργέω, *katargeō*) is compared with Rom 3:3 (that says that Paul does *not* "nullify" the law, also from καταργέω). This ambiguity is resolved only if one understands "law" in Eph 2:14 as the condemnation thereof, and not the law in its entirety, which, as was noted, Paul quotes approvingly in 6:3. In other words, the law—its condemnation—stood as "enmity" between the "far" (those not the people of God, the unsaved) and the "near" (the people of God, the saved, "the saints and members of God's household," 2:19). Unsaved Gentiles were worthy only of condemnation; and, of course, the condemnation of the law for sin was also a barrier between unsaved humans and a holy God. Those outside God's community, the unsaved, were separated from God (and from his people) by this enmity—the condemnation of divine law for sin. Only being "in Christ Jesus," only "by the blood of Christ," only "in his flesh," only "through the cross," only "in Himself," and only "through Him," could that enmity be removed and access to God gained.[31] By the work of Christ, "both" were made "*one*" (2:14); "two" were created into "*one* new person" (2:15); "both" were reconciled to God "in *one* body" (2:16); and "both" were given equal access to the Father "in *one* Spirit" (2:18). The grand benefits of salvation were brought by Christ to *all* (believing) humanity, with no distinction among them—an incredible part of the glorious work of God consummating all things in Christ.[32]

In sum, it was by this "nullification" of the law's *condemnation* that Christ accomplished the "destruction" of the enmity between God and man. And, at the same time, he "made both one"—Jewish believers and Gentiles who were once unbelievers—thus also removing the enmity between "far" and "near" (2:14). This was nothing short of a new "creation" of "one new person" (κτίζω, *ktizō*, "to create," 2:15, always indicates the work of God). The idea of a new "creation" was already broached in 2:10, a sovereign work of God in Christ. Again, this is a significant move towards the magnificent plan

---

29. Paul's declaration of believers as no longer under the condemnation of the law (Rom 6:14)—the law having come to bring about wrath, increase transgression, and arouse sinful passions (4:15; 5:20; 7:5)—is consistent with this view.

30. For an extensive discussion on the *theological* validity of all God's demands for all of God's people in every age, see Kuruvilla, *Privilege the Text!* 151–209.

31. The law condemned all law-breakers, but particularly poignant was the situation of unbelievers (Gentiles) who had no recourse to the sacrifices or means of atonement prescribed in Israel's Law.

32. Both "far" and "near" come to God by the same means, through Christ, as Eph 2:17 makes clear with a conflation of Isa 57:19 and 52:7 that talks of the "proclamation" (εὐαγγελίζω, *euangelizō*) of peace. Later, Paul will say that the Gentiles are "co-partakers of the promise in Christ Jesus through the *gospel* [εὐαγγέλιον, *euangelion*]" (Eph 3:6).

of God to consummate all things—here, all *people*—in Christ (1:9–10), in a sense by redoing creation!

What Christ accomplished in his single act of redemption (2:14–15b), then, had two related purposes, outlined in 2:15b and 2:16:

		Subjunctive		Participle
2:15	"… in Himself,	might create	the two into one new person,	making peace"
2:16	"in Himself …	might reconcile	both in one body to God …	killing the enmity"

By his work of removing the condemnation of divine demand (the "enmity"), two things were accomplished simultaneously by Christ. First, the barrier between "far" (Gentile unbelievers) and "near" (mostly Jewish believers) was removed: all (believing) humanity had become one! Second, the barrier between man and God was no more. "Enmity" in every direction, vertical and horizontal, and in every dimension, had been abolished. In other words, the perimeter surrounding the community of God's people was broken down by the work of Christ to include all (believing) humankind. Paul is describing a one-race humanity: the people of God (or two-race, if you will—the people of God and everyone else). This is a new unity that transcends old distinctions—the beginning of the consummation of all things in Christ.

Notice the almost precise balance between the descriptions of the status of the Gentiles as unbelievers (2:11–12) and their current standing as believers (2:16–22):

Ephesians 2:11–12: "Formerly"	Ephesians 2:16–22: "Now"
"In the flesh" (×2)	"In one/the Spirit" (2:18, 22)
	"in the Lord" (2:21)
"Separate from Christ"	Brought near "in Christ Jesus" (2:13)
	Brought near "by the blood of Christ" (2:13)
	Enmity destroyed "in His flesh" (2:14)
	Two made into one "in Himself" (2:15)
	Both reconciled to God "through the cross" (2:16)
	Enmity killed "in Himself" (2:16)
"Excluded from the *citizenship* of Israel"	"*Co-citizens* with the saints" (2:19)
"*Strangers*"	"No longer *strangers* and aliens" (2:19)
"Having no hope"	Becoming a holy temple in the Lord (2:21)
	Becoming a dwelling of God in the Spirit (2:22)
"Without God"	Reconciled to God (2:16)
	Peace with God (2:14, 15, 17)
	Access to God (2:18)

Once these Gentiles were separate from Christ; now they are brought near "in Christ Jesus," by the "blood of Christ," "in His flesh," "in Himself," and "through the cross." Once they were excluded from citizenship in the divine community; now they are "co-citizens" with the saints already within it. Once strangers, now they are "no longer strangers." Once hopeless, they now have a magnificent hope: they—Gentiles, too!—are becoming a temple for God. Once godless, they are now reconciled to him, in peace with him, and with access unto him. Yes, there is an assumption here that the community of God was, until Paul's day, mostly Jewish. But now Christ has made it possible for *all* nations to become part of God's people. The consummation of all things in Christ has begun!

Reconciliation now accomplished and peace now proclaimed, *all* humans (i.e., those who are believers), irrespective of tribe and tongue and nation, are now afforded access to God—through Christ, in the Spirit, to the Father, an obvious Trinitarian emphasis (2:18). The word "for" that commences 2:18 suggests that the evidence of the peace accomplished and proclaimed by Christ is the gaining of access to God by the reconciled ones. Whereas in a secular context, προσαγωγή (*prosagōgē*, "access") and its cognates often refer to audiences with emperors in their courts (e.g., Xenophon, *Cyropaedia* 1.3.8), here the access is for *all* humanity to the divine Ruler in the heavenlies (also see Rom 5:2 and Eph 3:12).[33] This incredible privilege of *all* humanity is emphasized in the use of "one" in Eph 2:14, 15, 16, as it points to the integral unity of God's people (both the older community of God—mostly Jews—and the *nouveaux arrivés* into that fold—the Gentiles), and by "one" in 2:18, as it refers to the Holy Spirit. This underscores the fact that the oneness of *all* believers is a Spirit-wrought unity of the body of Christ.[34]

4.3 Ephesians 2:19–22

THEOLOGICAL FOCUS OF PERICOPE 4.3

4.3   The grand hope of believers, as all things are being consummated in Christ, is that they are being grown together into a temple, a dwelling of God, in Christ, and in the Spirit (2:19–22).

TRANSLATION 4.3

2:19 *So then you are no longer strangers and aliens, but you are co-citizens with the saints, and members of God's household,*

2:20 *having been built upon the foundation of the apostles and prophets, Christ Jesus Himself being the cornerstone,*

2:21 *in whom the whole building, co-fitted, is growing into a holy temple in the Lord,*

2:22 *in whom you also are being co-built into a dwelling of God in the Spirit.*

33. The cultic sense of προσαγωγή is found in Lev 1:3; 3:3; 4:14 LXX; etc., indicating the offering brought with the worshiper seeking the presence of God.

34. "One Spirit" and "one body" also show up in Eph 4:4.

4.3   The grand hope of believers, as all things are being consummated in Christ, is that they are being grown together into a temple, a dwelling of God, in Christ, and in the Spirit.

In 2:19–22, readers are introduced to metaphors from domestic engineering ("household," 2:19),[35] architecture ("foundation," "cornerstone,"[36] "building," "being built," 2:20, 21, 22), and sacral institutions ("temple," "dwelling of God," 2:21, 22). As was noted, the terms denote an incredible change in the status and privileges of the Gentiles—once unbelievers, they are now believers and "members of God's household" (2:19).

The theme of the divine "household," in particular, echoes through this pericope and is one of the key motifs here, reflected in the six compound words in 2:19–22 that are built off the syllable οικ- (*oik-*; from οἶκος, *oikos*, "house"): πάροικος (*paroikos*, "alien," 2:19), οἰκεῖος (*oikeios*, "household," 2:19), ἐποικοδομέω (*epoikodomeō*, "build upon," 2:20), οἰκοδομή (*oikodomē*, "building," 2:21), συνοικοδομέω (*sunoikodomeō*, "co-build," 2:22), κατοικητήριον (*katoikētērion*, "dwelling," 2:22).[37] Within 2:19, one notices the contrasts: "strangers" vs. "co-citizens" and "aliens" (πάροικος, *paroikos*) vs. "members of God's *household*" (οἰκεῖος, *oikeios*). This is clearly a domiciliary passage, if you will, focusing on the integrated composition of humanity in the household of God, the church. Unbelievers have become "co-citizens with the saints" and "members of God's household" of all ages. And *all* humanity is invited to join this party—the consummation of all things is at hand! "Co-fitted" and "co-built" underscore the corporate aspect of this new "structure" that believers have become in Christ. This, then, is the key thrust of this pericope. The focus is not so much on Jew-Gentile unity, as it is upon the oneness of the body of Christ, irrespective of ethnicity or genetics. Clearly the οικ-words hark back to οἰκονομία (*oikonomia*, "administration") in 1:10; in other words, this union of humanity in Christ is an integral part of the grand scheme of God

35. This theme is also manifested in the mention of a Father (2:18; 3:14–15; 4:6) and of children (1:5).

36. The word ἀκρογωνιαῖος (*akrogōniaios*) is elsewhere found only in Isa 28:16 LXX; 1 Pet 2:6; also see *Barnabas* 6:2–3; Justin Martyr, *Dialogue with Trypho* 114.4; 126.1. Technically, the word could either indicate a cornerstone (the stone in the foundation, positioned at a corner and installed at the initiation of construction) or a capstone (the crowning stone at top of edifice and put in last of all). There is probably "very little at stake in opting for 'cornerstone' or 'capstone'" (Fowl, *Ephesians*, 99). In fact, Luke 20:18 seems to give such a structure *both* senses: people fall over this stone and the stone also falls on them! Nonetheless, the image of a cornerstone makes better sense in the current context, where the building activity is still ongoing and the structure is yet to be finished (the present tenses of the verbs "growing" and "being co-built" in 2:21, 22 attest to this). On the other hand, the equivalence of the building imagery here in 2:19–22 and the growing body imagery in 4:13–16 would match better if both stone and head are superior. See Thielman, *Ephesians*, 181. In either case, the thrust of the text remains unchanged: the whole building is in conformity with this (corner/cap)stone, Jesus Christ, "in whom" (2:21, 22 [×2]; also "in the Lord," 2:21) the building is becoming a dwelling and temple of God in the Spirit. And thus, there is another Trinitarian emphasis in the concluding verse, 2:22.

37. The one doing all the building is, of course, God; the divine passive in 2:20, "having been built," points to this Builder.

to consummate all things in Christ (1:10).[38] Thus, the Gentiles, the "you" of 2:11–13, have been assimilated into the community of God's people—the "one new person" (2:15), "one body" (2:16)—identified with the "saints" (2:19), incorporated into "God's household" (2:19), and integrated into a "holy temple in the Lord" (2:21), a "dwelling of God in the Spirit" (2:22). In OT prophecy, Jerusalem and its Temple would be the focus of all nations, the place of worship and where God would be glorified: Isa 2:2–3; 56:3–8; 66:18–20; Jer 3:17; Micah 4:2; Zech 8:22–23; 14:16–19. That is yet to come to pass—and it will, in the millennial reign of Christ—but in the present dispensation a certain degree of fulfillment of these promises is occurring: Gentiles have been brought near to God and have become, alongside and equally with Jews, the temple of God, the dwelling of God (Eph 2:21–22).[39]

As was mentioned in Pericope 2, the church is the fullness of Christ (1:23), i.e., the church is filled by Christ. This is best understood in tandem with the OT idea of God's *Shekinah* glory filling the Temple. Here in 2:19–22, the new body—Jews and Gentiles comprising the church, "God's household"—is becoming "a holy temple in the Lord" and "a dwelling of God *in the Spirit.*" Likely, "in the Spirit" indicates the agency, the instrument, by which the church becomes the divine dwelling: "the Holy Spirit is the means by which the presence of God is mediated to his people."[40] So here, as in 1:23, there is a sense of "already, but not yet." Though the church is already the fullness of Christ, there is a sense in which this is only gradually being accomplished: "being co-fitted" and "growing" (2:21; also seen in 4:15–16) and "being co-built" (2:22) are all in the present tense, indicating the continuous, ongoing activity of temple construction—into "a *holy* temple," for that is where a *holy* deity abides (2:19). "So, while the church as the dwelling place of God by the Spirit is an accomplished reality, it is also a process which stands in need of being increasingly actualised."[41] Of course, the consummation of all things in Christ is also, therefore, an ongoing process.

One has to read 2:19 as declaring that that Gentiles are no longer strangers/aliens, not because they have become Jews, but *because they have become a people of God.* Indeed, that is precisely what is claimed: "you are co-citizens with the saints." This is truly a dramatic change in the status of the Gentiles in Ephesus who came to Christ, and indeed of *all* humanity constituting the community of God. Now they are all filled with hope, for they—with the rest of the saints, both Jews and Gentiles—are becoming a holy temple of God and a dwelling of God in the Spirit (2:21–22). From a hopeless and godless circumstance (2:12) to this, as the consummation of all things in Christ proceeds inexorably onward. What privilege could be greater!

---

38. And see 3:2, 9 for further uses of οἰκονομία in this letter.

39. Other instances of the idea of the Holy Spirit indwelling the corporate body, the church, are found in 1 Cor 3:16; 2 Cor 6:16. The individual indwelling of individuals by the Holy Spirit is mentioned in Rom 8:9; 1 Cor 6:19; 1 John 2:27.

40. Gombis, "Being the Fullness of God," 261.

41. Ibid. Notice also that this growth occurs by believers being "co-fitted" and "co-built" *together*; the growth and building does not take place individually, but corporately.

SERMON FOCUS AND OUTLINES

> **THEOLOGICAL FOCUS OF PERICOPE 4**
>
> 4   All (believing) humanity has been united in one body, the work of Christ removing the condemnation of the law, winning access to God, and building believers together into the dwelling of God in the Spirit (2:11–22).

The fourth pericope of Ephesians also contrasts the past and present states of believers. Before salvation in Christ, Gentiles were Christless, stateless, "promiseless," hopeless, and godless. But "in Christ Jesus," "by the blood of Christ," they who were "far" have been brought "near" into the community of God's people. Christ accomplished this by removing the "enmity"—the condemnation of the law against sin—"in His flesh," "in Himself," and thereby united the community of believers into "one," and, at the same time, reconciled this "one body" to God, "through the cross," "in Himself." Now this united body has access "through Him" to the Father, in the Spirit. This unification of all (believing) humanity is part of the grand and glorious work of God consummating all things (and people) in Christ.

Possible Preaching Outlines for Pericope 4

I.   PAST: The Status of Unbelievers
        Christless, stateless, "promiseless," hopeless, and godless (2:11–12)
II.   PRESENT: The Station of Believers—their Union
        From far brought near (2:13); from strangers/aliens to co-citizens and household members (2:19)
        Both unified and created into one new person (2:15)
        Move-to-Relevance: Disunity in the church[42]
        The work of Christ to remove the condemnation of the law (2:13, 14, 15, 16, 18)
        Once separated from God, now reconciled with God, gaining access to him as a united body (2:16–18)
III. FUTURE: The "Structure" of Christians—their United Function
        Foundation: doctrine of the apostles and prophets (2:20a)
        Cornerstone: Jesus Christ himself (2:20b)
        Building: believers "co-built" and "co-fitted" (2:21–22)
        Function: the dwelling of God in Christ in the Spirit (2:21–22)
        The consummation of all things in Christ (1:10) furthered
        Move-to-Relevance: Dysfunction because of disunity
IV.   *Join Team Temple!*
        How specifically the unity of the new creation may be manifested in the community[43]

Extending the metaphor of building to bricks and mortar, one may create the following outline:

42. The "Move-to-Relevance" here (and in other outlines) is intended to keep the sermon from becoming a lecture; it serves to connect with the audience, answering their implicit question "Why are we listening to this?" Unless such moves are made often and that question answered, the sermon will remain a detached endeavor for the most part, unrelated to the audience, and adrift in a sea of words.

43. The worship service in which this sermon is preached may serve as a good opportunity to showcase church unity: a pulpit exchange (with the preachers preaching this same text)? Instituting a plan to pray regularly for sister-churches? Testimonies on the unity of the church? A program to address racial divides? Etc.

I.   FROM: Loose Bricks—Unbelievers' State

        Christless, stateless, "promiseless," hopeless, and godless (2:11–12)

II. TO: Assembled Bricks—Believers' Union

        From far brought near (2:13); from strangers/aliens to co-citizens and household members (2:19)

        Both unified and created into one new person (2:15)

        From separation from God to reconciliation with God, gaining access to him as a united body (2:16–18)

III. WITH: Mortar—Christ's Work

        The work of Christ to remove the condemnation of the law (2:13, 14, 15, 16, 18)

        Move-to-Relevance: Disunity in the church

IV. FOR: Building—Christians' Function

        Foundation: doctrine of the apostles and prophets (2:20a)

        Cornerstone: Jesus Christ himself (2:20b)

        Building: believers "co-built" and "co-fitted" (2:21–22)

        Function: the dwelling of God in Christ in the Spirit (2:21–22)

        The consummation of all things in Christ (1:10) furthered

        Move-to-Relevance: Dysfunction because of disunity

V.   SO: *Join Team Temple!*

        How specifically the unity of the new creation may be manifested in the community

PERICOPE 5

Church: Vehicle of God's Glory

Ephesians 3:1–13

[Paul's Ministry; Church's Ministry]

REVIEW, SUMMARY, PREVIEW

Review of Pericope 4: In Eph 2:11–22, believers are depicted as those who were once unbelievers now brought from the outside into the community of God's people, by the work of Christ. The barrier of the condemnation of sin was removed by Christ's atonement, thus unifying all (believing) humanity into a single body reconciled peacefully to God that is now being grown into the very dwelling of God.

Summary of Pericope 5: The fifth pericope of Ephesians (3:1–13) appears to be a digression. But by means of a personal testimonial, Paul—a prisoner in tribulation and "less than the least of all the saints"—proclaims what God has accomplished through him. And so the church is encouraged: every saint, engraced and empowered by God, is valuable to his purpose, no matter what the circumstance he or she may be in. For it is through the church, and through each individual making up the church, that God is made known to the cosmos, thus furthering his glorious plan to consummate all things in Christ.

Preview of Pericope 6: The next pericope (Eph 3:14–21) is an intercessory prayer in which Paul asks God that believers, strengthened by the Spirit, may have Christ dwelling in them—the establishment of

Christ's residence in his people as they are conformed to his image. As this ongoing dwelling takes place, the community comprehends the illimitable love of Christ and is increasingly filled with divine fullness, thus manifesting divine glory.

5. Ephesians 3:1–13

THEOLOGICAL FOCUS OF PERICOPE 5

5   Paul's divinely empowered role—paradoxically as a prisoner—in the divine administration of the mystery, to serve in the co-opting of all (believing) humanity into the community of God in Christ, forms a paradigm for the ministry of all believers, as God is made known to the cosmos through the church (3:1–13).

  5.1   Paul's paradoxical role, while yet a prisoner—a divinely engraced and empowered role in the administration of a hitherto unknown divine mystery—was to serve the co-opting of all (believing) humanity into the community of God in Christ (3:1–7).

  5.2   Paul's role in the administration of God's hidden mystery—the role of one less than the least of all the saints—forms a paradigm for the ministry of all believers, for through the church God is being made known to the cosmos (3:8–13).

OVERVIEW

This pericope is made up of two long sentences (Eph 3:2–7 and 3:8–12), a short one (3:13), and one that is incomplete (3:1). Paul begins in 3:1 intending to utter an intercessory prayer but breaks off immediately, to resume only in 3:14, where he repeats his opening phrase, "For this reason . . ." Also, the pericope is bounded by "for your sake": Paul's imprisonment for his Gentile readers' sake (3:1), and his tribulation for their sake (3:13). The digression of 3:2–13, that forms Pericope 5, describes the stewardship entrusted to Paul by God's grace—the apostle's ministry to the Gentiles and its relationship to the "mystery of Christ" (3:4). This is the most personal section of the Ephesian letter. But it is not simply a parenthetical, autobiographical digression; Paul's ministry in the service of God's grand work to consummate all things in Christ is, as will be seen, a paradigm of how believers' individual and corporate ministries are integral to this glorious plan of God.

In an earlier pericope (Pericope 2, 1:15–22), Paul had asserted that God had raised and seated Christ in the "heavenlies" far above every "rule" and "authority" (1:20–21). Here, in this pericope, he declares that God is making known his wisdom through the church, to the "rulers" and the "authorities" in the "heavenlies" (3:10). Thus, the magnificent plan to consummate all things in Christ (1:10) is shown in this pericope to be expanding in scope—from the unified humanity in Christ built into a divine dwelling in 2:11–22 (Pericope 4) to a grand exhibition of the wisdom of God to the hostile entities in the cosmos in 3:1–13 (especially 3:8–10). The connection with the six οικ- (*oik-*) words of 2:19–22 is firmly made with οἰκονομία (*oikonomia*, "administration") showing up in 3:2, 9. But even stronger is the link with the same word in

1:10: Paul's role in the "administration" of divine grace is the furthering of *God's* own "administration" of the ages, i.e., the consummation of all things in Christ.

Of note is that both Pericope 4 (2:11–22) and Pericope 5 (3:1–13) begin by explicitly addressing Gentiles (2:11 and 3:1). In the former, Paul had just asserted that all (believing) humanity, irrespective of ethnic origin and genetic makeup, had been united in Christ as "one body," created as "one new person" (2:15, 16). The three συν- (*syn-*, "co-") words in that pericope ("co-citizens," "co-fitted," "co-built"; 2:19, 21, 22) that reflected this unity now find their companions in another triplet of συν-words in 3:6: συγκληρονόμος, σύσσωμος, and συμμέτοχος (*synklēronomos, syssōmos,* and *symmetochos*; "co-heirs," "co-members," and "co-partakers," respectively). The access to God, won "through" Christ and "in one Spirit" (2:18), is mentioned in this pericope also: here it is "in" Christ and "through faith in Him" that that access is obtained (3:12). Also repeated in both contexts are the roles of apostles and prophets (2:20 and 3:5).[1]

As Paul is about to pray for the Gentile believers "for this reason" (3:1)—i.e., because they are now part of the united (believing) humanity becoming "a holy temple in the Lord" and "a dwelling of God in the Spirit" (see Pericope 4)—he is sidetracked. He enters into the digression of 3:2–13 by commencing a second new sentence (3:2–7) before the first (3:1) is completed. At first blush, this circumlocution is rather odd. Why in the midst of a discourse in Eph 1–2 that continues smoothly into 3:14–21, does Paul embark on an autobiographical diversion?[2] The answer to this question forms the theological thrust of this pericope.

5.1 Ephesians 3:1–7

THEOLOGICAL FOCUS OF PERICOPE 5.1

5.1   Paul's paradoxical role, while yet a prisoner—a divinely engraced and empowered role in the administration of a hitherto unknown divine mystery—was to serve the co-opting of all (believing) humanity into the community of God in Christ (3:1–7).

TRANSLATION 5.1

3:1   *For this reason I, Paul, the prisoner of Christ Jesus for the sake of you Gentiles—*

3:2   *if indeed you have heard of the administration of God's grace that was given to me for you,*

3:3   *that, by revelation, the mystery was made known to me, as I wrote before in brief,*

---

1. Other links with Pericope 4 include: "in [one] Spirit" (2:18 and 3:5); "promise" (2:12 and 3:6); and "in Christ Jesus" (2:13 and 3:6). Linking this pericope with others preceding it are: "co-heirs," 3:6, and "inheritance," 1:14, 18; "co-members" of the body, 3:6, and "body," 1:22–23; 2:16; "covenants of promise," 2:12, "Spirit of promise," 1:13, and "co-partakers of the promise," 3:6; divine "working" and "power," 1:19 and 3:7; "make known," 1:9 and 3:3, 5, 10; "riches," 1:7, 18; 2:7 and 3:8; "administration" and "all things," 1:10 and 3:9; and "purpose," 1:11 and 3:11.

2. The false start in 3:1, the pathos of Paul's self-reference in 3:1, and the length of the sentence 3:2–7 (105 words)—"these all look like a communication that was actually dictated with some emotion" (Thielman, *Ephesians*, 190).

3:4   *by which you are able, when you read [it], to understand my insight into the mystery of Christ,*

3:5   *which, in other generations, was not made known to the sons of men, as it has now been revealed to His holy apostles and prophets by the Spirit;*

3:6   *namely, that the Gentiles are co-heirs and co-members[3] and co-partakers of the promise in Christ Jesus through the gospel,*

3:7   *of which I was made a servant, according to the gift of God's grace that was given to me according to the working of His power.*

NOTES 5.1

5.1   *Paul's paradoxical role, while yet a prisoner—a divinely engraced and empowered role in the administration of a hitherto unknown divine mystery—was to serve the co-opting of all (believing) humanity into the community of God in Christ.*

Surprisingly, the prisoner of Caesar prefers to call himself "the prisoner of Christ Jesus" (3:1).[4] "In the literal sense he is a prisoner of Caesar, or of someone holding authority under Caesar. Yet he is kept a prisoner, not by physical restraint, but by his relation to Christ and his love for the Gentiles, on whose behalf he is a prisoner. He is Caesar's prisoner because he is first of all Christ's prisoner, not just a Christian who through some misfortune happens to find himself in prison."[5] The paradox is poignant. Here is a prisoner extolling the triumph of the God he serves, the God who has exalted Christ as cosmic lord and is consummating all things in him. How can the servant of such a great God be a humble captive in the dungeons of a pagan emperor? Paul's readers, as they went through Ephesians 1–2, may have wondered how it was that the author of these grand words dealing with sublime ideas was languishing in a lowly prison, his actual status belying his august statements. Indeed, Paul's captivity reflected the experience of God's people—outnumbered, insignificant, weak, and suffering. If these saints were co-citizens being co-fitted and co-built into the dwelling of the glorious God (2:19–22), should not this privileged position of Christians be reflected in actuality *now*? Indeed, this is the question asked by Christians in every age and in every place, one that will continue to be asked until the day all things are consummated in Christ.

But the truth is that for both Paul and for believers everywhere, their triumphant status in Christ trumps their tumultuous status in the world.

> In his current situation, Paul is in a position of utter defeat at the hands of the powers, being completely in their grasp. Seen in terms of the present age, he could not be in a weaker, more shameful, or more vulnerable position. Yet, as-tonishingly, it is by his preaching of the gospel that the creative power of God

3. "Co-members," i.e., co-members *of the body.*

4. The article "the" before "prisoner" emphasizes the special nature of his imprisonment for the cause of Christ, and "for the sake of you Gentiles."

5. Best, *Ephesians*, 296. Paul's imprisonment was noted in Acts 21:20–36; 24:23—25:12 (two years in Caesarea); and Acts 27–28 (two years in Rome).

> is unleashed and engaged, and the church, the arena of the triumph of God, is called into being, thereby displaying the wisdom of God to the powers.[6]

In other words, Paul's status as the prisoner of Christ completely transforms his station in the prison of Caesar. This is what the digression is all about: captivity to Christ changes everything—outlook, circumstance, and ministry—for every believer!

"Administration" (οἰκονομία, *oikonomia*) was encountered in Pericope 1 (1:10). It is commonly used of the management of households, cities, states, and in 1:10, of the universe, with the sense of ordering, arranging, or even implementing God's will for all the cosmos. Here in 3:2 (and in 3:9), Paul sees himself playing a definitive role as a preacher to the Gentiles in this divine management, a steward in God's grand plan.[7] Indeed, it is not just he, himself, who has an important role, but the entire church—the "one new person," the "one body" (2:15, 16), organized as a household (2:19), the very "dwelling of God in the Spirit" (2:22)—plays a key role in the divine administrative protocol. It is "through the church" that God's manifold wisdom is manifested to the hostile powers of the cosmos (3:9–10).

Paul had already commented on the "mystery" in 1:9–10—what he "wrote before in brief" (3:3). As was indicated in the commentary on those verses in Pericope 1, "mystery"—a previously hidden secret, now revealed—in Ephesians points to the divine scheme of salvation to be perfected in Jesus Christ: "the consummation of all things in Christ" (1:10), God's cosmic plan to bring all things to completion and in alignment to his will in the fullness of time. This is the trajectory of all creation, the ultimate end of all things.[8] The mystery had not been "made known" to humanity (3:5), as it had now been "revealed" to God's apostles and prophets by the Holy Spirit (3:5); this company included Paul himself, to whom the "revelation" was "made known" (3:3).[9] It had been hitherto unknown, as the contrast between 3:5a and 3:5b shows:

---

6. Gombis, "Ephesians 3:2–13," 322.

7. "If indeed you have heard" commences a first-class conditional sentence in 3:2 that takes the condition for granted: thus "surely you have heard," or "inasmuch as you have heard." This forms the protasis; the apodosis, with "therefore," comes only in 3:13, comprising the whole idea: "If . . . therefore." There is no assumption here that the Ephesians have *not* heard of Paul's ministry. Absent from that city for about six or seven years, Paul is here simply reminding the Gentile believers of what they had heard in the past.

8. See Eph 1:9; 3:3, 4, 9; 5:32; 6:19; and Rom 16:25–26; Col 1:25–27.

9. "Making known" the divine plan and mystery is a major theme in this pericope: 3:3, 5, 10 (also 1:9 and 6:19). In the Greek, the single article linking "holy apostles" and "prophets" groups this pair of leaders together (3:5); so also the single possessive pronoun "his," i.e., Christ's apostles-and-prophets. It was already noted in 2:20 that these two categories of leaders—also linked by a single article there—played a foundational role in the building of the church. Including himself in this respected company here in 3:5, Paul substantiates his point that God *is* working through him, even in his dire circumstances, just as God has been doing through other apostles and prophets. "Sons of men" (3:5) indicates humanity: Gen 11:5; Pss 12:1, 8; 45:2; 53:2; Mark 3:28.

	When?	What?	To Whom?
3:5a	in other generations	not *made known*	to the sons of men
3:5b	now	*revealed*	to His holy apostles and prophets
3:3		*revelation made known*	to me

In 3:4, the mystery is "of Christ," a genitival construction indicating the mystery *about* Christ, i.e., the consummation in Christ mentioned in 1:10, of which the unity of all (believing) humankind is a significant part (2:11–22). Outsiders (Gentiles) have now become "co-heirs" and "co-members" and "co-partakers of the promise in Christ Jesus through the gospel" (3:6; "with the saints," 2:19). Paul expresses the truth of this unity by employing those three συν-words, three different ways of stating the same basic idea. Each of these three blessings is experienced "in Christ Jesus" and "through the gospel" (3:6). Through the instrumentality of the good news of salvation, those who were once outside have now been introduced into a new sphere of life, the "in-Christ" sphere![10]

This integrated union of all (believing) humanity in a single community of God's people that included Gentiles and Jews was not foreshadowed in prior revelation.[11] The comparative conjunction, ὡς (*hōs*, "as"; Eph 3:5), therefore does not mean that the mystery was not made known in olden days "as clearly as" it has been made known now. Rather, 3:5 should be read as saying that the mystery was not made known then at all, *as opposed to* it being made known now.[12] Indeed, Paul goes on to say explicitly that the mystery had been "hidden for ages" (3:9; and see Col 1:26). The contrast between Eph 3:5a and 3:5b in the table above makes it a total contrast between the hiddenness of the past and the revelation of the present.[13]

The co-optation into the community of God's people assigns believers to a unique status: they are now "co-heirs" of the fullness of redemption, that involves the com-

10. As was discussed in Pericope 4, the emphasis there is on the unity of the body of (believing) humanity, not that the Gentiles have become Jews incorporated into Israel. Paul's view is that "the Church as a new entity which transcends old divisions and categories, and what for him is at the heart of God's disclosure is that the Gentiles are an essential constituent of this new entity" (Lincoln, *Ephesians*, 180). That this "heir-ship" and membership and "partaker-ship" were "through the gospel" (3:6) signifies that this unity is of believers. It is the unity of the church, the inclusivity and integrity of the body of Christ, not particularly a union between Gentiles and Jews, though, of course, "church" in those days was primarily Jewish in composition. But that is more incidental than deliberate.

11. However, divine intention to bless Gentiles is visible in both the OT and the NT. See, for instance Deut 10:18–19; 1 Kgs 8:41–43; Isa 2:2–4; 11:10; 19:24–25; 45:22; 49:6; 52:10; 56:6–7; 66:18–23; Amos 9:12; Micah 4:1–4; Zech 14:16; Acts 15:15–17; Rom 9:25; Gal 3:8. Also see the Abrahamic promise and its iterations that extend the scope of divine blessing to Gentiles (see Pericope 4), as well as Tob 14:6–7; *1 En.* 10.21; *T. Naph.* 8.3–4; *Sib. Or.* 3.716–723.

12. For example, take the statement: "I am not a teacher *as* you are." This may be read in a restrictive sense: "I am not a teacher as you are—I am a mediocre teacher." Or it might be read in a descriptive sense: "I am not a teacher as you are—I am an engineer." This latter sense operates here in 3:5. Modified from Hoehner, *Ephesians*, 439–40.

13. Best notes: "There is both continuity and discontinuity between the testaments; our passage stresses the discontinuity, perhaps over-stresses it " (*Ephesians*, 306).

prehensive scope of "every spiritual blessing" (1:3) at the "consummation of all things in Christ" (1:10), as well as the rewards awaiting faithful believers (see 1:14) and the magnificent privilege of being God's own possession (1:11, 14). Believers, in addition, are "co-members" of the body, i.e., the body of Christ, the church (1:23; 2:16; 4:12, 16; 5:23, 29–30). And, believers are also "co-partakers of the promise"—the Abrahamic and New Covenant promises and their iterations with implications for *all* humankind (see on 2:12). As was noted in Pericope 4, this is part of God's grand cosmic plan; specifically, here, the plan includes the uniting of all (believing) humanity in Christ.

Thus, the tangible evidence of God's glorious scheme is the unity of all (believing) humanity into "one new person," "one body" (2:15–16), co-heirs and co-members and co-partakers of the promise, who are being co-fitted and co-built into a dwelling of a glorious God (2:19–22; 3:6), rescued from the control of hostile powers and relocated from their dark realms into the sphere of "in-Christ."[14] Thus the "digression" is really not one that deviates from the trajectory of the ideas in the letter thus far. It is not particularly historical or autobiographical; neither is it apologetic, defending Paul's apostleship. And, markedly, Paul does not mention his suffering in the way he does in 2 Cor 3–4, to mark the authenticity and authority of his ministry. Here, his goal is different: Paul is the *model* of how God works "through the church" (3:10), and through individuals comprising it.

"To me," μοι (*moi*), occurs twice in 3:2, 3—the administration of God's grace was given *to Paul*, and the mystery, by revelation, was made known *to Paul*. The two are equated: it is the mystery made known to Paul that is his responsibility to administer, and in each case the passive indicates the initiative of God. "God did not simply give him the gospel message of grace to take to the Gentiles, but the assignment to do this is itself, in a special sense, God's grace given to Paul."[15] Both his mission and his commission to conduct that mission were manifestations of divine grace. The ministry of *all* God's people is likewise a matter of God's grace.

Thus the deputation of Paul as a servant of the gospel was commensurate with a divine standard: "I was made a servant, according to the gift of God's grace which was given to me" (3:7). The focus on divine grace is hard to miss. The single sentence that 3:2–7 is, is bounded on either side by "grace which was given to me" (3:2, 7). "This rhetorical device underscores the point that everything Paul has said in this passage, about the revelation to him of the mystery, the incorporation of Gentiles into the body of Christ, and his commission, arises from and can only be understood within the context of God's overflowing grace."[16] And it was this grace that appointed him to

---

14. This is not to say that these powers are now inactive; through the incorrigible and irredeemable "flesh" that each believer continues to possess until the day of his/her death, the forces of evil continue to influence humans even though their defeat is certain and has, in a sense, already been accomplished (2:20–23).

15. Thielman, *Ephesians*, 193. Also see Rom 1:5; 12:3; 15:15; 1 Cor 3:10; 15:10; Gal 2:7; Phil 1:7; and, in this pericope itself, in Eph 3:7–8.

16. O'Brien, *Ephesians*, 237.

"preach to the Gentiles the unfathomable riches of Christ" (3:8). It is no different for the ministry of the church and that of any other believer—it is all by grace.

Moreover, the giving of this divine grace to Paul was commensurate with yet another divine standard: "God's grace . . . given to me according to the working of His power" (3:7). As was noted earlier, power language elsewhere in Ephesians points to the mighty work of God. It was by the *same* "working" and "power" that God raised and exalted Christ (1:19–23). It is by this *same* divine "power" that the church grows in the love of Christ (3:16–20). It will be by this *same* power that believers will be "empowered" for victory against evil powers (6:10). And here it is Paul's own commission that is assigned a place with that same mighty work of God (Col 1:29). Thus, the equation of the empowerment of Paul's own ministry with the empowerment of all of these other cosmic events of great moment attests to the paradigmatic significance of what was happening to and through this single individual, Paul.[17] "Paul's imprisonment is no cause for alarm, nor is it an indication of divine disapproval of Paul or his ministry. Rather, God's working in power in the ministry of Paul continues despite his earthly circumstances."[18] As with Paul, so also with the rest of God's people: God continues to extend his grace and exercise his power, working in the church for his glory, no matter how adverse the circumstances. How Paul discharged his divinely appointed responsibility is considered in Eph 3:8–13.

5.2 *Ephesians 3:8–13*

THEOLOGICAL FOCUS OF PERICOPE 5.2

5.2 Paul's role in the administration of God's hidden mystery—the role of one less than the least of all the saints—forms a paradigm for the ministry of all believers, for through the church God is being made known to the cosmos (3:8–13).

TRANSLATION 5.2

3:8 *To me, less than the least of all the saints, this grace was given, to proclaim to the Gentiles the unfathomable riches of Christ,*

3:9 *and to enlighten everyone about the administration of the mystery hidden for ages in God, who created all things;*

3:10 *so that the manifold wisdom of God might now be made known, through the church, to the rulers and the authorities in the heavenlies,*

3:11 *according to the eternal purpose that He accomplished in Christ Jesus our Lord,*

3:12 *in whom we have boldness and access in confidence, through faith in Him.*

3:13 *Therefore I ask you not to lose heart at my tribulations for your sake, which is your glory.*

---

17. See Gombis, "Ephesians 3:2–13," 317.

18. Ibid., 317n15.

NOTES 5.2

5.2   *Paul's role in the administration of God's hidden mystery—the role of one less than the least of all the saints—forms a paradigm for the ministry of all believers, for through the church God is being made known to the cosmos.*

Ephesians 3:8–12 is the second complete sentence of this pericope. In it, Paul describes how he discharged his divinely engraced and empowered responsibility "to proclaim" and "to enlighten" (3:8, 9). Yes, Paul's was a unique commission. He claims, in 3:8–11, that he was the agent of proclaiming to the Gentiles the unfathomable riches of Christ (3:8), and that he was the instrument of revealing the grandness of the divine plan— the mystery (3:9)—so that God's wisdom may be made known to all the hostile powers in the cosmos (3:10), in keeping with God's eternal purpose in Christ Jesus (3:11). But the reader gets the distinct sense that even though Paul's commission was unique, all the saints are also involved in this magnificent project. Notice how Paul labels himself: "less than the least of all the saints" (3:8); elsewhere he is the "least of the apostles" (1 Cor 15:9) and the "foremost of sinners" (1 Tim 1:15).[19] The word translated "less than the least" is the comparative form of a superlative adjective, ἐλαχύς (*elachys*, "least"): thus, literally it reads "leaster"! Ironically, this imprisoned, "less-than-the-least"-ranked saint is the one who proclaims the "unfathomable riches of Christ" (Eph 3:8)—that the Gentiles have now, in Christ, become "co-heirs," "co-members," and "co-partakers of the promise" (3:6).[20]

But it is through Paul's "leastness" (3:8) that God's work is manifest. It is precisely because of Paul's weaknesses and incapacities, and because of his imprisonment and his sufferings, that divine power in his life and ministry is more vividly recognized. And therefore, everything that is accomplished through Paul is acknowledged to be of God, and of God alone. The paradox of Paul's weakness magnifies the portrait of God's power. Throughout this pericope, there is a preponderance of passive verbs: "was given" (3:2), "was made known" (3:3), "was not made known" and "has been re-vealed" (3:5), "was made a minister" and "was given" (3:7), "was given" (3:8), "has been hidden" (3:9), and "might be made known" (3:10). These passives underscore God as the subject of the divine actions, but the striking element is that most of these involve Paul as their object—God's direct role in the commissioning of Paul for this ministry of cosmic dimensions. Paul was engraced by God, as an individual, to be a part of the grand divine program to consummate all things in Christ. Thus it is implied that as with Paul, "less than the least of all the saints," so also with the people of God, all the other saints: they, too, are engraced and empowered for great things, for it is "through the church"—i.e., the unity of this body—that God's wisdom is manifested (3:10).

19. For his oppression of Christians before he became a believer, see Acts 7:58; 8:1–3; 9:1–8; 26:9–11, 14–15; 1 Cor 15:9; Gal 1:13, 23; Phil 3:6.

20. Another irony: the mystery that was once "hidden" (3:9) is now "revealed" (3:5), but it turns out to be "unfathomable" (3:8). Besides 3:8, "riches" show up in Ephesians in 1:7; 2:7 (riches of Christ's/God's grace), 1:18 (riches of God's glorious inheritance), and 3:16 (riches of God's glory).

The apostle's remarkable self-abnegation in 3:8 reminds the reader that if he, Paul, "less than the least of all saints," could be used so mightily, how much more the rest of the company of "all saints," ostensibly greater than Paul? Every believer, even the "leaster," is an integral part of God's great scheme as he brings about the consummation of all things in Christ (1:10). Notwithstanding Paul's special ministry as apostle to the Gentiles (Acts 9:15; 22:21; 26:17–18; Gal 1:16; 2:7–9; Rom 1:5; 11:13; 1 Tim 2:7), God's use of him as described in this pericope necessarily becomes a paradigm for God's use of *every* saint in his magnificent cosmic plan. Weak they may be, powerless, unrecognized, insignificant, and suffering. But through their weaknesses, the power of God is manifest, as the ages move on inexorably towards the grand consummation of all things in Christ. And in this movement, as God administers his grace and applies his power, the church fulfills its integral and crucial role in the divine endgame.

Once again in this section of Pericope 5, Paul's task of enlightening others is said to deal with the "administration of the mystery" (Eph 3:9; see 3:2). It was his responsibility to make known the work of God—i.e., the divine "administration" or management of God's grand plan. The apostle's ministry of enlightenment is directed to "everyone" (3:9).[21] But that is not all. In 3:10, a specific object of this enlightenment is named—the cosmic, hostile, anti-God powers, "the rulers and the authorities in the heavenlies" (3:10), the ones who, in comparison to God "who created all things" (3:9), are utterly impotent. "God's power is demonstrated by his ability to create the 'new humanity' (Eph 4:24), and to set it in the midst of enemy territory, thus confounding the evil powers."[22] This body, the church, is the corporate entity that God is filling with his presence, indeed, with his glory (1:23; 2:21–22). And this glory-filled temple of God (2:19, 21) is one of the prominent manifestations of divine wisdom, one of the important evidences of God's consummation of all things in Christ.[23] Thus, a powerful demonstration of God's multiplex wisdom is the united humanity of believers that forms the church.[24]

21. Early manuscripts do not have πάντας, *pantas*, "everyone" (3:9). But the word "has overwhelming support of all the text-types" (Hoehner, *Ephesians*, 455n1) and should be accepted, particularly since the preceding verb, "to enlighten," usually takes an accusative noun. The word πάντας is in the masculine gender, hence it is not just the Gentiles (from ἔθνος, a neuter word), but literally "everyone"—all (believing) humanity!

22. Gombis, "Ephesians 3:2–13," 321.

23. Evidence for the church being filled with the glory and presence of God is found in the Christlikeness that is to be the imprint upon every child of God, the image of the Lord Jesus Christ that each Christian is to bear (Rom 8:29).

24. "Manifold" (3:10) translates πολυποίκιλος, *polypoikilos*, "variegated." The rapturous notes sounded here cannot simply be expressions of wonder at the union of first-century Jews and Gentiles. There is more going on. As this commentary reads Eph 2–3, it is the integration of all (believing) humanity into "one new person" and "one body" (2:15–16) that evokes these expressions of awe. Granted, the church in Paul's day was composed mostly of Jews, thus the Jew-Gentile coalition is certainly a part of this unity. But the point being emphasized is that *all* of humanity—*believing* humanity, that is—has become one in Christ. Rather than merely an inter-ethnic reconciliation, this is a cosmic integration of humans, part of the "consummation of all things in Christ" (1:10). Several of the wordings of 3:9—"wisdom," "make known," "administration," and "mystery"—were employed in 1:8–10, in the discussion of this grand consummation.

One accomplishment of the digression of 3:2–13 is that it provides the context for integrating some of the ecclesiological and cosmic perspectives of the letter.[25] Such a coalescence was first depicted in 1:21–23, where Jesus Christ, the head above all inimical powers, and to whom all things are subject, becomes the head of the church. Now, in this pericope, we are told it is "through the church" that the wisdom of God is made known to these powers (3:10)—that their authority has been effectively neutered, particularly their control of humanity (2:1–3), as all things are being consummated in Christ (1:10). Church and cosmos thus intersect, their paths coincide, and one influences the other.

Thus the divine revelation "made known" to Paul (3:3) and "made known" to the apostles and prophets (3:5), so that it may be "made known" to all believers (1:9), is now "made known" to rulers and authorities in the heavenlies (3:10).[26] These are the very powers that overwhelmed unbelievers and kept them in the bonds of sin (2:1–2), and that continue to battle believers (6:12). Their location, "in the heavenlies" (3:10), is the same station of God (1:3, 20), of Christ (1:20; 2:6), and of believers (1:20–23; 2:6) and their blessings (1:3). And if the believers—and thus the church—are in the heavenlies, then the church becomes the ideal agent for the display of God's wisdom to the powers that are also located in the same space.[27] The body of believers, the church, thus becomes the agent announcing the magnificence and perfections of divine wisdom to those powers in the heavenlies. Indeed, it is "*through* the church," not "*in* the church," that this display occurs, suggesting that it happens "by what the church collectively does, rather than via its mere existence."[28] But even by its very existence, as a unified body, the church declares that God's grand scheme of consummating all things in Christ is going according to plan—the church is evidence of the uniting of all (believing) humanity. No hostile power can stand against this body or thwart God's purpose.

In sum, this enlightenment, here in 3:9, is not only informative (for "everyone"), but also demonstrative (to the evil spiritual entities)—it is a proclamation of victory, "through the church" (3:10).[29] In the Greek, the subject of 3:10 comes at the end of verse, delayed for emphasis thus: "so that it might be made known now to the rulers and authorities in the heavenlies, through the church—the manifold wisdom of God." And thereby, "church" and divine "wisdom" are juxtaposed. The antagonistic forces arrayed against God seek to aggravate the divisions within humanity; but these powers are confounded by God and are now subjected to his Son (1:20–23). And as this proclamation of divine wisdom continues, and as unbelievers are joined to the church,

---

25. Lincoln, *Ephesians*, 188–89, 194.

26. Are other supernatural beings, like angels, also not in the know about God's plans? It appears so: Mark 13:32; 1 Tim 3:16; 1 Pet 1:12; also see *1 En.* 16.3; *2 En.* 24:3.

27. Best, *Ephesians*, 325. Both good and evil supernatural entities are often described as being located in heaven or in the air: Job 1:6; Dan 10:13, 21; 2 Macc 5:2; *1 En.* 61.10; 90.21; also see Philo, *De plantatione* 14; *De gigantibus* 6–7.

28. Wallace, *Greek Grammar*, 430.

29. Gombis, "Ephesians 3:2–13," 320.

divine triumph continues to be heralded, and God's plan for consummating all things in Christ continues to move forwards. Thus the powerful working of God achieves the impossible: all (believing) humanity united as one, displaying, by their existence and life and growth, what great things God has done, is doing, and will do. In other words, as has been stated before, the lives of the people of God are not a negligible factor in the divine calculus, but an integral component in the divine plan and the working out of divine purpose. Far more than most Christians realize, the supernatural battle for the cosmos impinges upon the seemingly mundane, and often painful, lives of believers here on earth. And, God declares through the Apostle Paul, these lives and how these lives are lived are critical to the divine enterprise: it is not for aught that God has maintained his outpost—the church—on this plot of the cosmos. Believers are participants in the most glorious plan of God as he consummates all things in Christ, harmonizings all things in accordance with his will: Christians are the ongoing and live evidence of divine victory and the pledge of ultimate triumph to all supernatural hosts and entities.

Ephesians 3:11 clearly connects with 1:11 with the phrase "according to the purpose" that is found in both locations, thus linking the divine activities in this pericope with God's grand scheme of "consummating all things in Christ" (1:10). This "purpose" (πρόθεσις, *prothesis*) was an eternal one (3:11; and notice also the cognate verb, "he purposed," προέθετο, *proetheto*, used in 1:9). Evidently it was not a last-minute operation conceived by God to salvage his cosmic plan from failure.

The triplex title of the Son of God here—Christ, Jesus, and Lord (3:11)—is used in solemn utterances and always in connection with explicit mention of the Father (1:2, 3, 17; 5:20; 6:23–24): the pronoun "He" clearly refers to the First Person of the Godhead. The mention, then, of the Father's eternal purpose is intended to be momentous and awe-inspiring.[30] And with that, there is an unexpected use of the first person plural in 3:12: "we." The last time this was encountered was in 2:18, where also "access" to God was mentioned, and that also "through Him [Christ]," just as here in 3:12—"through faith in Him [Christ]."[31] Even as the process of "consummation of all things in Christ" is ongoing, even as the manifold wisdom of God is being displayed to hostile powers in the heavenlies through the church—even now, believers have bold access to God, untrammeled and unhindered, an unimaginable privilege.

---

30. Perhaps that consequential statement also prompted the alliteration with π (*p*) in the next verse (3:12): ἐν ᾧ ἔχομεν τὴν παρρησίαν καὶ προσαγωγὴν ἐν πεποιθήσει διὰ τῆς πίστεως αὐτου (*en hō echomen tēn parrēsian kai prosagōgēn en pepoithēsei dia tēs pisteōs autou*).

31. This last phrase has caused much debate. Is the faith of *believers* in Christ in view here (i.e., the genitive in διὰ τῆς πίστεως αὐτοῦ as objective: "faith *in* Him"), or is it the faithfulness of *Christ* himself that is described (i.e., the genitive as subjective: "faith *of* Him")? While it is not an easy decision, that Christ is mentioned as dwelling "in your hearts through faith [διὰ τῆς πίστεως, *dia tēs pisteōs*]" (3:17) suggests that it is faith *in* Christ, rather than the faithfulness *of* Christ, that is being referred to, here in 3:12. Also note that believers' faith *in* Christ has already been mentioned with some regularity in this letter: 1:13, 15, 19; 2:8.

But the irony is pungent: Paul claims to have "boldness and access in confidence" to God (3:12) while he languishes in prison![32] It is this apparent discrepancy between privileged position and present predicament that is addressed in this pericope, as Paul demonstrates the magnificent scope of his divinely ordered ministry. "[H]is imprisonment—far from hindering his ministry—actually serves to magnify the triumph of God. Paul's strategy throughout the digression is to develop the paradox of his situation—at the same time that Paul occupies an utterly weak and shameful position as a prisoner, he fulfills his cosmically crucial commission as the administrator of the grace of God."[33] And as it is for Paul the servant of God, so also for the rest of the saints of God: God is accomplishing through them ("through the church," 3:10) his vast cosmic scheme. No matter what the situation believers find themselves, no matter how dire the circumstances, they can be confident that God is working through them and manifesting himself through them to the cosmos.

So, finally, in 3:13, Paul arrives at the apodosis for the protasis in 3:2: "if indeed you have heard [3:2] . . . therefore I ask you not to lose heart [3:13]." God's grand plan, his eternal purpose, of "consummating all things in Christ," has involved, Paul declared, the mystery of the unity of all (believing) humanity, a message he had been commissioned to proclaim for the enlightenment of all and for the display to the inimical powers of God's manifold wisdom through the church. In light of such a magnificent plan and Paul's own momentous role—albeit the role belonging to one "less than the least of all the saints"—he beseeches them not to be disheartened or downcast about his tribulations. After all, he is suffering for their sake, in God's service, unto God's glory. In fact, there may be a hint here that if the one who is "less than the least of all the saints" is suffering even as he participates in the grand mission of God, those who are higher in saintly ranking—i.e., the rest of all the saints—can expect no less, in their own commissions from God. Thus even in their afflictions, believers are to see the triumph of God, even as Paul does in the midst of his own tribulations. Paul seems to be insisting that his imprisonment is not a crisis, but simply another event that serves God's eternal purposes, inscrutable though these happenings may be in the short-term view.[34]

In Ephesians, glory belongs to God: 1:6, 12, 14, 17, 18; 3:16, 21. But here it is "your glory" (3:13). Perhaps this reflects the glorious inheritance that they are to God—"the riches of the glory of His inheritance in the saints" (1:18). There might be an eschatological nuance here, too: Paul's tribulations for the Ephesians are "your glory" because his faithful proclamation has led to their incorporation into that glorious united body of (believing) humanity, the church—the temple in which dwells the

---

32. The phrase "boldness and access in confidence" (3:12) is qualified by the single article in the Greek, hinting at a hendiadys: "boldness, i.e., confident access."

33. Gombis, "Ephesians 3:2–13," 316.

34. By now—i.e., if Paul wrote Ephesians during his imprisonment described in Acts 28—he has probably been incarcerated for about five years: Acts 24:27; 27:9; 28:11, 16, 30. See Thielman, *Ephesians*, 221. Paul's attitude to suffering may be glimpsed in these verses: Rom 5:3; 8:17–18, 35; 2 Cor 4:16–17; 12:10; Col 1:14; 2 Tim 2:8–10; 3:10–11.

glory of God in its fullness (1:23; 2:21, 22). The partial glory they experience now will reach its perfection with the "consummation of all things in Christ" at the fullness of time (1:10). Paul's suffering, in short, leads to the glory of the church! And with that he moves, quite naturally, into a posture of prayer, 3:14–21.

SERMON FOCUS AND OUTLINES

THEOLOGICAL FOCUS OF PERICOPE 5

5   Paul's divinely empowered role in the administration of God's plan forms a paradigm for the ministry of all believers, as God is made known to the cosmos through the church (3:1–13).

On the surface, Pericope 5 appears to be a digression from Paul's train of thought begun in Pericope 1 and continued through Pericope 4. Indeed, what Paul has discussed in these earlier pericopes leads him naturally to a prayer of thanks in Pericope 6 (3:14–21). But that is *after* Pericope 5 (3:1–13), the seeming digression. On closer examination, it is not a detour at all. After discussing the contrasts between what they were formerly and what they are now, Paul illustrates the role of believers in God's grand scheme of consummating all things in Christ. For this purpose, in 3:1–13, Paul uses himself as a paradigm. God's grace working through him and empowering him, enables him, one "less than the least of all the saints," to be the agent of enlightenment of the "mystery"—the union of all (believing) humanity in the body of Christ—thus glorifying God. Likewise, the rest of the saints are to consider their roles in the manifestation of divine wisdom to the hostile powers of the cosmos as engraced and empowered by God, and redounding to his glory. In other words, the church plays an integral part in God's plans in the vast arena that encompasses the entirety of the universe.

Possible Preaching Outlines for Pericope 5

I.   Paradox of Ministry

    Paul, the prisoner of Caesar vs. Paul, the prisoner of Christ (3:1)
    Paul experiencing tribulation vs. Paul experiencing divine revelation (3:2–3, 13)
    Paul, "less than the least of all the saints" vs. Paul, engraced, empowered for ministry (3:4–9)

II.   Paradigm of Ministry

    God using those in any circumstance, even a prisoner
    God using any saint, even one "less than the least of all the saints"
    Move-to-relevance: The causes of discouragement as we follow Christ

III.   Purpose of Ministry

    God manifested to the cosmos through the church (3:10)
    God's eternal purpose furthered: the consummation of all things in Christ (3:11)
    Ministry undertaken confidently (3:12)

IV.   *Value God's purpose in you!*

    The value of saints from the least to the greatest
    The value of ministry, irrespective of circumstances
    Specifics on how to value divine purpose in/for our lives in every situation[35]

35. It might not be a bad idea to introduce the concept of spiritual gifts in the application section of this sermon. Spiritual gifts specifically show up in Pericope 7 (4:1–16), but there the thrust is on the

Beginning with a direct connection to the situation of listeners in the first move (pessimism/discouragement), the next two moves give reasons for hope (optimism). The last two points duplicate the corresponding ones in the outline above.

I.   Pessimism in Ministry
        The causes of discouragement as we follow and serve Christ: focusing on persons/ positions
II.   Persons in Ministry
        Paul, the least of the saints vs. Paul, engraced and empowered for ministry (3:4–9)
        God using any saint, even one "less than the least of all the saints"
III. Positions of Ministry
        Paul, the prisoner of Caesar vs. Paul, the prisoner of Christ (3:1)
        Paul experiencing tribulation vs. Paul experiencing divine revelation (3:2–3, 13)
        God using those in any circumstance, even a prisoner
IV.   Purpose of Ministry
        God manifested to the cosmos through the church (3:10)
        God's eternal purpose furthered: the consummation of all things in Christ (3:11)
        Ministry undertaken confidently (3:12)
V.   *Value God's purpose in you!*
        The value of saints from the least to the greatest
        The value of ministry, irrespective of circumstances
        Specifics on how to value divine purpose in/for our lives in every situation

---

use thereof in a selfless and loving fashion for the edification of the body—a more corporate focus. Here the idea may be broached on the value of each person and his/her spiritual gift(s). And of course, some specific suggestion on how exactly one can value one's gift (or, even better, value *another's* gift) should form part of the application. In Pericope 7, we will see that there are deliberate links between 4:1–16 and 3:1–13.

PERICOPE 6

Church: Conformed, Loved, Filled

Ephesians 3:14–21

[Indwelling by Christ; Love of Christ; Fullness of God; Glory of God]

REVIEW, SUMMARY, PREVIEW

Review of Pericope 5: In Eph 3:1–13, with a personal testimonial, Paul—a prisoner in tribulation and "less than the least of all the saints"—proclaims what God has accomplished through him. And so the church is encouraged: every saint is valuable to God's purpose. For it is through the church, engraced and empowered by him, that God is made known to the cosmos, furthering his glorious plan to consummate all things in Christ.

Summary of Pericope 6: This sixth pericope of Ephesians, an intercessory prayer (3:14–21), resumes Paul's train of thought after his digression: (3:1–13). He asks God that believers be strengthened by the Holy Spirit so that Christ may dwell them—the established residence of Christ as he is formed in his people and they are conformed to his image, a facet of sanctification, also achieved by faith. And as this ongoing indwelling occurs, saints in community come to comprehend the illimitable love of Christ. Through all this, the church is increasingly filled with the divine fulness, manifesting God's glory.

Preview of Pericope 7: The next pericope, Eph 4:1–16, addresses how believers can walk worthy, reflecting the Godhead, and living in loving, selfless unity. To this end, Christ, the Head of the body gives grace-gifts. Leaders employ their gifts to equip the saints, who in turn use

99

their gifts to build up the body in love, resulting in maturity—growing into the Head, to the measure of the stature of Christ.

6. Ephesians 3:14–21

THEOLOGICAL FOCUS OF PERICOPE 6

6   **Believers, strengthened by the Spirit and thereby increasingly conformed to Christ by faith, grasp, in loving community, the immensity of Christ's love for them, becoming filled to the fullness of God—God glorified and dwelling in them (3:14–21).**

   6.1   Believers, strengthened by the Spirit and thereby increasingly conformed to Christ by faith, grasp the immensity of Christ's love for them by experientially comprehending it in the loving community of the saints (3:14–19a).

   6.2   The goal for believers is that they be filled to the fullness of God—God glorified in them (and in Christ Jesus), as the church increasingly becomes the temple of God (3:19b–21).

OVERVIEW

This pericope is actually Paul's *report* of a prayer than an actual prayer. It has two long sentences, 3:14–19 and 3:20–21. Together they make up the second intercessory prayer in Ephesians; the first was in 1:15–23, with which this one has several similarities.

Ephesians 1:15–23	Ephesians 3:14–21
"that the God …	"that …
the Father of glory	the Father …
may give to you	may give to you …
the Spirit …	through His Spirit …
riches of the glory of His inheritance …	riches of His glory …
greatness of His power"	strengthened with power"
"fullness"	"fullness"
"strength," "power," "might"	"strengthened," "power," "might be able"

The first prayer, 1:15–23, was for the comprehension of divine power; the second, 3:14–21, is for the comprehension of divine love (by means of divine power, 3:16). This second prayer (Pericope 6), contains elements of the first: both are addressed to the Father (1:17; 3:14–15); the petitions are for the Spirit (1:17; 3:16) and, through him, for knowledge (1:18–19; 3:19, using different words) and power (1:19; 3:16); both mention riches of divine glory (1:18; 3:16) and the fullness of God (1:23; 3:19). And, as in 1:18–19, there are a number of synonyms for "power" in this prayer: "strengthened," "power" (3:16), "might be able" (3:18). The first prayer (1:15–23) followed a blessing (1:3–14); one might say that the second (3:14–21) also follows a statement of divine blessings (2:1–22), albeit only after the "digression" of 3:1–13. Moreover, linking 2:11–22 and 3:14–21 (the pericopes before and after the digression of 3:1–13) are the word pairs κατοικητήριον (*katoikētērion*, "dwelling," 2:22) and κατοικέω (*katoikeō*, "to dwell," 3:17); and θεμέλιος (*themelios,* "foundation," 2:20) and θεμελιόω (*themelioō,* "to found/ground," 3:17).

After having portrayed himself in the previous pericope (3:1–13) as a paradigm for how God uses believers to execute his grand scheme—"the consummation of all things in Christ" (1:10)—it is only natural that Paul expects his readers to let themselves now be divine instruments in this glorious divine plan for the cosmos and the ages. The one who became part of God's grand purpose by the "working of His *power*" (3:7), now prays that God would grant his readers to be "strengthened with *power*" (3:16). In other words, he would have the Ephesians join in with him in this divine plan for the cosmos, empowered by the same God. This pericope, then, is Paul's hope that the Ephesian believers will participate in the mystery and its tremendous ramifications. "Indeed, one might go so far as to say that this would be Paul's desire and prayer for the church universal, past, present, and future, because he recognizes that understanding and participating in this mystery is foundational for faithful worship and faithful action."[1]

The church clearly plays a significant role in the consummation of all things in Christ. It is the fullness of Christ who as head over all things is given to the church (1:22); it is the body of Christ (1:22); it is the dwelling of deity, a "holy temple in the Lord" (2:21); and it is "through the church" that God's wisdom is being displayed to all the hostile forces in the heavenlies (3:10). Now with a reiteration of the indwelling of the church by Christ (3:17), Paul prays that the church, the body and fullness of Christ (1:22–23), may be "filled up to all the fulness of God" himself—the glory of God inhabiting his temple (3:19).[2] The church is undoubtedly caught up in a grand cosmic drama.

Heil structures the current pericope, 3:14–21, this way[3]:

> **A**   *every* (πᾶς, *pas*) family (3:14–15)
> > **B**   strengthened with *power* (δύναμις, *dynamis*) (3:16)
> > > **C**   that *Christ* may dwell; rooted and founded in *love* (3:17)
> > > > **D**   breadth and length and height and depth (3:18)
> > > **C'**   *love* of Christ (3:19)
> > **B'**   to Him who is *able* (δύναμαι, *dynamai*); according to the *power* (δύναμις) (3:20)
> **A'**   to *all* (πᾶς) generations (3:21)

This pericope resumes the false start made at the beginning of the previous pericope (3:1), and with the same words, "For this reason." The actual prayer request/report comes in 3:16–19, and has some ambiguity in its syntax. There are three ἵνα- (*hina*-) clauses: "that He may grant . . ." (3:17), "that you might be able . . ." (3:18),[4] and "that you may be filled . . ." (3:19). The clauses are not linked with "and" to produce: "I bow

---

1. Fowl, *Ephesians,* 116.

2. See Heil, *Ephesians,* 160–61.

3. Ibid., 25–26. Similar elements are italicized.

4. I have deliberately used "*might* be able" to allude to one of the synonyms for power employed in 3:18—ἐξισχύω (*exischyō,* "be strong enough, be able").

my knees before the Father that . . . *and* that . . . *and* that." In other words, the three clauses may not be three parallel requests in Paul's prayer. Rather, "we should think of the prayer report's clauses as building on each other and of the prayer report itself becoming increasingly intense."[5] Paul's desire for their filling is the culmination of his prayer (3:19; what remains is a doxology in 3:20–21). One notices that this is similar to the conclusion of the first prayer: in 1:23 also, Paul had stated that the church is the fullness of Christ. It also links with the conclusion of Pericope 4: in 2:21–22, Paul had pictured believers becoming a holy temple and dwelling (κατοικητήριον, *katoikētērion*) of God. Here in 3:14–19, he prays that Christ may dwell (κατοικέω, *katoikeō*) in their hearts. Note also that the first two *hina*-clauses (3:16–17 and 3:18–19a) each have a finite verb (an aorist subjunctive) followed by two infinitives (see table below). It might then be best to see all the various elements in these three verses, 3:16–19, as functioning sequentially or in series this way: request (3:16) → result (3:17) → purpose (3:18) → result (3:19a) → purpose (3:19b).[6]

	Hina-Clause	Aorist Subjunctive	Infinitive	
Request	that	He may grant you …	to be strengthened …	3:16
Result			so that Christ may dwell …	3:17
Purpose	that …	[you] might be able	to comprehend …	3:18
Result			and to know …	3:19a
Purpose	that	you may be filled up		3:19b

The second sentence of the pericope, 3:20–21, is a concluding doxology. In short, Paul is interceding for the Ephesians, for what he thinks they will need "to faithfully negotiate their place in the drama of salvation that is unfolding before them."[7] Thielman observes that the mention of posture (bowed knees, 3:14), the wordiness, the rather ambiguous syntax, and the crescendo of ideas and sentences that build up, "betray Paul's emotional investment in the subjects of the prayer and those for whom he prays. The apostolic responsibility he felt for the encouragement of his readers, combined with a deeply seated conviction that they could be encouraged by the power of God and the vast love of Christ, gives the intercessory prayer report and the concluding doxology their unusual character."[8]

6.1 Ephesians 3:14–19a

THEOLOGICAL FOCUS OF PERICOPE 6.1

6.1 Believers, strengthened by the Spirit and thereby increasingly conformed to Christ by faith, grasp the immensity of Christ's love for them by experientially comprehending it in the loving community of the saints (3:14–19a).

5. Thielman, *Ephesians*, 228.

6. From Hoehner, *Ephesians*, 476.

7. Fowl, *Ephesians*, 119.

8. *Ephesians*, 225.

TRANSLATION 6.1

> 3:14 *For this reason I bow my knees before the Father,*
>
> 3:15 *from whom every family in heaven and on earth is named,*
>
> 3:16 *that He may grant you, according to the riches of His glory, to be strengthened with power in the inner person through His Spirit,*
>
> 3:17 *so that Christ may dwell in your hearts through faith, so that, having been rooted and founded in love,*
>
> 3:18 *you might be able to comprehend with all the saints what [is] the breadth and length and height and depth,*
>
> 3:19a *and to know the love of Christ surpassing knowledge,*

NOTES 6.1

6.1   *Believers, strengthened by the Spirit and thereby increasingly conformed to Christ by faith, grasp the immensity of Christ's love for them by experientially comprehending it in the loving community of the saints.*

Paul begins the first part of his prayer by detailing his posture and demarcating his divine addressee (3:14–15). Though kneeling in prayer was not uncommon (see 1 Kgs 8:54; Ezra 9:5; Ps 95:6; Luke 22:41; Acts 9:40; 20:36; 21:5), the typical prayer posture was on one's feet (Mark 11:25; Luke 18:11, 13). God as Father is referred to in Ephesians in 1:2, 3, 17; 2:18; 3:14; 4:6; 5:20; 6:23, designating him with both authority and intimacy. The wordplay of πατήρ (*patēr*, "father") and πατριά (*patria*, "family/fatherhood") in 3:15 must be noted.[9] In light of the use of "name" in the ancient Near East as a means of depicting the true nature of an individual (see Gen 25:26; 1 Sam 25:25), the link between "Father" and "family" affirms the former's status as Creator of all things (Eph 3:9; 1 Cor 8:6; Col 1:15–18; also see Eph 4:6), the one upon whom all things depend, and by whom all things are sustained. And this would include every living being, all humanity, every bit of flora and fauna, as well as any and all other (supernatural) beings.[10] That the "Father" is the Creator of "family" also indicates his position of authority over all creation.[11] God's creatorship was already mentioned in Eph 3:9.

The prayer proper begins in 3:16 with Paul asking that God grant strength to his readers, commensurate with the vast resources and abundance of God's glory—i.e., that his giving may be "as unbounded as his glory is."[12] In fact, here in context,

9. Besides here, "family" is found in the NT only in Luke 2:4 and Acts 3:25: in the latter, the substitution of the LXX's usual designation of Gentiles, ἔθνη (*ethnē*, "nations"), with πατριαί (*patriai*, "families") is significant. The word likely indicates an extended social unit than a smaller nuclear family (see 1 Chr 16:28; Pss 22:27; 96:7 LXX). Indeed, "every family *in heaven*" may indicate even units of those hostile powers mentioned often in Ephesians (1:21; 3:10; 6:12).

10. O'Brien, *Ephesians*, 256.

11. Plato calls God "Maker and Father of this Universe" (*Timaeus* 28c), and Philo labels him as "the Father who created the world" (*On the Special Laws* 3.189).

12. Fowl, *Ephesians*, 120.

"glory" might be related to God's power (as it is in Rom 6:4; Col 1:11). In any case, readers are assured that the Father is fully capable of meeting their needs for strength. This strengthening with power is by the agency of the Holy Spirit and happens in the "inner person," the core of each believer. This "inner person" is not a psychological component of an individual, but indicates the essence of a person—"the focal point at the centre of a person's life"—and thus, the *whole* person.[13] In Paul's first prayer, he wished the Ephesians to *know* the greatness of divine power (Eph 1:18–19; this was to be accomplished by the Spirit, 1:17); here it is their *strengthening* by that same power that is petitioned of God (3:16).[14]

The parallels in Paul's first *hina*-clause (3:16–17a) are enlightening:

3:16	to be strengthened (aorist infinitive)	through the Spirit διὰ τοῦ πνεύματος (*dia tou pneumatos*)	with power	in the inner person
3:17a	so that … may dwell (aorist infinitive)	through faith διὰ τῆς πίστεως (*dia tēs pisteōs*)	Christ	in your hearts

Lincoln observes that the similarities between these two infinitive clauses indicate that "Christ functions as equivalent to the role of the Spirit," a concept reflected elsewhere in Paul: Rom 8:9, 10; 1 Cor 15:45; 2 Cor 3:17; 4:10; Gal 4:6; Eph 2:22. "Believers do not experience Christ except as Spirit and do not experience the Spirit except as Christ."[15] But why is it that believers need to be "strengthened with power in the inner person through His Spirit" in order for Christ to dwell in their hearts (3:16–17)? In light of the parallels between these two infinitive clauses in 3:16–17, it must be that the strengthening of the Holy Spirit is the means of that indwelling by Christ—the indwelling by Christ is accomplished through of the strengthening by the Spirit.[16] Clearly, then, this is not the indwelling of Christ that occurs when a believer places his/her trust in Christ as Savior, a one-time event (Rom 8:10; 2 Cor 13:5; Gal 2:20; Col 1:27). Instead, Paul here is praying for an ongoing indwelling. And the plural "hearts" (Eph 3:17) points to this being a continuing event *for each believer*. So this is saying that the perfections of Christ's humanity are progressively and increasingly to be manifest in every believer— a "deeper" dwelling of Christ—by means of the Spirit's powerful work in their lives:

13. O'Brien, *Ephesians*, 258. Notice that "heart" in 3:17 is parallel to "inner person" in 3:16. This parallelism is also evident in 2 Cor 4:6 and 5:12. In Ephesians the "heart" stands for the whole person—1:18; 3:17; 4:18; 5:19; 6:5, 22—"employed in its customary Old Testament sense of the centre of one's personality, the thoughts, will, emotions, and whatever else lies at the centre of our being" (ibid., 259). "Be strengthened," a passive verb, points to this being the work of God.

14. The instrumentality of the Holy Spirit in dispensing divine power to God's people is also established in Acts 1:8; Rom 1:4; 15:19; 1 Cor 2:4; 1 Thess 1:5.

15. Lincoln, *Ephesians*, 206. Best explains that 3:16 would have been more easily comprehensible in a Hellenistic world, while 3:17 would have been more familiar to the Semitic way of thought (*Ephesians*, 341).

16. While both "to be strengthened" and "to dwell" are infinitives, the absence of a coordinating conjunction between the two infinitive clauses makes the first the means of the second.

i.e., Christ being formed in the believer and the believer being conformed to Christ (Rom 8:29). "The implication, as far as this prayer is concerned, is that greater experience of the Spirit's power will mean the character of Christ increasingly becoming the hallmark of believers' lives."[17] It is by the ongoing work of the Spirit that "Christ may 'be at home in,' that is, at the very center of or deeply rooted in believers' lives."[18] Christ must become the controlling factor in believers' attitudes and actions. Thus "to be empowered by the Spirit in the inner person means that Christ himself dwells in their hearts" and that the believer is being conformed to the image of Christ more and more.[19]

And why is this indwelling of Christ—the conformation of the believer with Christ—said to occur "through faith" (3:17)? We are not given any explanation here, but in keeping with this interpretive thrust of the dwelling of Christ, faith here must be linked to the obedience of believers as they are conformed to Christlikeness, by the strength of the Spirit (see Rom 1:5 with 15:18; 1:9 with 16:19; 9:30–32; 14:23; Ps 78:7–8, 11, 17–19, 32–58).[20] "If Christ has taken up residence in our hearts, he is at the centre of our lives and exercises his rule over all that we are and do. . . . The implication of the apostle's prayer, then, is that the more the Spirit empowers their lives the greater will be their transformation into the likeness of Christ."[21] And this happens by the strength of the Spirit that the believer taps into "through faith." It takes an act of faith to acknowledge and receive the working of the Godhead in our lives: trust in God's granting—according to his rich resources—strength in the inner person, trust in the Holy Spirit's working, and trust in Christ being formed in the believer. Thus even sanctification is by faith, not just justification (as was established in Pericope 3, 2:1–10).

Ephesians 3:17b commences the second *hina*-clause (that clause actually comes in 3:18). There are two perfect nominative participles here—"rooted and founded," one an agricultural metaphor, the other, architectural.[22] Their nominative cases appear to connect them to the second person plural, "you," of the following verb, "that you might be able" (3:18a).[23] Thus the rooting and founding, that are the *consequences* of what preceded (the strengthening by the Spirit and indwelling by Christ), also form the

---

17. Lincoln, *Ephesians*, 206.

18. Hoehner, *Ephesians*, 481. Such a picture of Christ in the Christian is found in Rom 8:29; 1 Cor 15:49; 2 Cor 3:18; 4:10–11; 13:3; Gal 2:20; 4:19; Eph 4:13–16; Col 1:28.

19. O'Brien, *Ephesians*, 258. Substantiating this interpretation is Best's observation that "dwell," κατοικέω (*katoikeō*), in Eph 3:17, "indicates a settling in or colonising tenancy." Notably, its cognate noun, κατοικητήριον (*katoikētērion*), describes the "dwelling" of God in the community of believers (2:22). In contrast, the verb, παροικέω (*paroikeō*), also means "dwell," but in a more temporary fashion; its cognate noun is found in 2:19, translated as "alien" (Best, *Ephesians*, 341).

20. See Kuruvilla, *Privilege the Text!* 195–207, for this concept of "obedience of faith" or "faithful obedience."

21. O'Brien, *Ephesians*, 259.

22. "Founded" (θεμελιόω, *themelioō*), as was noted, connects to the "foundation" (θεμέλιος, *themelios*) in 2:20.

23. As also does the perfect tense of these two participles, emphasizing a resulting and ongoing state—being "rooted" and "founded" in love enables believers to comprehend.

condition of what follows in 3:18 (the second *hina*-clause). The Spirit's strengthening/ Christ's indwelling results in believers being firmly grounded upon Christ's love. And being firmly grounded upon Christ's love, they can now "comprehend" and "know" this love: "having been rooted and founded in love, you may be able to comprehend."

It was "in love" that God predestined believers (1:4); "in the Beloved" God bestowed grace upon believers (1:6); "in love" they are asked to conduct themselves (4:2); "in love" Christians are to speak the truth (4:15); "in love" the body is built up (4:16); and "in love" believers are asked to walk (5:2). And now, in addition, in 3:17b, it is "in love" that believers are "rooted and founded."[24] Thus "love" in Ephesians refers to both human and divine love, but since 3:19 deals with the love of Christ, it is likely that the love in 3:17b is divine love as well.

Also, since both 3:17b and 3:19a deal with love, 3:18 must be dealing with love as well—its breadth and length and height and depth—even though this is not explicitly noted in the text. Moreover, the indwelling of Christ was mentioned in 3:17, followed by the love of Christ in 3:19; thus, 3:18 must also be dealing with something relating to the Second Person of the Trinity. In context, it is most likely Christ's love that is in focus here. All four spatial dimensions are governed by a single article and thus are to be taken as "a unity, a totality which evokes the immensity of a particular object"— the love of Christ, illimitable and immeasurable and infinite (and incomprehensible, 3:19).[25] Foster makes an interesting suggestion regarding these four dimensions. The dimensions of the altar of the eschatological temple are given by Yahweh in Ezek 43:13–17 (see below for the significance of this), employing, in the LXX, all four of the dimensions mentioned in Eph 3:18. "Thus, the dimensions outlined in the prayer of Eph 3:14–19 might refer to the sacrificial altar as described in Ezekiel 43. If the author does refer to the dimensions of the altar as a metaphor for the love of Christ, then perhaps the author intends to point to 'the sacrificial love' of Christ in his death."[26] In any case, the magnitude of the love of Christ is clearly being exalted.

In sum, this second *hina*-clause in 3:17b–19 petitions that believers, "having been rooted and founded in love," might actually "comprehend" and "know"[27] this love of Christ in all its grand dimensions—a love that, paradoxically, surpasses knowledge (3:19)! This is probably why this knowledge has to be a divine gift, and why it is being prayed for by the apostle.

> [T]o comprehend the love of Christ is beyond the capability of any human being. The very fact that Christ's love expressed itself in his willingness to die on behalf of sinners is in itself beyond one's comprehension. . . . No matter how much knowledge we have of Christ and his work, his love surpasses that knowledge. The more we know of his love, the more we are amazed by it. Paul is not deni-

24. "Love" as a noun also shows up in 1:15; 2:4; 6:23.

25. Lincoln, *Ephesians*, 212. Romans 8:39 mentions "height" and "depth" in connection with "the love of God which is in Christ Jesus."

26. Foster, "A Temple in the Lord," 92.

27. The two infinitives, unlike the pair in 3:16–17a, are coordinated with each other by means of the particle, τέ (*te*, "and").

grating knowledge, for it is greatly emphasized in this epistle (1:9, 17, 18; 3:3–5, 9; 4:13; 5:17). He even requests it in this very prayer (vv. 18, 19a), but here he wishes to stress Christ's love as that which is beyond human comprehension.[28]

Yet there is an imperatival element here. This comprehension of the dimensions of Christ's illimitable love surely implies a manifestation of this love in their lives towards one another. That implicit element is subsequently made clear: the comprehension of Christ's love is *communal*, shared "with all the saints" (3:18). And with that we have yet another employment of the preposition σὺν (*syn*, "with"; also see 2:19, 21, 22; 3:6), underscoring the unity of all (believing) humanity, part of the divine work of consummating all things in Christ (1:10). "Since we learn from other people, knowledge is generally communal; this is especially true of love whose nature can only be grasped through interaction with others. The true understanding of Christ's love is not then an individual experience but takes place in the community."[29] It is only when mutual love is manifested and expressed in the community of God's people, that the love of Christ—its illimitability—is glimpsed. In other words, to truly comprehend Christ's love is to experience it in a practical way in the community of the people of God, "with all the saints": the body of Christ portrays the love of Christ. This is quite a striking truth: the incredible and inexhaustible vastness of Christ's love is not felt in isolation as some fuzzy, idiosyncratic feeling, but in community, by the experience of the love of fellow believers. How important it is, then, that Christians in community should be diligent in their love for one another! In other words, "rooted and founded" in Christ's love—a divine love that goes back to eternity past (3:4–5)—believers experientially and practically comprehend this love in the communal loving fellowship (the implicit imperative) that they enjoy "with all the saints" (3:18).

6.2 Ephesians 3:19b–21

THEOLOGICAL FOCUS OF PERICOPE 6.2

6.2 The goal for believers is that they be filled to the fullness of God—God glorified in them (and in Jesus Christ), as the church increasingly becomes the temple of God (3:19b–21).

TRANSLATION 6.2

3:19b *that you may be filled to all the fullness of God.*

3:20 *Now to Him who is able to do superlatively, beyond all that we ask or think, according to the power that works in us,*

3:21 *to Him [be] the glory in the church and in Christ Jesus to all generations, forever and ever. Amen.*

---

28. Hoehner, *Ephesians*, 489–90.

29. Best, *Ephesians*, 344.

NOTES 6.2

6.2   *The goal for believers is that they be filled to the fullness of God—God glorified in*
them (and in Christ Jesus), as the church increasingly becomes the temple of God.

The third and final *hina*-clause of Paul's prayer is in 3:19b that is the culmination of
the previous two. The strengthening by the Spirit/the indwelling by Christ, and the
communal comprehension and knowledge of Christ's love, move believers towards a
unified and integrated final goal: that they may be "filled to all the fulness of God." The
"fullness of God" indicates the fullness of his nature and perfections; and this fullness
is the criterion or standard by which believers are to be filled—"*to* all the fullness of
God" (3:19). In 1:23, the church as Christ's body is mentioned as already sharing in
that divine fullness, yet, here, Paul prays that they *may be* so filled (also see 4:13). This
tension between the "already" and "not yet" is also seen in 2:19–22, where the building in which God dwells is only *becoming* a temple of God. "[T]hough the church as
the dwelling place of God by the Spirit is already a reality, it is not yet fully realised
and—practically, at least—stands in need of being manifested with ever increasing
effectiveness."[30] Believers are becoming what they already are!

In sum, Paul prays that God would strengthen believers in the inner person, resulting in Christ's indwelling them and his being formed in them more and more. As
a result, having been rooted and founded in Christ's love, they would comprehend
this infinite love—experientially knowing it in the church "with all the saints"—thus
being filled to the fullness of God, i.e., being filled up with God's character, reflecting
God himself. Paul is praying "that they may 'be all that God wants them to be,' that is,
spiritually mature. Since God himself, Christ himself, is the standard, then this means
being perfect as he is perfect, being holy as he is holy."[31] While the prayer ends with
3:19b, this idea of fullness is now carried into the following doxology, 3:20–21.

The doxology of 3:20–21 identifies God as the one who can do all that is asked of
him and even more, and concludes with a wish for God's glorification. Again, power
shows up here (3:20; as it did in 1:19–21): τῷ δὲ δυναμένῳ (*tō de dynamenō*) is literally, "to Him who is powerful/able"; and there is also δύναμις (*dynamis*, "power")
and ἐνεργέω (*energeō*, "to work"). "The doxology not only follows Paul's petitionary
prayer; it is also integrally connected with it: the ascription of power to God in the designation 'to him who is able,' the mention of his power at work within the readers (cf.
v. 16), and the fact that they can achieve more than they can ask (in prayer), all show
plainly that this ascription of praise [in the doxology of 3:20–21] is closely linked with
the preceding intercession."[32] And the magnitude of God's capacity to answer prayer
is underscored by the two uses of the preposition ὑπέρ (*hyper*) in 3:20—ὑπὲρ πάντα

---

30. Gombis, "Being the Fullness of God," 262.

31. O'Brien, *Ephesians*, 265–66. "Though in Christ this divine fullness ideally [i.e., positionally]
belongs to a believer, Paul prayed that it might be experientially [i.e., practically] realized in each one"
(Hoehner, *Ephesians*, 491).

32. O'Brien, *Ephesians*, 267. For other mentions of divine power working on believers' behalf, see
1:19–21; 3:7–8, 16–18, 20; 6:10–20. This is a recurrent theme in Ephesians.

ὑπερεκπερισσοῦ (*hyper panta . . . hyperekperissou,* "beyond all . . . superlatively"). One gets the sense that Paul's vocabulary is being stretched beyond normal bounds, in proportion to God's power that is even more boundless.[33] God can do not only beyond what his people ask, but also beyond what his people can *think* (or imagine)! Indeed, this is quite appropriate to describe the working of a God who is consummating all things in the cosmos in Christ Jesus and co-opting his people into this grand and glorious plan.

> In the earlier petition of chapter 1, God's effective power towards believers (1:19) was said to be nothing less than "the operation of his mighty strength" exerted in the resurrection of Christ (1:20). Now that same power which raised Christ from the dead, enthroned him in the heavenlies, and then raised and enthrones us with him, is at work *within us* to achieve infinitely more than we can ask or imagine. In the doxology Paul thus praises God for the bestowal of strength by his Spirit on his people, and affirms that the full realization of God's gracious purposes for them and in them becomes possible.[34]

In Ephesians, the church is depicted as Christ's body and "the fullness of Him who fills all things in all ways"—with Christ as its head (1:22–23; also 5:30); it is a holy temple and the dwelling of God in the Spirit being built in Christ—with Christ as its cornerstone (2:20–22); it is the organism that is growing into the measure of its head—Christ (4:13–15); and it is the bride of the divine groom—Christ (5:23–30). The linkage between Christ and the church is undeniably prominent in this letter. Thus when the doxology wishes for God to be glorified "in the church and in Christ Jesus" (3:21), it appears to be quite a natural juxtaposition of two entities that are closely related to each other.[35] Thus, "God's glory *in the church* cannot be separated from his glory *in Christ Jesus.*" It is because the church is in Christ Jesus that God is glorified in the church. Thus Christ is not only the mediator of God's action to believers, he is also the mediator of believers' response of worship to, and glorification of, the Father.[36] In a sense, what this letter has been saying all along is: church + Christ = body + Head. It is this duality, this combination, through which (in which) God is glorified.

Foster notes that, in the OT, the construction of the tabernacle and temple was followed by their filling with divine glory.[37]

Divine Dwelling	Construction	Filling
Tabernacle	Exod 25–31, 35–40	Exod 40:34–35
Temple	1 Kgs 5–9; 2 Chr 2:1—7:10	1 Kgs 8:10–11; 2 Chr 7:1–2
Body of Christ	Eph 2:19–22	Eph 3:16–19 (also 1:23)

33. Paul "becomes so redundant and expansive that he seems to be grasping to express the ineffable" (Thielman, *Ephesians,* 225).

34. O'Brien, *Ephesians,* 267.

35. Fowl, *Ephesians,* 123. This is the only NT doxology that has both "church" and "Christ Jesus" in proximity.

36. O'Brien, *Ephesians,* 268–69.

37. Foster, "A Temple in the Lord," 89–90.

And so if the church is the locus of the fulness of Christ (Eph 1:23), the place of the dwelling of God in the Spirit (2:22), the entity which Christ indwells (3:17), and the body that is filled up to the fullness of God (3:19), it appears quite similar to the situation with the tabernacle/temple: where God is, his glory is/will be.[38] Thus, God is glorified "in the church" (3:21). Paul is, in short, praying that "this temple of the community at Ephesus will find itself filled to the fullness of God, just as the glory of God filled the tabernacle and temple in the days of Moses and Solomon."[39] And, of course, this is true of every local body of Christ, the dwelling of God.

Foster also points to the reversal, in Ezekiel, of the normal pattern of temple-building followed by glory-filling. The people of God are indicted in Ezek 4–9, climaxing in Ezek 8–9 with the accusation of idolatry in the temple. In Ezek 10, the cloud of divine glory "fills" the temple, but only to depart (10:3–4, 18–19). "The irony here is quite dramatic when one remembers the tradition traced up to this point. Apparently the climactic sin of Israel pertained to the idols found in the temple, so that instead of the glory coming and filling the sanctuary, the filling of the temple with glory serves as a prelude to glory departing that sanctuary."[40] But in the eschaton, the glory of God would return to the temple (43:3–4) and the temple would again be "full" of divine glory (43:5). It is quite possible that Paul, here in Ephesians, sees the church as a foreshadowing of Ezekiel's new temple of the eschaton.

Just as God expected, in the past, to receive glory in the locus where he dwelt—i.e., in the tabernacle and in the temple—so also, he expects to receive glory in the "temple" that he dwells in, in this current age—the church. That was evident even in Eph 1, where the blessing of Pericope 1 resounded with "to the praise of the/His glory" (Eph 1:6, 12, 14), all relating to the church as the agency of glorification. Foster observes that "the filling of the tabernacle or temple in the Jewish Scriptures at one level signifies God's legitimization of the sanctuary in question as the place where his presence dwells, where people might legitimately encounter God." The powerful impact of this allusion is intended to convince the church of its significant role in the divine drama and in the plan of God to consummate all things in Christ.[41] There is no doubt that the temple-and-indwelling metaphor is central to Christians' self-understanding of their place in God's grand scheme for the cosmos. "Thus, not only should the Ephesians [and all believers] view themselves as a dwelling place of God (2:22), even more they ought to understand that God intends this to fulfill the promise of his glory in the New Temple recorded in Ezekiel 43, a promise which they, as a community, experience [at

---

38. Best, *Ephesians*, 351.

39. Foster, "A Temple in the Lord," 91. That no space can contain God is clear: 1 Kgs 8:27; 2 Chr 2:6; Isa 6:3; 66:1; Jer 23:24; Ps 72:19. Indeed, all of creation is portrayed as a temple in Gen 1–2 (see Kuruvilla, *Genesis*, 29–51). Also see Pericope 2 for the OT notion of "fullness" language indicating divine glory. "Fullness" and "filling" echo throughout this letter—the noun in Eph 1:10, 23; 3:19; 4:13; and the verb in 1:23; 3:19; 4:10; 5:18.

40. Foster, "A Temple in the Lord," 90.

41. Ibid., 93, 94.

least partially, in this dispensation]."[42] And not only that, they themselves are active participants in this temple-building enterprise (Eph 2:22; 4:12, 16): this is a call for them to be engaged in the construction of the divine temple, the dwelling place of God, and how to fulfill their mandate to become that sanctuary. This is how believers are to understand their identity, role, and ministry as a unified body, the church—as the dwelling of God in Christ and by the Spirit, that glorifies the triune Godhead.[43]

Thus, the idea of 1:23 that divine glory fills all things in all ways and *also* fills the church is reinforced in this pericope: the church, filled up to all the fullness of God, is, with Christ, an instrument of divine glorification (3:21). It is the holiness and blamelessness of the church, its spotlessness and "wrinklelessness" (i.e., its Christlikeness, conformation to the image of Christ), that manifests the glory of God (5:27).[44]

SERMON FOCUS AND OUTLINES

THEOLOGICAL FOCUS OF PERICOPE 6

6 **Believers, increasingly conformed to Christ in faith by the Spirit, and comprehending, in community, the immensity of Christ's love, glorify God who dwells in them (3:14–21).**

The "digression" that Pericope 5 was, now culminates with Paul's intercessory prayer in Pericope 6. The thrust of this pericope is that through the power of the Spirit and in faith, believers may increasingly be conformed to Christ (his indwelling them). Thus they are able, as they live in community, to comprehend the immeasurable extent of Christ's love: their conformation to Christ's image enables this love, manifest in love in the community, to grow and flourish. And through all this, they become, more and more, the temple of God, his fullness in them. And thus God is glorified by the body of Christ.

For the sake of clarity and simplicity, it is probably best to integrate the concept of conformity to Christ with the idea of loving fellow-believers (thus manifesting the love of Christ): *look like Christ by loving like Christ!*

Possible Preaching Outlines for Pericope 6

I.   Conformity to Christ: Indwelling[45]

42. Ibid., 95.

43. From ibid.

44. Ephesians 3:10 already noted that it is through the church that God's wisdom is displayed to the hostile powers of the cosmos.

45. As is obvious, this is a straightforward "textual" outline, following the sequence of verses in this pericope. There is nothing magical about having a sermonic outline that parallels the structure of the text. Spoken sermons are a different form of media than scripted biblical texts. The former do not necessarily have to follow the sequence of argument or parallel the narration of the latter. What kind of outline is appropriate for the audience in the pew, in a sermon uttered by the preacher in the pulpit, must be decided upon preaching event by preaching event. On the other hand, there is something to be said for ease of following along (from a congregant's point of view) with a sermon whose structure closely parallels the structure of the biblical text. Parallelism of structure between text and sermon means fewer ungainly leaps around the text by the preacher. The fewer these leaps, the greater the clarity, and thus,

By the granting of the Father (3:14–16a)
By the power of the Spirit (3:16b)
By the indwelling of Christ (3:17a)

II.   Love of Christ: Communality
The necessity of experiencing the love of Christ in community (3:17b–18a)
The vastness of Christ's love grasped only in community, not in isolation (3:18–19a)
Move-to-relevance: Our less than diligent expression of Christ's love to others

II.   Body of Christ: Function
Conformation to Christ and the manifestation of his love: filling with divine fullness (3:19b)
God's glorification (3:20–21): function of the Body of Christ
God's glorification: consummation of all things in Christ

IV.   *Look like Christ by loving like Christ!*
Specifics on loving fellow-believers, thus manifesting the love of Christ

The outline below is not too different from the one above, but deals with the idea from a different angle. It, too, is essentially a textual outline.

I.   God's Goal for the Believer: Conformity
The indwelling and conformity to God's Son, Jesus Christ
By the granting of the Father (3:14–16a)
By the power of the Spirit (3:16b)
By the indwelling of Christ (3:17a)

II.   God's Means for Achieving the Goal: Love
Experiencing and expressing the love of Christ in community (3:17b–19a)
Move-to-relevance: Our less than diligent expression of Christ's love to one another

III. God's Glory the Purpose in Achieving the Goal: Glory
Conformation to Christ and the manifestation of his love: filling with divine fullness (3:19b)
God's glorification (3:20–21): function of the Body of Christ
God's glorification: consummation of all things in Christ

IV.   *Look like Christ by loving like Christ!*
Specifics on loving fellow-believers, thus manifesting the love of Christ.

---

hopefully, the firmer the assimilation of truth in the hearts, minds, and lives of listeners.

PERICOPE 7

Unity in Diversity for Maturity

Ephesians 4:1–16

[Christ, the Gift-Giver; Leaders, the Facilitators; Saints, the Builders]

REVIEW, SUMMARY, PREVIEW

Review of Pericope 6: In Eph 3:14–21, Paul prays that believers, strengthened by the Spirit, may become the established residence of Christ, as he is formed in his people and they are conformed to his image. Thus the community will comprehend the illimitable love of Christ and be increasingly filled with divine fulness, manifesting God's glory, becoming his temple.

Summary of Pericope 7: The seventh pericope of Ephesians (4:1–16) addresses how believers should walk worthy of their calling. Reflecting the Godhead, they are to live in loving, selfless unity. A primary characteristic of such a walk of selfless love is the exercise of grace-gifts given by Christ, the head of the body, the victor. Leaders, themselves gifted to the church, employ their gifts to equip the saints, who in turn use their gifts to build up the body. The result is maturity, no longer remaining as children and being led astray by false doctrine, but growing into the head, Christ, to the measure of his stature, accomplished by each part of the body doing its bit, in love.

Preview of Pericope 8: The next pericope, Eph 4:17–32, has Paul exhorting a lifestyle that is conducive to unity in the body. Now that believers have come to Christ, they have put off the "old person" and put on the "new person," and are thus being continually renewed into the

113

divine image of Christ. This ongoing transformation is to be expressed by appropriate words, deeds, and thoughts that manifest the divine life.

7. Ephesians 4:1–16

THEOLOGICAL FOCUS OF PERICOPE 7

7 **Selfless love that leads to peaceful unity and oneness of the body—reflecting the oneness of the Godhead—and the exercise of grace-gifts, builds the body to the full stature of its head, Christ (4:1–16).**

7.1 Selfless love makes for the peaceful unity of the body that is characterized by oneness in organization, hope, belief, and identification, all reflecting the oneness of the Godhead (4:1–6).

7.2 The exercise of the grace-gifts of Christ, appropriately given to each believer and to church leaders, involves the latter facilitating the ministerial work of the former, thus building up the body of Christ in unity and love, to the full stature of its head, Christ (4:7–16).

  7.2.1 *Appropriate grace-gifts are given to each believer by Christ, the one who died and rose again, the triumphant divine warrior (4:7–10).*

  7.2.2 *The grace-gifting of Christ to church leaders enables them to facilitate the ministerial work of the saints, thus building up the body of Christ, in unity of faith and of knowledge, to maturity—the stature of Christ (4:11–13).*

  7.2.3 *The appropriate exercise of Christ's grace-gifts by each one moves believers from immaturity to maturity, avoiding false doctrine, demonstrating truth in love, and being built in love—thus growing the body into its head, Christ (4:14–16).*

OVERVIEW

Pericope 7 (4:1–16) deals with two elements of the functioning of the body of Christ: 4:1–6 concerns unity, and 4:7–16 concerns unity *in diversity.*

In continuity with Eph 3, one sees in this pericope: "prisoner" (4:1; and 3:1, 13), and calling and gifts (4:4, 11–12; and 3:2, 7–10).[1] This signifies that themes Paul had discussed in Eph 3—call, gifting, and ministry—will be continued in Eph 4. His thrust here will be the call, gifting, and ministry of the body as a whole and of individuals within it, as opposed to his *personal* call, gifting, and ministry in the previous chapter. Call and gifting and ministry mandate "particular forms of life and action from believers," and this emphasis turns out to constitute most of Eph 4–6. "Seen in this light, the transition between chapter 3 and 4 is not the transition from doctrine to ethics. Rather, it is the transition from Paul's reflection on his own calling and how he views the world and conducts himself in the light of that call—to Paul's reflection on God's

---

1. In fact, links with previous pericopes are many: "Father" (4:6 and 3:14); "walk" (4:1 and 2:10); "calling" (4:1, 4 and 1:18); "peace" (4:3 and 2:14, 17); "faith" (4:5 and 1:15; 2:8, 18; 3:12, 17); "given"/"gift" (4:7 and 3:7–8); "apostles" and "prophets" (4:11 and 3:5); "work" (4:12 and 2:10); "working" (4:16 and 1:19; 3:7); "ministry" (4:12 and 3:7), "fullness" (4:13 and 3:19); and "growth" (4:15, 16 and 2:21).

call to the Ephesians and how they should see the world and conduct themselves in the light of that call."[2]

Several times thus far, reference has been made to inimical and menacing supernatural powers (1:21; 2:2; 3:10; also see 6:10–20). In 3:10, the unified community that the church is, becomes a testimony of the manifold wisdom of God to these forces— evidence of the inevitability of the successful execution of God's grand plan of consummating all things in Christ (1:10). This cosmic manifestation of divine wisdom calls for the public display of the unity of the body of Christ, primarily as the dwelling of God, a holy temple (2:21–22). It is this unity and, particularly, unity *in diversity*, that occupies Paul in Pericope 7. Subsequently, the remaining pericopes of the letter will address how this unity may be expressed, with exhortations to "particular forms of life and action" that sustain this unity.

Heil structures the pericope this way[3]:

> **A** Bearing with one another *in love* (4:1–2)
> **B** Unity of the Spirit; one *faith*; *measure* of the gift of Christ (4:3–7)
>   **C** When He *ascended*; He *ascended*; He also *descended* (4:8–9)
>   **C'** The one who *descended;* the one who *ascended* (4:10)
> **B'** Unity of the *faith;* to the *measure* of the stature … of Christ (4:11–14)
> **A'** Truthful *in love*; building of itself *in love* (4:15–16)

The central focus, thus, is on the grace-gifting by Jesus Christ, the victorious, ascended Lord.

7.1 Ephesians 4:1–6

THEOLOGICAL FOCUS OF PERICOPE 7.1

7.1 Selfless love makes for the peaceful unity of the body that is characterized by oneness in organization, hope, belief, and identification, all reflecting the oneness of the Godhead (4:1–6).

TRANSLATION 7.1

4:1 *Therefore I, the prisoner of the Lord, exhort you to walk worthy of the calling with which you were called,*

4:2 *with all humility and gentleness, with patience, bearing with one another in love,*

4:3 *being diligent to keep the unity of the Spirit in the bond of peace;*

4:4 *one body and one Spirit, just as also you were called in one hope of your calling;*

4:5 *one Lord, one faith, one baptism,*

4:6 *one God and Father of all who [is] over all and through all and in all.*

---

2. Fowl, *Ephesians*, 126–27.

3. Heil, *Ephesians*, 26–27. Similar elements are italicized.

NOTES 7.1

7.1 Selfless love makes for the peaceful unity of the body that is characterized by oneness in organization, hope, belief, and identification, all reflecting the oneness of the Godhead.

The pericope begins with a call to a worthy walk characterized by four graces—humility, gentleness, patience, and forbearance in love (4:1–3). Then follows an exhortation to unity with a sevenfold declaration of the unifying elements of the faith, in which the members of the Trinity are present (4:4–6).

Of note is Paul's reference in 4:6 to the "one God and Father of all who is over all and through all and in all" ("all" translates πᾶς, *pas*), echoing "the Father, from whom every [also from πᾶς] family in heaven and on earth is named" (3:14–15).[4] This echo reminds readers that "the 'one' God is the ultimate origin of the unity they share with all other believers." This God, who is Father *of* all, sovereign *over* all, dynamic *through* all, and immanent *in* all, is working "all" things according to his glorious design to consummate "all" things in Christ (1:10–11): "this cosmic unity is the ultimate destiny of the unity of the Spirit that they [the readers] share with all other believers."[5]

The "therefore" that begins 4:1 refers to the previous pericope: because God is glorified in the church (and in Christ), its "walk" is to be worthy of its calling to be such an agency of divine glory (i.e., the fullness of God, the locus of God's glory: 1:23; 3:19), the dwelling and holy temple of God (2:21–22) that manifests the wisdom of God to the cosmos (3:10).[6] The church is thus an exceedingly important entity in the divine economy. *Therefore*, they are to walk worthily, for a relationship with God (the calling, 4:1, 4) mandates responsibility towards God (the walking, 4:1).[7] "God's calling establishes the norm or criterion to which their conduct should conform."[8] The call is not the result of a worthy walk; rather, the worthy walk is the result of, and the response to, believers' call.

"Walking" (4:1) has four adverbial modifiers: two prepositional phrases with μετὰ (*meta*, "with"): "with all humility and gentleness" and "with patience"; and two parallel nominative participial clauses: "bearing with one another in love,"[9] and "being diligent to keep the unity of the Spirit in the bond of peace" (4:2–3)—i.e., a bond that consists of/is peace. Paradoxically, it is a "prisoner" (δέσμιος, *desmios*, 4:1) who talks of the "bond" (σύνδεσμος, *syndesmos*, 4:3) of peace.[10]

---

4. "Father" also shows up in 1:2, 3, 17; 2:18.

5. Ibid., 171.

6. This grand status is likely part of what Paul discussed in 1:12, 14, 18: the church's call to the marvelous hope of its inheritance and its being *God's* inheritance ("hope of His/your calling" is found in 1:18 and 4:4).

7. "Walking" as a way of life occurs also in Eph 2:2, 10; 4:17 (x2); 5:2, 8, 15. In 2:10, it was noted that God himself prepares those good works in which believers are to "walk."

8. O'Brien, *Ephesians*, 275–76.

9. "One another" is found in Eph 4:2, 25, 32; 5:21.

10. Mentions of peace in this letter occur in 1:2; 2:14, 15, 17 (x2); 4:3; 6:15, 23.

"Humility," "gentleness," and "patience" are active dispositions of selflessness that result in harmony in community. Pride, aggressiveness, impatience, and intolerance, on the other hand, serve to destroy such a unity. Being humble, gentle, and patient is to demonstrate loving forbearance ("bearing with one another in love"). And "in the bond of peace" in 4:3 is parallel to "in love" in 4:2; thus the two are equated: it is "in love" that the "bond of peace" is strengthened. The unity of the church is preserved by loving interpersonal relationships and interactions that are characterized by self-lessness. This loving unity is "of the Spirit" (4:3)—i.e., created by the Spirit but, here, continued by humble, gentle, and patient people; it is wrought by Christ (2:14, 15, 17), and worked out by the saints. All that to say, if such unity and peace is *not* maintained, the church would be a visible contradiction of God's design and plan (3:10).

> Since the church has been designed by God to be the masterpiece of his goodness and the pattern on which the reconciled universe of the future will be modelled . . . believers are expected to live in a manner consistent with this divine purpose. To *keep* this unity must mean to maintain it *visibly*. If the unity of the Spirit is real, it must be transparently evident, and believers have a responsibility before God to make sure that this is so. To live in a manner which mars the unity of the Spirit is to do despite the gracious reconciling work of Christ. It is tantamount to saying that his sacrificial death by which relationships with God and others have been restored, along with the resulting freedom of access to the Father, are of no real consequence to us![11]

In sum, such loving and peaceful unity, fostered by selflessness (humility, gentleness, and patience), is to be a preeminent characteristic of all Christian relationships. It is a significant feature of the vast scheme of God to consummate all things in Christ, particularly in the life of the church and for the important role it plays in this operation. This unity is not an artificial construct, forced and unnatural.[12] On the contrary, Paul asserts in 4:4–6 that unity is the natural outcome of the church's oneness in organization ("one body"), hope ("one hope"), belief ("one faith"), and identification ("one baptism"[13]), and reflected in the oneness of the Godhead ("one Spirit," "one Lord," "one God and Father").[14] These seven acclamations of the core unities of the Christian faith appear to be deliberately created to reflect the significance of the number seven. Besides, they begin without introduction, conjunction, or governing verb in any of the three verses. Another striking element is the employment of "one" in all three genders in 4:5: "one [masculine] Lord, one [feminine] faith, one [neuter] baptism." All of this

11. Ibid., 279–80.

12. Notice the connections between Eph 4:1–3 and 4:4–6: "called" and "calling" (4:4) echo the words in 4:1, as also does "Spirit" (4:4 reflecting 4:3). "Hope of . . . calling" also appeared in 1:18. Fowl calls 4:4–6 "a dense and concise explication of the bases for the dispositions and the unity advocated in 4:1–3" (*Ephesians*, 133).

13. I.e., the identification with Christ, accomplished by believers' baptism into him, at the point of their trust in him as their only God and Savior (see below).

14. The members of the Trinity in 4:4–6 appear in reverse order from the usual creedal formulation; they show up as Spirit, Son, and Father, probably because 4:3 had just mentioned the role of the Spirit as the author of unity.

hammers home the same point, with "one" occurring seven times in the thirty-four words of 4:4–6, expressed in three triads in these verses.[15]

"One body" and "one Spirit" (4:4) recalls 2:16 and 2:18. The thrust of that earlier pericope (Pericope 4: 2:11–22) was the unity of all (believing) humanity in Christ as "one body" and as "one new person" (2:15), with the privilege of access to the Father "in one Spirit" (2:18). And it is this same Spirit in whom this one body is being built into a "dwelling of God" (2:22); as well, this Spirit strengthens individual believers in the inner person enabling the increasing manifestation of Christ in them—i.e., bringing them into conformity to Christ's image (3:16–17).[16]

From a state of hopelessness (2:12), they had been given "one hope" by their calling (4:4; also 1:12, 18)—the joint hope for the future shared by all (believing) humanity with regard to their inheritance pledged by the Spirit, and their becoming *God's* inheritance (1:12–14), and with regard to their status as a dwelling of God in his glory (1:23; 2:20–22; 3:19). Altogether, this hope points to the glorious plan of God to consummate all things in Christ (1:10) as the "the kingdom of Christ and of God" is established (5:5). So if the future destiny of this body is a singular one in Christ, then should not individuals within the body be living as one right now?

> The eschatological dimension to the call can now be seen to set the exhortation to unity in the Church in a broader context, since it recalls the cosmic unity which is the goal of the salvation God provides in Christ. . . . The one hope of Ephesians is not something individual and private but corporate and public, hope for a cosmos that is unified and reconciled, a world in which everything is brought together in harmony through that which God has done in Christ. This hope has already been related to the Church and its unity in 3:9, 10, where, as we have seen, the existence of the Church is God's announcement to the principalities and powers in the heavenly realms that he is going to make good on his multifaceted and wise plan for cosmic unity. The Church is depicted as providing the powers with a tangible reminder that their authority has been decisively broken and that everything is going to be united in Christ. It can play this role because it is the one new humanity in place of two (2:15) and the one body (2:16).[17]

Indeed, the very existence of this unified body, the church, is a visible and tangible guarantee that cosmic unity will soon be achieved. And this sense of imminence, expectancy, and anticipation of the *future* ought to motivate their practical walk of unity in the *present*, as they manifest this divine unity to all antagonistic forces.

"Faith" in 4:5 is the objective substance of one's subjective faith (as in Rom 1:5; 10:8; Gal 1:23; Col 1:23; 1 Tim 3:9; 4:1, 6; Jude 3), the body of common belief—the "unity of faith" of all (believing) humanity (Eph 4:13). Though, in those early days of

---

15. "The repetition [of 'one' in 4:5] shows that his [Paul's] emphasis lies on the numeral itself and not on the three terms to which it is attached. This should caution us against finding a subtle significance in the order of the terms or theological reasons why precisely these three terms and not others were chosen"—a recommendation valid for all the terms in 4:4–6 (Thielman, *Ephesians*, 257).

16. It was that same Spirit that was also the pledge of the inheritance believers are promised and hope for (1:12–14).

17. Lincoln, *Ephesians*, 239.

the church, water baptism immediately followed one's coming to faith, that ordinance is likely not what is being referred to by "baptism." Rather it is the identification of believers with the one Lord by whom they have been baptized in the Spirit (Rom 6:1–14), thus incorporating them into the body of Christ.[18]

The breadth of the unity envisaged in these verses is emphasized by the repetitions of "all" (×4) in Eph 4:6. The whole universe is encompassed in the word "all" (as in 1:10, 11, 21, 22, 23; 3:9, 21; 4:10). The transcendent God, sovereign Creator (3:9), the one after whom all families are named (3:15), is "over all" the cosmos. The omnipotent God who subjects all things under Christ (1:22), who is consummating "all things" in Christ (1:10), and who works "all things" according to his will (1:11), is "through all" the cosmos. This omnipresent God who, in Christ, "fills all things in all ways" (1:23; 4:10), is "in all" the cosmos. This is the God who is "over all and through all and in all," whose manifold wisdom is being made known universally (3:10), and whose name will be glorified for ever (3:21) as his kingdom comes to pass (5:5).[19]

> God's universal sovereignty and presence are set forth as the climactic ground for the unity of the Spirit that believers are to maintain. His universal rule is being exercised to fulfill his ultimate purpose of unifying all things in Christ. The unity of the church is the means by which the manifold wisdom of God is being displayed to the universe. The church is the eschatological outpost, the pilot project of God's purposes, and his people are the expression of this unity that displays to the universe his final goal.[20]

With these powerful declarations of unity and the reasons for such unity, and with this magnificent depiction of the triune Godhead, 4:1–6 prepares the way for 4:7–16—unity *in diversity.*

7.2   *Ephesians 4:7–16*

THEOLOGICAL FOCUS OF PERICOPE 7.2

---

18. In Acts and the Epistles, one sees that the baptizer is most always Christ, the medium is the Holy Spirit, and the goal is the incorporation of believers into Christ/the body of Christ (Mark 1:8; 1 Cor 12:13; Gal 3:27; etc.). Indeed, there is a sense of transfer to Christ as his possession or property as a result of this baptism (Gal 3:27–29). The Spirit is the sphere into which one is baptized and/or the means by which the union with the body of Christ is accomplished (1 Cor 12:13). The goal for the "baptizee" is thus is to be identified with Christ, even to his death and resurrection—the end of an old life and the beginning of a new one (Rom 6:4). Paul, though not devaluing the ordinance, considered the *ritual* secondary in importance compared to the *reality* that it represented—the transforming and incorporating work of the Holy Spirit (1 Cor 1:13–17; and see Eph 1:13).

19. Other similar NT confessions with a chain of prepositions indicate a comprehensive and cosmic sweep for "all" (Rom 11:36; 1 Cor 8:6; Col 1:16–17). Thus, "all" is being read as neuter, rather than masculine. If masculine, pertaining to believers, then God in Christ is the head over the church (Eph 1:23; 3:9): "over" all. He is accomplishing his purposes through the church (1:11, 23; 2:21–22; 3:10, 21): "through" all. And he is immanently present in the church (1:23; 2:21–22; 3:17): "in" all.

20. O'Brien, *Ephesians*, 285–86.

> 7.2   The exercise of the grace-gifts of Christ, appropriately given to each believer and to church leaders, involves the latter facilitating the ministerial work of the former, thus building up the body of Christ in unity and love, to the full stature of its head, Christ (4:7–16).
>
> > 7.2.1   *Appropriate grace-gifts are given to each believer by Christ, the one who died and rose again, the triumphant divine warrior (4:7–10).*
> >
> > 7.2.2   *The grace-gifting of Christ to church leaders enables them to facilitate the ministerial work of the saints, thus building up the body of Christ, in unity of faith and of knowledge, to maturity—the stature of Christ (4:11–13).*
> >
> > 7.2.3   *The appropriate exercise of Christ's grace-gifts by each one moves believers from immaturity to maturity, avoiding false doctrine, demonstrating truth in love, and being built in love—thus growing the body into its head, Christ (4:14–16).*

TRANSLATION 7.2

4:7   *But to each one of us grace was given according to the measure of the gift of Christ.*

4:8   *Therefore it says, "When He ascended on high, He took captivity captive; He gave gifts to men."*

4:9   *(Now what is "He ascended," but that He also descended into the lower parts of the earth?*

4:10   *The one who descended is Himself also the one who ascended far above all the heavens, in order that that He might fill all things.)*

4:11   *And it was He who gave some as apostles, and some as prophets, and some as evangelists, and some as pastors and teachers,*

4:12   *for the equipping of the saints for work of ministry, for building up of the body of Christ;*

4:13   *until we all attain to the unity of the faith, and of the knowledge of the Son of God, to a mature person, to the measure of the stature of the fullness of Christ,*

4:14   *so that we may no longer be children, being tossed by waves and carried about by every wind of doctrine by the trickery of people, by the craftiness of the deceptive scheme,*

4:15   *but being truthful in love, we are to grow up in all things into Him who is the head, Christ,*

4:16   *from whom the whole body, co-fitted and conjoined through every supporting connection according to the working in measure of each individual part, causes the growth of the body[21] for building itself in love.*

NOTES 7.2

This section, 4:7–16, continues to deal with unity, but the focus is on unity *in diversity*—in fact, "each" forms an *inclusio* at the beginning and end of the section (4:7, 16).[22]

21. The "of the body" is redundant after mention of "the whole body" at the beginning of the verse.

22. "Each" would have been sufficient, but "each *one*" in 4:7 emphasizes the uniqueness of the individual believer. Though there is yet another "one" in 4:7 that echoes the repeats of that word in 4:4–6, after the resounding "all" in 4:6 it is the word "each" in 4:7 that catches the reader's eye by contrast. There

"The unity of the Church, which has been prominent to this point, is now shown to be that of an organism in which Christ's sovereign distribution of grace produces the diversity."[23] Unity, in other words, is not uniformity. Individuals are unique, and here Paul affirms that gifting is also unique. Indeed, the uniqueness helps promote unity, for the various gifts act in concert to build the body into what God intends it to be—united in faith, growing in love, achieving the measure of the fullness of Christ's stature (4:13–16).[24] In sum, this section discusses the giving of the various gifts in 4:7–12, and the working of those gifts for the goal of unity in 4:13–16. After 4:7 introduces the issue, 4:8 cites Ps 68:18; then Eph 4:9–10 elaborates its application to Christ, and 4:11–16 shows how the work of Christ (his grace-gifting) applies in the present context of unity *in diversity*.

7.2.1 Appropriate grace-gifts are given to each believer by Christ, the one who died and rose again, the triumphant divine warrior.

First it was God who "gave" Christ as head over all things to the church (1:22); now it is Christ who "gives" gifts to the church (4:7, 8, 11).[25] This latter giving of grace by Christ is measured out sovereignly by the gift-giver himself, perfectly fitted for each person: "according to the *measure* of the gift of Christ" (4:7). "Rather than thinking of grace as a supply (either limited or unlimited) of undifferentiated cloth, this verse encourages us to think of God's gift of grace as a precisely tailored suit that fits each of us perfectly."[26] "Measure" is found again in 4:13, 16: the church grows into the "measure" of Christ's stature, and it is according to the "working in measure" (i.e., appropriate working) of each part of the body that this growth occurs. *Measured* gifts of grace, working concertedly in *measure* through each individual, leads to growth that is in *measure* with the stature of Christ.[27]

Reading this section, one is reminded of the similar gifting of grace to Paul, mentioned in 3:1–10: "grace," "to give," and "gift," the three key words in 4:7–12, are also found in 3:2, 7–8. That a deliberate link is being forged between Paul's experience and that of other believers is clear from his intentional use of χάρις (*charis*, "grace") in both Eph 3 and Eph 4; elsewhere, when discussing spiritual gifts, Paul employs χαρίσματα (*charismata*; Rom 12:6; 1 Cor 12:4, 9, 28, 30–31). And, as in Paul's own case (Eph

---

is also a shift from the second person plural in 4:1–6, to the first person plural in 4:7–16. The second person plural returns in 4:17.

23. Lincoln, *Ephesians*, 241.

24. Of note, 4:11–16 is a single sentence in the Greek.

25. Heil, *Ephesians*, 173. Such spiritual gifts are for all people: see, besides here, Rom 12:6–8; 1 Cor 12:1–30; 1 Pet 4:10–11. As Best notes: "Only those receiving redemptive grace [2:5, 8] receive charismatic graces [4:7]" (*Ephesians*, 377).

26. Fowl, *Ephesians*, 136.

27. This also suggests that Christ's grace-gifting is part of a strategic divine design of the body, not an arbitrary randomization of handouts (see Rom 12:3; 1 Cor 12:11). While specific gifts per se are in view in Eph 4:7–11 and 4:14–16, it is people-as-gifts that are the focus of 4:11–13, i.e., the leaders of the church. Of course, it is implied that these leaders have those particular gifts. In essence, these gifted people represent the offices that enable the growth of the church into the unity of the Spirit (4:3).

3:1–10), χάρις here also implies that along with the gift come "the powers and capabilities requisite" to successfully exercise that gift.[28]

It must be confessed that 4:7 could have continued seamlessly into 4:11, without burdening the reader with the interpretive difficulties loaded in 4:8–10—"a notorious crux" with the citation of Ps 68:18.[29] But that would shift the focus from Christ the grace-gift giver. In the place where it is, Eph 4:8–10 keeps our gaze fixed on Christ, making the link with the growth of the body into the measure of this gift-giver's stature quite appropriate.

The citation, Ps 68:18, in its original context is part of a victory psalm; proclaiming God's triumph, the psalmist addresses God and celebrates his having led his captives high (Mt. Zion?) and received gifts (tribute? booty?) from them. The sticking point of Paul's version of Ps 68:18 are his words "and He *gave* gifts to men." The corresponding verse in the Hebrew psalm has "You have *received* gifts among humankind"; the LXX also reflects this reading.[30] Apparently, ancient Jewish interpretation saw Ps 68:18 as a reference to the ascent of Moses ("you" in the text) to heaven (not Mt. Zion) to receive the Torah ("captivity," and not prisoners of war) from the hand of God. Of course, Moses's receiving the Torah was to *give* it to humankind, an assumption made clear in the Targum on Ps 68:19 and the Peshitta: both have "you have given/you gave."[31] But whether Paul was familiar with the Targums is questionable; while perhaps older in tradition, their circulation in writing post-dates Paul.

Of course, spoils of war are usually distributed by the victor to those in his party (Gen 14:17–24; Jdg 5:30; 1 Sam 30:26–31), so it is not inconceivable that Paul, in Eph 4:8, modified the LXX text to reflect this giving of gifts by the triumphant Christ.[32] The victorious warfare motif in 1:20—2:22 was noted in Pericope 3 (2:1–10), a pattern that included conflict, victory, kingship, house-/temple-building, and celebration.[33] Frequently in this ancient Near Eastern motif, the deity's ascension to the throne is followed by his blessing his people.[34] It is likely that Ps 68 follows this scheme, with

28. "χάρις," BDAG 1080.

29. O'Brien, *Ephesians*, 289. Besides, Ps 68 is considered "textually and exegetically the most difficult and obscure of all the psalms" (Dahood, *Psalms II*, 133).

30. Also, what God has done is recorded in the Hebrew in an address to God in the second person; in Eph 4:8, Christ's deeds are mentioned, but in the third person. "Humankind" is a collective singular (in both the Hebrew and the LXX—ἀνθρώπῳ, *anthrōpō*); "men" makes it plural in Eph 4:8 (ἀνθρώποις, *anthrōpois*). Note: in the Hebrew the verse is 68:19; in the LXX, it is 67:19; in the translations in English, 68:18. This commentary will cite the location of the English version of the OT, except in references to the Targums.

31. *Tg. Ps.* 68:19: "You ascended to heaven, Prophet Moses, You led captive captivity, You learned the words of Torah, You gave them (as) gifts to the sons of men" (translation from Harris, "The Ascent and Descent," 209).

32. Hoehner, *Ephesians*, 529. Paul's introduction of Ps 68:18 with "therefore it says" is not his usual prelude to OT citations; it is found only here, in Eph 5:14, and in Jas 4:6. The quotation in Eph 5:14 is a composite of a variety of Isaianic texts: a free, interpretive paraphrase may well be what the opening phrase introduces, both there and here in 4:8.

33. Gombis, "Ephesians 2," 405–8.

34. Gombis gives examples of these blessings from *Enuma Elish*, as well as from Ps 29, where victory

Yahweh as the conquering Divine Warrior who, after his triumph, blesses his people with gifts. The ascension is to his throne, and on his way, he receives tribute, presumably followed by his distribution of gifts. In fact, the Psalm ends with a statement about Yahweh *giving*: "O God, awesome in Your sanctuary. The God of Israel Himself *gives* might and strength to the people. Blessed be God!" (Ps 68:35).

> [T]he imagery of Yahweh ascending to his heavenly throne from which he blesses his people is what the author aims to capture in this quotation in Eph 4:8. He is not simply quoting one verse—Ps 68:19 [in the Hebrew text] in abstraction from the remainder of the psalm—but rather appropriating the narrative movement of the entire psalm. In this manner, the author portrays Christ as the victorious Divine Warrior who has the right to give gifts to his people because of his triumphs.[35]

In another intriguing attempt to explain Paul's citation, Smith links Ps 68:18 with Num 8, and postulates that the psalmist was actually thinking of the Levites who were *taken* from among the sons of Israel (Num 8:6, 16, 18) for liturgical service to Yahweh (8:11, 19). These Levites are, then, the "captives": "the Levites shall be Mine" (Num 3:45; 8:14). And strikingly, these individuals are also labeled "gifts" in 8:19: "And I have *given* the Levites as *gifts* to do the service of the sons of Israel in the tent of meeting" to the nation of Israel. Thus captives—Levites—are taken and given as gifts.[36] "God has, throughout history, chosen special men as leaders of the community of believers," a concept which is exactly what Paul is developing in Eph 4:7–16.[37]

In any case, it appears that the best explanation for the descent of Christ in Eph 4:9 is that it is a reference to a descent to his grave or, metaphorically, to his death.[38] Phrases similar to "into the lower parts of the earth" (εἰς τὰ κατώτερα μέρη τῆς γῆς, *eis ta katōtera merē tēs gēs*; Eph 4:9) in the LXX also indicate the locus as a grave: e.g., Ps 63:9 (τὰ κατώτατα τῆς γῆς, *ta katōtata tēs gēs*, "into the lowest/depths of the earth").[39] However, the "descent" could also be broad enough to encompass Jesus Christ's incarnation and passion. This would mean seeing "lower parts *of the earth*" as an appositional genitive: "lower parts, *i.e.*, the earth" (for other appositional genitives in this letter, see Eph 2:14, 15, 20; 6:14, 16, 17). "A comparison is drawn, not between one part of the earth and another, but between the whole earth and heaven; as if he had said, that from that lofty habitation Christ descended into our deep gulf" (Calvin, *Commentary on Ephesians* 4:9).

---

is followed by blessing (29:11), and from Isa 43:16–21. See his "Cosmic Lordship," 374.

35. Ibid., 375.

36. "Gift" in both Num 8:10 and Ps 68:18 are cognates of the same verb "to give."

37. Smith, "Paul's Use of Psalm 68:18," 186–88.

38. Underworld as grave: 1 Kgs 2:6; Pss 49:14; 55:15 ("Sheol"); Luke 16:23; Acts 2:27, 31 ("Hades"). Even in Greco-Roman religions the underworld was prominent as a place of residence for the dead (Bales, "The Descent of Christ," 89). The church fathers connected this descent of Christ with 1 Pet 3:19 and 4:6, and with the announcement of the gospel to those in Hades (Irenaeus, *Adversus haereses* 4.22.1; Tertullian, *De anime* 55.2; Ambrosiaster, *Commentary on Ephesians* 4; Chrysostom, *Homilies on Ephesians* 11).

39. Also see Num 16:30; Ps 139:8, 15; Isa 14:11, 15.

So, in sum, Eph 4:9 likely refers to the descent/death of Christ and his ascent/resurrection—perhaps a comprehensive view of his earthly ministry—no doubt evoking his victory over the hostile powers, his enemies (1:20–22).[40] Thus Paul can apply to Christ the idea of the divine warrior from Ps 68 who also ascended after his victory in battle, and proceeded to distribute gifts to his people.[41] That this theme ends with mention of Christ filling all things (Eph 4:10) also points to his cosmic victory and the ultimate divine plan of consummating all things in Christ.

The pivotal point of the momentum of Ps 68 is in 68:18—the verse cited in Eph 4:8—where God is enthroned in his temple. At that point—and *because* of that fact—the recital of God's past deeds (redemption of his people, Ps 68:1–8; gaining of land, 68:9–14; enthronement of God, 68:15–18) shifts to his present (68:19–20) and his future (68:21–23, 28–31) provision for his people.[42] All "kingdoms of the earth" will sing praises to God who rides on the "highest heavens" (68:32)—all of this bespeaking the sense of God's "filling of all things" mentioned in Eph 4:10.

> Seen in this light, it is quite plausible that Paul employs this verse because it summarizes the historical parallel between God's actions in the psalm and those accomplished by Jesus. Consistent with the eschatological fulfillment of the OT typology, Paul shifts the verbal referents of the verse to fit their new fulfillment moment. As Yahweh ascended to his temple on Zion, so also does Jesus ascend to the highest place—even to the right hand of God . . . [Eph 1:20; 2:6]. As Yahweh supplied strength and power to his people as a result of his enthronement in the temple [Ps 68:35], so also does Jesus provide his people with enabling gifts as a consequence of his ascension to the highest place. The christological implications of this paralleling between Yahweh and Christ are quite profound, especially since Jesus' ascent brings Yahweh's actions in the psalm to their cosmic *telos* and accomplishes a dominion that outstrips even the psalmist's eschatological vision [Eph 1:10, 20–23; 4:10].[43]

Thus, Lunde and Donne understand all of Christ's work described in Eph 4:9–10 as "a christological *mediation* of Yahweh's actions," drawing from statements in this letter of God's actions *in Christ* (1:3, 4, 6, 7, 9, 10 [×2], 20; 2: [5], 6, 7, 10, 13; 3:11, 12, 21; 4:32) and *through Christ* (1:5, 7; [2:13]).

> In light of this identification, it is not surprising that the description of the Father's sovereign dominion (4:6) is paralleled by Christ (4:10b), nor that Paul

40. Affirming this connection, "far above," occurs both in Eph 4:10 and in 1:21, as well as "heaven"/"heavenlies," and the notion of Christ actively filling all things; also see Col 2:15.

41. Gombis, "Cosmic Lordship," 377–78. He notes how the descent-ascent theme, i.e., the humiliation-exaltation motif, is also found in Rom 1:4; 8:34; 1 Cor 15:20–26; Phil 2:6–11; Col 3:1.

42. Psalm 68:24–27 returns to the theme of enthronement; 68:1–3 and 68:32–35 begin and end the psalm in a paean of song, respectively. Also note that 68:29 makes it clear that it is *because* of divine enthronement that God receives gifts from the nations.

43. Lunde and Dunne, "Paul's Creative and Contextual Use of Psalm 68," 107–8. There is, of course, no explicit language of "descent" in Ps 68 comparable to that in Eph 4. But that aspect of divine activity is implicit in God's coming to the aid of his people (Ps 68:1–14). Besides, there never was, and there never will be, a "descent" like that of Jesus Christ in his incarnation and his passion. Of note, Lunde and Donne conclude that the gift of Christ is the Holy Spirit (ibid., 111).

ascribes the "kingdom" to both "Christ and God" (5:5). Since Christ's mediation of the Father's work is woven into the fabric of Paul's argument from the very outset of the letter, it is quite likely that the insertion of Christ in 4:8 into the role once occupied by Yahweh indicates that Paul redacted the verse in view of its OT context.[44]

Not only do we see a loving Christ who descends down to the lower parts of the earth, to die for his people, we also see a powerful Christ who ascended far above the heavens wherein are the hostile forces (this comparison alone may justify Paul's use of "*lower parts* of the earth" to stand in opposition to "*far above* all the heavens," 4:9–10). And from his exalted position as the divine victor, he blesses his people. Christ's grace-gifts are those that unite the church, growing it into the stature of Christ (4:12–13), the body growing into the head (4:14–15), with every part functioning optimally and in synchrony with every other part to build the body in love (4:15, 16). "The building of the body is inextricably linked with [Christ's] intention of filling the universe with his rule, since the church is his instrument in carrying out his purposes for the cosmos."[45]

> [The gifts] are seen as the royal largesse which Christ distributes from his position of cosmic lordship after his triumphant ascent. In fact Christ has given these ministers as part of the overall purpose for which he ascended—that his work of filling all things might be brought to completion. The link with the previous verse indicates that in the writer's vision Christ's giving of ministers of the word to build up the whole body into his fullness is interwoven with the goal of his pervading the cosmos with his presence and his rule. This underlines the point the writer has already made in 1:22, 23. God *gives* Christ as head over all to the Church, and it becomes his instrument in carrying out his purposes for the cosmos. The readers are to see themselves as part of this Church which has a universal role and which is to be a pledge of the universe's ultimate unity in Christ. Now, the one who has been given to the Church as cosmic Lord, himself gives to the Church to equip it fully for its cosmic task.[46]

Again one gets the strong sense of a coordinated action of the Godhead to achieve the ultimate divine purpose of consummating all things in Christ, a purpose in which the church plays a key role.

7.2.2 *The grace-gifting of Christ to church leaders enables them to facilitate the ministerial work of the saints, thus building up the body of Christ, in unity of faith and of knowledge, to maturity—the stature of Christ.*

"Evangelist" occurs elsewhere in the NT only in Acts 21:8 and 2 Tim 4:5. But Eph 4:11 has the only instance of "pastor" in this leadership sense in the NT, though ποιμήν (*poimēn*) is frequently employed in the sense of "shepherd," and then always in proximity to "sheep" or "flock."[47]

---

44. Ibid., 111, 112. I might add that in Ephesians, not only the Son, but also the Spirit mediates the work of the Father: 1:13; 3:16–19; 4:11–12, 30; 6:11, 17–18.

45. O'Brien, *Ephesians*, 297.

46. Lincoln, *Ephesians*, 248.

47. For leaders functioning as shepherds see 2 Sam 5:2; 1 Chr 11:2; Ps 78:71; Jer 23:2; Ezek 34:11; the

The titles of the offices/gifts in Eph 4:11 are not mutually exclusive; one might conceivably bear more than one office or have more than one gift: Paul, for instance, was both apostle and teacher (1 Tim 2:7; Acts 15:35). Nevertheless, the functions of these ministerial offices can be distinguished. "Pastors and teachers" are qualified by a single definite article, in contrast to the other gifts, making these two categories closer to each other than to the others. Wallace considers the syntax as indicating that the first is the subset of the second, thus: "all pastors were to be teachers, though not all teachers were to be pastors."[48] In any case, all four (or five) of these gifted ones denote people who are verbally talented—in a sense all were teachers as, in fact, all in the congregation were to be: Col 3:16; Heb 5:12. Notwithstanding this wide sense of all being teachers, gifted individuals are being specifically singled out here (likely for public ministry), as in Acts 13:1; Rom 12:7; 1 Cor 12:28; Gal 6:6; 1 Thess 5:12; Jas 3:1. That not every believer exercises ministry in these offices is evident from the shift from "each one" in Eph 4:7, to a select few in 4:11.

There are three prepositional phrases in 4:12, with only the first having an article: "for [πρός, *pros*] *the* equipping of the saints," "for [εἰς, *eis*] work of ministry," and "for [εἰς] building up of the body of Christ."[49] According to Hoehner, the change in prepositions indicates the first expressing an immediate purpose, with the other two denoting a direction or goal. "The progression indicates, therefore, that he gave gifted people for the immediate purpose of preparing all the saints with the goal of preparing them for the work of ministry, which in turn has the final goal of building up the body of Christ."[50] In other words, the Head gives, leaders equip, saints minister, and thereby, the body is built (4:11–12). Note that the "work" (ἔργον, *ergon*) of building in 4:12 cannot be that exclusively undertaken by leaders; rather it is the "working" (ἐνέργεια, *energeia*) of "each" individual part (which includes the "working" of leaders, too, of course) that causes the building, as 4:16 makes clear. In support of such a reading is the fact that at the beginning of the pericope "*each* one of us" was given grace gifts, and at the conclusion also it is "*each* individual part" that causes the growth of the body. Thus 4:7–16 seems to be primarily concerned with the role of *all* believers in the growth and unity of the church, not just that of leaders. The focus of 4:10–11 is simply that a few individuals with particular gifts enable "each" believer to employ his/her own gifts for the building program. Thus bodybuilding is primarily the responsibility of the saints, as is also implied in 4:16: "building *itself.*" The leaders, as saints themselves,

---

NT uses the cognate verb, ποιμαίνω (*poimainō*, "to shepherd"), in John 21:16; Acts 20:28; 1 Pet 5:2. Of course, these are modeled after God, often depicted as a shepherd himself (Gen 48:15; 49:24; Pss 23:1; 80:1; 89:1; Isa 40:11; 49:9–10; Jer 23:1–6; 50:19; Ezek 34:11, 23–24; Zech 10:8–9), and Jesus, the Good Shepherd (Matt 10:16; 15:24; 18:12–14; Luke 15:3–7; John 10:3, 11–14, 27; Heb 13:20; 1 Pet 2:25; 5:4; Heb 13:20).

48. Wallace, *Greek Grammar*, 284.

49. Examples of several prepositional strung together in *parallel* in Ephesians include those in 1:3; 2:6; 6:12; and especially in 4:13 and 4:14. But there are those that are catenated, not in parallel, but in *series*, for e.g., 1:5–6, 20–21.

50. Hoehner, *Ephesians*, 549. Others argue that the prepositions are interchangeable, as in Rom 3:25–26, and that no particular sequence is intended.

also engage in this activity, but the role for which these individuals are gifted is the equipping of the saints to undertake that grand construction.[51] This is the "work of ministry" (4:12); notably, "ministry" is related to spiritual gifts in 1 Cor 12:5–7 (also see Rev 2:19), explicitly mentioning that each one's gift is for the common good of the larger body.

Ephesians 4:12 thus delineates the threefold pattern of the exercise of various gifts—"equipping," "working," and "building"; 4:13 then depicts the threefold goal of this exercise—the attainment of unity of faith and knowledge, maturity, and the stature of Christ. Not that a few in the church will attain to these ends, but that *all* will (4:13). There might also be an implication here that such growth occurs not in isolation, but in the company of fellow-believers, each one exercising his/her gifts for the benefit of the corporate body. That one of the goals is to "attain . . . to a mature *person*"—singular—also hints at this corporate growth (see "one new person" and one body" in 2:15–16).[52]

The "faith" (4:13) is best seen as indicating the body of faith, the objective sense of what is believed, as in 4:5 (the context has the notion of instruction by gifted individuals, 4:11; false teaching is also mentioned in 4:14). "Knowledge" (4:13) is likely the personal and experiential knowledge of Jesus Christ; that they may know the *love* of Christ surpassing knowledge, was Paul's prayer in 3:19. Both faith and knowledge here is to be attained under the guidance of the grace-gifted leaders of 4:11. Thus what is sought is "unity . . . in a common set of doctrines and in a common experience of knowing the Christ."[53]

The church is *already* united as "one new person" and "one body" growing into a holy temple and dwelling of God (2:15–16, 20–22); the unities mentioned in 4:4–6 also indicates an *already* united church. Yet it appears that that state has *not yet* been fully attained. Thus, here too, we see "the tension between the 'already' and the 'not yet'; it [the unity] has been proclaimed as a given fact, but is now presented as the goal of Christian endeavour, a goal which can only be reached by *all* collectively, and will

---

51. The noun καταρτισμός (*katartismos,* "equipping," Eph 4:12) is a hapax legomenon; its cognate verb, καταρτίζω (*katartizō*) is found in several places in the NT, with the sense of "repair/restore" (Matt 4:21; Mark 1:19; Gal 6:1), "prepare/equip" (Matt 21:16; Luke 6:40; Rom 9:22; Heb 13:21), or "complete/perfect" (1 Cor 1:10; 2 Cor 13:11; 1 Thess 3:10). Appollonius Citiensis (ca. 1st/2nd century CE), in a commentary on Hippocrates's *On Joints,* uses καταρτισμός for the setting of a limb or bone or joint (1.1, 2; 2.1, 4; 3.4; 4.2). One also notices a number of other medical terms in Eph 4:13, 14, 16 (see below); after all, this is a missive that makes believers into a "body" and places Christ as its "head"—1:22–23; 2:16. So much so, "the five specially gifted groups of 4:11, like the ancient physician, are charged with setting the body in order so that it can grow and function properly" (Thielman, *Ephesians,* 279n27). Overall, "equipping" is a good translation of καταρτισμός to denote that responsibility. There seems to be considerable evidence that "the καταρτ-word group could be used to refer to moral or spiritual maturation" (Page, "Whose Ministry?" 34). This lines up well with 4:13 that explicitly mentions growth and maturity.

52. Nevertheless, one notes that the word here translated "person" in 4:13 is ἀνήρ (*anēr,* "man"), specifically male; it is not the more generic ἄνθρωπος (*anthrōpos,* "man"). Perhaps this specificity reflects the desire of the author to parallel "man" with "Christ" in 4:13–16; likewise the choice of the word also matches the masculine gender of νήπιοι (*nēpioi,* "children") in 4:14. In keeping with this interpretation, ἄνθρωπος shows up in 4:14 in the generic sense (the plural is translated "people").

53. Thielman, *Ephesians,* 281.

finally occur at Christ's coming, when he brings his people to complete maturity."[54] So also for the fullness of Christ, already noted to be a possession of the church in 1:23. Yet it is towards this stature of fullness that the church continues to move—i.e., unto maturity, as opposed to the immature state of the children in 4:14—another "already, but not yet" element (so also in 3:19, where Paul prays for the church to be so filled).

7.2.3 *The appropriate exercise of Christ's grace-gifts by each one moves believers from immaturity to maturity, avoiding false doctrine, demonstrating truth in love, and being built in love—thus growing the body into its head, Christ.*

The ἵνα- (*hina-*) clause that begins 4:14 ("so that") is coordinate with "He . . . gave" in 4:11. Thus, Christ *gave* grace-gifted individuals to the church (4:11) who would facilitate the building of the body of Christ to the maturity of Christ (4:12–13), *so that*, protected from false teaching (4:14), they would grow up into the head, Jesus Christ, built up in love (4:15–16). There is, thus, a negative picture and a positive one painted in 4:14 and 4:15, respectively. The contrast between these two verses is clearly seen in the opposition of subjunctives: the static "we may no longer *be* children" (4:14) vs. the dynamic "we are to *grow* up in all things into Him" (4:15). The first is governed by "trickery of people" (literally, "men"), while the second is superintended by the headship of Christ. Notice, as well, the structural contrast between 4:14b and 4:15a:

A	ἐν πανουργίᾳ (*en panourgia*, "by the craftiness")
B	πρὸς τὴν μεθοδείαν τῆς πλάνης, (*pros tēn methodeian tēs planēs*; "of the deceptive scheme")
B'	ἀληθεύοντες (*alētheuontes*; "being truthful")
A'	ἐν ἀγάπῃ (*en agapē*; "in love")`

The antidote to scheming deceitfully in craftiness (4:14) is being truthful in love, and this is an important means of growing into Christ in all things (4:15), i.e., becoming conformed more and more to the image of Christ. "Being truthful" in 4:15 refers to both word and deed, just as the falsity and deceit of 4:14 is both in word and deed. Though the negative picture sounds deprecatory, it might just be that—a picture, and not an accusation; one remembers Paul's praise of these same believers in 1:15–16. So 4:14 is likely a rhetorical ploy to exhort them to never fall into the trap of immaturity, led astray by false doctrine. Nothing should jeopardize or threaten their progress towards growing into Christ, i.e., becoming Christlike.

No specific false teaching is spelled out in this pericope; Paul is being deliberately general, his words capable of encompassing any number of fakes and fictions that undermine "the unity of the faith and of the knowledge of the Son of God" (4:13). All of these potential deceits and detours of 4:14 are to be countered under the guidance of the grace-gifted ones of 4:11. That "craftiness of the deceptive scheme" is singular may

54. O'Brien, *Ephesians*, 306.

indicate that "[d]espite their variety, the false teachings of which Paul speaks serve one great, erroneous plan."[55] And so, unlike the trickery and craftiness and false winds of doctrine, believers, "being truthful in love," are to grow up into Christ. "In love" in Ephesians is found in 3:17, 19; 4:2, 15, 16; 5:2. Indeed with 4:2 and 4:16, "love" forms an *inclusio* for Eph 4. "The truth as proclaimed should not be dissociated from love or promoted at the expense of love, while a life of love should embody the truth of the gospel."[56]

In 2:21–22, it was noted that *in Christ* the whole building was growing into a holy temple *in the Lord.* And *in Christ* believers were being co-built into a dwelling of God—all bespeaking Christ's control over the process, the sphere in which the process occurs. In 4:15, the growth was to occur *into Christ*—he is the goal, the end-point, of the process. Now in 4:16 it is *from Christ* that this growth of the body occurs—he is the one who supplies all that is required for this process. It is *in* him, and *into* him, and *from* him that the church grows, building itself in love.[57] Christ is thus the giver of grace-gifts that enable the growth and building of the body (4:7–12): "from him" each individual part of the body working in concert with every other part, as those gifts are exercised properly, causes the body to grow in love. The empowering is Christ's, but the "working" is that of the individual parts, as 4:16 further clarifies. Accordingly, the divine passive, "you are being built" (2:22), becomes, here, "the body . . . building itself" (4:16).[58]

"Each individual part" (ἑνὸς ἑκάστου, *henos ekastou*) works "in *measure*" (4:16)— obviously related to the gifting to "each one of us [ἑνὶ . . . ἑκάστῳ, *heni . . . ekastō*] . . . according to the *measure* of Christ's gift" (4:7).[59] And the prepositional phrase, "according to the working in measure of each individual part" qualifies "through every supporting connection." In other words, the body of Christ is fitted and joined to-

---

55. Thielman, *Ephesians,* 284. The word πανουργία (*panourgia,* "craftiness") is also used to describe the deception of Eve by the serpent (2 Cor 11:3); and μεθοδεία (*methodeia,* "scheme") is employed of the devil in Eph 6:11. "If this connection is in view, then behind the false teaching are not simply evil men and women who pursue their unscrupulous goals with a scheming that produces error. There is also a supernatural, evil power who seeks to deceive them with devilish cunning; his 'intrigues' are to be resisted energetically with the aid of God's armour (6:11)" (O'Brien, *Ephesians,* 310).

56. Ibid., 312.

57. Ibid., 314. In Paul's day, the head was thought to be the source of the body's growth (Hoehner, *Ephesians,* 577).

58. Both divine sovereignty and human responsibility are biblical truths to be held in tensive balance. The body image (4:12, 16) following a discussion of gifts (4:11) is a pattern found also in 1 Cor 12 (gifts in 12:1–11; body in 12:12–31). But in Eph 4:16 multiple metaphors are utilized: "The architectural, physiological, and sociological terms are jointed together in a happy, if puzzling, whirl" (Barth, *Ephesians,* 445). This verse is quite dense, made even more obscure by period medical terminology. One can also never be certain that ancient authors employed those terms in conformity with then-contemporary technical understanding. Scientific verbiage tends to be employed less precisely in common layman's usage (see Best, *Ephesians,* 409). Thus several of the words in the passage are unclear; the best option is to see διὰ πάσης ἀφῆς τῆς ἐπιχορηγίας (*dia pasēs haphēs tēs epichorēgias,* literally, "through every joint/ligament of supply," 4:16) as "through every supporting connection/contact" (see Hoehner, *Ephesians,* 571–74).

59. "Measure" was also used in 4:13.

gether through "every supporting connection"—these connections are made by means of the appropriate "working . . . of each individual part." The result is the body causing the growth of itself, building itself in love.[60] So each believer functions in the body of Christ in proportion to the gift given to him or her by Christ; each believer forms the "supporting connection," all such "connections" from every believer working together—in proportion to the gifting of each part—causing the growth of the body. Strikingly, prior instances of "working" in Ephesians dealt with *divine* power (1:19; 3:7); here, in 4:16, in its final employment in the letter, it deals with the "working" of individual *believers*, empowered, no doubt, by the grace-gifting of Christ through the Spirit. In sum, each individual, discretely and uniquely gifted by Christ, plays an important role in the maintenance of unity, sustenance of growth, and continuance of the building of the body in love.[61] As noted, this pericope begins and ends with mentions of "in love" (4:2, 16; also 4:15), the sphere of existence of the unified body of Christ.

Again, in 4:16, we spy the tension between the "already" and the "not yet" that has been observed in prior pericopes:

> In one sense the body of Christ is already complete: it is a true body, not simply part of one. In another sense that body is said to grow to perfection, a process that will be completed only on the final day. The body metaphor reflects the "already–not yet" tension of the two ages. It is both complete and yet it grows. It is a heavenly entity and yet it is an earthly reality; and it is both present and future, with a consummation occurring at the parousia.[62]

The concept of "fullness" in Ephesians has been tracked in each prior pericope (see on 1:23; 2:19–22; and 3:14–19). In this pericope, in 4:13, the fullness of Christ is the standard and criteria against which the maturity of the church is gauged. Thus the ascension and grace-gifting by Christ turns out to be for the express purpose of moving the church towards bearing the "fullness"—divine glory—of God: a case of "already, but not yet." Gombis concludes: "In Ephesians, then, the combination of 'fullness' and 'Spirit' language refers to *the abiding presence of God in Christ with, in, and among his people.* While Christ 'fills' all things in that his rule as Lord is cosmic in scope, his presence resides uniquely in the church (1:23; 4:10–13). God has created the church to be his new temple, the place on earth where he dwells 'by the Spirit' (2:22)."[63] And this is a key part of his consummation of all things in Christ (1:10).

SERMON FOCUS AND OUTLINES

THEOLOGICAL FOCUS OF PERICOPE 7

---

60. Ibid., 576.

61. While there is a focus in 4:16 on "each individual part," ultimately the emphasis is on the corporate structure of the body and its unified growth: "the whole body"; "building itself"; and the two συν- (*syn-*, "co-") words—"co-fitted" and "conjoined" (4:16).

62. O'Brien, *Ephesians*, 317.

63. "Being the Fullness of God in Christ," 262.

> **7 Selfless and loving exercise of grace-gifts, that leads to peaceful unity, builds up the body to the mature stature of its head, Christ (4:1–16).**

In an earlier pericope (Pericope 5: 3:1–13), the suggestion was made to introduce the concept of spiritual gifts in the application section of a sermon on that text. Here, in Pericope 7, spiritual gifts are explicitly mentioned, forming the core of this passage. After introducing this pericope with the importance of selflessness to promote unity, the exercise of such gifts is discussed. Christ, the Head of the church and the victor over all forces antithetical to God and his plans, distributes gifts to his people, to each believer in appropriate measure. In the church, gifted leaders are themselves gifted to the body to equip believers to minister with their own gifts, ultimately to the building up of the body to attain to the mature stature of its Head, Jesus Christ. That this is a construction based "in love" is clear in that the pericope begins and ends with that phrase (4:2, 15, 16).[64] And so it is recommended that a sermon on this pericope focus on the selfless, loving exercise of spiritual gifts, one for another, to build the church.

Possible Preaching Outlines for Pericope 7

I. Selflessness in Love
     A walk worthy of the divine call marked by selflessness (4:1–2)
     Selflessness, powered by love, promoting unity (4:2–3)
     Selfless, loving unity, a reflection of the unity of the Godhead (4:4–6)
     Move-to-relevance: selfishness, a hindrance to unity
II. Service through Love
     Christ, the gift-giver, the Head of the body (4:7–10)
     Leaders, the equippers, the body-facilitators (4:11–12a)
     Saints, the ministers, the body-builders (4:12b, 16)
     Move-to-relevance: Spiritual gifts recap[65]
III. Success of Love
     Growing into maturity commensurate with the status of Christ, the Head (4:13, 15)
     Avoiding being lead astray (4:14)
     Move-to-relevance: Dangers of not growing/maturing
IV. *Bodybuilders exercise gifts!*[66]
     Specifics on the loving exercise of gifts to build the body to maturity[67]

Focusing on the protagonists—Christ, leaders, and the saints—yields another outline:

I. CHRIST: The Body's Head
     Christ, the gift-giver, the Head of the body (4:7–10)
     God's goal: selfless, loving unity that reflects the Godhead (4:1–6)
     Move-to-relevance: selfishness, a hindrance to unity

---

64. "Love" was also a focus of Pericope 6: 3:14–21.

65. A brief recap of what was touched on in the sermon on Pericope 5: 3:1–13 would be helpful here. Or one could address here aspects of spiritual gifts *not* covered in that earlier sermon.

66. While this statement could be seen as an imperative—especially with the addition of a comma after "bodybuilders"—it is not. Sermon applications as imperatives are generally a good idea: it focuses listeners on specific actions *they* should engage in. For clarity's sake, that may be the best way to proceed. But there is nothing amiss in having the imperative implied, as in the application statement in this sermon outline.

67. To keep this sermon distinct from the one on Pericope 5, the focus is best kept on the foundation of ministry—love, and the final goal of ministry—maturity.

EPHESIANS

II. LEADERS: The Body's Facilitators
>   Leaders, the equippers, the body-facilitators (4:11–12a)
>   Leaders' goal: move to maturity, no longer being children (4:13–14)
>   Move-to-relevance: Dangers of not growing/maturing

III. SAINTS: The Body's Builders
>   Saints, the ministers, the body-builders (4:12b, 16)
>   Saints' goal: Growth into Christ, the Head, in love (4:15–16)
>   Move-to-relevance: Spiritual gifts recap

IV. *Bodybuilders exercise gifts!*
>   Specifics on the loving exercise of gifts to build the body to maturity

PERICOPE 8

Manifesting Divine Life

Ephesians 4:17–32

[Old Person vs. New Person; Divine Likeness]

REVIEW, SUMMARY, PREVIEW

Review of Pericope 7: In Eph 4:1–16, Paul addresses how believers can walk worthily, reflecting the Godhead, and living in loving, selfless unity. To this end, Christ, the head of the body gives grace-gifts. Leaders employ their gifts to equip the saints, who in turn use their gifts to build up the body in love, resulting in maturity—growing into the head, to the measure of Christ's stature.

Summary of Pericope 8: The eighth pericope of Ephesians (4:17–32) continues with Paul exhorting a lifestyle that is implicitly conducive to unity in the body. Now that believers have come to Christ, they are reminded that they have put off the "old person" and put on the "new person." And with this new clothing, they are being continually renewed into the divine image of Christ. This ongoing transformation is to be expressed by appropriate words, deeds, and thoughts that manifest the divine life. Thereby unity is sustained in the body and the divine consummation of all things in Christ is furthered.

Preview of Pericope 9: The next pericope, Eph 5:1–20, continues the contrast between the lifestyle of the believer and that of the unbeliever. The former, imitating God and the selfless love of Christ, walks wisely and by the Spirit, thus inviting divine pleasure. The believer walking in light also exposes the deeds of darkness, and, comprehending the will of God, worships him devotedly.

8.   Ephesians 4:17–32

> **THEOLOGICAL FOCUS OF PERICOPE 8**
>
> **8**   **Believers, no longer living licentiously, ignorant and devoid of divine life, are now, after learning Christ, being divinely renewed into the likeness of God, which is manifested as they maintain unity and build up one another by activities conducive to community (4:17–32).**
>
> 8.1   Believers no longer live hardheartedly ignorant and devoid of divine life, willfully given to all manner of licentious behavior (4:17–19).
>
> 8.2   Believers learning Christ—being taught that they have put off the old person and put on the new—are now being divinely renewed into the likeness of God (4:20–24).
>
> 8.3   The likeness of God is manifested by believers as they maintain unity and build up one another, eschewing anger, sharing resources, speaking grace, controlling tempers, and forgiving divinely (4:25–32).

OVERVIEW

This pericope concludes at 4:32. The next two verses, 5:1–2, form the introduction to a new section, as also do 4:1 and 4:17: all three opening statements have "therefore" and a form of the verb "to walk." Since the negative exhortations in the following section (5:3–14) deal generally with sexual immorality—illicit love—the preamble of 5:1–2, expressing how *divine* kind of love ought to be manifested in the body, is germane to that topic.

Heil structures Pericope 8 (4:17–32) this way[1]:

> **A**   Life *of God*; *every* (πᾶς, *pas*) kind of impurity (4:17–19)
> **B**   You *heard*; just as *truth* is in Jesus (4:20–21)
> **C**   Put *off* the *old person ... in accordance with ...* (×2) (4:22)
> **C'**   Put *on* the *new person ... in accordance with ...* (4:23–24)
> **B'**   Speak *truth*; grace to *those who hear* (4:25–29)
> **A'**   Spirit *of God*; *all* bitterness; *all* malice (πᾶς ×2); *God* in Christ (4:30–32)

The unity of believers, that was in focus in 4:7–16, now shifts to the corresponding separation from unbelievers in 4:17–32: how believers should *not* live/walk—what they should put off, and what they should put on (*C, C'*). Remarkably enough, "the peril facing Gentile believers is neither persecution brought on by their new attitude to paganism nor the influence of heretical intellectual ideas but a relapse into their former pre-Christian ways, which are the ways of the world around them."[2] Each of the ethical commands in this pericope shows a negative action to be avoided and a

---

1. Heil, *Ephesians*, 27–29. Similar elements are italicized.

2. Best, *Ephesians*, 415.

positive action to be adopted (a pattern also seen in 5:3–14). And all of this is possible for the children of God because they have put on the "new person" characterized, like God, by "righteousness and holiness of the truth" (4:24).

There is strong precedent for these NT recommendations of lifestyle change. Relationship calls for responsibility.[3] Notable is the fact that even the Decalogue is prefaced by an announcement of relationship: "I am the Lord your God, who brought you out of the land of Egypt, out of the house of slavery" (Exod 20:2). The list of divine demands came afterwards. Likewise, Lev 18:1–5 ("I am Yahweh your God. You shall not do . . . I am Yahweh your God. So you shall keep My statutes and My judgments, by which a man may live if he does them; I am Yahweh") suggests that *because* this God was Yahweh, the Israelites' covenantal God, *therefore* the Israelites were to behave in a certain fashion.[4] That God's setting apart of his people (the divine-human relationship) came prior to their responsibility to be holy was asserted in Lev 20 (20:26—"Thus [according to the specifics detailed in 20:1–25] you are to be holy to Me, for I, Yahweh, am holy; and I have set you apart from the peoples to be Mine" (also see 22:32–33; 23:41–43). The emphasis of Pericope 8 (Eph 4:7–32) is that this changed life is to correspond with who God is (4:24).

8.1 Ephesians 4:17–19

THEOLOGICAL FOCUS OF PERICOPE 8.1

8.1   Believers no longer live hardheartedly ignorant and devoid of divine life, willfully given to all manner of licentious behavior (4:17–19).

TRANSLATION 8.1

4:17 *Therefore this I say, and implore in the Lord, that you no longer walk just as the Gentiles also walk, in the futility of their mind,*

4:18 *having been darkened in their understanding, having been excluded from the life of God because of the ignorance that is in them, because of the hardness of their heart;*

4:19 *who, having become callous, have given themselves over to licentiousness for the practice of every kind of impurity with greed.*

---

3. See Kuruvilla, *Privilege the Text!* 189–93.

4. Also Lev 19:1–3 ("You shall be holy, for I, Yahweh, your God am holy. . . . I am Yahweh your God") and the numerous echoes throughout Leviticus of "I am the Lord" (19:3, 4, 10, 12, 14, 16, 18, 25, 28, 29, 30, 31, 32, 34, 36, 37; etc.). And see Deut 11:26–28; 30:15–20; Ps 1; Jer 21:8; *T. Asher* 1.3–5; and *Didache* 1–5, for the contrasts between a life with and without God.

NOTES 8.1

8.1 *Believers no longer live hardheartedly ignorant and devoid of divine life, willfully given to all manner of licentious behavior.*

The beginning of this pericope (4:17) has a number of similarities with the beginning of the previous one (4:1).[5]

4:1	*"Therefore* I, the prisoner *of* [ἐν, *en*] *the Lord,* **exhort** *you to walk* worthy of the calling with which you were called."
4:17	*"Therefore* this I say, and **implore** *in* [ἐν] *the Lord, that you* no longer *walk* just as the Gentiles also *walk."*

This is a serious and solemn exhortation from Paul, emphasized by his affirmation "in the Lord" (4:17). "The moral exhortation here is not merely advice that Paul's readers can take or leave at their discretion but is critical instruction for becoming the human beings and the community that God intends for them to be."[6] The urging also shows that life-change does not immediately follow conversion.

Heil notes that the extended description of the "interior mentality" regarding how unbelievers walk—in the "futility of their *mind*," "darkened in their *understanding*," "ignorance *in them*," "hardness of their *heart*" (4:17–18)—is in contrast to what was going on within believers: "strengthened with power through His Spirit in *the inner man*," Christ dwelling "in your *hearts*" (3:16–19). Moreover, unbelievers are characterized by ignorance (4:18), but believers know the love of Christ that surpasses knowledge (3:19).[7] "[A]long with futile reasoning and darkened understanding, ignorance and hardness of heart [4:17–19] all work together to present a picture of Gentiles as alienated from their true end in God in a comprehensive way, touching on the intellect, perceptions, affections, desires, and judgments."[8] They are, in every respect, "far" from God, as a previous pericope put it.

The cognitive and perceptive dimensions of unbelievers are the focus of 4:17–19. Their mind-set is futile and their understanding is in darkness. They are alienated from God ("excluded from the life of God"); their ignorance and hardheartedness are labeled as the cause of such alienation. The two participles, "having been darkened" and "having been excluded" (4:18) are both in the dative, indicating the sphere in which these unbelievers operate. Both are also perfect participles, pointing to past actions with ongoing results.[9] So this situation is not a temporary blindness but a lasting one, powerfully signaled in the first clause of 4:18 with the use of an emphatic

---

5. Heil, *Ephesians*, 189.

6. Thielman, *Ephesians*, 296. In 4:17, "Gentiles" essentially stands for "unbelievers."

7. Heil, *Ephesians*, 189–90.

8. Fowl, *Ephesians*, 148.

9. These perfect participles are masculine (as also is the perfect participle in 4:19, ἀπηλγηκότες, *apēlgēkotes*, "having become callous"), while the subject, "Gentiles" (τὰ ἔθνη, *ta ethnē*) in 4:17 is neuter, perhaps signaling a "transition from a class to persons" (Hoehner, *Ephesians*, 585).

periphrastic expression—the passive perfect participle, ἐσκοτωμένοι (*eskotōmenoi*) + a supplemental participle, ὄντες (*ontes*): "having been darkened." "[T]he light of their understanding had gone out so that they were now in a state of being incapable of grasping the truth of God and his gospel."[10] Believers, on the other hand, have eyes that can see (1:18)!

"Having been excluded from the life of God" depicts these unbelievers as separated from the life that comes from God. In other words, they are effectively "dead" (as 2:1, 5 had already asserted), and are "without God" (2:12). The reasons given for this alienation are "because of the ignorance that is in them" and "because of the hardness of their heart" (4:18). Such ignorance is a willful and rebellious refusal to know God, an internal cause ("in them") for their alienation.[11] "To know God means to be in a close personal relationship with him. Knowledge has to do with an obedient and grateful response of the whole person, not simply intellectual assent. Likewise, 'ignorance' . . . describes someone's total stance, and this includes emotions, will, and action, not just one's mental response."[12]

While 4:1 also began with "therefore . . . walk" here in 4:17 it is essentially "therefore . . . *don't* walk."[13] The sequence of events in 4:17–18 may be considered as being written in reverse. Reordering the series, the progression looks like this:

hardness of heart (4:18d) →
Ignorance (4:18c) →
exclusion from the life of God (4:18c) →
darkness in understanding (4:18a) →
futility of mind (4:17d)

The hardness of heart renders them ignorant; ignorance keeps them excluded from God ("from the life of God"); exclusion from God prevents them from understanding; and lack of understanding makes their cognitive endeavors futile.[14] "[B]ecause it lacks the right relationship to God, Gentile thinking suffers from a fatal flaw. It has lost its grasp on reality and fallen prey to folly."[15] Moral apathy results—callousness, insensitivity to moral issues, incapacity for shame, a sort of "conscience-lessness" (4:19). The

10. O'Brien, *Ephesians*, 321. Life and light are also linked in Ps 36:9; John 1:4; 8:12. Darkness in Ephesians is frequently used of unbelievers and connected with demonic beings: 2:3, 11–12; 5:8, 11; 6:12. Perhaps the *passive* perfect participles in 4:18, "having been darkened" and "having been excluded," indicate some demonic influence?

11. Hoehner, *Ephesians*, 587.

12. O'Brien, *Ephesians*, 321.

13. "Walking" sections (and verses) occur in 2:1–10 (2:2, 10); 4:1–6 (4:1); 4:17–24 (4:17); 5:1–2 (5:2); 5:3–14 (5:8); and 5:15–17 (5:15).

14. "Futility" (ματαιότης, *mataiotēs*) is also found in Rom 1:21. Interestingly, μάταιος (*mataios*) can mean "idols," when used in the plural (Acts 14:15). "Mind" indicates knowing, understanding, and judging—almost equivalent to "mind-set." Thus unbelievers are unable to grasp cognitively the revelation of God.

15. Lincoln, *Ephesians*, 277.

ultimate result is the unbeliever's lifestyle ("walk," 4:17), given over to all manner of uncontrolled licentious behavior (4:19). There are echoes here of the condemnation of unbelievers in Rom 1:21–23. In that passage the issue was the culprits' refusal to recognize natural revelation in creation. Here, however, it is their hardheartedness that is at the top of this downward spiral into immorality. In Romans it was God who "gave them over" (Rom 1:24, 26, 28); here, they "have given *themselves* over" (Eph 4:19), further underscoring their own culpability.[16] The two prepositional phrases in 4:18—"because of the ignorance that is in them" and "because of the hardness of their heart"—clearly denote the responsibility of the subjects and their willfulness in this matter.

As a result, every kind of sexual "impurity" with greed is manifested (4:19).[17] And as in Rom 1 (see 1:24, where also "impurity" is used), Eph 4:19 also likely focuses on immoral activities. But how does "greed" fit in? Though it could be read as a third vice, after licentiousness and impurity, the prepositional structure "with greed" indicates that "the indecent conduct already described was practised *with a continual lust for more*. The pagan way of life was characterized by an insatiable desire to participate in more and more forms of immorality."[18] According to Hoehner, "greed," πλεονεξία (*pleonexia*), is derived from πλέον and ἔχω (*pleon* and *echō*)—literally: "I want more!" This is covetousness stemming from a total consumption with self and its immediate satisfactions.[19]

8.2 Ephesians 4:20–24

> **THEOLOGICAL FOCUS OF PERICOPE 8.2**
>
> 8.2 Believers learning Christ—being taught that they have put off the old person and put on the new—are now being divinely renewed into the likeness of God (4:20–24).

TRANSLATION 8.2

4:20 *But you did not learn Christ this way,*

4:21 *if indeed you heard Him and were taught in Him, just as truth is in Jesus,*

---

16. Fowl, *Ephesians*, 147–48.

17. "Licentiousness," ἀσέλγεια (*aselgeia*; 4:19), in Hellenistic Jewish texts often refers to sexual deviance (Wis 14:26; Josephus, *Antiquities* 8.318; 15.98; 16.185; 20.112). Elsewhere in Paul, the word is used in the context of sexual immorality (Rom 13:13; 2 Cor 12:21; Gal 5:19); also see 1 Pet 4:3. "Impurity," ἀκαθαρσία (*akatharsia*), also appears to have sexual connotations, as in Rom 1:24; 2 Cor 2:21; Gal 5:19; Col 3:5; 1 Thess 4:7; *T. Jud.* 14.5.

18. O'Brien, *Ephesians*, 323. Best notes that all of these pejorative descriptions of the pagan world in 4:17–19 are "governed more by theology than by observation." Surely there were commendable practices in the ancient world of that time. Paul himself had much to say about the system of Roman justice (Rom 13:1–7); it stood him in good stead often: Acts 16:35–39; 18:12–17; 21:31–37; 22:22–29; 25:8–12) (*Ephesians*, 425).

19. *Ephesians*, 591–92. "Greed" and "greedy person" also show up again in the context of immorality in 5:3, 5.

4:22 *that you have put off the old person—in accordance with your former lifestyle— who is being corrupted in accordance with deceitful lusts,*

4:23 *and are being renewed in the spirit of your mind,*

4:24 *and have put on the new person who is created in accordance with God['s likeness] in true righteousness and holiness.*

NOTES 8.2

8.2   *Believers learning Christ—being taught that they have put off the old person and put on the new—are now being divinely renewed into the likeness of God.*

Ephesians 4:20–21 is chiastic in structure[20]:

> **A**   Learned *Christ* (4:20)
> **B**   You heard *Him* (4:21a)
> **B'**   And were taught in *Him* (4:21b)
> **A'** Truth is in *Jesus* (4:21c)

Both "you" and "this way" are emphatic in 4:20: literally, "But you—not this way did you learn Christ." With that, a stark contrast is created between the walk of unbelievers (4:17–19) and the walk expected of believers (4:20–24).

There is an oddity of syntax here, in 4:20–21, that has not been documented elsewhere in period Greek literature: the verbs of learning and hearing here are not followed by the *content* of that learning and hearing—pieces of information or data about Christ. Instead, what they have learned and heard is a *person*—Jesus Christ himself, the object of their education and audition. Believers, Paul assumes, "learn Christ" and have "heard Him" (also see Luke 10:16). But how would this next generation of believers in Ephesus (and subsequent ones down to our day all over the world), have "learned" and "heard" Christ?

This might well have been the result of the evangelistic preaching *of* Christ (Acts 5:42; 1 Cor 1:23; 15:12; 2 Cor 1:19; 4:5; 11:4; Phil 1:15): Christ is preached and thus Christ is learned—"you were taught in Him," i.e., "we preached Christ and you learned and heard Christ," Paul might be saying here in Eph 4:21.[21] Thus there is clearly an implication that Christ is learned and heard when the gospel is preached. But there seems to be more: Jesus Christ is learned and heard as lives are being transformed into his likeness. "Truth is in Jesus" (4:21) refers to the truth of Christian life in its entirety—its faith and its practice—as embodied in Jesus Christ, the standard of truth, the image *par excellence* to which believers are to be conformed (Rom 8:29). This is the truth they have "learned" and "heard," which, of course, includes salvific truth, but goes beyond to indicate sanctification truth. This truth—of how to live in Christ,

---

20. From Heil, *Ephesians*, 191.

21. See O'Brien, *Ephesians*, 324. Perhaps this learning and hearing is also equivalent to "knowing" Christ: John 17:3; 1 Cor 2:2; Phil 3:8, 10; 1 John 2:3, 13, 14; 5:20; etc.

conformed to Christlikeness—was what they had been "taught in Him" (Eph 4:21).[22] Truth taught "in Him" also demarcates the sphere of learning and hearing: it is possible to learn and hear Christ and to be taught this truth in Jesus only if one has a relationship with him. This active and ongoing sense of learning and hearing in the Christian's life, makes sense in contrast with the active and ongoing life of unbelievers—completely disconnected from God and his truth: minds futile, understanding darkened, ignorant, hardhearted, callous (4:17–19). Unlike them, believers "learned Christ," and "heard Christ," and are "taught in Christ," for "the truth is in Jesus." These truths in Jesus that are learned, heard, and taught in him, deal with the living of the totality of Christian life, after the fashion of the perfect Man, Jesus Christ.

Not surprisingly, 4:21 is the only place in this letter where Christ is referred to simply as "Jesus"; perhaps it emphasizes "the foundation of Christian teaching, particularly its ethics, in the teaching and conduct of Jesus during his earthly ministry." After all, the historical *Jesus* is the embodiment of truth, the exemplary human.[23] He is the model for all humanity, the gold standard/image into which children of God are being transformed. This is the goal of preaching: to align the people of God to the theological demand of every pericope of Scripture, for each pericope depicts a facet of the image of Christ, the perfect Man. The composite of all these facets portrays the canonical image of Christ, to which believers are being conformed (Rom 8:29).[24] That is what it means to learn and hear Christ, to be taught in him the truth that is in Jesus (Eph 4:20–21). This is a lifelong process and is how "Christ may dwell in your hearts" (3:17)—an increasing experiential knowledge of Christ and his love (3:18–19) and a progressive conformation to Christlikeness.[25]

What believers were "taught in Him" is first spelled out broadly with three infinitives that form the thrust of 4:22–24: "to put off" (aorist middle, 4:22); "to be renewed" (present passive, 4:23[26]); and "to put on" (aorist middle, 4:24). All relate to "you were taught" (4:21) and provide the content of that teaching.[27] It is advisable to see all three infinitives not as imperatives, but as indicatives: "you have put off," "you are being renewed," and "you have put on." This best suits the context, with 4:25–32 then providing eleven specific imperatives in light of the preceding three general indicatives (see below). Also note the "therefore" (διό, *dio*) in 4:25; the other times it appears, a point is made based upon prior content of teaching, not upon a prior exhortation or imperative (2:11; 3:14; 4:8; 5:14). Paul's pattern in this letter has consistently been

---

22. "Truth" in this pericope occurs in Eph 4:21, 24, 25.

23. Thielman, *Ephesians*, 302.

24. For this notion of conforming to the "image" (εἰκών, *eikōn*) of Christ, see Rom 8:29, and for a full discussion of such a *christiconic* hermeneutic, see Kuruvilla, *Privilege the Text!* 238–68.

25. Also see Gal 2:20; Phil 1:21; 4:13; Col 3:3.

26. It could be a present *middle,* but the absence of an accusative object following the verb makes it more likely to be a passive (Hoehner, *Ephesians*, 607)

27. Later, in 4:25–32, and in the remainder of the Ephesian letter, Paul spells out the practical consequences of living according to how believers learned and heard Christ and according to what they were taught in him.

indicatives followed by imperatives (4:1–6; 5:1–6; 6:10–20); thus 4:22–32 is following that same sequence. It is also unlikely that believers are currently, in the present, being "corrupted in accordance with deceitful lusts" (4:22): that is a trait of unbelievers (4:17–19). Besides, as far as believers are concerned, the old is gone: Rom 6:2, 4, 6; 2 Cor 5:17; Gal 3:27.[28] Thus the old person—the person in the realm of sin and in the flesh—has been put off; the new person—the person in Christ—has been put on. There is therefore no need for imperatives here, to urge believers to undertake what has already been accomplished by Christ's redemptive work and applied to them by the Holy Spirit at the point of their conversion.[29]

The "old"/"new" persons are "individuals who are identified with these orders of existence," the entirety of the person in those states of life or spheres of subsistence.[30] The contrasts are vivid: the old person "is being corrupted in accordance with deceitful lusts" (Eph 4:22)[31]; the new person "is created in accordance with God['s likeness] in true righteousness and holiness" (4:24).[32] The "old" person descends into deterioration and decay; the "new" person ascends in piety and purity. The parallels make the contrasts vivid:

	Ephesians 4:22	Ephesians 4:24
Infinitive	ἀποθέσθαι (apothesthai) "you have put off"	ἐνδύσασθαι (endusasthai) "you have put on"
Person	τὸν παλαιὸν ἄνθρωπον (ton palaion anthrōpon) "the old person"	τὸν καινὸν ἄνθρωπον (ton kainon anthrōpon) "the new person"
Participle	φθειρόμενον (phtheiromenon) "being corrupted"	κτισθέντα (ktisthenta) "is created"
kata	κατὰ (kata) "in accordance with"	κατὰ (kata) "in accordance with"
Genitive Clause	ἐπιθυμίας τῆς ἀπάτης (epithymias tēs apatēs) "deceitful lusts"	ὁσιότητι τῆς ἀληθείας (hosiotēti tēs alētheias) "true … holiness"

---

28. Ibid., 601–2.

29. While the "old person" is gone, the ethical entity, the flesh, still remains with believers until the day of glory—sinful and incorrigible. However, the Christian now also has the indwelling Holy Spirit who enables one to gain victory over the flesh.

30. O'Brien, *Ephesians*, 328.

31. "Deceit," ἀπάτη (apatē), that characterizes the lusts of the old person, can also be used with sexual overtones (4 Macc 18:8; Jdt 9:3; 16:8); that would link Eph 4:22 with 4:19.

32. No doubt there is a connection here with 2:10: believers were "*created* in Christ Jesus for good works."

Between the aorist middle infinitives for "put off" and "put on" (4:22, 24) is a present passive infinitive, "being renewed" in 4:23. "The present tense suggests that the renewal of the mind is a repeated process throughout the believer's life, which is in contrast to the inceptive act involved in putting off the old person (v. 22) and putting on the new person (v. 24)," as indicated by their aorist forms.[33] Moreover, it is in the passive, suggesting God's work in the ongoing renewal of his people (2 Cor 4:16; Titus 3:5).[34] The sphere of this renewal is "in the spirit of your mind"; this is the only place in Ephesians where "spirit" refers to the human spirit.[35] This too is a genitive—"spirit *of your mind*"—and likely another example of this letter's proclivity to accumulate synonyms. Thus, "spirit of your mind" points to the sphere of renewal as being the believer's innermost being, the immaterial part, the "inner person" (3:16). Nonetheless, with the outcome being "true righteousness and holiness," there is no doubt that an outward expression of this inner renewal is also expected.

> The contrast with the preceding section of the paragraph (vv. 17–19) could hardly be sharper. There, the desperate condition of Gentiles outside of Christ is depicted in terms of their being darkened in their understanding so that they are blind to the truth, and their alienation from God is the result of the ignorance within them. In consequence, they abandon themselves to all kinds of degrading activities. Here, the ongoing transformation of the mind leads to just [i.e., righteous] and holy living which reflects the character of God himself (cf. Rom 12:2).[36]

The outward expression of this inward renewal is already taking place for the "new person" has been "put on." This "new person" has been "created in accordance with God['s likeness] in true righteousness and holiness"—this is what Christians are to look like.[37] In other words, believers are given new life in Christ to live commensurate with the attributes of the Creator, who is "righteous" and "holy" (Deut 32:4; Neh 9:33; Pss 95:13; 119:75; 145:17; *Pss. Sol.* 10.5; Luke 1:75; Rev 16:5; 19:2). This is to say that "God is not only the author of this mighty work; he is also the pattern or model of the new creation. . . . Within the christological and eschatological dimensions of Paul's gospel the vices are regarded as the outworking of the 'old person,' while the virtues or graces are produced in the 'new person,' and these reflect the character of Christ."[38] And that is perfectly consonant with the fact that it is to the "image" (εἰκών, *eikōn*) of

33. Hoehner, *Ephesians*, 607.

34. On the other hand, the middle voices of the infinitives in 4:22 and 4:24 indicate the subject receiving the benefit of *his/her own* actions—i.e., the doffing and the donning of the old and new person, respectively.

35. Elsewhere, "spirit" is always the Holy Spirit: Eph 1:17; 3:16; 4:2; 5:18; 6:18.

36. O'Brien, *Ephesians*, 331.

37. Literally, "in accordance with God," but best understood as "in accordance with God['s likeness]," as in Col 3:10. "True righteousness and holiness" (Eph 4:24) is a stark contrast to the "deceitful lusts" of unbelievers (4:22). The "new person" in 2:15 had a corporate connotation—the entirety of (believing) humanity, united in Christ. Here, however, in keeping with a more individualistic context (see 4:7, 11, 12–16, 25, 28, 32), the "new person" is the new creation that each believer becomes in Christ (see 2 Cor 5:17; Gal 5:16).

38. Ibid., 332, 336.

Christ, the paradigm and ultimate standard, that believers are to be conformed: Rom 8:29; 1 Cor 15:49; 2 Cor 3:18; Eph 3:19; 4:13–16; Col 1:28. Having put on the new person, their model for life is the righteousness and holiness of God in Christ.

In sum, believers were taught (Eph 4:21) that they had put off the old person (4:22) and put on the new person (4:24) at their conversion, which began the ongoing process of divinely wrought renewal into the likeness of God (4:23)—to be specific, into the image of Christ. This is what it means to "learn Christ." The practical consequences of this "learning" (or "receiving," see Col 2:6) Christ, at least the consequences that Paul is interested in spelling out, are found in the remainder of this letter.

8.3 *Ephesians 4:25–32*

THEOLOGICAL FOCUS OF PERICOPE 8.3

8.3   The likeness of God is manifested by believers as they maintain unity and build up one another, eschewing anger, sharing resources, speaking grace, controlling tempers, and forgiving divinely (4:25–32).

TRANSLATION 8.3

4:25 *Therefore, putting off falsehood, speak truth each with his neighbor, for we are members of one another.*

4:26 *Be angry and do not sin; do not let the sun go down on your wrath,*

4:27 *nor give the devil an opportunity.*

4:28 *He who steals must no longer steal, but rather he must labor, working with his own hands what is good, so that he may have [something] to share with the one having need.*

4:29 *Let no unwholesome word come out from your mouth, but only what is good for building up of the one in need, so that it may give grace to those who hear.*

4:30 *And do not grieve the Holy Spirit of God, by whom you were sealed for the day of redemption.*

4:31 *Let all bitterness and wrath and rage and clamor and slander be put away from you, with all malice.*

4:32 *But be kind to one another, compassionate, forgiving each other, just as God in Christ also has forgiven you.*

NOTES 8.3

8.3   *The likeness of God is manifested by believers as they maintain unity and build up one another, eschewing anger, sharing resources, speaking grace, controlling tempers, and forgiving divinely.*

Notice that 4:25 begins with "therefore"—i.e., *because* believers "are being renewed . . . according to God['s likeness]." In other words, the practicalities of what this ongoing renewal of life is all about (4:23), and what "a new person who is created in accordance with God['s likeness] in true righteousness and holiness" looks like (4:25), takes up the rest of the pericope. And at the commencement of the next pericope, this idea of conformity to divine likeness is returned to, launching another series of what this new person's life resembles: "Therefore be imitators of God" (5:1).

There are five exhortations in this section, 4:25–32 (4:25, 26–27, 28, 29, 30–32), each with a negative and a positive command, and a motivation for the latter. They deal with lying, anger, theft, unwholesome speech, and other impure kinds of utterances, respectively. After the exalted concepts of "learning" and "hearing" Christ, being "taught in Him," and being renewed in the likeness of God, now Paul lands back on the earth, to address more mundane matters of daily Christian life. All of these facets of behavior concern the maintenance of "the unity of the Spirit in the bond of peace" (Eph 4:3). Ultimately, of course, all of this is part of God's grand and glorious plan to consummate all things in Christ.

Negative behaviors are to be "put off" (4:25)—a recurrence of the verb from 4:22. Indeed, this repetition of the verb in the same tense and voice points to an important truth: conduct is integrally linked with condition. If one has "put off" a condition, then one must "put off" conduct that stems from that doffed condition. And, the contrary: if one has "put on" a condition, then one must "put on" conduct that befits that donned condition: the "new person" is to demonstrate a lifestyle that is "in accordance with God['s likeness] in true righteousness and holiness" (4:24).

"Falsehood" in 4:25 alludes to the "deceitful lusts" in 4:22; "truth" (4:25) also showed up earlier in 4:24 (and 4:15). As well, the language of the unified body (4:12, 16) recurs in 4:25: "for we are members of one another." The OT quote in Eph 4:25 is from Zech 8:16. In the context of Zech 8, 8:16 follows upon a series of promises regarding the future of Jerusalem in the millennial kingdom (8:1–15), particularly the one about God pledging to dwell with his people there (8:3). After a sequence of utterances that describe what *God* will do, the prophet moves to what "*you* should do" (8:16), beginning with speaking truth to one another (or "neighbor," in the LXX) within the community of God's people. So, borrowing Zech 8:16, Paul, here in Eph 4:25, declares that within the communal and harmonious relationship of the body (1:23; 2:16; 4:7–16), there can be no place for anything but the truth.

Anger, too, is a serious and substantial hurdle to harmony in community (4:26–27). The exhortation "be angry and do not sin" provides the only quote of Ps 4 in the NT (Ps 4:4). That OT text describes the psalmist's anger against those who have unjustly accused him; he now exhorts others to relinquish such anger. This is not a command that requires one to "be angry," rather it has the sense of "when you are angry"—when such anger is justifiable—do not let it lead you into sin. So Eph 4:26 may be dealing with "righteous" anger, whereas 4:31 likely points to unrighteous anger (see below): "If ours [i.e., our anger] is not free from injured pride, malice, or a spirit of revenge, it has degenerated into sin" (Jas 1:19–20).[39] And to talk about anger fermenting

---

39. Ibid., 340. And Eph 4:26 "does not mean that a person may be legitimately angry until sunset; were this taken literally it would mean that those who lived in the Arctic or Antarctic would at certain

into sinful "wrath," Paul uses the noun, παροργισμός (*parorgismos*) in Eph 4:26—anger of a violent kind. There is no explicit unity-of-community motif in the exhortation of 4:26–27, though giving the devil a toehold with such paroxysms of anger is certainly not conducive to communality and harmony befitting the body of Christ united by the Spirit.

The next two exhortations are recorded without an initial conjunction (4:28, 29). Each one is in the singular, unlike the plural verbs that precede (4:27) and follow it (4:30). Both stealing and unwholesome speech are clearly detrimental to unity and the building up of the body. The prohibition of the cardinal sin of theft was enshrined in the Decalogue and elsewhere in both the OT and the NT (Exod 20:15; 22:1; Deut 5:19; Lev 19:11; Jer 7:9; Hos 4:2; Rom 2:21; 1 Cor 6:10; 1 Pet 4:15). Instead, labor and work was valued (Exod 20:9; Prov 6:6; 28:19; 1 Thess 4:11–12; 2 Thess 3:6–12). "Thieves fail to play their part in the life of the community, not because they steal from fellow members, but because they make no financial contribution to it; the new conduct demanded of them would positively benefit the community."[40] Paul is therefore exhorting believers in Eph 4:28 to do "good" and to give, rather than cheat others to get. In 2:10, God was said to have prepared ἔργοι ἀγαθοι (*ergoi agathoi,* "good works") for his people to do; here, in 4:28, they are to "do" (ἐργάζομαι, *ergazomai*) what is "good" (ἀγαθός, *agathos*).[41] The connections are obvious: what God has prepared for believers to do (2:10) must be done by believers (4:28).

In 4:29, once again the issue of speech is addressed: 4:25, and possibly 4:26–27, dealt with communication as well. There seems to be a parallel between all these speech-related exhortations (4:25–27 and 4:29–30) in this pericope: both have a corporate metaphor ("members," 4:25; "building," 4:29), and both have a motive related to a supernatural being ("devil," 4:27; "Holy Spirit of God," 4:30).[42] But while the earlier antithesis was "falsehood" vs. "truth" (4:25), here in 4:29 it is "unwholesome" vs. "good." In other words, falsity is not in question here; it is the wisdom in choice of words that is being appealed for, with the stress on edification ("building up") by the giving of grace through speech. Hence, we have the explicit picture of speakers guarding the words that exit their mouths (4:29). Appropriately enough, the giving of grace now becomes the responsibility of those who have received grace from God (1:6; 2:5, 6). Or to put it another way, to give grace (in speech) is to exhibit "God['s likeness]," the one who first gave grace. This exhortation is emphatic, beginning literally with

---

times of the year have no temporal limitation on their anger" (Best, *Ephesians,* 450). Here, Paul appears to be employing a common proverb. Plutarch exhorted: "We should next pattern ourselves after the Pythagoreans who, though related not at all by birth, yet sharing a common discipline, if ever they were led by anger [ὀργή, *orgē*] into recrimination, never let the sun go down before they joined right hands, embraced each other, and were reconciled" (*On Brotherly Love* 17 [*Moralia* 488C]). The cognate verb of ὀργή is used in Eph 4:26: ὀργίζεσθε (*orgizesthe,* "be angry"); there is also παροργισμός (*parorgismos,* "wrath") in the same verse.

40. Best, *Ephesians,* 453.

41. See Acts 20:35; Gal 6:10; 1 Tim 5:8; Titus 3:14; 1 John 3:17; *Didache* 4.6.

42. The Holy Spirit is associated with speech elsewhere in Ephesians, too: 5:18–20 and perhaps 6:17.

"every [from πᾶς, *pas*] unwholesome word."[43] "Unwholesome" translates σαπρός (*sapros*), that can mean rotting, decayed, and harmful: it clearly is antithetical to "building up" (i.e., edification). Destruction is the result of "unwholesome" words; construction is the result of gracious words that are "good for building up one in need."[44] The community focus is obvious.

The seriousness of this exhortation is underscored with a coordinating conjunction, "and" in 4:30, that links 4:29 to 4:30. That 4:29 warns about not grieving the "Holy Spirit of God" provides a powerful incentive for producing only "good" words of "grace" that "build up." "The Spirit, who is the divine agent of reconciliation and unity in the body (2:18, 22; 4:3–4), is especially grieved when unwholesome speech is uttered by members against one another."[45] Disunity distresses the Holy Spirit of God.

The allusion in Eph 4:30 is to Isa 63:10 that deals with the rebellious nature of the Israelites of the exodus generation, the ones who had been redeemed by Yahweh, their Savior, and made his people (Isa 63:8). To them God guaranteed his presence and showed his love (63:9). Yet they rebelled and "offended His Holy Spirit" (63:10). The story is the same in Ephesians. The community of God's people—redeemed by the blood of Christ (Eph 1:7), saved by grace through faith (2:8), and indwelt by divine presence and fullness/glory (1:23; 2:21–22)—would, like the ancients, be rebelling against God and grieving his Holy Spirit, were they to be dealing in unwholesome words that only tear down and destroy what was divinely intended to be built up. And how greater would that grievance be, since God's grand plan of consummation of all things in Christ involved this very body of believers, united by that same Holy Spirit (2:22; 4:3–4), and by him "sealed for the day of redemption" (4:30; also 1:13–14).[46] So this is a strong warning in 4:30: "it refers not to a direct attack on the Spirit but to believers engaging in sinful activities mentioned in the previous verses (especially harmful speech) which destroy relationships within the body and so mar the Spirit's work in building Christ's people. . . . Anything incompatible with the unity or purity of the church is inconsistent with the Spirit's own nature and therefore grieves him."[47] Of course, the "grieving" of the Spirit does not mean ultimate frustration or thwarting of divine purpose. Nonetheless, it is a serious matter to distress the divine presence in believers.

> Thus it appears that a primary purpose of the Spirit's work in the Ephesian church is building up the body into that which God intends. In the context of 4:25–5:2, then, grieving the Spirit refers to the practices of falsehood, theft, corrosive speech, and anything else that frustrates the Sprit's work of building up the Ephesians into one body (4:4), the work of strengthening them so that Christ

43. See also how 4:31 begins: "all [also from πᾶς] bitterness and wrath and anger and clamor and slander."

44. "Building" was already encountered in 2:20–22; 4:12, 16.

45. O'Brien, *Ephesians*, 345. "Resisting" and "quenching" the Spirit are found in Acts 7:51 and 1 Thess 5:19, respectively.

46. The "day of redemption" is the fulfillment of salvation, equivalent to the "day of the Lord/Christ," likely more than a twenty-four-hour day (1 Cor 1:8; 5:5; 2 Cor 1:14; Phil 1:16, 10; 2:16; Thess 5:2; 2 Thess 2:2): it indicates the time of the consummation of all things in Christ (Eph 1:10, 14; 5:5, 27).

47. Ibid., 348.

may dwell in their hearts through faith as they are rooted and grounded in love (3:17), "until we all come to the unity of the faith and knowledge of the Son of God" (4:13).[48]

Indeed, those sealed by the Spirit (4:30) are those with the imprint of divine character upon them. This is therefore a mandate to live lives worthy of that God and his sealing, especially, in this context, by eschewing activities that militate against the Spirit-driven unity of the body.

As noted earlier, the return to the topic of anger in 4:31–32 may distinguish this as being an unrighteous sort of anger; after all, anger, per se, is not prohibited in 4:26–27, only its sinful expression. All of the varieties of speech in 4:31—bitterness, wrath, rage, clamor, slander, and malice—are manifestations of an angry demeanor and a hot temper; they are all vices potentially destructive to a community life of unity. The vice list appears to be a crescendo, from inner attitudes to outward explosions, with the word "all," at the beginning and at the end of 4:31, qualifying every item in the catalog. "Paul's list, then, is an elaborate way of describing angry verbiage, not a taxonomy of anger or an outline of its psychological development."[49]

In contrast are the virtues of 4:32, promoting a united community. The list outlines the manifestations of a godly character—the lifestyle of the "new person" exhibiting God's likeness (4:24). But here attitudes and thoughts are in focus, as opposed to words (4:25, 29) and deeds (4:26–29). God is himself "kind" (Pss 24:8; 33:9; 68:17; 85:5; 99:5; 106:1; 108:21; 118:68; 136:1; 145:9; Luke 6:35; Rom 2:4; 1 Pet 2:3), "compassionate" (using the cognate verb: Matt 9:36; 14:14; 18:27; Luke 1:78; 7:13; 10:33; 15:20), "engracing/forgiving" (Rom 8:32; 1 Cor 2:12; Col 2:13; and using a related verb: Luke 1:28; Eph 1:6[50])—describing tender-heartedness as opposed to the hard-heartedness of the ungodly (4:18). Thus "[t]he basis of Christian action lies in what God has done for Christians."[51] Indeed, one might go further: the ground of all Christian behavior is the character of God himself, as 4:24 makes abundantly clear!

SERMON FOCUS AND OUTLINES

THEOLOGICAL FOCUS OF PERICOPE 8

8   Believers, no longer living licentiously, are being divinely renewed into the likeness of God that is manifest as they maintain unity and engage in activities that build up one another (4:17–32).

---

48. Fowl, *Ephesians*, 158.

49. Thielman, *Ephesians*, 319.

50. Elsewhere in Ephesians, the verb χαρίζομαι (*charizomai*) is employed for the concept of God giving grace: 1:2, 6, 7; 2:5, 7, 8; 3:2, 7, 8; 4:7; 6:24. Commonly used to denote "forgiving" (Luke 7:42; 2 Cor 2:7, 10; 12:13; Col 2:13; 3:13), the verb is related to χάρις (*charis*, "grace")—the "gracious bestowal of something unmerited," and the antithesis of bitterness, wrath, rage, clamor, slander, and malice (Hoehner, *Ephesians*, 639). Here the participial form functions as one of manner, denoting *how* believers are to kind and compassionate—i.e., by being forgiving.

51. Best, *Ephesians*, 464.

The explicit focus on the unity of the believing community shifts, in this pericope, to recommend lifestyles implicitly conducive to that unity. A contrast is made between unbelievers and believers, the old person and the new person. The latter in each pair is undergoing an operation of renewal into the likeness of God, i.e., the image of Christ.

We are thus given a list of items that are inveighed against: licentious living, falsehood, anger leading to sin, theft, unwholesome speech—bitterness, wrath, rage, clamor, slander, malice. Instead, believers are to be kind, compassionate, and graciously forgiving—the imitation of God in Christ. Lists are rather hard to preach. It is best not to decimate them into individual items and deliver sermonettes on each. An attempt must be made to integrate the contents into a whole, so that a single thrust may be isolated and efficiently preached. Here the renewal into divine likeness—i.e., that of God the Son, conformation into his likeness and its consequence—is key. The new person no longer lives licentiously, but in words, deeds, and thoughts (the emphases in this pericope) engages in activities that, reflecting Christ, maintain unity and build up the body.

Possible Preaching Outlines for Pericope 8

I. PAST: The Lifestyle of Unbelievers
      Licentious living rooted in hardheartedness (4:17–19)
      Move-to-relevance: The possibility of believers regressing into such a degenerate lifestyle[52]
II. PRESENT: The New Status of Believers
      Learning, hearing, being taught in Christ (4:20–21)
      Jesus Christ, the embodiment of truth, the exemplary Man (4:21)
      The ongoing renewal of believers into the likeness of God (4:22–24)
      Move-to-relevance: Relationship mandates responsibility
III. FUTURE: The Lifestyle of Believers
      Evil words to be eschewed (4:25–27, 29, 31–32)
      Evil deeds to be abandoned (4:28)
      Evil thoughts to be rejected (4:31–32)
      The grieving of the Spirit by evil words, deeds, and thoughts (4:30)
IV. *Delight the Spirit!*[53]
      Specifics on engaging in divinely modeled words, deeds, and thoughts[54]

Focusing on the protagonists—Christ, leaders, and the saints—yields another outline:

I. Right Words
      The wrong model (4:25a, 26, 29a, 31a) vs. the right model (4:25b, 26–27, 29b)
      Move-to-relevance: how wrong words inhibit unity
II. Right Deeds
      The wrong model (4:19b, 27a) vs. the right model (4:27b)
      Move-to-relevance: how wrong deeds inhibit unity
III. Right Thoughts
      The wrong model (4:17–18, 31b) vs. the right model (4:32)
      Move-to-relevance: how wrong thoughts inhibit unity

---

52. Not to imply loss of salvation, of course. But the very fact that Paul is exhorting them against such a lifestyle implies that it is possible even for believers to fall back into such deplorable conditions.

53. This is a take on "Do not grieve the Holy Spirit."

54. In the application one might perhaps focus on a single item in the list, depending on where the congregation is in its spiritual walk: doing good, speaking edifyingly, being gracious.

IV.   *Delight the Spirit!*[55]

        The wrong result (4:30) vs. the right result

        Specifics on engaging in divinely modeled words, deeds, and thoughts

V.   The Power for Right Living

        The wrong model (4:17, 22) vs. the right model (4:23–24): divine likeness

---

55. There is no compulsion to make the application move the last one of the sermon. It probably fits best as the last move, but there are other creative options.

PERICOPE 9

Living Wisely, Pleasing God

Ephesians 5:1–20

[Pleasing God vs. Angering God]

REVIEW, SUMMARY, PREVIEW

Review of Pericope 8: In Eph 4:17–32, Paul exhorts a lifestyle that is conducive to unity in the body. Believers are reminded that they have put off the "old person" and put on the "new person," and that they are now being renewed continually into the image of God in Christ. This ongoing transformation is to be expressed by appropriate words, deeds, and thoughts that manifest the divine life.

Summary of Pericope 9: This pericope (Eph 5:1–20) continues the contrast between the lifestyle of the believer and that of the unbeliever. The former, imitating God and the selfless love of Christ, walks wisely and by the Spirit, and, as a result invites divine pleasure. The believer in light also exposes the deeds of darkness—convicting (and converting) unbelievers—and, comprehending the will of God, worships him with a heart of gratitude.

Preview of Pericope 10: The next pericope, Eph 5:21–33, continues the broader theme of the filling by the Spirit of the divine fullness of God in Christ. This particular pericope considers the responsibilities of husbands (to love) and wives (to submit), constantly referring back to the divine model—the relationship of Christ and his bride, the church.

9. *Ephesians 5:1–20*

THEOLOGICAL FOCUS OF PERICOPE 9

9   The imitation of God and of Christ's selfless love, that invites the pleasure of God, entails the abandonment of sexual immorality—illicit "love" that incurs the wrath of God—and the adoption of a wise and worshipful lifestyle, filled by the Spirit with the divine fullness of God in Christ (5:1–20).

9.1   The imitation of God, and of Christ's selfless love, entails the abandonment of all kinds of sexual immorality, both in word and in deed—illicit "love" that incurs the wrath of God (5:1–6).

9.2   Believers, children of light and light themselves, walk accordingly, pleasing God, without participating in the works of darkness, thereby exposing such works and even being agents of transformation to those who engage in them (5:7–14).

9.3   The wise walk of believers, making the most of time in evil days and understanding God's will, involves being filled by the Spirit with the divine fullness of God in Christ, manifested in the worship of the church (5:15–20).

OVERVIEW

In the previous pericope, after reminding readers of the stark difference in lifestyles between unbelievers and believers, and the state of the latter as being renewed in the "new person who is created in accordance with God['s likeness]" (4:17–24), Paul went on to delineate a number of specific sins (4:24–32). He returns here, in the current pericope, to the same theme of *imitatio Dei* (5:1–2), before launching into the particulars of avoiding immorality (5:3–6), and walking as children of light (5:7–14) as those who are wise, filled by the Spirit (5:15–21).[1]

In 5:3, two of the three sins mentioned, impurity and greed, are borrowed from 4:19. These were not considered in any detail there in Pericope 8, so Paul addresses them now in this pericope, giving both behaviors connotations of sexual immorality (see below). Also, in this pericope, the antitheses of darkness-light (5:8–14), folly-wisdom (5:15–17), and wine-Spirit (5:18–20) resemble the antithesis of the old person-new person (4:22–24).

One might lay out Pericope 9 this way:

5:1–2	Motivation
5:3–7	Vices
5:8–17	Transition: vices to virtues
5:18–20	Virtues

Following the motivation that deals with the *love* of Christ, it is appropriate to discuss the vices of sexual immorality—what the world thinks "love" is all about. The proper operation of the virtues of Christian love is critical to the appropriate and optimal

---

1. Connections with previous pericopes are many: "walk" is utilized in 5:2, 8, 15 (earlier seen in 2:2, 10; 4:1, 17); "in love," used in 5:2, was also employed in 1:4; 3:17, 19: 4:1–2, 15, 16; "beloved," in 5:1, was seen before in 1:6; "inheritance," in 5:5, was also encountered in 1:14, 18; 3:6; divine "will," in 5:17, reminds the reader of 1:1, 9, 11; and "thanksgiving," mentioned in 5:4, 20, was first seen in 1:16.

functioning of the community: the morality of individuals and that of the corporate body are closely related.

Several items in this pericope are grouped in threes: three terms list the vices in 5:3 ("immorality," "impurity," and "greed"), three terms are employed for immoral speech in 5:4 ("filthiness," "silly talk," and "coarse jesting"), three terms in 5:5 describe those who engage in these activities ("immoral," "impure," and "covetous"), and three terms name the fruit of light in 5:9 ("goodness," "righteousness," and "truth"). There is also a triplet of antitheses (noted above), each with μή . . . ἀλλά . . . (mē . . . alla . . .; "not . . . but . . ."; 5:15, 17, 18); as well as a triplet of alpha-privative terms: : ἄσοφοι (asophoi, "unwise"; 5:15), ἄφρονες (aphrones, "foolish": 5:17), and ἀσωτία (asōtia, "unchastity"; 5:18).[2]

9.1 Ephesians 5:1–6

> **THEOLOGICAL FOCUS OF PERICOPE 9.1**
>
> 9.1   The imitation of God, and of Christ's selfless love, entails the abandonment of all kinds of sexual immorality, both in word and in deed—illicit "love" that incurs the wrath of God (5:1–6).

TRANSLATION 9.1

5:1   *Therefore be imitators of God, as beloved children,*

5:2   *and walk in love, just as Christ also loved us and gave Himself up for us, an offering and a sacrifice to God as a fragrant aroma.*

5:3   *But immorality and all impurity or greed must not even be named among you, as is proper among saints—*

5:4   *and [let there be no] filthiness, and foolish talk, or coarse jesting, which are not fitting, but rather thanksgiving.*

5:5   *For this you know for certain, that no immoral or impure or greedy person (who is an idolater) has an inheritance in the kingdom of Christ and of God.*

5:6   *Let no one deceive you with empty words, for because of these things the wrath of God comes upon the sons of disobedience.*

NOTES 9.1

9.1   *The imitation of God, and of Christ's selfless love, entails the abandonment of all kinds of sexual immorality, both in word and in deed—illicit "love" that incurs the wrath of God.*

The first two verses, 5:1–2, introduce this pericope, as also did 4:1 and 4:17 their respective pericopes; all three introductions have "therefore," and the verb "to walk"

---

2. Other triads in Ephesians include: 1:6, 12, 14; 1:18–19; 3:6; 4:2, 4, 5, 6, 13, 19, 32; 5:3, 4, 5, 9, 19; also note the three sections of the household code, 5:22–33; 6:1–4, 5–9.

(also see 5:7–8, below). In 4:1, believers were called to a walk worthy of their calling; in 4:17, they were to walk no longer as unbelievers. Here we are explicitly told what that walk entails: the walk "in love," the imitation of God and of Christ, who loved with a love beyond compare.[3] The love of Christ was exemplified in his atonement for sin—an "offering and sacrifice" (a hendiadys; also in Ps 40:6 LXX; Phil 4:18).[4] The two nouns are predicate accusatives, thus pointing to Christ giving himself up "[*as*] an offering and a sacrifice to God."[5] That this self-giving was pleasing to God is indicated in the description of the act as "a fragrant aroma"—often used of divine acceptance of sacrifice (Gen 8:21; Exod 29:18, 25, 41; Lev 1:9, 13, 17; 2:9, 12; 3:5; Num 15:3, 5; Ezek 6:13, 19; Phil 4:18 etc.).

This notion of divine imitation (Eph 5:1) had already been introduced in the previous pericope, with the "new person" being created in God's likeness in true righteousness and holiness (4:24). Believers "have been adopted into God's family . . . and are his beloved children [1:5]. . . . Since they have richly experienced that love, they should be imitators of him and reproduce the family likeness." Having Jesus Christ as both the ground and model of love (5:2), such self-sacrificial love is to be the mark of believers, the "beloved children" of God (5:1).[6]

After this grand model of love has been introduced, Paul turns to contrast the behavior of believers and unbelievers for the remainder of the pericope (5:3–20). He commences by pointing to the illegitimate and illicit love of the world as the point of difference, as well as the self-indulgence of unbelievers ("greed," 5:3) as opposed to the self-sacrifice of Christ and, hopefully, the selflessness of believers who imitate him (5:2). With "immorality"[7] heading the list, it appears that the rest of the vices are colored by this sense of sexual misconduct.[8] "Indeed, Paul already understands that sex is never really a separate category of activity. Then as now, sex was always tied up with issues such as purity, identity, power, and desire, which touch on most aspects of life. Thus misconduct in one's sexual practices reflects a wider and deeper level

---

3. Only here does one find the "imitation" of God; the related "following" of God was a major motif in the OT: Num 14:24; 32:11, 12; Josh 14:8, 9, 14; 1 Sam 12:14; etc. However, the "imitation" motif shows up often in Paul—the imitation of Paul himself, or of Paul as he imitates Christ: 1 Cor 4:16; 11:1; Phil 3:17; 4:9; 1 Thess 1:6; 2 Thess 3:7–9; besides here in Eph 5:1 (also see Gal 4:12; Eph 5:25–27). In fact, God's children have a mandate to "be perfect, as your heavenly Father is perfect" (Matt 5:48; also see Luke 6:36; John 17:11, 21; Col 3:13; 1 Pet 1:15). Also see 1 Thess 1:7; 2:14; Heb 6:12–15; 13:7, for exhortations to mimic the saints of God. Jesus, however, remains the ultimate model: Rom 15:1–5; Phil 2:5; 1 John 2:6; 3:16; 1 Pet 2:21; etc. That, of course, is not to deny that Jesus Christ is more than a model. But for the purposes of preaching, the focus is on his perfect humanity that humankind is called to conform to—the εἰκών (*eikōn*, "image") of Christ (Rom 8:29): hence *christiconic* interpretation. See Kuruvilla, *Privilege the Text!* 264–68.

4. Christ's "giving up" himself is noted in Eph 5:2 and 5:27.

5. Hoehner, *Ephesians*, 650.

6. O'Brien, *Ephesians*, 352, 355.

7. "Immorality," πορνεία (*porneia*), indicates any kind of illicit sexual activity: 1 Cor 6:18; 6:9; 5:9–11; Gal 5:19; Col 3:5; 1 Thess 4:13.

8. "Impurity," ἀκαθαρσία (*akatharsia*), can also indicate sexual impurity. See, for example, 2 Cor 12:21; Gal 5:19; 1 Thess 4:3, 7. "*All* impurity" encompasses every kind thereof.

of disorder."[9] Self-indulgence is commonly manifest in sexual sins that have roots in the desire to *satisfy* self rather than to sacrifice self. That, too, is a form of greed, of a most dangerous kind, the inner spring of many evil passions.[10] Perhaps that is why greed is set apart in 5:3 with a different conjunction: "immorality and all impurity *or* greed." Indeed, in 5:5, where the triad of vices in 5:3 is repeated, this time labeling those who commit them—"immoral or impure or greedy person"—this last kind of individual is explicitly called "an idolater." "[S]exual lust is an idolatrous obsession; it places self-gratification or another person at the centre of one's existence, and thus is the worship of the creature rather than the Creator (Rom 1:25)."[11] And no wonder: such attitudes and actions are entirely antithetical to God and to the imitation of God/Christ who loved with a perfect love. Therefore these vices are not even to be named among Christians (Eph 5:3)![12]

The ideas of 5:3 are taken up verbatim in 5:5, almost rendering 5:4 parenthetical as it deals with less serious sins. But in all likelihood, the kinds of speech indicated in 5:4 are also related to "immorality" that headed the vice list in 5:3. Heil observes a chiastic structure for 5:1–6 that supports the contention that both words and deeds of a sexual kind are hinted at here in 5:3–5[13]:

> **A** Imitators *of God,* as *beloved children* (5:1)
>   **B** *Immorality; impurity; greed* (5:3)
>   **C** *Shamefulness; foolish talk; sarcastic ridicule; but rather thanksgiving* (5:4)
>   **B'** *Immoral; impure; greedy person* (5:5)
> **A'** Wrath *of God* is coming upon the *sons of disobedience* (5:6)

In any case, the three kinds of speech in 5:4 are dependent on the verb in 5:3 ("not to be named"), making them part of the same list: thus, *immoral* utterances: "filthiness and foolish talk [the vulgar product of a dull mind?] or coarse jesting [the obscene product of a sharp mind?]."[14] "All three terms refer to a dirty mind expressing itself in vulgar conversation. This kind of language must be avoided as utterly inappropriate among those whom God has set apart as holy." So, abstaining from these kinds of immoral

9. Fowl, *Ephesians,* 165.

10. "Greed" in the context of immorality also showed up earlier in 4:19. It was mentioned in the commentary on that verse that "greed," πλεονεξία (*pleonexia*), is derived from πλέον and ἔχω (*pleon* and *echō*)—i.e., "I want more" (Hoehner, *Ephesians,* 591–92).

11. O'Brien, *Ephesians,* 363. Jewish literature has frequently linked immorality with idolatry: Wis 14:12; *T. Reub.* 4:6; *T. Jud.* 23:1; *T. Benj.* 10:10; also see Rev 2:20.

12. Clearly Paul is addressing only certain sins; one might conceive of others that could potentially disrupt community and unity, like pride and envy (perhaps these were implied in Eph 4:2); but they are not part of his thrust in this pericope.

13. Heil, *Ephesians,* 29–30. Similar and contrasting elements are italicized.

14. All three Greek words here are hapax legomena in the NT. The connecting conjunctions are as in 5:3: "filthiness *and* silly talk *or* coarse jesting." Perhaps this is because the last two items explicitly relate to speech (though some textual variants have "or" in both cases). However, "filthiness," αἰσχρότης (*aischrotēs*), can also be related to speech; the word is similar to αἰσχρολογία (*aischrologia,* "filthy words," Col 3:8). The word εὐτραπελία (*eutrapelia,* "coarse jesting") can have the positive connotation of wittiness; hence facetiousness and, in the current context, risqué wit.

speech, believers are to engage in thanksgiving, "the fundamental Christian response of gratitude, expressed by those who have experienced God's grace in Christ."[15] Unlike self-satisfying unbelievers, believers are conscious of the self-giving of God, his goodness and generosity in Christ, and so, rather than engage in obscenities and vulgarities, they express thanks to their Creator and Redeemer, the ultimate source of all their blessings. Perhaps this thanksgiving is specific for the subject under discussion: sex. In that case, it is a call for Christians to maintain a grateful attitude to God for what is a divine gift, unlike the pagan attitude towards sex—immorality, obscenity, vulgarity, and an engagement to satisfy the flesh and the self, often at the expense of others: self-satisfaction, not self-sacrifice, as recommended here and modeled by Christ. In sum, "each of these vices in one way or another reflects a level of disorder in one's desires and loves. Thanksgiving reorders a believer's loves so that they are focused on God. Further, cultivating the habit of thanksgiving also enables believers to love others in God properly."[16]

Because Paul is dealing with the character and lifestyle of unbelievers (as opposed to that of the "saints," 5:3), 5:5 is a reaffirmation that these unbelievers have no inheritance in the kingdom of Christ and God.[17] And believers are warned not to be deceived with "empty words" (5:6), i.e., those that rationalize the acceptance of those evil mores that were described in 5:3–5. "Arguments of this kind are 'empty' and devoid of the truth . . . because they do not reckon with God's holy judgment on sin."[18] It is "because of these things"— immorality, impurity, idolatrous greed, and the improper chatter (5:3–5)—that the wrath of God comes upon unbelievers, the "sons of disobedience" (5:6).[19]

---

15. O'Brien, *Ephesians*, 360, 361. The alliteration is keen: εὐτραπελία vs. εὐχαριστία (*eucharistia*, "thanksgiving").

16. Fowl, *Ephesians*, 167.

17. A failure to receive an inheritance in the divine kingdom simply stands for loss of eternal reward, a situation that affects all unbelievers. However, certain believers may also lose out on rewards in eternity (though not eternal life, of course). Therefore, it is possible that one could take this as a warning to *believers* who choose to live lives of immorality, impurity, and greed, that what will be the certain lot of all unbelievers, could possibly also be theirs—loss of eternal reward. "Inheritance" has thus far been set in the future: 1:14, 18. Here, in 5:5, "has an inheritance" is in the present tense, i.e., unbelievers *do not have* an inheritance in the divine kingdom, whereas, by implication, believers, in general, do. This is likely another instance of the "realized eschatology"—already, but not yet—of Ephesians. Likewise, elsewhere in the NT, "the kingdom of Christ and of God" (5:5) is both in the present (Rom 14:17; 1 Cor 4:20; 15:24; Col 1:13; 4:11) and in the future (1 Cor 6:9–10; 15:50; Gal 5:21; 2 Tim 4:1, 8). That divine wrath "comes" is also consistent with the fact that unbelievers "do not have" inheritance—both are in the present tense. Thus the wrath of God (Eph 5:6) also may be both present (John 3:36; Rom 1:18; 13:4–5; 1 Thess 2:16), and future (Luke 21:23; Rom 2:5; 5:9; 9:22; 1 Thess 1:10; 5:9). Aspects of the "already" are being experienced now; but the fullness of the inheritance, kingdom, and of divine wrath are "not yet."

18. O'Brien, *Ephesians*, 364. The cognate of the verb "to deceive" was used in 4:22.

19. O'Brien reads "sons of disobedience" as "not those who commit the occasional act of disobedience but to men and women whose lives are characterized by disobedience"—in this context, unbelievers, as also in 2:2 (ibid., 365).

9.2 Ephesians 5:7–14

THEOLOGICAL FOCUS OF PERICOPE 9.2

9.2 Believers, children of light and light themselves, walk accordingly, pleasing God, without participating in the works of darkness, thereby exposing such works and even being agents of the transformation of those who engage in them (5:7–14).

TRANSLATION 9.2

5:7 *Therefore do not be co-partakers[20] with them;*

5:8 *for you were formerly darkness, but now you are light in the Lord; walk as children of light*

5:9 *(for the fruit of the light [is] in all goodness and righteousness and truth),*

5:10 *discerning what is pleasing to the Lord.*

5:11 *Do not co-participate in the unfruitful works of darkness, but instead even expose [them];*

5:12 *for it is shameful even to speak of the things done by them in secret.*

5:13 *But all things, when exposed by the light, become manifest, for everything that becomes manifest is light.*

5:14 *Therefore it says, "Awake, sleeper, And arise from the dead, And Christ will shine on you."*

NOTES 9.2

9.2 *Believers, children of light and light themselves, walk accordingly, pleasing God, without participating in the works of darkness, thereby exposing such works and even being agents of transformation to those who engage in them.*

It is likely that Eph 5:7–8 begins a new section: like 4:1; 4:17; 5:1; and 5:15, these verses also have "therefore" and a form of the verb "to walk." After the contrast between unbelievers and believers in 5:1–6, Paul now makes a subtle shift: 5:7–20 deals with then vs. now. And in this section, 5:7–14 focuses pointedly upon the symbolism of light (now) and darkness (then).

The exhortation not to be partakers with unbelievers, buying into their lifestyle (5:7), is an appropriate one in every generation: far too easily the world seeps into the church, influencing its attitudes and behaviors. "Co-partakers," συμμέτοχος (*symmetochos*; 5:7), was also used in 3:6, where the partaking was of Christ; here, Paul is urging the saints not to partake of the actions of unbelievers.[21] These two forms of participation—with Christ and with unbelievers (i.e., their actions)—are mutually exclusive. "Given that one has been transferred from the realm of darkness into the

---

20. No doubt the "co-" prefix is redundant here (and in "co-participate" in 5:11), but I am retaining it in all translations of the Greek words that begin with συν- (*syn-*) in this letter.

21. Ephesians 5:8 also supports this identification of the non-inheritors of 5:5, the "sons of disobedience" of 5:6, and the "them" of 5:7 with unbelievers.

kingdom of Christ, it is unintelligible for one to act as if one still participated in the realm of darkness. The Ephesians' allegiance, their citizenship, has been transformed and transferred into Christ's realm. It is only reasonable that they act accordingly," demonstrating values diametrically opposed to those of the world.[22] In fact, it would quite a contradiction for those in the sphere of light to live like those in the domain of darkness.

Themes related to darkness and light have already shown up in 1:18 (light = knowledge) and 4:18 (darkness = ignorance).[23] But here it is believers and unbelievers themselves who are light and darkness, respectively (5:8). "Those ruled by the dominion of *darkness* or of *light* represent that dominion in their own persons. So when they were converted, it was their lives, not their surroundings, that were changed from darkness to light. This radical transformation had taken place *in the Lord* [5:8]. He is the one who has made the decisive difference, and it is through their union with him that they have entered a new dominion and become *light*."[24] The identification of individuals themselves with the spheres of their existence indicate their wholehearted commitment to the values of those realms, whether of darkness or of light.

5:8a	For you were	formerly	darkness	
5:8b		but now	light	in the Lord.

Apart from the shared conjunction and verb at the beginning of the verse ("for you were"), 5:8a and 5:8b are antithetically parallel. There is, however, the last clause—"in the Lord"—that describes the unique sphere in which those who are light exist. And that clause makes all the difference in their walk![25] No longer "sons of disobedience" (5:6), they are to live/walk as "children of light" (5:8)—i.e., children characterized by light in the Lord, since they imitate God who is light.

Then follows a parenthetical remark in 5:9 that contains a triplet of attributes: "for the fruit of the light [is] in all goodness and righteousness and truth." The last two elements of the triplet, righteousness and truth, were shown as divine characteristics in 4:24[26]; "goodness," too, is an attribute of God: 1 Chr 16:34; Pss 27:13; 135:3; Mark 10:18; etc. "Fruit of the light" indicates the virtues that are the result of being light, and stands in contrast to the "unfruitful deeds of darkness" (Eph 5:11). Thus, fruit produced by believers—goodness, righteousness, and truth—reflects God himself; this essentially is an exhortation for them to be godly. "The description of the works of darkness as unfruitful, then, is part of the theme of the futility of existence in the unbelieving world that Paul has already developed in 2:1–3 and 4:17–19. It stands in utter contrast to the purposeful, goal-oriented existence that characterizes the believ-

22. Fowl, *Ephesians*, 169.

23. "Darkness" will be encountered again in 6:12, where it describes the domain of the hostile forces arrayed against God, his people, and his plans.

24. O'Brien, *Ephesians*, 367.

25. As was noted, "walk" occurs in Ephesians in 2:2, 10; 4:1, 17; 5:2, 8, 15.

26. Also see Deut 32:4; Neh 9:33; Pss 95:13; 119:75; 145:17; *Pss. Sol.* 10.5; Luke 1:75; Rev 16:5; 19:2.

ing community because of its union with Christ (1:9–12; 2:19–22; 4:11–16)."[27] And such deeds of darkness are essentially ungodly, not reflecting the attributes of deity.

The attitude with which this "walk" (5:8) is to be conducted is clearly stated in 5:10—"discerning what is pleasing to the Lord."[28] This statement is at the center of a chiastic structure that forms 5:7–14, asserting its importance in the life of a believer.[29]

> **A**   Now you are *light*; walk as children of *light* (5:7–8)
>   **B**   *Fruit* of *the light* (5:9)
>   **C**   Discerning what is pleasing to the Lord (5:10)
>   **B'** *Unfruitful* works of darkness; exposed by *the light* (5:11–13)
> **A'** Everything that becomes manifest is *light* (5:14).

Engaging in what is "pleasing to the Lord" means not "co-participating" in the "unfruitful deeds of darkness" (5:11)[30]; in fact, quite emphatically—"instead even"—Paul urges exposure of those dark deeds (5:11, 13).[31] There is nothing here about speech, so while verbal exposure of evil has its place, here the focus is on light exposing darkness: good deeds (and believers themselves who are light) showing up evil deeds (and unbelievers themselves who are darkness) for what they are. "This is a body of Christians whose common life and practice stand as a sharp yet appealing alternative to the surrounding world," a challenge to evil and evildoers.[32] In a way similar to the countering of immoral words with thanksgiving (5:3–4), here deeds (and people) of darkness are countered by deeds (and people) of light (5:11). And just as immorality, impurity, and greed ought not even to be named among the saints (5:3), so also to speak of the deeds of darkness that are done in secret is "shameful" (5:12).[33]

The meaning of the complex structure of 5:13 is not entirely clear. Essentially, Paul is asserting that light (either believers or their deeds, or both) exposes the deeds of darkness, those shameful sexual sins done in secret (5:12). And thereby a transformation takes place, "for everything that becomes manifest is [i.e., becomes] light." Perhaps this is the result of some of those unbelievers abandoning their dark realm for the kingdom of light (see John 3:19–21; also Ps 139:11–12; John 1:5; 2 Cor 4:6) and

---

27. Thielman, *Ephesians*, 342–43.

28. For "pleasing God," see Rom 12:2; 14:18; 2 Cor 5:9; Eph 5:10; Phil 4:18; Col 1:10; 3:20; Heb 13:21; Wis 4:10; Sir 55:16; *T. Dan.* 1:3. The same notion was reflected in the previous section, Eph 5:1–6, in the mention of "fragrant aroma" (5:2).

29. Heil, *Ephesians*, 30–31. Related elements are italicized.

30. Both "co-participate" here and "co-partake" in 5:7 are συν- (*syn-*) words: συγκοινωνέω (*synkoinōneō*) and συμμέτοχος (*symmetochos*), respectively. For other συν-words, see 2:5, 6, 19, 21–22; 3:6; 4:3, 16.

31. The word translated "expose" (ἐλέγχω , *elenchō*; 5:11) can also mean "reprove" or "convict" (as in Matt 18:15; 1 Cor 14:24). Hoehner thinks it most likely that it is the dark deeds of lapsed *believers* that are to be exposed in this fashion (*Ephesians*, 679).

32. Fowl, *Ephesians*, 171.

33. "Shameful," translates αἰσχρός (*aischros*); a related word, αἰσχρότης (*aischrotēs*, "filthiness"), was used in 5:4.

thereby becoming light themselves—the same conversion Paul's readers went through, described in Eph 5:8 (and perhaps as hoped for in 1 Cor 14:24–25).

Ephesians 5:14 appears to be introducing an OT quote with "Therefore it says" (as 4:8 did), but though the content appears to be biblical, the exact locus of the citation is indeterminable.[34] In any case the awakening, arising, etc., seem to be recalling the process of conversion noted in 2:1, 5–6, 8 (with sleep, death, and darkness as conditions of spiritual death). "[U]nbelievers should awake to the truth of the gospel and rise from their former lives of sin, and if they do this, Christ will shine his powerful light on them. This is how we know that every unbeliever illuminated by the gospel is transformed into light."[35] The emphatic placement of "the Christ" at the end of the sentence emphasizes Paul's point; literally, it reads: "and he will shine on you—the Christ." He it is, who shines and transforms, converts and recreates.

The symbolism of light and darkness allows for no shades of grey in between; the boundaries are well demarcated:

> The apostle wants his Christian readers to realize that they are to live by values that are diametrically opposed to the standard of their contemporary world, values that include sexual purity and wholesome speech. Instead of being corrupted by the surrounding darkness, believers are to exercise their influence on it. Paul adopts no defeatist attitude towards the society around him. Christ is the light who has summoned the readers to wake up and rise from the dead. He has shone upon them so that they have become light in the Lord. As children of light their lives are to shine as a beacon, exposing the darkness around for what it really is. Some who sit in darkness may be attracted to the light and even choose to enter it.[36]

The ethical demands of a believer's lifestyle are clear: they, living in the realm of light, in Christ, live to a different code, follow an exalted standard, and thus influence a dark world.

---

34. In Paul, the present tense verb λέγει (*legei,* "it says") is found thirty-five times and except for three instances (1 Cor 1:12; 12:3; 1 Tim 4:1), all are connected with Scripture. So what is introduced here in Eph 5:14 with λέγει may be a paraphrase of an OT verse—speculations include Isa 9:2; 26:19; 60:1; Jonah 1:6. But perhaps all that Paul intends by this introduction ("Therefore it says") is that what follows carries the authority of Scripture, without designating any specific OT text (see 1 Cor 2:9; 9:14; 1 Tim 4:1; 5:18 [a composite citation of Deut 25:4 and a word from Jesus, Luke 10:7]). Lincoln, *Ephesians,* 332, considers the quote a line from a baptismal confession. O'Brien sees it as part of an early Christian hymn, or one composed by Paul himself (*Ephesians,* 376–77).

35. Thielman, *Ephesians,* 351. He observes that in the religious atmosphere of Palestine, metaphors relating to waking from sleep, resurrection from death, and enlightenment from darkness, were commonly employed for proselytes, for idolaters who turned to worship the true God, and for those repenting of long-standing sin. That likely accounts for Paul's frequent use of these images to describe conversion: Rom 6:3–11; 2 Cor 4:4–6; Gal 2:19–20 (see ibid., 349). Christ himself as light is found in John 1:4, 9; 8:12; 9:5; 12:46; Luke 1:78–79; 2 Cor 4:6.

36. O'Brien, *Ephesians,* 377.

9.3 Ephesians 5:15–20

> **THEOLOGICAL FOCUS OF PERICOPE 9.3**
>
> 9.3 The wise walk of believers, making the most of time in evil days and understanding God's will, involves being filled by the Spirit with the divine fullness of God in Christ, manifested in the worship of the church (5:15–20).

TRANSLATION 9.3

5:15 *Therefore watch carefully how you walk, not as unwise persons but as wise,*

5:16 *making the most of time, because the days are evil.*

5:17 *So then do not be foolish, but understand what the will of the Lord is.*

5:18 *And do not get drunk with wine, for that is dissipation, but be filled by the Spirit,*

5:19 *speaking to one another in psalms and hymns and spiritual songs, singing and making melody in your heart to the Lord;*

5:20 *always giving thanks for all things in the name of our Lord Jesus Christ to God, even the Father,*

NOTES 9.3

9.3 *The wise walk of believers, making the most of time in evil days and understanding God's will, involves being filled by the Spirit with the divine fullness of God in Christ, manifested in the worship of the church.*

Once again, as in 4:1; 4:7; and 5:7, we see a new section commencing with "therefore" and a form of "walk" (5:15)—the last occurrence of the verb in this letter.[37] This section, 5:15–20, outlines the walk of wisdom: this is how the "children of light" (5:8) should live. The wise walk is a Spirit-filled walk, and how that is accomplished is the subject of the remainder of this pericope and of the entirety of the next two pericopes, 5:21–33 and 6:1–9 (Pericopes 10 and 11). To live a life filled by the Spirit is to engage in worship (5:19–20; see below) and to practice mutual submission in the body of Christ, particularly between the basic relationships of humankind—those between spouses, between parents and children, and between employers and employees (5:21–6:9).

There are three contrasts that dominate 5:15–20, each employing μή . . . ἀλλά . . . (*mē . . . alla . . .*; "not . . . but . . ."): unwise vs. wise walking (5:15), becoming foolish vs. understanding the Lord's will (5:17), and getting drunk with wine vs. being filled by the Spirit (5:18)—the last evidenced by worship (God-ward) and submission (man-ward; 5:21–6:9). The three contrasts are likely to be parallel. In the first contrast, believers are urged to "*watch* carefully how you walk," wisely, and not unwisely (5:15). Watching is, of course, an appropriate imperative for those who are "light." The wisdom for walking is not simply intellectual knowledge, but rather practical and experiential skill for living. This is equivalent to understanding (and doing) the will of God, the divine

---

37. These "walks" are to be in worthiness/unity (4:1), in holiness (4:17), in love (5:2), in light (5:8), and here, in carefulness/wisdom (5:15).

demand for believers' lives (5:17).[38] "The doing of his will is not a matter of irrational impulse but of intelligent reflection and action."[39] In turn, knowing God's will (and doing it) is to be "filled by the Spirit," as the divine presence is manifest more and more in their lives (5:18; see below).

Wise living also involves the recognition that time is short and that the days are evil (5:16)—perhaps an acknowledgement by believers that they are living in the last days.[40] "Evil" and "day" are linked together also in 6:13, in connection with spiritual warfare against the devil, and the rulers, powers, and world forces of darkness—all evil spiritual entities (6:11–12). Thus the wickedness of the last days is clearly anti-God and demonic in origin (also see 2:2). But there is no thought here that believers should live in fear or that they should insulate themselves from the world. Rather they are to walk wisely, "making the most of time"[41] to live lives understanding "the will of the Lord," without being "foolish"—the second contrast (5:16–17).

Indeed, the will of God is that believers be "holy and blameless before Him" (1:4), for they are "created in accordance with God['s likeness] in true righteousness and holiness" (4:22); and one day Christ intends to present his bride to himself "holy and blameless" (5:27). The broad trajectory of God's will has already been made known—to consummate all things in Christ (1:9–10). It is by the specifics of living wisely, understanding the particularities of God's will (divine demand with regard to the concrete circumstances of daily life), and filled by the Holy Spirit, that believers can participate in the grand *telos* of God's will. And their participation involves being formed into the likeness of God (4:24), i.e., into the image of Christ (Rom 8:29).

The final contrast, between getting drunk with wine and being filled with the Spirit, is found in Eph 5:18.[42] Drunkenness is thus paralleled with walking unwisely and being foolish (in the two earlier contrasts of 5:15 and 5:17, respectively), and is explicitly labeled ἀσωτία (*asōtia,* "dissipation")—self-gratifying and self-indulgent behavior that only results in debauchery.[43]

Ephesians 5:18–21 is a single sentence that has five anarthrous participles modifying the main imperative verb "be filled" (5:18): "speaking," "singing," "making melody," "giving thanks," and "submitting."[44] "Filled," πληροῦσθε (*plērousthe,* from

---

38. God's "will" in Ephesians is found in 1:1, 9–11; 5:17; 6:6.

39. Bruce, *The Epistles to the Colossians, to Philemon, and to the Ephesians,* 379.

40. Lincoln, *Ephesians,* 342, notes that in Jewish and early Christian literature the last days were characterized by evil: see *T. Dan* 5.4; *T. Zeb.* 9.5, 6; 2 Tim 3:1; 2 Pet 3:3.

41. The verb is ἐξαγοράζω (*exagorazō*) that, in the mercantile language of the day, meant "to buy out" or "redeem."

42. Elsewhere in the NT, "spirit" and "wine" are associated in Luke 1:15; Acts 2:4, 13, 27.

43. This word is used elsewhere in the NT only in Titus 1:6 (and 1:7 mentions addiction to wine) and 1 Pet 4:4 (and 4:3 has drunkenness). Wine, while its use is not condemned in the NT (see 1 Tim 5:23), is clearly not to be abused (1 Tim 3:3, 8; Titus 1:7; 2:3): inebriation is folly, and a characteristic of those who operate in the lifestyle of the "old person."

44. The last verse, Eph 5:21, containing the fifth participle of the sequence, "submitting," is a hinge verse that connects what precedes (the other four participles qualifying the verb "filled") and what follows (the specificities of "submitting" in key contexts of daily life). Since it ties in more closely with what

πληρόω, *plēroō,* "to fill") is an imperative present passive second person plural verb. While the passive denotes that the filling is accomplished by another, the imperative places the responsibility on believers to "cooperate with the Spirit in their own filling"—divine and human agency operating in tandem.[45] Seeing that most, if not all, of the five participles that qualify "filled" have the sense of exhortations, they are likely to be participles of means, the manner in which the imperative of 5:18 regarding filling by the Holy Spirit may be actualized—and that is by "speaking," "singing," "making melody," "giving thanks" (these four may conveniently be characterized as elements of worship) and "submitting" (see below).[46] Thus, worship and submission, encompassing the implied exhortations of the five participles and the descriptions of the manner in which "filling" is to take place, are appropriate engagements for a body that is "a holy temple in the Lord" and "a dwelling of God in the Spirit" (2:21–22).

Instead of being drunk, therefore, the Ephesians are enjoined to be "filled by the Spirit" (ἐν πνεύματι, *en pneumati*).[47] The verb "to fill" (πληρόω, *plēroō*) occurs in 1:23; 3:19; 4:10; 5:18, and always in connection with a member of the Godhead. In 1:23, Christ is the one filling the church (the "filler"), he is also the content of the filling (the "fullness"); in 3:19, likewise, God is the "filler" and the "fullness"; and in 4:10, Christ is the "filler." Thus in 5:18 there is no reason the Spirit could not be "filler" or "fullness," or both. But while the analogy with wine may suggest that the Spirit is the content of the filling ("the fullness")—after all, both imperatives, not to be drunk and to be filled, are followed by the dative—here the construction of πληρόω + ἐν (*en*, "in/with/by") + dative best indicates the Spirit as the instrument of the filling (the "filler").[48] The

follows, i.e., Pericopes 10 (5:21–33) and Pericope 11 (6:1–9), 5:21 will be discussed with those texts.

45. Thielman, *Ephesians*, 360.

46. Yet one must confess that how exactly one obeys the imperative to be filled is unclear, even though we are given five suggestive participles. "One of the remarkable currents of NT theology is a studied reserve on the *method* of sanctification. That is, the biblical authors speak positively about the ministry of the Spirit but typically refrain from telling how that ministry is to be implemented into the believer's life." Wallace speculates that this approach may reflect Jer 31:31, 34 that has Yahweh promising that his people will not have to teach one another or exhort one another to know Yahweh. "This new covenant mentality of what might be labeled a 'soft mysticism' is prevalent in the NT" (Wallace, *Greek Grammar*, 639). More likely, this biblical reticence for prescription is because of the impossibility of providing specifics for every possible congregation in every possible age in every possible space. Offering specifics for application is, therefore, the responsibility of the preacher, the shepherd of the flock. For this conception of preaching see Kuruvilla, *A Vision for Preaching*.

47. The emphasis on the Holy Spirit percolates throughout this letter: 1:3, 13, 14, 17; 2:18, 22; 3:16; 4:30; 5:18; 6:17–18.

48. "There are no other examples in biblical Greek in which ἐν + the dative after πληρόω indicates content ['fullness']" (Wallace, *Greek Grammar*, 375). However, the church fathers did employ that syntax: e.g., Ignatius, in the greeting in *To the Smyrnaeans,* describes the church as "filled with faith and love." Normally, verbs of filling take a genitive of content (πληρόω + genitive, as in Acts 2:28; 13:52; Rom 15:13, 14; etc.) (Hoehner, *Ephesians*, 703). Against this, Chrysostom in *Homilies on Ephesians* 19 interprets 5:18 as having the effect of a genitive: οἱ ψάλλοντες γὰρ πνεύματος [genitive of content = "fullness"] πληροῦνται ἁγίου (*hoi psallontes gar pneumatos plērountai hagiou,* "for they who make melody are filled with the Holy Spirit"). In any case, seeing the dative in 5:18 as instrumental, denoting the "filler," fits the context better and is in line with similar uses of ἐν with "Spirit" in this letter: 2:18, 22; 3:5; 4:30; 6:18; also see Rom 15:16; 1 Cor 12:3, 13.

instrumental use of the preposition ἐν indicates that the Holy Spirit is the means and agent by which divine presence is mediated, just as the instrumentality of wine mediates the state of inebriation.

Of course, this makes the content of the filling (the "fullness") unstated in 5:18, but in light of the notion of divine fullness that has been encountered previously in this letter, it can be understood that the Spirit, the "filler," fills believers with the divine "fullness." "In other words, Paul's readers are to be transformed by the Spirit into the likeness of God and Christ, ideas which are entirely consistent with the earlier exhortations of 4:32–5:2."[49] This was expressly stated in 4:13—the "fullness of Christ" is the final goal into which the body of Christ is growing. Perhaps the best way to put it is that what believers are being filled with is *the fullness of God in Christ (mediated) by the Spirit.* As has been discussed under Eph 1:23; 2:19–22; 3:19; and 4:13, divine fullness is closely linked to the OT concept of divine glory abiding in the tabernacle and temple; the "fullness" language in the OT (LXX of Isa 6:1–4; Ezek 10:4; 43:5; 44:4; Hag 2:7; etc.) often indicates the immanence and presence of God amongst his people. In exhorting the Ephesians to be filled by the Spirit rather than be drunk with wine, the biblical writer is essentially commanding them to become, corporately, the unique temple of God, the dwelling place of God in Christ, a state of glory mediated by the Spirit. As they do so, they manifest the attributes of God ("goodness and righteousness and truth," Eph 5:9), and bring glory to him, as they live wisely, by the will of God, pleasing him. This section (5:18–20) is thus obviously Trinitarian—all three members of the Godhead are represented: Spirit (5:18), Christ (5:19, 20), and the Father (5:20)—for this is a glorious venture that is being undertaken.[50] The church is the new temple of God serving his presence, where the fullness of Christ abides (1:23)—"a holy temple in the Lord," "a dwelling of God in the Spirit" (2:19–22; also 3:16–19).[51]

It must also be noted in this connection that the context of this text is the functioning of the corporate body of believers, a thread that runs all throughout 4:1—6:9. "[T]he thrust of the passage is corporate, not merely individualistic. All of the expressions of lives full of the [S]pirit are in relationships, be it among Christians at worship, in the home, or at the workplace. This corporate dimension to 'being filled with the Spirit' is often inadequately recognized in a theology of a 'Spirit-filled life' that deals primarily with an individual's personal—even private—experience."[52] Filling by the Spirit, therefore, refers to the abiding presence of God in Christ mediated by the Spirit with, in, and among God's people as a body (also see 1:23; 3:19; 4:13).

This filling is characteristic of the wise and of those who understand the will of God, i.e., those displaying the lifestyle of the "new person." Those who have been "sealed" by the Spirit (1:13) and have been exhorted not to "grieve" the Spirit (4:30), are now urged to be "filled" by the Spirit (5:18), equated to wise living and comprehend-

---

49. O'Brien, *Ephesians*, 392.

50. Besides here, Trinitarian elements in Ephesians are also found in 1:4–14, 17; 2:18, 22; 3:4–5, 14–17; 4:4–6.

51. See Gombis, "Being the Fullness of God," 268; and Lincoln, *Ephesians*, 348.

52. Köstenberger, "What Does it Mean to be Filled with the Spirit?" 233.

ing the divine will. "If believers were only filled with wisdom, the influence would be impersonal; however the filling by the Spirit adds God's personal presence, influence, and enablement to walk wisely, all of which are beneficial to believers and pleasing to God. With the indwelling each Christian has all of the Spirit, but the command to be filled by the Spirit enables the Spirit to have all of the believer," as the divine presence increasingly manifests itself in the life of the Christian. A walk of wisdom that comprehends divine will is therefore characterized by a filling by the Spirit, a situation parallel to *walking* by the Spirit (Gal 5:16, 25), a state of being under the Spirit's control.[53] This is a work in progress, not completed on this side of eternity. O'Brien notes wisely:

> [T]he exhortation to be filled by the Spirit is part of the eschatological tension between the "already" and the "not yet." The church as Christ's body *already* shares his fulness ([Eph]1:23). Yet Paul's petition for his readers (3:14–19) . . . is that they might be filled to all the fulness of God [3:19] . . . Paul's intercession presupposes that the readers have *not yet* been filled; God begins to answer this petition in the here and now, and he will consummate his work on the final day when the readers are filled with *all* his fulness. Similarly, the body of Christ has *not yet* reached mature manhood; it is moving towards the fulness of Christ (4:13). And in the process the Holy Spirit is powerfully at work transforming believes both individually and corporately into the likeness of Christ.[54]

The chiastic structure of 5:19–20 is instructive:

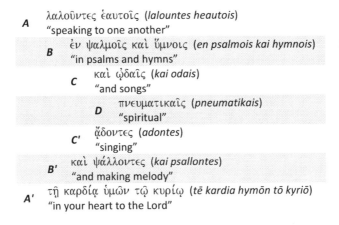

A   λαλοῦντες ἑαυτοῖς (*lalountes heautois*)
     "speaking to one another"
   B   ἐν ψαλμοῖς καὶ ὕμνοις (*en psalmois kai hymnois*)
      "in psalms and hymns"
     C   καὶ ᾠδαῖς (*kai odais*)
       "and songs"
       D   πνευματικαῖς (*pneumatikais*)
        "spiritual"
     C'   ᾄδοντες (*adontes*)
       "singing"
   B'   καὶ ψάλλοντες (*kai psallontes*)
      "and making melody"
A'   τῇ καρδίᾳ ὑμῶν τῷ κυρίῳ (*tē kardia hymōn tō kyriō*)
     "in your heart to the Lord"

This textual shape is centered on what is "spiritual" (*D*), quite appropriate after having the filling by the "Spirit" head this section. Also note the balance between *B* and *B'*, and between *C* and *C'*: "making melody" is a verb derived from "psalms"; and "singing" is related to "songs." All that to say, the three participles, "speaking," and "singing," and "making melody," are simply describing different facets of the same activity, conducted "to one another" and "to the Lord" (*A* and *A'*), i.e., with both vertical and horizontal orientations.[55]

53. Hoehner, *Ephesians*, 705.

54. O'Brien, *Ephesians*, 393.

55. This synonymy between the participles is in keeping with the syntactical redundancies already

In 5:20, Paul introduces the fourth participle of means (of the Spirit's filling): thanksgiving through Christ to the Father is to be made "always" and for "all things."[56] "Our English word 'thank' means to express gratitude to a person because of personal benefits received, and can therefore be rather self-centred; thanksgiving for the apostle, however, approximated what we normally understand by 'praise.'"[57] That being the case, even this participle, "thanksgiving," approaches the function of the prior three—"speaking," "singing," and "making melody"—for "a life filled with thanksgiving will find spontaneous expression in psalms, hymns, and songs."[58] Therefore, this commentary uses the broad category of "worship" to encompass all four of the activities mentioned in 5:19–20. In other words, "God is not just saving individuals and preparing them for heaven; rather, he is creating *a people* among whom he can live and who in their life together will reproduce God's life and character. This view of salvation is consistent throughout Paul's letters. It is demonstrated most clearly in his references to the Spirit, who plays the key role not only in forming the people of God, but also in their life together and in their worship."[59] This, too, is part of the consummation of all things in Christ.

SERMON FOCUS AND OUTLINES

THEOLOGICAL FOCUS OF PERICOPE 9

9   The imitation of God and Christ's selfless love call for abandonment of sexual immorality, and the adoption of a wise and worshipful lifestyle (5:1–20).

The new lifestyle of the believer continues to be the focus of this pericope (as it is in the remaining pericopes of this letter, as well). The wise walk of the believer, in light, and by the Spirit, will, the apostle declares, stand as a witness to unbelievers, furthering their enlightenment. This is also a walk in love, reflecting the love of Christ, the antithesis of the illicit love of sexual immorality that believers are not even to talk about. Immorality of this kind incurs the wrath of God, while the walk of true love, with the divine qualities of goodness, righteousness, and truth, brings about the pleasure of God. Besides, this wise walk is also a powerful witness to unbelievers. In sum, here is a lifestyle that is worshipful, being filled by the fullness of God in Christ (mediated) by the Spirit.[60]

---

noted in this letter.

56. The idea of thanksgiving also appears in 5:4; and 1:16 had Paul's personal thanksgiving to God for his Ephesian readers.

57. O'Brien, *Ephesians,* 397n150.

58. Ibid., 398.

59. Fee, *Paul, the Spirit,* 66. Indeed, God is seeking such worshipers (John 4:23). The fifth participle, "submitting" (Eph 5:21) is also part of this group of participles that lists the means of filling by the Spirit. However, since the entailments of "submitting" are expounded in the next two pericopes, 5:21 will be discussed in Pericope 9 (5:21–33).

60. The submission aspect of such a walk is treated in the next two pericopes.

Possible Preaching Outlines for Pericope 9

I.   Walk of Folly, Darkness, and Wine: The Lifestyle of Unbelievers
                Immorality (5:3–8a, 17a, 18a)
                Result: the loss of reward (5:5)
                Result: the wrath of God (5:6)
                Move-to-relevance: The danger of believers engaging an immoral lifestyle
II.   Walk of Wisdom, Light, and Spirit: The Lifestyle of Believers
                Imitation of God (5:1–2, 8b–12, 15–16, 17b, 18b–20)
                Result: the salvation of unbelievers (5:11–14)
                Result: the pleasure of God (5:2, 10)
III.   *Worship with your life!*
                Specifics on living a life of worship[61]

By focusing on the three sections of the pericope instead, the three contrasts can be brought out and three facets of the lifestyle of believers underscored (each section begins with "therefore": 5:1, 7, 15).

I.   Exhibiting Deity
                Imitation of God in true love, leading to reward[62] (5:1–2)
                Contrast: false love = immorality, and loss of reward (5:3–6)
                Move-to-relevance: the dangerous possibility of lapsing
II.   Exposing Darkness
                Living fruitfully as children of light, inviting the pleasure of God (5:8b–10, 13–14)
                Contrast: unfruitful works of darkness, incurring the wrath of God (5:6, 11–12)
                Move-to-relevance: the distinct possibility of converting unbelievers
III.   Expressing Devotion
                A wisely lived life of worship (5:15–20)
                Contrast: a life of folly (5:15–18)
                Move-to-relevance: our lack of worship
IV.   *Worship with your life!*
                Specifics on living a life of worship[63]

---

61. Thanksgiving and praise are probably the most straightforward applications to offer here.

62. The reward for believers is implied in 5:5.

63. Here, it should be emphasized that worship is the core of the Christian life, out of which springs the "exhibition" of God, the "exposure" of darkness, and the "expression" of devotion.

PERICOPE 10

Emulating the Christ-Church Relationship

Ephesians 5:21–33

[Submission and Love in Marriage; the Divine Model]

REVIEW, SUMMARY, PREVIEW

Review of Pericope 9: In Eph 5:1–20, the contrast between the lifestyle of the believer and that of the unbeliever is continued. The former, imitating God and the selfless love of Christ, walks wisely, in light and by the Spirit and, as a result, invites divine pleasure, exposes the deeds of darkness and, comprehending the will of God, worships him with gratitude.

Summary of Pericope 10: This tenth pericope of Ephesians (5:21–33) continues the broader theme of the filling by the Spirit of the divine fullness of God in Christ. Of the two broad manifestations of such filling, the first (worship) was dealt with in Pericope 9. Pericopes 10 and 11 deal with the second: submission. This particular pericope considers the responsibilities of husbands (to love) and wives (to submit), constantly referring back to the divine model—the relationship of Christ and his bride, the church.

Preview of Pericope 11: The next pericope, Eph 6:1–9, carries on the theme of the filling by the Spirit of the divine fullness of God in Christ. Children are to obey their parents, and parents are to raise their children with care; slaves, too, are to obey their masters, and masters are to treat their slaves with sincerity. Ultimate obedience and accountability of all parties concerned are to God in Christ, who will reward them appropriately.

10. Ephesians 5:21–33

<table>
<tr><td colspan="2">THEOLOGICAL FOCUS OF PERICOPE 10</td></tr>
<tr><td>10</td><td>The filling by the Spirit of the divine fullness of God in Christ manifests in the mutual submission of believers in the fear of Christ, and in the modeling of the husband-wife relationship after the Christ-church relationship (5:21–33).</td></tr>
<tr><td>10.1</td><td>The filling by the Spirit of the divine fullness of God in Christ manifests in mutual submission of believers, in the fear of Christ (5:21).</td></tr>
<tr><td>10.2</td><td>The husband-wife relationship is modeled after the Christ-church relationship, husbands demonstrating the kind of sacrificial love shown by Christ, and wives submitting to authority as unto Christ, thus manifesting that divine union (5:22–33).</td></tr>
<tr><td>10.2.1</td><td>Wives submit to their husbands, their heads, in everything, as unto Christ, and as the church submits to its head, Christ (5:22–24).</td></tr>
<tr><td>10.2.2</td><td>Husbands love their wives as Christ sacrificially loved the church to present it to himself one day, holy, blameless, and all-glorious (5:25–27).</td></tr>
<tr><td>10.2.3</td><td>Husbands love their wives as their own bodies—just as Christ loved the church, nourishing and cherishing it—and manifest this love in an exclusive union with their spouses, representing the union of Christ and the church (5:28–33).</td></tr>
</table>

OVERVIEW

It must be confessed that linking 5:21 with 5:22–33, and not reading 5:21 with what precedes, tends to isolate these household codes dealing with spouses, children and parents, and slaves and masters, as discrete pericopes (Pericopes 10 and 11) disconnected with the ethical exhortations of Pericope 9 (5:1–20). Indeed, "submitting" in 5:21 is the fifth participle of means that is dependent upon the main verb "be filled" (5:18.); the other four were: "speaking," "singing," "making melody," and "giving thanks" (see Pericope 9, especially 5:19–20).

> **A** "speaking": between believers (5:19a)
>   **B** "singing," "making melody": between believers and God (5:19b)
>   **B'** "giving thanks": between believers and God (5:20)
> **A'** "submitting": between believers (5:21)

In fact, one can also see the similarity in that "speaking to one another" is paralleled here by "submitting to one another" (5:19 and 5:21; A and A').[1] Thus the entire section of 5:21–6:9 must be seen as a means of being "filled by the Spirit." For preaching purposes, of course, this large chunk of text must be broken up, as has been done in this commentary. However, the preacher must be careful to maintain the thread of the theological thrust begun earlier. That 5:21 is connected with what follows is obvious:

---

1. The Greek words indicating "one another" are ἑαυτοῖς (*heautois*) and ἀλλήλοις (*allēlois*), respectively, in 5:19 and 5:21.

the verb "submit" is explicitly noted in 5:21 and 24; it is implied in 5:22; and its idea is expressed with a synonym in 5:33; 6:1, 2, 5.

The current pericope commences in 5:21, a hinge verse, with the fifth participle, "submitting," that modifies the verb "be filled" (5:18). And with this key participle Paul gives us an extended treatise on the organization of the household that is grounded upon the attitude of submission. This was a frequently addressed topic in the philosophical literature of Greco-Roman times, for the ordering of society was based upon the ordering of the household.[2] Inevitably this focus found its way into Christian literature as well.[3] In the household code in Ephesians, the wife-husband relationship takes the most space; spousal relationships reflect the relationship between Christ and the church. In fact, the relationship that is preeminent in this pericope is the one between Christ and the church; it forms the model for the secondary one, the relationship between husband and wife.

What is rather unusual in the NT household codes is the fact that wives, children, and slaves are addressed equally with husbands, fathers, and masters, and, moreover, these codes assume a degree of self-determination and self-responsibility possessed by the first group of individuals. For a society that was patriarchal and hierarchical even in Christian circles, this is countercultural. These household codes accept the dignity of every human being before God, whether husband or wife, parent or child, slave or master. One is responsible for one's own conduct before an impartial God. "The value, dignity, or worth of the members of the Christian household in a subordinate position is no less than that of those in authority."[4] Indeed, the model to be followed is not patriarchal or hierarchical, but christological and creational (with reference to Gen 2:24 that is cited in this pericope in Ephesians).

These two pericopes (Pericope 10, Eph 5:21–33 and Pericope 11, Eph 6:1–9) also assume that readers and members of the body of Christ are part of Christian households and that they are committed to maintaining the relationships therein in God's way. Going with that assumption, several areas remain outside the scope of the discussion in these passages: a believer married to an unbeliever; abuse of spouses; what a husband or wife, parent or child, master or slave should do if the other party does not live by these codes; marriage between a free person and a slave; slave abuse; child abuse; celibacy; etc. None of these issues are addressed; in other words, these pericopes are not comprehensive treatises on the conduct of such relationships. Rather, they are quite narrowly focused on how the particular interpersonal interactions further the agenda of God for the church, the world, and the cosmos.

The pattern of the household code in this pericope is straightforward: the member of the pair that is to submit is addressed first with an exhortation to submission,

---

2. See Hoehner, *Ephesians*, 720–29, for an excursus on "Household Code."

3. Thielman, *Ephesians*, 366. See Eph 5:22—6:9; Col 3:18—4:1; 1 Tim 2:1—3:13; 6:1–2; Titus 1:5–9; 2:2–10; 3:1; 1 Pet 2:13—3:7; as well as *Didache* 4.9–11; Ignatius, *To Polycarp* 4–5; Polycarp, *To the Philippians* 4.2–6:3; *Barnabas* 19.5, 7; *1 Clement* 1.3; 21.6–8. Also see Philo, *Hypothetica* 7.3; Josephus, *Against Apion* 2.24 §199; etc.

4. O'Brien, *Ephesians*, 408.

followed by a command to the individual to whom submission is due. The latter, too, is reminded of his responsibilities in the created order before God. Christological and ecclesiological themes abound in this pericope, integrating what has been stated in prior pericopes, as the relationship between Christ and church is displayed here in a climactic account.

> Here, as earlier, Christ is the exalted head (cf. 1:22; 4:15). He is the one who loves and gives himself for believers (cf. 3:19; 5:2), who brings the Church into being by his saving death (cf. 1:7, 13; 2:5, 6; 2:14–18), who cares for its needs and growth (cf. 4:11, 16), who is intimately related to the Church as he fills it, dwells in believers' hearts, and is the source of their life (cf. 1:23; 2:21; 3:17; 4:15, 16). But now these elements are given a new focus as Christ is specifically called Savior (v 23), as his care for the Church is talked of in terms of nourishing and cherishing it (v 29), as his sanctifying activity is elaborated (vv 26, 27), and as he is seen as the bridegroom whose concern is for his bride's glory and purity (v 27) and whose relation to his Church can be depicted as a spiritual marriage union (vv 31, 32). Here as earlier, the Church is Christ's body (cf. 1:23; 2:16; 3:6; 4:4, 12, 16), is associated with glory (cf. 1:6, 12, 14, 18; 3:21), and is to be holy and blameless (cf. 1:4; 2:21; 4:24; 5:3–14). What had been assumed previously in depicting Christ as head in talking of learning Christ (cf. 4:20, 21) is now expressed explicitly—the Church is subject to Christ (v 24).[5]

Indeed, one might say that in this pericope, the important subject is not marriage and the relationship of husbands and wives, but the relationship of Christ and his church.

10.1 Ephesians 5:21

THEOLOGICAL FOCUS OF PERICOPE 10.1

10.1 The filling by the Spirit of the divine fullness of God in Christ manifests in mutual submission of believers, in the fear of Christ (5:21).

TRANSLATION 10.2

5:21 *submitting to one another in the fear of Christ.*

NOTES 10.1

10.1 The filling by the Spirit of the divine fullness of God in Christ manifests in mutual submission of believers, in the fear of Christ.

The submission enjoined in 5:21 is likely related to the selfless walk of humility, gentleness, patience, and forbearance in love, urged in 4:2–3, the result of which would be the "unity of the Spirit in the bond of peace." That goal is, no doubt, being sought in the exhortations of the household codes in Eph 5–6, for, in a sinful and broken world, hierarchy at multiple levels of daily life and subordination to appropriate authorities

5. Lincoln, *Ephesians*, 388–89.

are essential for keeping order. But 5:21 is surprising: though the verb, "submit," implies organizational hierarchy and the authority of some over others, what is called for here is *mutual* submission, "to one another." The verb in 5:21 is a present participle, best read as being in the middle voice that indicates a voluntary, rather than a forced, submission, as in Rom 8:7; 10:3; 13:1, 5; 1 Cor 16:16; Col 3:18; Titus 2:5, 9; 3:1. This then is a subjecting of oneself to another, a willing subordination.

The final clause of Eph 5:21 gives the rationale (or manner) of this mutual submission: "in the fear of Christ." "[T]he believer . . . filled by the Spirit, submits to others out of fear or reverence for Christ. Such fear conveys more than just respect. . . . On the other hand, it is doubtful that it is a fear that comprises terror."[6] This "fear of *Christ*," is appropriate towards the one to whom God has "subjected" all things (1:22 uses the same verb, ὑποτάσσω, *hypotassō*, employed in 5:21). In context, the "all things" in 1:22 are the cosmic hostile forces of evil who have no choice but to submit in obedience to this divine One with universal authority. How much more then should believers obey, though their fear is one that is tempered with the comprehension of Christ's incomparable and unfathomable love (3:17–19)! Thus, mutual submission is, in essence, a reverence for Christ and *his* authority over the church; therefore, those who are part of his body must reflect this "fear" by submitting one to another: to submit to one another is to "fear" Christ. This is the foundational model of all relationships within the body of Christ, and it functions without undermining the hierarchical roles of the various players and actants.

Thus this implied imperative for mutual submission in 5:21 is not that those in authority cede that authority as they submit to those who are subordinate, but that they, in some sense, serve and submit even as they simultaneously govern and lead. As Calvin noted on Eph 5:21 (*Commentary on Ephesians*): "No one ought to free themselves from submission. And where love reigns, there is mutual servanthood. I do not except even kings and governors, for they rule that they may serve." The authority of the one to whom submission is called for in the following verses (husbands, parents, and masters) is constrained by their attitude of submission to those over whom they are placed (wives, children, and slaves).[7] After all, the true model of leadership was that modeled by the serving Savior, Jesus Christ (Mark 10:42–45), a model that "relativizes the conventional authority structures" of the world, requiring almost a divine degree of humility to be practiced (Phil 2:3–4).[8]

---

6. Hoehner, *Ephesians*, 719. The "fear of Christ" is the motivation for submission and "in the fear of Christ" is how submission ought to be practiced. This is equivalent to the "fear of Yahweh/the Lord/God" in the OT, as in Gen 22:12; Lev 25:17; Deut 6:2, 13; 13:4; Josh 4:24; 1 Sam 12:14; Pss 15:4; 19:9; 67:7; Prov 1:7; 3:7; 10:27; etc. (in the NT "fear" and "God" are in juxtaposed only in Acts 9:31; Rom 3:18; 2 Cor 5:11; 7:1; and Eph 5:21). Such awe of the divine and deference to God leads to obedience.

7. Thielman, *Ephesians*, 373.

8. Fowl, *Ephesians*, 186. Both submission and humility to one another in the body of Christ are exhorted in 1 Pet 5:5, too. Also, while all believers are commanded to love (Eph 5:2), here the command to love is specifically for husbands (5:25, 28, 33); wives are not expressly called to love their husbands. In other words, the broad scope of mutual submission to, and mutual love for, one another does not vitiate the specific thrust in this pericope—submission and love operating only in one direction in particular

[H]ere in Ephesians mutual submission coexists with a hierarchy of roles within the household. Believers should not insist on getting their own way, so there is a general sense in which husbands are to have a submissive attitude to wives, putting their wives' interests before their own, and similarly parents to children and masters to slaves. But this does not eliminate the more specific roles in which wives are to submit to husbands, children to parents and slaves to masters.[9]

Again, all of this continues the section from the previous pericope, discussing how one is "filled by the Spirit" (5:18). And the next verse, 5:22, begins without a conjunction; neither does it have a verb. In other words, 5:22 is integrally connected to 5:21 and carries on the theme of submission.

10.2 Ephesians 5:22–33

THEOLOGICAL FOCUS OF PERICOPE 10.2

10.2   The husband-wife relationship is modeled after the Christ-church relationship, husbands demonstrating the kind of sacrificial love shown by Christ, and wives submitting to authority as unto Christ, thus manifesting that divine union (5:22–33).

    10.2.1   *Wives submit to their husbands, their heads, in everything, as unto Christ, and as the church submits to its head, Christ (5:22–24).*

    10.2.2   *Husbands love their wives as Christ sacrificially loved the church to present it to himself one day, holy, blameless, and all-glorious (5:25–27).*

    10.2.3   *Husbands love their wives as their own bodies—just as Christ loved the church, nourishing and cherishing it—and manifest this love in an exclusive union with their spouses, representing the union of Christ and the church (5:28–33).*

TRANSLATION 10.2

5:22 *Wives [submit] to your own husbands, as to the Lord,*

5:23 *for the husband is the head of the wife, as also Christ [is] the head of the church—He [being] the Savior of the body;*

5:24 *but as the church submits to Christ, so also the wives to their husbands in everything.*

5:25 *Husbands, love your wives, just as Christ also loved the church and gave Himself up for her,*

5:26 *that He might sanctify her, having cleansed [her] by the washing of water in the word,*

5:27 *that He might present to Himself the church glorious, not having spot or wrinkle or any such thing, but that she might be holy and blameless.*

---

relationships. However, another line of interpretation sees 5:21 as not calling for *mutual* submission; rather, it is simply a heading, and the specifics of "to one another" is unpacked in the subsequent sections: it entails submission by wives, children, and slaves, to husbands, parents, and masters, respectively. "To one another" is used in this non-reciprocal fashion in Luke 2:15; 12:1; 24:32; 1 Cor 11:33; Rev 6:4 (O'Brien, *Ephesians*, 405).

9. Lincoln, *Ephesians*, 366.

5:28 *So also husbands ought to love their own wives, as their own bodies. He who loves his own wife loves himself;*

5:29 *for no one ever hates his own flesh, but nourishes and cherishes it, just as Christ also the church,*

5:30 *because we are members of His body.*

5:31 *For this reason a man shall leave father and mother and shall be joined to his wife, and the two shall become one flesh.*

5:32 *This mystery is great; but I speak with reference to Christ and to the church.*

5:33 *Nevertheless, you also, one by one—each must love his own wife thus: as himself; and the wife [is to see] that she fear the husband.*

NOTES 10.2

Throughout this section, Eph 5:22–33, that deals with spousal relationships, the focus swings back and forth between the union of husband and wife and the union of Christ and the church:

A	Husband–wife (5:22–23a)
B	Christ–church (5:23b–24a)
A'	Husband–wife (5:24b–25a)
B'	Christ–church (5:25b–27)
A''	Husband–wife (5:28–29a)
B''	Christ–church (5:29b–30)
A'''	Husband–wife (5:31)
B'''	Christ–church (5:32)
A''''	Husband–wife (5:33)

The frequent use of comparative particles in 5:22–33—ὡς (*hōs,* "as," 5:23, 24, 28), οὕτως (*houtos,* "so"/"thus," 5:24, 28), and καθώς (*kathōs,* "just as," 5:25, 29)—attest to the significance of the comparison between husband-wife and Christ-church. The two duos coalesce in 5:31–32, and the pericope concludes with a summary of the husband-wife relationship.

A new note of unity is struck in this pericope. Cosmic unity, the consummation of all things in Christ, was first mentioned in 1:10, and the unity of all (believing) humankind was described in 2:11–22. How this latter unity is part of the larger scheme of the former unity was treated in 3:9–10. But here, in describing the unity of specific members of a household—husband and wife, and their "one-fleshedness" (5:28–31)—yet another facet of unity is brought to the surface: the "oneness" and "bodiness" between Christ and his bride, the church.[10] "[I]f the Church's display of unity is to act as a pledge of God's purposes of unity for the cosmos, then marital unity in particular will also be a reflection of God's cosmic purpose."[11] Thus the commands to husband

---

10. While we certainly are to learn something about human marriage from the divine relationship between Christ and the church, there is no question that we also learn something crucially important in this pericope about Christ's union with the church.

11. Lincoln, *Ephesians*, 389–90.

and wife stand at the top of the household code, for no other human relationship so closely reflects Christ's union with the church.

The exhortations to wives and husbands are similar in structure: both commence with the command (5:22, 25), illustrate with a model (5:24, 25), and close with a reiteration of the command (5:24, 28). Broadly, even with the interspersed paeans to Christ's relationship to his bride, the imperatives for wives and husbands are given in a chiastic fashion:

> **A**   To wives (5:22–24)
>   **B**   To husbands (5:25–29)
>   **B'**   To husbands (5:33a)
> **A'**   To wives (5:33b)

10.2.1   *Wives submit to their husbands, their heads, in everything, as unto Christ, and as the church submits to its head, Christ.*

The command to wives takes on a chiastic structure: command (*A*), rationale with mention of a human head and a divine one (*B* and *B'*), and a reiteration of the command (*A'*)[12]:

> **A**   "Submit"; "wives to their own husbands" (5:21–22)
>   **B**   "Head" (5:23a)
>   **B'**   "Head" (5:23b)
> **A'**   "Submits"; "wives to their husbands" (5:24)

The continued force of the middle-voice verb, "submit," carried over from 5:21 into 5:22 indicates that what is called for is the submission of a free agent. Even as the church is never forced to submit to its head, Christ, so also the wife is never to be forced to do so to her husband. "Paul's admonition to wives is an appeal to free and responsible persons which can only be heeded voluntarily, never by the elimination or breaking of the human will, much less by means of a servile submissiveness."[13] The verb ὑποτάσσω is used of Christ's submission to the Father (1 Cor 15:28), thus proving that subordination in economy (i.e., functional subordination) does not equal inferiority in essence (i.e., ontological subordination). "[T]he headship of the husband does not connote any sense of qualitative superiority to the wife. . . . In God's administration the role of the husband's headship is positional power. His headship and the wife's submission are for the sake of harmony."[14]

---

12. Girard, "Love as Subjection," 128.

13. O'Brien, *Ephesians,* 411–12.

14. Hoehner, *Ephesians,* 740. Josephus (*Against Apion* 2.201) considered women to be inferior to men. The mental capacity of that gender was supposed to be defective according to the first-century BCE philosopher, Arius Didymus (cited in Stobaeus, *Florilegium* 2.7.26; 2.149.5); so also Aristotle (*Politics* 1.1254b13–14, 1:1259b1–2; 1.1260a9–14). Thus this exhortation by Paul to wives is quite countercultural, giving them the responsibility to submit voluntarily, not to mention their being treated equally with their husbands as both parties are addressed and assigned imperatives in this household code.

The vertical component of the wife's submission to her husband is clear: it is to be "as to the Lord" (5:22), parallel to the motivations of mutual submission "in the fear of Christ" (5:21), that of children to obey their parents "in the Lord" (6:1), and of slaves to render faithful service "as to the Lord" (6:7). In other words, in her submission to her husband, the wife submits to the Lord. The one kind of submission cannot be separated from the other. If the latter, then the former, and so submission to her husband "is part and parcel of the way that she serves the Lord Jesus."[15] Notice the model for the wife's submission: both the headship of Christ over the church, and the latter's submission to the former, are mentioned, in 5:23b–24a. Altogether, this exhortation in 5:22–24 turns out to be more than a point of proper marital conduct; it is a spiritual issue.[16]

Besides 5:23, there are only two other uses of "head" in Ephesians, in 1:22 and 4:15; both denote the head of the church, Christ. In fact, in 1:22, the same verb ὑποτάσσω is employed to denote the submission of all things under the feet of this "head." And in 4:15, it is from this "head" that the growth of the whole body, the church, occurs—he supplies all that is needed for this process. The parallels between the usage of "head" in 1:22 and 4:15–16, and its employment in this passage are evident: Christ is the one to whom the church submits (5:24), and Christ is the one who "nourishes and cherishes" the church (5:29)—his authority and leadership used for the benefit of the church. Thus the headship of the husband is what is being referred to here, i.e., his authority and leadership over his wife for her benefit.[17]

Christ's headship is closely associated (equated?) with his being "the Savior of the body," i.e., it is his salvific work that demonstrates, and even proves, his status as head: Eph 1:7; 2:13, 16; 5:2, 25—all these verses point to his self-sacrificial atonement that qualifies him for headship over the church. "Paul pictures the wife's submission as the recognition of the authority of a husband who imitates the self-sacrificial, nurturing, and supporting roles that Christ fills with respect to the church."[18]

---

15. O'Brien, *Ephesians*, 412.

16. Interestingly enough, the responsibility of children and slaves is not simply to submit voluntarily as wives are to do; indeed, they are to "obey"—ὑπακούω (*hypakouō*; 6:1, 5) is a more powerful imperative, making the exhortation an explicit command and a mandate. Indeed, it is worth noting that in 1 Pet 3:5, 6, the command to "submit" (from ὑποτάσσω) is illustrated in Sarah's "obeying" (also from ὑπακούω) her husband.

17. There has been some dispute as to whether "head" here means "source" (husband/Adam the *source* of the wife/Eve), rather than "authority." Grudem surveyed 2,336 instances of κεφαλή (*kephalē*, "head") in thirty-six authors from the eighth century BCE to the fourth century CE. Of all its metaphorical uses (i.e., not as an actual anatomical head), not a single one referred to "head" as being the "source" or "origin" of something; instead, in a number of instances it had the sense of "ruler" or "person of superior authority or rank." See "Does Κεφαλή ('Head') Mean 'Source,'" 51–52. For contemporary uses of "head" as authority, see Philo, *Life of Moses* 2.30 (Ptolemy over kings); 2.82 (mind over senses); *On the Special Laws* 3:184 (head over body); Plutarch, *Pelopidas* 2.1.3 (general over the army); Hermas, *Similitudes* 7.6 (man over household); Josephus, *Jewish War* 4.261 (Jerusalem over nation); etc. Also see, in the LXX, Deut 28:12–13, 43–45; Jdg 10:18; 11:8, 9, 11; 2 Sam 22:44; Ps 18:43; Isa 7:8, 9; 9:14–16; Jer 31:7; Lam 1:5; and in the NT, 1 Cor 11:3; Eph 1:22; 4:15; 5:22–24; Col 1:18; 2:10, 18–19. The use of the word "fear" in Eph 5:33 also substantiates this sense of "head" as authority.

18. Thielman, *Ephesians*, 379.

The Church receives God's gift of Christ as head over all on its behalf (1:22). In the building imagery of 2:20, 21 the Church looks to Christ as the crowning stone of its structure and the one who holds it all together. It opens itself to his constant presence (3:17) and comes to know his all-encompassing love (3:19). The Church receives his gift of grace (4:7) and his gifts of ministers for its own upbuilding (4:11, 12). It grows toward its head and receives from him all that is necessary for such growth (4:15, 16), including teaching about him (4:20, 21). The Church imitates Christ's love (5:2) and tries to learn what is pleasing to him (5:10) and to understand his will (5:17). It sings praises to him (5:19) and lives in fear of him (5:21). The Church's subordination, then, means looking to its head for his beneficial rule, living by his norms, experiencing his presence and love, receiving from him gifts that will enable growth to maturity, and responding to him in gratitude and awe. It is such attitudes that the wife is being encouraged to develop in relation to her husband.[19]

While Paul seems to have been intent on making the husband's headship analogous to Christ's, he introduces a parenthetical point here with the emphatic "He [being] the Savior of the body" (5:23). Likely, then, this particular facet of Christ's headship is *not* to serve as a model for the husband's headship. How could a husband conceivably "save" his wife? This disjunction is reinforced by the "but" that begins the next verse, 5:24.[20]

"In everything" (5:24) indicates an unlimited submission that is expected of wives—in the same way that the church submits to its head, Christ (5:24)—i.e., irrespective of merit, deservedness, or response on the part of the husband. But of course, there is at least one limit: sin—the wife need not submit if asked to sin, for, in essence, her submission to her husband is to be "as to the Lord" (5:23), who would never ask her to sin.[21] Neither is there any qualification of the statement to permit wives to submit only to good husbands, caring husbands, loving husbands, Christian husbands, etc. "Just as the church should willingly submit to Christ in all things and, if it does so, will not find that stifling, demeaning, or stultifying of growth and freedom, so also wives should willingly submit to their husbands in all things and, if they do so, will not find that stifling, demeaning, or stultifying."[22] The same issues will crop up with the subsequent exhortation to husbands to love their wives—there is no qualification there as to what kind of wives deserve to be loved. As expected, this is an ideal view of a Christian marriage of "onefleshedness" (5:28–31), where both husband and wife treat each other they way they ought to, as urged in this pericope. "[T]he church's submission to Christ leads to blessing, growth, and unity for God's people. Similarly,

19. Lincoln, *Ephesians*, 372.

20. However, see 1 Cor 7:16, where "to save" is used of both wife and husband, each as subject and as object of the other's action of "saving." Also see Tob 6:17 ("You [husband] will save her [wife]").

21. See Acts 5:29. One must add that spousal abuse cannot, and should not, be tolerated; help must be sought from appropriate sources and authorities in such cases. But one must bear in mind, as has been stated earlier, that this pericope does not intend to cover all contingencies of marriage in every society, culture, or time. See 2 Cor 4:8; 7:5, for the same kind of hyperbole with "every." This caveat also operates for the relationships discussed in the subsequent pericope, those of children and parents, and of slaves and masters.

22. Knight, "Husbands and Wives," 170.

the wife's submission to her husband, as she seeks to honour the Lord Jesus Christ, will *ultimately* lead to divine blessing for herself and others."[23]

*10.2.2   Husbands love their wives as Christ sacrificially loved the church to present it
to himself one day, holy, blameless, and all-glorious.*

Interestingly, the "head" of Roman society, the emperor, was to be protected at all costs, said Seneca, the first-century Roman philosopher (*De Clementia* 1.4.3). The members of the emperor's "body," Roman citizens, were expected to sacrifice themselves for his sake, even to "thrust a right hand into the flame," or plunge "willingly into a chasm," or even "throw themselves before the swords of assassins" (ibid., 1.3.3–4). Indeed, the head was not called to be the one who loved; rather, he was the one *to be loved* (ibid., 1.3.4; 1.5.1–2). Aristotle would have agreed with Seneca: "[I]t is the part of a ruler to be loved, not to love" (*Ethica eudemia* 7.3.4). Since the common good was contingent on the wellbeing of the head, for the head to endanger itself was not noble, but foolish. But Paul turns this traditional idea on its head: the "head" (the husband) is to be sacrificial and loving towards his bride, unlike contemporary "heads" in the hierarchies of the Greco-Roman world.[24] In keeping with the mores of the day, rarely does one see an exhortation to husbands to love their wives outside of the NT context.[25] O'Brien notes that the ἀγάπη (*agapē*, "love") word-group "does not appear in a any extra-biblical Hellenistic rules for the household."[26]

One might have thought that with the command to wives to submit to their husbands, husbands would be, in turn, commanded to *rule* their wives. Instead, they are urged repeatedly to love them: Eph 5:25, 28, 33—it is decidedly an important command! Thus there is an inherent asymmetry in the relationship: one submits to the other (but is not exhorted to love him), and the other loves the one (but is not exhorted to rule her).

What exactly the husband's love entails is not specified. But the intent of such love is "to seek the highest good in the one loved."[27] In light of the subsequent verses (5:25b–30), such love clearly calls for the husband's self-sacrifice in the "unceasing care and loving service for his wife's entire well-being." Such a love, a divine demand that is made of the husband, is therefore an act of the will, and not an emotional or physical response.[28] In any case, all believers are called to love one another (4:2, 15, 16; 5:2); but in this pericope it is the special responsibility of the husband towards his wife

---

23. O'Brien, *Ephesians*, 418.

24. Lee-Barnewall, "Turning Κεφαλή on its Head," 599–614.

25. However, *Sentences* 195, 196, by Pseudo-Phocylides (likely apocryphal; Phocylides was a Greek philosopher, ca. first-century BCE to first-century CE, whose writing was Jewish in style and dependent on the LXX) makes such a reference (but using στέργω, *stergō*, for "love," not ἀγαπάω, *agapaō*); so does Plutarch, *Conjugalia Praecepta* 4.34 (using ἐράω, *eraō*, for "love"), and also *b. Yebam.* 62b ("Concerning a man who loves his wife as himself").

26. O'Brien, *Ephesians*, 418–19n233.

27. Hoehner, *Ephesians*, 747.

28. O'Brien, *Ephesians*, 419.

that is in focus, a love modeled upon that of Christ for his bride, the church.[29] Appropriately, then, 5:25–28 is chiastically centered upon this divine pattern[30]:

> **A** "Husbands, love your wives" (5:25)
>   **B** "That He might sanctify [ἀγιάζω, *hagiazō*] her" (5:26)
>   **C** Christ presents the church glorious and blemishless (5:27ab)
>   **B'** "That she might be holy [ἅγιος, *hagios*] and blameless" (5:27c)
> **A'** "So also husbands ought to love their won wives" (5:28)

That it was Christ who "gave Himself up" for the church (5:25; also 5:2[31]) emphasizes his initiative, and urges that such an initiative be taken by the husband as well, to love his wife selflessly.

> Clearly there are certain respects in which husbands cannot exactly replicate the relationship between Christ and the church. . . . Nevertheless, the self-giving, other-regarding love that Christ displays for the church is the same love that husbands are to display for their wives. . . . The analogies between Christ-and-the-church and husbands-and-wives are not exact in every respect, but the admonition here in 5:28 indicates that this analogy is to be taken in all seriousness as the standard against which a husband's love for his wife is measured.[32]

The purpose of Christ's death for the church (5:25b) is outlined in three ἵνα- (*hina*, "that") clauses in 5:26–27[33]: "that He might sanctify her,"[34] "that He might present to Himself the church glorious," and "that she might be holy and blameless."[35] It is very possible that the background to this sanctification and glorification by washing in the context of marriage (5:26) is Ezek 16:1–14, where God is described as washing the nation—the divine bride—in water, anointing her with oil, clothing her with embroidery and fine linen, adorning her with ornaments, crowning her head, feeding her lavishly, and bestowing upon her his splendor.

The participle, "cleansing," indicates how the "sanctifying" was accomplished—"having cleansed [her] by the washing of water with the word" (Eph 5:26). That this is not baptism is obvious, for nowhere in the NT is the *church* ever said to be baptized; neither does the ritual of baptism cleanse sin. The use of water simply explicates the "washing" (as in Heb 10:22). Moreover, "word" (ῥῆμα, *rhēma*) is never used elsewhere

---

29. Marriage as a spousal relationship between Yahweh and Israel is noted in Isa 54:5–8; Jer 2:1–3; 31:31–32; Ezek 23; Hosea 1–3. Of course, Jesus called himself the bridegroom: Mark 2:18–20; John 3:29; also see 2 Cor 11:1–3.

30. Girard, "Love as Subjection," 130.

31. In 5:2, the example of Christ was to motivate all believers to "walk in love" for each other; here in 5:25, a special case is identified where the model of Christ's love has to be emulated: the husband-wife relationship.

32. Fowl, *Ephesians*, 190.

33. As well, there is a cutaneous triplet in 5:27: "spot," "wrinkle," and "any such thing."

34. The verb ἀγιάζω (*hagiazō*, "to sanctify") is found only here in Ephesians; the cognate noun ἅγιος (*hagios*, "holy," "saint") is employed in 1:1, 15, 18; 2:19; 3:8, 18; 4:12; 5:3; 6:18.

35. It was to be "holy and blameless" (5:27) that God chose believers before the foundation of the world (1:4).

in the NT in connection with baptism. Thus this washing is likely to be a spiritual cleansing as in 1 Cor 6:11 and Titus 3:5, and analogous to the prenuptial bridal bath alluded to in Ezek 16, part of Jewish matrimonial tradition. This is substantiated by the use of λουτρόν (*loutron,* "washing," Eph 5:26) for ceremonial washings, as in Philo, *Cherubim* 95; *De mutatione nominum* 124; Josephus, *Against Apion* 1.282; etc. "Having cleansed [her] by the washing of water in the word" (Eph 5:26) is therefore a metaphorical reference to the cleansing accomplished upon salvation through believ-ing the gospel—"in the word" of the gospel, the account of Christ's atoning work for his bride.[36] In sum, "the reason that Christ gave himself for the church (redemption) was in order that he might sanctify her because he has cleansed her with the washing of the water, speaking metaphorically of his sacrificial death and this is in connection with the proclaimed word of Christ's death."[37] The entire image here is reminiscent of the nuptial activities of ancient times; however, unusually, here in Eph 5 it is the groom who bathes the bride and who presents her to himself (5:27; see below).

The next verse, 5:27, continues the theme of the church's bridal bath. The purpose of the cleansing/washing is so that Christ "may present to Himself the church glori-ous" (5:27). "It is he himself who prepares her, he alone presents her, and he alone receives her all-glorious."[38] And as the dermatological terms, "spot" and "wrinkle" imply, Christ is the skin doctor here.[39] What it means to be "glorious" is explained both negatively ("not having spot or wrinkle or any such thing") and positively ("holy" and "blameless"). While the word "glory" is not used there, Ezek 16:10–14 describes, metaphorically, Yahweh's beautifying operations with the virgin that he has cleansed and espoused. The divine spouse concludes: "'Then your name went forth among the nations because of your beauty, for it was perfect because of My splendor which I set upon on you'" (16:14). And in its eschatological sense, the presentation of believers by Christ to himself will occur on the day of Christ; see Rom 14:10; 2 Cor 4:14; 11:2; Col 1:22, 28; Rev 19:7–10; 21:2, 9–10; etc. "Finally, that which was planned in eternity past ([Eph] 1:4) will be accomplished when Christ presents to himself the church that is holy and without blame ([Eph] 5:27)."[40]

---

36. Thielman, *Ephesians,* 384. Paul employs ῥῆμα eight times; with the exception of 2 Cor 13:1, he uses it to refer to the word(s) of God or Christ: Rom 10:8 (x2), 17, 18; 2 Cor 12:4; Eph 5:26; 6:17; also see Heb 6:5; 1 Pet 1: 25; etc.

37. Hoehner, *Ephesians,* 757. The importance of proclamation/word is noted in the Talmud; if a groom gives his bride a gift and says to her, "'Behold, thou art consecrated unto me,' [or] 'thou art betrothed unto me,' [or] 'Behold, thou art a wife unto me'—then she is betrothed" (*b. Qidd.* 5b). The subsequent washing of the bride before the actual wedding symbolized her cleansing that would set her apart for her groom (Hoehner, *Ephesians,* 756).

38. Ibid., 759. In 2 Cor 11:2, the Corinthians are presented by Paul to Christ as "a pure virgin." Here it is Christ making the presentation to himself, not just of a holy and blameless bride, but also a *glorious* one! The church's glory (Eph 5:27) was mentioned earlier in 3:21—there God was being glorified in the church.

39. This verse has a special meaning for me, a practicing dermatologist. Derivatives of the two Greek words, σπίλος and ῥυτις (*spilos,* "spot," and *rhytis,* "wrinkle"), are still in use in my specialty to refer to a certain kind of spotted mole (nevus spilus), and to wrinkles (rhytides).

40. Ibid., 761.

10.2.3   Husbands love their wives as their own bodies—just as Christ loved the church nourishing and cherishing it—and manifest this love in an exclusive union with their spouses, representing the union of Christ and the church.

The word οὕτως (*houtos*, "so," "thus," or "in the same manner"; 5:28) indicates how husbands are to love their wives: as they love their own bodies. And clearly this is how Christ viewed the church, his bride—as his own body. Notice the back and forth references to "body" and "flesh" to point to both the unity of husband and wife, as well as that of Christ and church.[41]

> **A**   "Body"—husband and wife (5:28)
> **B**   "Flesh"—Christ and church (5:39)
> **A'**   "Body"—Christ and church (5:30)
> **B'**   "Flesh"—husband and wife (5:31)

Every other instance of "body" in Ephesians is in the singular, and connotes the body of Christ, the church: 1:23; 2:16; 4:4, 12, 16; 5:23, 30. Here in 5:28, in the plural, it is the "own bodies" of husbands that is in view. However, analogically, Paul is saying that if Christ loved his own "body" (the church) with intense care (5:29), then so also should husbands love their "own bodies." This is clearly an obligation of husbands: "husbands *ought to* love their own wives," as their own bodies (5:28). The man and woman in a spousal relationship are to be seen and considered as a single person, one entity. Thus the call for the husband is not to love *another* person (his wife) as he loves himself; no, to love his wife is to love *himself,* for she is one body with him (5:28–31).[42]

To "nourish and cherish" is to nurture physically and emotionally. The tenderness of Christ's nourishment and cherishing of his body, the church with all its imperfections, is a manifestation of his amazing love. "As it is natural for man not to hate his own flesh but to nurture and take care of it, so it is also the natural thing for Christ to nurture and take care of his body, the church. He redeemed it (1:7–12; 2:1–10), sealed it (1:13–14), empowered [and protected] it (1:19–23), brought it into one body (2:16), filled it with God's fullness (3:19), gifted it (4:7–16), and loved and sanctified it (5:25–26)."[43] A constant, continual, and consistent care is implied in Christ's "nourish-

41. At least here, then, "body" and "flesh" are to be considered synonymous. The Greek word σάρξ (*sarx*, "flesh") is also feminine; so the same pronoun can refer to the flesh, to the church, and to the wife (all feminine in the Greek), thus maintaining the continuity of thought and coherence of argument in this section.

42. This "onefleshedness" of spouses is also noted in Matt 19:5–6; Mark 10:7–8; and 1 Cor 6:16. Of all the things God may call a disciple to give up in order to follow Jesus, a spouse is *not* one of them (Mark 10:29). Once one has entered into marriage, two have become one, even for the purposes of discipleship. See Kuruvilla, *Mark,* 202–10. "Your own" in Eph 5:22 and "their own" in 5:28 "highlight the exclusive nature of the relationship between husbands and wives: they are to have a level of commitment to each other that is qualitatively different from their commitments to other men and women" (Thielman, *Ephesians,* 387).

43. Hoehner, *Ephesians,* 768.

ing and cherishing" of his bride and his body, the church. Such a poignant manifestation of great love is what must be emulated in a husband-wife relationship.

> [T]he primary point of connection here is not between the specific practices of care and nurture of our human bodies and Christ's practices of care for the church. Rather, the point seems to be to indicate that Christ's care and nurture of his body, the church, is as natural, normal, and uncoerced as humans' care for their own bodies. Christ's care of the church is not so much a duty grudgingly performed as a joyful act of love. . . . This care that Christ lavishes freely on his body is the model of the nurture and care that husbands should display toward their own "flesh."[44]

It is thus clear that "body" is not just a metaphor for Paul; the relationship between Christ and the church is characterized by the integrity and unity possessed by a body. Such a notion is so powerful and personal that at this juncture, in 5:30, Paul suddenly switches to the first person plural: "*we* are members of His body."[45]

To substantiate his point, the apostle throws in Gen 2:24, directly quoting it in Eph 5:31, without any of the standard preambles that often introduce an OT quote in the NT.[46] "For this reason" in 5:31 likely points back to the prior discussion of the Christ-church and husband-wife entities each being a single body. "[S]urprising as it may seem, Paul is saying in 5:31 that God has instituted marriage 'because' the church is Christ's body. This probably means that the union of husband and wife in 'one flesh' was originally intended to prefigure and to illustrate the union that Christ now has with the church."[47] In other words, the relationship between Christ and his bride the church is the paradigm for that between human spouses; the latter is the symbol or token of the former. This truth could only have been expounded on after the atoning work of Christ had been completed—thus it was a "mystery" until now, and a "great" one at that (5:32). "Further, within the wider context of Ephesians as a whole the union between Christian husband and wife which is part of the unity between Christ and the church is thus a pledge of God's purposes of unity for the cosmos."[48] The idea of "two" becoming "one"—here of husband and wife (5:31, citing Gen 2:24)—was also employed earlier to portray the unity of all (believing) humanity (Eph 2:15). Both these unions are crucial to the fulfillment of God's grand plan to consummate all things in Christ (1:10). And both these unions are part of the "mystery" in Ephesians. Indeed, all the references to "mystery" in Ephesians deal with unity of some sort: relating to God's grand plan to consummate (unite) all things in Christ (1:9–10); the union of

44. Fowl, *Ephesians*, 191.

45. Earlier this truth was expressed as "we are members of one another" (4:25). Now the concept of the unified and integrated body is expressed as "we are members of His body" (5:30).

46. There are minor changes here in the quotation from the LXX version of Gen 2:24.

47. Thielman, *Ephesians*, 389. The preposition εἰς (*eis,* "into") before "one flesh" (5:31) reflects the Semitism behind the LXX—the Hebrew particle preposition ל (*l,* "into/in/of/by"); for obvious reasons, the preposition is omitted in the English translation here. Paul cites Gen 2:24 only once more, in 1 Cor 6:16, to deal with the union of those who cohabit.

48. O'Brien, *Ephesians*, 434.

all (believing) humankind (3:3–4, 9); the union of husband and wife reflecting that between Christ and the church (5:32); and the proclamation of the good news that brings everything together—the "mystery" of the gospel (6:19).

The word πλὴν (*plēn*) that commences 5:33 is usually an adversative conjunction—"but" or "nevertheless." But it may also be employed, as here, as a summative transition to close out the discussion, something like the contemporary use in English of "in any case." The pericope concludes with a reiteration of the commands to husband and wife. For the husband, the command to love is clearly being underscored: ὑμεῖς (*hymeis*, "you" [plural]) is in the emphatic position, supplemented in force by "one by one" and "each": "Nevertheless you also, one by one—each must love" (5:33). For the wife, there is a return to the "fear" that commenced the pericope in 5:21. There it was the "fear of Christ"; here the wife is to "fear the husband." "Fear" is a critical element in the relationship of humans to all hierarchical and authority structures: see Rom 13:3, 4, 7; Eph 6:5; 1 Pet 2:18. Clearly there is more implied here than just respect—even a reverence for and deference to the husband's position and role, as deputized by divine fiat.

Thielman notes that the syntax, ἵνα (*hina*) + subjunctive, φοβῆται (*phobētai*, "that she fear") has, in the NT, "a softer, more respectful nuance than the simple imperative" (see Matt 20:33; Mark 5:23; 10:51; 2 Cor 8:7; Gal 2:10; Eph 5:33). Thus the husband has a clear imperative to love his wife, but the wife gets a milder command. Such a softening is also noticeable in Eph 5:22 and 5:24, where the actual verb is missing; the imperative thus is more implied than explicitly stated.

> In a society in which women had less say over who they married than men, and less power within the relationship once the marriage had taken place, it was important for a household code that had been transformed by the gospel not to be heavy-handed in its instructions to the less-powerful partner. . . . Perhaps the softness of the imperative is a recognition that the wife's obedience to Paul's instructions will often involve complexities introduced by the inevitable mixture of her husband's sinfulness with his position of authoritative head.[49]

Thus, by such a God-ordained unity of relationship between husbands and wives, God's grand plan to consummate all things in Christ is furthered.

SERMON FOCUS AND OUTLINES

THEOLOGICAL FOCUS OF PERICOPE 10

10   The filling by the Spirit manifests in the mutual submission of believers, and in the modeling of the husband-wife relationship after the Christ-church relationship (5:21–33).

This pericope and the next continues the theme of the filling by the Spirit of the fullness of God in Christ. Particularly, both pericopes deal with the "submitting" aspect of such filling, one of the five participles qualifying the main imperative, "be filled" (5:18); the others are "speaking," "singing," "making melody," and "giving thanks," integrated together as "worshiping."

49. Thielman, *Ephesians*, 391–92.

The pericope begins with a call to mutual submission, but quickly moves on to spend most of its time and space upon the relationship between husband and wife. This relationship is to be modeled after the one between Christ and his church. In fact, with the numerous comparisons being made to the latter divine model, one might consider this pericope as primarily pointing to that divine relationship and only secondarily to the human one. Nonetheless, this sermon is best billed as one on marriage.[50]

Possible Preaching Outlines for Pericope 10

I.   The Divine Model
      Christ as head of the church and its Savior (5:23b)
      Christ's love for the church (5:25b)
      What Christ accomplished for the church (5:26–27)
      Christ's care for the church (5:29b–30)
      Church's submission to Christ (5:24a)
      The Christ-church relationship, a mystery (5:32b)
      Move-to-relevance: What marriage teaches us about the relationship of Christ and the church
II. The Human Copy
      Wives' submission to their husbands, as to Christ (5:22, 33b)
      The scope of wives' submission (5:24b)
      Husbands' position as head (5:23a)
      Husbands' role: to love (5:25a, 28–29a, 33a)
      Husbands' exclusive commitment (5:31)
III. *Recognize your role!*
      Specifics on husbands and wives living out their responsibilities

A simpler outline focuses, separately, upon the role of husbands and that of wives, each half of the sermon concluding with an application to the appropriate unit of the spousal pair. This outline creates two "sermonettes"—somewhat unavoidable when two separate groups of people (here, husbands and wives) with distinct responsibilities are addressed.

I.   Role of Husbands (and Christ): *Recognize your role!*
      Christ as head of the church and its Savior (5:23b)
      Christ's love for the church (5:25b)
      What Christ accomplished for the church (5:26–27)
      Christ's care for the church (5:29b–30)
      Husbands' position as head of their wives (5:23a)
      Husbands' role: to love their wives (5:25a, 28–29a, 33a)
      Husbands' exclusive commitment to their wives (5:31)
      Application: Specifics on husbands living out their responsibilities
II. Role of Wives (and the church): *Recognize your role!*
      Church's submission to Christ (5:24a)
      The Christ-church relationship, a mystery (5:32b)
      Wives' submission to their husbands, as to Christ (5:22, 33b)
      The scope of wives' submission to their husbands (5:24b)
      Application: Specifics on wives living out their responsibilities

50. Conceivably, it might be part of a series on marriage (and singleness, of course), a series that fills the hiatus of a couple of weeks taken from the Ephesians program. Perhaps the responsibilities of husbands and wives towards each other could be addressed in separate sermons, too.

PERICOPE 11

Children and Parents; Slaves and Masters

Ephesians 6:1–9

[Children's Obedience, Parents' Care; Slaves' Obedience, Masters' Sincerity]

REVIEW, SUMMARY, PREVIEW

Review of Pericope 10: In Eph 5:21–33, Paul continues the broader theme of the filling by the Spirit of the divine fullness of God in Christ. This particular pericope considers the responsibilities of husbands (to love) and wives (to submit), constantly referring back to the divine model—the relationship of Christ and his bride, the church.

Summary of Pericope 11: This pericope (Eph 6:1–9) carries on the theme of the filling by the Spirit of the divine fullness of God in Christ, and deals with a facet of one of the manifestations of such filling: submission. Children are to obey their parents and parents are to raise their children with care; slaves, too, are to obey their masters and masters are to treat their slaves with sincerity. Ultimate obedience and accountability of all parties concerned are to God in Christ, who is pleased by such submission and who will reward them appropriately.

Preview of Pericope 12: The next pericope, Eph 6:10–24, concludes the letter. Powerful supernatural foes attempt to thwart divine purpose, and their attack is directed against the people of God who are to stand firm. Divine empowerment is provided in the form of God's own armor—a commitment to, and dependence upon, God. With the provision of that armor is also a call to intense and comprehensive prayer. And thereby the church attains divine peace.

11. *Ephesians 6:1–9*

THEOLOGICAL FOCUS OF PERICOPE 11

11   **Relationships of believers conducive to unity in the household are characterized by obedience of children to parents as unto the Lord and the gentle instruction of children by parents, and by slaves obeying their masters and masters treating slaves with sincerity as they both do God's will and serve him, all of which brings reward (6:1–9).**

    11.1   Children, obeying their parents and being rewarded for their obedience, and parents bringing up children in the ways of God, foster the unity of the household, a manifestation of the filling by the Spirit (6:1–4).

        11.1.1   Children obey their parents as if obeying God, and are rewarded for it, even with long life (6:1–3).

        11.1.2   Parents bring up children with gentleness, instructing and disciplining them in the ways of God (6:4).

    11.2   Slaves, obeying their masters with sincerity, and masters treating their slaves likewise, do God's will and serve him, receiving their reward from their impartial Master in heaven (6:5–9).

        11.2.1   Slaves obey their masters with sincerity, doing God's will devotedly and serving him, thus obtaining their reward (6:5–8).

        11.2.2   Masters treat their slaves with sincerity, remembering that they, too, have a Master in heaven who rewards and punishes impartially (6:9).

OVERVIEW

The theme of submission continues in this pericope. It must be remembered that this theme, introduced in Eph 5:21, is the extension of the fifth participle—"submitting"—that qualifies the "filling by the Spirit" (5:18).[1] Such submission is part of what it means to be "filled by the Spirit" with the divine fullness of God in Christ. The first major section that specified how this submission was to take place considered the roles of husbands and wives in marriage (Pericope 10; 5:21–33). However, there the focus was more on one member of the pair—husbands. In this pericope, where the roles of children and parents, and slaves and masters are dealt with, the subordinate ones in each pair—children and slaves—get most of the attention. "Christian children and slaves who heed this apostolic exhortation to obey, and wives who voluntarily submit to their husbands (v. 22), show that they are receptive to the Spirit's work of transforming them into the likeness of God and Christ. They demonstrate that they understand the Lord's will (v. 17)."[2]

---

1. The others—"speaking," "singing," "making melody," and "giving thanks"—were dealt with in Pericope 9 (5:1–20), integrated as "worship."

2. O'Brien, *Ephesians*, 439.

The very fact that all the protagonists were addressed directly—wives (5:22), husbands (5:25), children (6:1), fathers (6:4), slaves (6:5), and masters (6:9)—is itself countercultural, for it is evidence of their presence together in the assembly, at least for the reading of this letter. Besides, it also presupposes some self-determination, assuming the rights of wives, children, and slaves to make decisions for themselves, as to how they would behave towards those in authority over them.

There is a sense of continuity with previous pericopes: what is "right" is recommended in 6:1; earlier, what was "proper" was considered in 5:3, and what was "fitting," in 5:4. "Right" translates δίκαιος (*dikaios*), a cognate of which is δικαιοσύνη (*dikaiosynē*, "righteousness"), employed in 4:24; 5:9; and later in 6:14. "To provoke to anger" is παροργίζω (*parorgizō*; 6:4); παροργισμός (*parorgismos*, "wrath") and ὀργίζω (*orgizō*, "be angry") showed up in 4:26, as well as ὀργή (*orgē*, "wrath") in 4:31. The notion of divine will, in 6:6, has already appeared in 1:1, 5, 9, 11; 5:17; what is "good" (6:8), in 4:28, 29; future judgment (6:8–9), in 5:5–6; "nourish" (6:4), in 5:29; "fear" (6:5), in 5:21, 33; and the contrast with "not . . . but . . ." (6:4, 6), in 5:15–18. Moreover, "in the Lord" (6:1) is also found in 2:21; 4:1, 17; 5:8, 19; 6:10, 21.

11.1 Ephesians 6:1–4

> **THEOLOGICAL FOCUS OF PERICOPE 11.1**
>
> 11.1 Children, obeying their parents and being rewarded for their obedience, and parents bringing up children in the ways of God, foster the unity of the household, a manifestation of the filling by the Spirit (6:1–4).
>
> 11.1.1 *Children obey their parents as if obeying God, and are rewarded for it, even with long life (6:1–3).*
>
> 11.1.2 *Parents bring up children with gentleness, instructing and disciplining them in the ways of God (6:4).*

TRANSLATION 11.1

6:1 *Children, obey your parents in the Lord, for this is right.*

6:2 *"Honor your father and mother" (which is the first commandment with a promise),*

6:3 *"so that it may be well with you, and that you may be long-lived on the earth."*

6:4 *And fathers, do not provoke your children to anger, but bring them up in the discipline and instruction of the Lord.*

NOTES 11.1

11.1.1 Children obey their parents as if obeying God, and are rewarded for it, even with long life.

The instruction to children and fathers has an *inclusio* at either end, with "children" and "Lord" showing up in both 6:1 and 6:4, surrounding an OT citation:

> **A** *"Children,* obey your parents *in the Lord"* (6:1)
> **B** OT citation (6:3)
> **A'** "Do not provoke your *children";* "instruction *of the Lord"* (6:4)

In syntax, the commands to children and slaves resemble those to wives: in all cases such subjection to their respective authorities is "as to the Lord" (5:22), "in the Lord" (6:1), "as to Christ," or "as to the Lord" (6:6, 7). However, unlike the wife who is only asked to submit herself—there is a degree of voluntariness in the middle voice of the verb (in 5:21, and implied in 5:22)—the other two, children and slaves, are required to "obey," with the verb in the active voice (6:1, 5).

We are given no clue as to the age of the "children" (τέκνα, *tekna*) addressed in Eph 6:1. Besides the obvious connotation of those who are young in age and under the responsibility and care of their parents (Matt 2:18; 7:11; 15:26; 19:29; 22:24), the word can also be used of one old enough to be a believer (Matt 10:21), to labor in the field (Matt 21:28), to be responsible for one's actions (Mark 2:5; Luke 15:31; 16:25; John 8:39), to commit murder (Matt 10:21), to follow Jesus as a disciple (Mark 10:24), and to teach others (1 Cor 4:17). As well, τέκνα is generically used of offspring without any indication of age (Matt 3:9; 23:37; 27:25; Mark 7:27; Luke 7:35; John 1:12; Rom 8:16; etc.); such is the case with the word used elsewhere in Ephesians (2:3; 5:1, 8). Of course, it is also used of Jesus Christ, the "Son" of God (Acts 13:33). At any event, that children are directly addressed here in Eph 6:1–4 suggests that they were at least old enough to understand and obey. In light of contemporary Roman and Hellenistic Jewish understanding of parental obedience as encompassing the submission of even adult children, this is likely to be the intention in 6:1–4, too: a wide variety of ages of children is envisaged. Indeed, disobedience to parents was a mark of the depravity of the Gentiles (Rom 1:30) and a sign of the chaotic evil pervading the last days (2 Tim 3:2).

The phrase "in the Lord" qualifies the verb "obey" rather than "parents."[3] The sense is that to obey one's parents is tantamount to obeying God, for it is God's word in the Decalogue that requires such honoring of parents. Except parents, no other set of humans are deemed worthy of this esteem. Elsewhere in the OT, disobedience and rebellion against parents is to dishonor Yahweh, and is equated with treason and idolatry: Exod 21:15, 17; Lev 19:3; 20:9; Deut 21:18–21; 27:16.[4] So much so, the relationship between Yahweh and his people is likened to that between a father and his children (Deut 1:31; 8:2–5; Prov 3:11–12).[5] Indeed, in Lev 19:3, children are called to "fear" their fathers and mothers, a reverence usually reserved for God (19:14, 32),

3. Some manuscripts, versions, and church fathers do not use the phrase "in the Lord," though it is well represented in others. It is unlikely to have been added in, since the usual form in the Ephesian household code is "as to," rather than "in," the Lord/Christ.

4. The death penalty was recommended for children who dishonored their parents: Lev 20:9; Deut 21:18–21. Philo alludes to this in *On the Special Laws* 2.232, as also does Josephus, *Against Apion* 2.206, 217; *Antiquities* 4.264. Thus, with capital punishment for these offenses, there is, in God's economy, a shortening of life for dishonoring parents—a fact pertinent to the topic of this section.

5. O'Brien, *Ephesians*, 442n13.

and for God's sanctuary (19:30). Such a view of one's parents as being only below God in the hierarchy of authorities to be obeyed was common in contemporary Judaism.[6] The OT also called for obedience to parents in Prov 1:8–9; 3:11–12; 17:25; etc.[7] And this obedience "in the Lord" is "right" (Eph 6:1), i.e., it is demanded in the Torah as what God requires.

In other words, obedience is part of spiritual formation and discipleship to God, a mark of a follower of Christ, and not simply a response to authority. And, not least, such submission to parents is integral to, and a sign of, being filled by the Spirit (Eph 5:18). It promotes the unity of the home, and thus of the church and of society, and is an important step forward in the consummation of all things in Christ (1:10), the overarching thrust of Ephesians.

Here also, as other parts of the household code in this letter, the discussion is not intended to be exhaustive: the limits of filial obedience are not stated. Clearly such obedience would not include sin, for that would not be "in the Lord" (Eph 6:1). Many things go unmentioned: age of children, quality of parents, specific situation and the parental command involved, etc.

The citation of the Decalogue in Eph 6:2–3 appears to be closer to Deut 5:16 than to Exod 20:12. The clause "that it may be well with you" is absent in Exod 20:12; however, it does show up in the LXX of both Exod 20:12 and Deut 5:16. In any case, the OT reference in both Deuteronomy and Exodus to the land as a portion "which the Lord, your God, has given you" is omitted here in Eph 6:2–3.[8] The theological thrust of that OT command is thereby brought out in its universalization to all peoples, beyond the scope of a particular nation that was living upon a particular tract of land granted to them by Yahweh in a particular part of the world. In other words, the shift of context from ancient text (Decalogue for the Israelites in Canaan) to modern audience has necessitated a *theological* interpretive movement to include all the people of God, irrespective of era and station.[9] This, too, is a reflection of the consummating work of

---

6. As Philo notes: "[I]n my opinion, what God is to the world, that parents are to their children; since, just as God gave existence to that which had no existence, they also, in imitation of his power, as far at least as they were able, make the race of mankind everlasting" (*On the Special Laws* 2.225). Also see ibid., 2.235; *Decalogue* 119–120; and *Life of Moses* 2.198, for similar sentiments.

7. In contemporary Roman culture, the father had absolute power over his children, whatever their age or status in life—the *patria potestas* ("power of the father"). Dionysius of Halicarnassus (*Antiquitates romanae* 2.26.4) wrote: "[T]he lawgiver of the Romans gave virtually full power to the father over his son, even during his whole life, whether he thought proper to imprison him, to scourge him, to put him in chains and keep him at work in the fields, or to put him to death, and this even though the son were already engaged in public affairs, though he were numbered among the highest magistrates, and though he were celebrated for his zeal for the commonwealth." Such a father was allowed to sell his son, not once but thrice—if that enslaved individual were freed twice, that is—a power greater than that of any master over a slave (ibid., 2.27.1).

8. This omission of the Decalogue's reference to the Promised Land was apparently also the practice in later Judaism: Sir 3:1–16 expounds on children's responsibilities to parents and never mentions the promise of land. Neither does Philo in *On the Special Laws* 2.261, as he quotes the commandment from the Decalogue: "'Honor father and mother, that it may be well with you, and that it may be long life.'"

9. See Kuruvilla, *Privilege the Text!* 89–150.

God in Christ, as all (believing) humanity is included in the category of God's people (see Pericope 4; Eph 2:11–22).

The question of why this is labeled "the first commandment with a promise" (Eph 6:2) is puzzling. It has been noted that the second commandment in the Decalogue that forbids idolatry (Deut 5:8–10), and the third that forbids taking the name of Yahweh in vain (5:11), appear to carry "promises" of punishment for their respective violations. In matter of fact, such "promises" are actually threats. The first "promise" (= reward) comes only with the fourth commandment, that mandates honoring of parents (Deut 5:16).[10]

When are these promises of Eph 6:3 fulfilled? The retention of "on the earth" in Eph 6:3 from the Decalogue suggests that fulfillment occurs in this life. That it does not deal with eternal life is obvious: eternal life is *eternal*, and those possessing it would not need to be described as "*long-lived* on the earth." All that to say, as with many of God's promises, there are practical consequences for the behavior of God's people in this life, with rewards in the here and now accompanying obedience (along with discipline for disobedience).[11] What the promised "wellness" of 6:3a will look like, or what shape it will take, is not specified. It is best to accept this as a promise that a trustworthy God will keep; indeed, he will, even regarding the longevity of life promised in 6:3b.

But does obedience to parents really yield long life? The common scholarly approach to this is to consider it proverbial and aphoristic, i.e., what the commandment declares is only a general truth with a number of exceptions (innocent children dying early deaths, disrespectful children living long, etc.). As against this interpretive mindset, I suggest that one consider this commandment—and others of this sort in any genre of Scripture—in a more holistic fashion. One must acknowledge that there are a number of causes for longevity: inherited genes, refraining from addictions, eating well, exercising appropriately, driving carefully, treating illnesses, etc. And Eph 6:2–3 adds yet another condition to this list: obedience to/honoring of parents. There is no reason to suspect that this promise is false or that it comes to pass only infrequently or that it is only partially true. I would much rather affirm that, *all other causes and conditions being the same,* obeying one's parents *will* increase one's lifespan.[12] I do

---

10. One might argue that Deut 5:10 has God "promising" lovingkindness to those who serve him, but that seems simply to be a description of God—one who *visits* iniquity on the rebellious and *shows* lovingkindness to those who serve him. Both verbs are participles, qualifying the main clause: "I, Yahweh, your God, [am] a jealous God." With regard to the Decalogue in Exod 20:1–17, the command to honor father and mother is also the first with a promise (= reward), though threats similar to those in Deut 5 are appended to commandments #2 and #3 in Exod 20. However, in Exodus, unlike in Deuteronomy, there are a number of other commandments with promises (= reward) *before* the Decalogue: Exod 12:13; 15:26; 19:5–6. Thus it is probably best to stick with reading Eph 6:2 as reflecting the Deuteronomic version of the Decalogue.

11. For this concept of blessing in this life for obedience, see Kuruvilla, *Privilege the Text!* 252–58. That, of course, does not rule out abundant blessings in the life to come, including rewards for obedience.

12. To these causes, one might well add the numerous utterances in Proverbs that promise life by eschewing violence (Prov 1:19), avoiding naiveté (1:32; 10:21; 14:12; 21:16), obeying God (Prov 3:1–2; 4:10), being wise (Prov 3:16; 9:11; 13:14; 15:24), resisting adultery (Prov 5:5, 23; 7:27; 9:18), fearing God

not venture to say by how many milliseconds, minutes, hours, days, weeks, months, or decades, but I would maintain that honoring parents *does* prolong life, by some amount. The contrary is true as well: sin reduces lifespan. Again, I would not quantify the amount of decrease per unit of sin and by degree or extent of sin. But I would aver that sin *does* reduce length of life. That might not be far from being scientifically demonstrable either.

11.1.2   *Parents bring up children with gentleness, instructing and disciplining them in the ways of God.*

As head of the household, only the father is addressed in Eph 6:4. Yet πατέρες (*pateres*, "fathers") could very well include mothers as well, as in Heb 11:23, where the word means "parents." That Eph 6:4 begins with "and" emphasizes the mutuality of the relationship and focuses on the respective responsibilities of the parties involved: children obey their parents *and* parents (fathers) foster their children.

In light of the mores of contemporary Roman society and those of Hellenistic Judaism, that afforded parents considerable power over the lives of their children (as was noted earlier[13]), it is quite countercultural that Paul sanctions no such authority in the hands of parents. Here they are asked to treat their wards with utmost care and concern.

Anger had already been condemned as inappropriate for the people of God, especially if it led to sin (Eph 4:26, 31). Here, fathers' provocation of their children to anger is proscribed, perhaps to prevent such anger from leading to sin and providing opportunities for the devil (4:27). Thus "excessively severe discipline, unreasonably harsh demands, abuse of authority, arbitrariness, unfairness, constant nagging and condemnation, subjecting a child to humiliation, and all forms of gross insensitivity to a child's needs and sensibilities" is ruled out.[14] While there is nothing here about paternal love for children, perhaps that may safely be assumed.

Instead of provoking to anger, parents are to "bring up" (ἐκτρέφω, *ektrephō*, "nourish," was also used in 5:29 of Christ's concern and care for his bride) their children in the "discipline and instruction of the Lord" (6:4). "Discipline and instruction" likely reflects the tendency of Paul in this letter to use synonyms; it is best not to distinguish too finely between the two facets of childrearing. Yet some distinction may be safely made: "discipline" (παιδεία, *paideia*) can indicate both training/instruction (Acts 7:22;

(Prov 10:27; 14:27; 19:23: 22:4), displaying righteousness (Prov 11:4, 19, 30; 16:17; 19:16: 21:21), refusing wickedness (Prov 12:7; 15:27; 22:22–23), speaking guardedly (Prov 13:3; 21:6), as well as honoring parents (Prov 20:20; 30:17). Rather than consign these to the category of sententious moralisms that are not necessarily true all the time, I would affirm that they are *always* true. Again, I would not dare to speculate on the length of time these habits add to one's life, but I am convinced that they *will* do so, *all other factors remaining equal.*

13. The Israelite patriarchal structure also afforded the father considerable control of his children of any age: they could be stoned (Deut 13:6–11; 21:18–21), or sold into slavery (Exod 21:7).

14. Lincoln, *Ephesians*, 406. Pseudo-Phocylides (ca. sixth century BCE), *Sentences* 207, warns against treating children severely: "Be not harsh with your children, but be gentle." So also Plutarch, *On the Education of Children* 12: "This also I assert, that children ought to be led to honorable practices by means of encouragement and reasoning, and most certainly not by blows or ill-treatment, for it surely is agreed that these are fitting rather for slaves than for the free-born."

22:3; 2 Tim 3:16; Titus 2:12) and correction/punishment (1 Cor 11:32; 2 Cor 6:9; Heb 12:5, 7, 8, 11). Probably the latter, correction, is the emphasis here—Heb 12:8 uses παιδεία to describe how God deals with his children. On the other hand, "instruction" (νουθεσία, *nouthesia*) may be focusing on the training aspect.[15] So the father (standing in for both parents) was responsible to educate his sons in the way of the Lord (Exod 10:2; 12:25; 13:8; Deut 4:9; 6:7, 20–21; 11:19; 32:7, 46; Prov 19:18; 22:6; Sir 7:23; also see Heb 12:6–7), with discipline playing a key role (Deut 8:5; 2 Sam 7:14; Prov 13:24; 22:15; 23:13–14; 29:15, 17; Sir 30:1–13).[16]

The discipline and instruction are to be "of the Lord," i.e., a subjective or possessive genitive: discipline and instruction coming from the Lord or prescribed by him. "The fathers are the Lord's agents and, therefore, raise their children according to his mandates."[17] In other words, fathers, surrogates for God the Father—after all, God is the ultimate Father, Eph 3:14–15; 4:6—care for their children as God does for his. Such "discipline and instruction" is equivalent to "learning Christ" and being "taught in him" (4:20–21). Thus we have a "Christian education" program not only at the church-wide level, but also within familial units that compose the larger body.

> Within the pagan household the training of the children, especially sons, would be directed to the end of preparing them to fulfill their proper role in the household and in the community at large. In Ephesians, fathers are admonished to form their children to fulfill their proper ends as people of the Lord. That is, the formation of children in the household should be in the light of their identity as Christians, not primarily as members of a specific family or citizens of a particular city. The primary role of the phrase "of the Lord" is properly to locate the primary loyalty of Christians and the importance of making that known in the formation of children and all others.[18]

Thus both children and fathers (parents) contribute to the solidarity and unity of the home, thus strengthening the pillars of society, ultimately helping bring about the "consummation of all things in Christ," a grand unity of the cosmos under God, for God.

11.2 Ephesians 6:5–9

THEOLOGICAL FOCUS OF PERICOPE 11.2

11.2 Slaves, obeying their masters with sincerity, and masters treating their slaves likewise, do God's will and serve him, receiving their reward from their impartial Master in heaven (6:5–9).

---

15. Philo uses both words together in *On God* 54; *On the Special Laws* 2.239; 4.96.

16. Hoehner, *Ephesians*, 794–95. Mothers and grandmothers apparently exercised these same responsibilities, as evidenced in 2 Tim 1:5; 3:15. Corporate discipline is clearly involved, though the issues of what kind of corporal discipline and how much of it, the age of children this could be administered to, etc., are not the concerns of the apostle here. In any case, the Christian must bear in mind that over 1,500 child fatalities due to abuse were recorded in the U.S. in 2012, 80 percent of the cases involving parents as abusers! For statistics, see www.childwelfare.gov.

17. Ibid., 799.

18. Fowl, *Ephesians*, 195.

> **11.2.1** *Slaves obey their masters with sincerity, doing God's will devotedly and serving him, thus obtaining their reward (6:5–8).*
>
> **11.2.2** *Masters treat their slaves with sincerity, remembering that they, too, have a Master in heaven who rewards and punishes impartially (6:9).*

TRANSLATION 11.2

6:5 *Slaves, obey your masters according to the flesh, with fear and trembling, in sincerity of your heart, as to Christ,*

6:6 *not with eye-service, as people-pleasers, but as slaves of Christ, doing the will of God from the soul,*

6:7 *serving with zeal, as to the Lord, and not to people,*

6:8 *knowing that whatever good each one does, this he will receive back from the Lord, whether slave or free.*

6:9 *And masters, do the same things to them, giving up threatening, knowing that both their Master and yours is in heaven, and there is no partiality with Him.*

EXCURSUS ON SLAVERY

Though legally, Roman law distinguished between slaves and the free in terms of power, in practice such distinctions were not sharp, a smooth gradation of status existed between the two categories. "For example, slaves of Greek owners could own property, including their own slaves, and could obtain permission to take other employment in addition to their duties as slaves. . . . [I]n general slaves were treated reasonably well, if only because their masters recognized that this was the way to get the best out of them."[19] The institution of slavery was a fixture in Mediterranean economic life, part and parcel of the labor structure of that day. Besides, "the change of legal status out of enslavement into liberty, by way of manumission, was as constant and as easy in Greco-Roman life as the reverse transition over the short passage from individual freedom of action into the constraints of nonfreedom; and the methods employed for making either transition were many."[20] That is quite unlike modern conceptions of slavery in many parts of the world where movement from one class to another—or at least from slavery to freedom—is almost impossible. Indeed, in ancient days, "many slaves had talents and skills useful to their owners; they might work at some craft in a business; while in larger households some did the 'dirty' work, others found openings as musicians, medical advisers, educators, stewards, mistresses, companions of the elderly. Sometimes owners hired them out to work for others and were paid for their work."[21] It has been estimated by some that up to a third of the population of the Roman Empire were slaves.[22] All that to say, slavery in the Greco-Roman times was not

19. Lincoln, *Ephesians*, 416–17.

20. Westermann, "Between Slavery and Freedom," 215.

21. Best, *Ephesians*, 574.

22. Scheidel, "Human Mobility in Roman Italy, I," 9; also see "Human Mobility in Roman Italy, II," 64–71.

what modern-day slavery is. With all this in mind, the closest analogy to this ancient situation in modern times is the employer-employee relationship, though there are differences, of course. In any case, this will be the focus of application for a sermon on this pericope (see below).

That is not to say that the ancient institution was not deplorable, or that it needed no change. The reality was that slaves were looked upon as economic tools, to satisfy the selfish desires of their masters. Aristotle noted that there is no need to consider justice in the relationship between "craftsman and tool, soul and body, master and slave"—"there is no friendship nor justice towards lifeless things. . . . [T]he slave is a living tool and the tool a lifeless slave" (*Nicomachean Ethics* 8.11). He did not consider the use of slaves and of tame animals very different, "for both with their bodies minister to the needs of life" (*Politics* 1.1254). But this was not uniformly the case in Greco-Roman society. The first-century Stoic philosopher Seneca was far more humanitarian in his recommendations (*Epistle* 47): "'These people are slaves.' No: they are human beings. 'These people are slaves.' No: they are those with whom you share your roof. 'These people are slaves.' No: when you consider how much power Chance can exert over you both, they are fellow-slaves. . . . But this is the kernel of my advice: Treat your inferiors as you would be treated by your superiors." For the most part, Hellenistic Judaism concurred: masters were not to abuse slaves.[23] Philo (*Decalogue* 167), discusses various Mosaic commandments—"some to servants, encouraging them to show an affectionate service towards their masters, others to the masters recommending them to practice that gentleness and mildness towards their slaves, by which the inequality of their respective conditions is in some degree equalized." Regarding the value of slaves, Seneca also declared (*De Beneficiis* 3.18): "The path of virtue is closed to no one, it lies open to all; it admits and invites all, whether they be free-born men, slaves or freed-men, kings or exiles; it requires no qualifications of family or of property, it is satisfied with a mere man."

No, there is no direct condemnation of slavery in this section of Pericope 11 (Eph 6:5–9), but the level of mutual respect and reciprocity of actions exhorted here erodes the "function" (the traditional conduct of slaves and masters) that makes the "form" (the very institution of slavery) harder to sustain.[24] Thus the failure here in Ephesians is not on the part of the text (or its author); rather the failure is of those who refuse to live by the demands of its radical Christianity that, because of the impartiality of God, view humans as equal in essence as bearers of the divine image (6:9).[25] Hoehner declares: "The abolition of slavery is a modern phenomenon. Certainly Paul and the early Christian church did not advocate the abolition of slavery as an insti-

---

23. See Sir 7:20, 21; 33:31; Philo, *On the Special Laws* 2.66–68, 89–91; 3.137–43; Pseudo-Phocylides, *Sentences* 223–27.

24. Other passages dealing with slaves have similar thrusts: 1 Cor 7:21–24; Col 3:22–24; 1 Tim 6:1–2; Titus 2:9–10; Philemon; 1 Pet 2:18–25.

25. It seems likely that the Ephesians (and others in Paul's circle) had received further instruction on these matters: notice the participle "knowing" in both 6:8 and 6:9; there is an assumption that both slaves and masters knew more than what was written here about these matters.

tution. Christianity's emphasis has always been on the transformation of individuals who will in turn influence society, not the transformation of society which will then transform individuals (1 Cor 1:8—2:16)."[26] I might note, *pace* Hoehner, that the abolition of slavery—or at least attempts at abolition—are *not* modern. One of the first references in Christian literature—indeed, perhaps in *all* literature—calling for the abolition of slavery comes from Gregory of Nyssa in the fourth century CE (*Homilies on Ecclesiastes* 4 [on Eccl 2:7]). He considered a slave-owner as one "who appropriates to himself what belongs to God and attributes to himself power over the human race as if he were its lord."

> You condemn man who is free and autonomous to servitude, and you contradict God by perverting the natural law. Man, who was created as lord over the earth, you have put under the yoke of servitude as a transgressor and rebel against the divine precept. You have forgotten the limit of your authority which consists in jurisdiction over brutish animals. Scripture says that man shall rule birds, beasts, fish, four-footed animals and reptiles. How can you transgress the servitude bestowed upon you and raise yourself against man's freedom by stripping yourself of the servitude proper to beasts? . . . Do not these [i.e., suffering and cheerfulness, joy and sadness, grief and pleasure, wrath and fear, pain and death] belong to both slave and lord who breathe the same air and look upon the sun? Does not food nourish them both? Do not they have the same intestines? Do not both become dust in death? Is there not one standard? Is there not a common rule and a common hell? How can you who are equal in all things have superiority so that as man, you consider yourself as man's ruler and say "I have servants and maidens" as if they were goats or cattle?

So perhaps it is not surprising—though it is certainly countercultural—that slaves are addressed here in Eph 6:5–8 on an equal footing with masters, as those with the same standing as their owners in the body of Christ, before God (in Phlm 1, 7, 16, 20, both master and slave are called "brother"), and with an assumption of at least some degree of self-determination. Some of these slaves might well have been leaders in the church. Pliny, in a letter to the Emperor Trajan (*Epistle* 10.97.8), writes of torturing two Christian female slaves, "who were called *ministers*" (from *ministra,* which is synonymous with *diāconus,* "deacon"). The Pastoral Epistles do not list freedom as a qualification for holding church office.

The Ephesian text we are dealing with brings out equality among the social classes of the day in other ways, too: slaves "do" (Eph 6:6), slaves and freedmen "do" (6:8), and masters "do" (6:9): all are equally "doers," and all these "doings" of the various individuals are equally taken into account by the impartial Master in heaven (6:9). Besides, both slave and masters receive parallel commands:

	Slaves (Ephesians 6:5–8)	Masters (Ephesians 6:9)
Imperative	"Obey" (6:5a)	"Do the same things" (6:9a)
	"doing the will of God" (6:6b)	"giving up threatening" (6:9b)
Participles	"serving" (6:7)	
	"knowing ..." (6:8)	"knowing ..." (6:9c)

26. Hoehner, *Ephesians,* 804.

The final participle in each section, "knowing" (6:8, 9c), emphasizes the equal standing of each party before God. Slaves are to obey "knowing that" recompense is just (6:8), and masters are to do the same things "knowing that" the heavenly Master is fair (6:9). As well, slaves will receive "back" (παρά; *para*) from the Lord (6:8), and masters are aware there is no partiality "with" (also παρά) the Lord (6:9): they, too, will receive back their due. Thus, there is a constant emphasis in this section on "the leveling effect that Christ's lordship has on human relationships, and the reciprocity that should result from this among members of the household."[27]

NOTES 11.2

11.2.1   Slaves obey their masters with sincerity, doing God's will devotedly and serving him, thus obtaining their reward.

The command to slaves and masters in 6:5–9 is chiastic in structure:

> **A**   *Masters* (6:5)
>> **B**   *Eye-service* (ὀφθαλμοδουλία, *ophthalmodoulia*);
>> as *slaves* (δοῦλοι, *douloi*) of Christ, *doing* the will of God (6:6)
>>> **C**   *Serving* (δουλεύω, *douleuō*) with zeal, as to the Lord (6:7)
>> **B'**   Whatever good each one *does*;
>> whether *slave* (δοῦλος, *doulos*) or free (6:8)
> **A'**   *Masters;* their *Master* (6:9)

Notice the consistent focus on serving—the words with δουλ- (*doul-*): "eye-service" and "slaves" (6:6); "serving" (6:7); and "slave" (6:8). But ultimately it was not their earthly masters being "served," but Christ, the heavenly Master (6:9). A contrast is made between "masters according to the flesh" (6:5) and the "Master . . . in heaven" (6:9). It is to this latter Master of all—even of slaves *and* masters—that slaves owe their ultimate allegiance and loyalty. It is to be noted that Paul uses κύριος (*kyrios*) for "master" in 6:5 and 6:9, not the more common and unambiguous δεσπότης (*despotēs*) as in some of the other passages dealing with slave-master relationships (1 Tim 6:1; Titus 2:9; 1 Pet 2:18). Pointedly, then, κύριος sustains the wordplay: slaves are to serve the κύριος in heaven, not the κύριος according to the flesh.

Thus what Paul commanded the slaves—to obey their masters with "fear and trembling" and "as to Christ," "doing the will of God from the soul" (6:5–6)—had already been demanded of all members in the community of Christians, who were to learn "what is pleasing to the Lord" (5:10), to "understand what the will of the Lord is" (5:17), and to be "submitting to one another in the fear of Christ" (5:21). God's will comes to pass in the life of Paul (1:1), it predestines believers in eternity past (1:5), it is being carried out in the consummation of all things in Christ (1:9, 11), it is to be comprehended and executed by believers (5:17), and now by slaves (6:6): at every level God's will is being done, from one end of the cosmos to the other, from the beginning

---

27. Thielman, *Ephesians*, 404.

of time till its end, in the life of an apostle and in the life of a slave. That also mandates the responsibility of God's children to abide by the divine will and, in a sense, to bring it to pass. The comparisons in 6:5–7 show how slaves are to behave towards their masters in light of their acknowledgement of Christ as "Lord":

> **A** "As [ὡς, *hōs*] to Christ" (6:5)
> **B** "Not … as [ὡς] people-pleasers" (6:6a)
> **B'** "But as [ὡς] slaves of Christ" (6:6b)
> **A'** "As [ὡς] to the Lord" (6:7)

How slaves should obey their masters is thereby described in four phrases, each with ὡς (*hōs*, "as"): "with fear and trembling, in sincerity of your heart *as* to Christ"; "not with eye-service *as* people-pleasers"; "*as* slaves of Christ, doing the will of God from the soul"[28]; and "serving with zeal, *as* to the Lord." "[A]lthough their actions are often governed by the will of another, the nature of his admonitions indicates that Paul takes them to be in full control of their inner dispositions."[29]

"Fear" (6:5) was already mentioned in the household code in 5:21, 33. The joint terminology of "fear and trembling" is elsewhere used in the NT to designate not terror or panic, but the attitude of an inferior before a superior—a recognition, by the former, of the authority of the latter (Mark 5:33; 1 Cor 2:3; 2 Cor 7:15; Eph 6:5; Phil 2:12; Heb 12:21).[30] Since it is Christian masters who are subsequently addressed, this "fear" has the same force as that of the wife for her husband (Eph 5:33), a demeanor of deferential respect. "Sincerity of your heart" (6:5) qualifies the attitude of "fear and trembling": it denotes purity of motive and singleness of purpose. And such an obedience is to be displayed "as to Christ," "as slaves of Christ," and "as to the Lord" (6:5, 6, 7). And by expressing such an attitude, "from the Lord" they would get their reward (6:8). It is not that the master represents Christ to the slave, but that "the master is factored out of the equation and replaced with the Lord."[31] This kind of intense commitment of slaves to Christ comes with an equally powerful recognition of their ultimate Master and his rule over, and governance of, not only their lives, but everything in the cosmos. "Ultimately, then, the distinction between the sacred and the secular breaks down. Any and every task, however menial, falls within the sphere of his lordship and is done in order to please him."[32]

---

28. Or "innermost being," or even "heart."

29. Fowl, *Ephesians*, 195.

30. The phrase is also common in the LXX: Gen 9:2; Exod 15:16; Deut 2:25; Ps 2:11; Isa 19:16.

31. Thielman, *Ephesians*, 406. This is true of the submission of wives to husbands as well—"as to the Lord" (5:22). But in that case, in the command to husbands, these men are, in a sense, to represent Christ to their wives (5:25–30). Perhaps the reason for almost removing the master from the picture is a recognition by Paul of the inherent injustice of the entire system; that would also explain the redundancies in 6:5–8, drawing attention to the true Master and the divine one to whom slaves (and those free) ultimately owe their allegiance.

32. O'Brien, *Ephesians*, 450.

This obedience of slaves, in fear and trembling and with sincerity of heart as to Christ, is given a negative counterpart: obedience merely as "eye-service"[33] performed by fawning "people-pleasers" (6:6). Slaves are not to be "people-pleasers," but "slaves of Christ"—in effect, "Christ-pleasers"—"doing the will of God from the soul" (6:6), for it is in doing his will that his pleasure is gained (5:10, 17). That slaves are called to be obedient to their masters also means that masters (at least those who were Christian) should not be forcing such obedience upon their slaves (just as husbands are not given the right to force the submission of their wives). Ultimately, however, these slaves were "slaves of Christ" (6:6), performing their services with "zeal" (6:7). Rather than "performing [from ποιέω, *poieō*] the desires [θελήμα, *thelēma*] of the flesh" as unbelievers (2:3), here believers (slaves) are "doing [ποιέω] the will [θελήμα] of God from the soul" as slaves of Christ (6:6).[34] Rendering service to God with "zeal," not to men (6:7), they would be rewarded by God who sees and values heartfelt ("from the soul") commitment to him (6:8). In this verse and the next, Paul treats future motivation of rewards as present incentive for behavior, first of slaves (6:8), and then of masters (6:9).[35] There is an emphasis on "each one" that shows up early in 6:8 (literally: "knowing that each one, whatever good he does"[36]): God does not forget; he rewards both those who are slaves *and* those who are free. Social status and degree of freedom are no constraints for divine rewards. God, after all, is not partial to such things (6:9).[37] There is no hint that such rewards include manumission for slaves: that may or may not happen, but this promise of rewards will be fulfilled on the day of Christ (Rom 2:6; 2 Cor 5:10), though what exactly those rewards will be is unclear.

11.2.2 *Masters treat their slaves with sincerity, remembering that they, too, have a Master in heaven who rewards and punishes impartially.*

Masters are, in turn, exhorted to "do the same things" to their slaves (6:9)—i.e., to demonstrate the same sincerity of heart as they relate to their slaves, "as to Christ," "doing the will of God from the soul," serving "as to the Lord" (6:5–7), and expecting similar rewards from an impartial judge (6:9). That Christ, the "Lord" (κύριος, 6:7, 8), is the true "Master" (κύριος, 6:9b) of both slave and "master" (κύριος, 6:9a) is a reminder that masters, themselves, are slaves, too, fellow-slaves with their own slaves of the same Master in heaven.

Paul's exhortation must have been quite shocking in a culture where the abuse of slaves was not entirely uncommon (noted earlier). Tacitus (*Annales* 14.44) writes of slaves: "[Y]ou will never coerce such a medley of humanity except by terror." Seneca,

33. Here and in Col 3:22 are found the only instances of the word ὀφθαλμοδουλία (*ophthalmodoulia*) in the NT and, indeed, in all extant Greek literature.

34. Heil, *Ephesians*, 264.

35. The concept of future motivation for present behavior was already broached in 5:5–6.

36. For good works, performed in the power of God, see: Eph 2:10; Col 1:9–12; 2 Cor 9:8; 2 Thess 2:16–17; Heb 13:20–21.

37. God's impartiality is noted in Deut 10:17; 2 Chr 19:7; Sir 35:12–13; *Jub.* 5.16; 21.4; 30.16; 33.18; *T. Job* 43.13; Gal 2:6; Col 3:25, as well as in Eph 6:9.

though, questions the right of a master to punish a slave with whipping and shackling (*De Ira* 3.24.1), and bids one wait till anger has subsided before imprisoning, flogging, or breaking the legs of a slave (ibid., 3.32.1). Hellenistic Jewish literature tended to be in the same vein (Sir 4:30; 7:20; 33:31). But Paul goes in a diametrically opposite direction: his exhortation to masters in Eph 6:9 ("giving up threatening") "rejects all forms of manipulating, demeaning, or terrifying slaves by threats. In the immediate context, slaves have already been instructed to show respect, sincerity of heart, and goodwill; now masters are urged to treat them in a similar manner."[38] Paul's advice to believing slave masters thus subtly undermines the whole system of slaveholding. Slave-owning believers are, in a sense, to submit to their slaves (5:21), serving their slaves in the same way they desire their slaves to serve them. The threat of violence is impossible in such an arrangement, and without the threat of violence, the whole system of abusive slavery breaks down.

The sense of mutuality affirmed by "do the same things" (6:9), already underscored in 5:21, should not be neutralized. Early Christianity consistently saw true leaders as primarily servants themselves (Matt 20:24–28; Mark 10:41–45; Luke 12:37; John 13:1–17; also see 1 Cor 9:19; Gal 5:13). Moreover, the theology of Ephesians includes all humanity, without exception, in the category of sinners who rebelled against God—husbands and wives, children and parents, slaves and masters (Eph 2:2–3, 11–12; 4:17–19, 22; 5:7–8a). And they are also united as one body in their apprehension of the gospel of grace by faith in Christ and all of the benefits appertaining thereunto (1:7; 2:5, 8–9, 14–22; 4:1–6, 7, 23–24; etc.).[39] Mutual respect and submission in every category of household hierarchy is therefore an integral part of the consummation of all things in Christ.

SERMON FOCUS AND OUTLINES

> **THEOLOGICAL FOCUS OF PERICOPE 11**
>
> 11   Children obey their parents and parents gently instruct their children, and slaves obey their masters with sincerity and masters treat their slaves likewise as they both serve God—all furthering unity and promising reward (6:1–9).

This pericope concludes the theme of the filling by the Spirit of the fullness of God in Christ. Along with Pericope 10 (5:21–33), this one also deals with the "submitting" aspect of such filling, one of five participles qualifying the main imperative, "be filled" (5:18); the others are "speaking," "singing," "making melody," "giving thanks," which were integrated as "worshiping" (see Pericope 9: 5:1–20).

---

38. O'Brien, *Ephesians*, 454. Of course, as with the husband-wife relationship, many questions remain: if threats are illegitimate, how would a master control a rebellious slave? What about slaves in authority over other slaves? Or a Christian slave owned by a non-Christian master? What if a slave held a church office with authority over his owner—how would that change the master-slave relationship? And what are the limits of obedience and submission? Needless to say, this is not an exhaustive treatise on such relationships. And neither should the Bible as whole, be treated as such; it does not—nay, *cannot!*—spell out every possible application for humankind in every age in every quarter of the globe. For the Bible to direct explicitly every possible twist and turn in the life of every individual Christian and of every community of God in every millennium would be absolutely impossible.

39. See Thielman, *Ephesians*, 408–10.

Two pairs of relationships are addressed here: children-parents and slaves-masters. Children are to obey their parents and parents are to rear their children with gentleness; slaves are to obey their masters sincerely and masters are to treat their slaves likewise. All these exhortations are based "in the Lord" (or its variants): ultimate obedience and accountability, of both inferior and superior, is to Christ. And proper exercise of these responsibilities pleases God and brings reward to each party.

The distinctive nature of the two pairs might make it difficult for both areas to be covered in a single sermon. However, if one considers the broader thrust of submission and respect, and the need for inferiors to submit to superiors (whether children or slaves, to parents or masters) and for superiors to treat inferiors with gentleness and concern, a single sermon will suffice. In the outline below, it is in the application that the distinct situations are brought out as arenas in which to actualize the theological thrust of submission and respect. As was noted, the master-slave relationship is best applied here as the employer-employee relationship. The fact remains that in the nine verses of this pericope there are nine references to God: Lord (6:1, 4, 7, 8), Christ (6:5, 6), God (6:6), Master (6:9), Him (6:9). Without a doubt, the broader theological thrust refers to the maintenance of household relationships as unto God.

Possible Preaching Outlines for Pericope 11

I.   The Responsibility
            Submission to superiors as unto Christ (6:1–2, 5–7)
            Concerned oversight by superiors with sincerity (6:4, 9)
            Move-to-relevance: Failure to submit as inferiors and to have concerned oversight as superiors
II.   The Reward
            Promised rewards for submission (6:3, 8)
            Promised rewards for concerned oversight (6:9)
            Move-to-relevance: Consequences of failure to submit and to have concerned oversight
III. The Routine:[40] *Submit to your true Master!*
            Specifics on submitting to God in all relationships
            Specifics for children, for parents, for employees, for employers

It is not unlikely that everyone in a congregation is a child, or a parent, or an employee, or an employer (or various combinations thereof). Therefore, the preacher could conceivably address each category (or each pair, as below) separately.

40. Besides seeking alliteration, I use "Routine" here for another reason: applications in sermons are not intended to be one-time actions that can be done and checked off. Hopefully, such actions as are pastorally recommended—based on the theological thrust of the pericope preached—will become *routine*, incorporated into one's life, so that both the action and the attitude it expresses form habits, and dispositions, and character, ultimately to conform the Christian to the image of Christ (Rom 8:29).

EPHESIANS

I. Children and Parents
- Submission of children to parents (6:1–2)
- Concerned oversight of children by parents (6:4)
- Promised rewards (6:3)
- Move-to-relevance: Failure to submit as children and to have concerned oversight as parents

II. Employees and Employers
- Submission of employees to employers (6: 8)
- Concerned oversight of employees by employers (6:9)
- Promised rewards (6:8–9)
- Move-to-relevance: Failure to submit as employees and to have concerned oversight as employers

III. *Submit to your true Master!*
- Specifics on submitting to God in all relationships
- Specifics for children, for parents, for employees, for employers

PERICOPE 12

Victory in Battle

Ephesians 6:10–24

[Battle; Armor; Prayer; Peace]

REVIEW, SUMMARY

Review of Pericope 11: In Eph 6:1–9, the theme of filling by the Spirit of the divine fullness of God in Christ is continued. Children are to obey their parents and parents are to raise their children with care; slaves, too, are to obey their masters and masters are to treat their slaves with sincerity. Ultimate obedience and accountability of all parties concerned are to God in Christ, who will reward them appropriately.

Summary of Pericope 12: The twelfth and final pericope of Ephesians (6:10–24) brings to a close the letter that has laid out the implications of God's grand and glorious plan to consummate all things in Christ. In the meantime, powerful supernatural foes are attempting to thwart divine purpose, and their attack is directed against the people of God who are to stand firm against these inimical forces. Divine empowerment is provided in the form of God's own armor—a commitment to and dependence upon God, to conform to his virtues and to rely upon him totally. With that also comes a call to intense and comprehensive prayer. And thereby divine peace is attained by the church.

12. Ephesians 12:10–24

> **THEOLOGICAL FOCUS OF PERICOPE 12**
>
> **12   Victory against supernatural foes is achieved by divine empowerment in the form of God's armor—related to the attributes, deeds, and utterances of God—and by constant, alert engagement in Spirit-driven prayer, resulting in divine peace, love, and grace suffusing the lives of believers (6:10–24).**
>
> 12.1   Victory in warfare against supernatural foes is achieved by divine empowerment in the form of God's armor: belt-truth, breastplate-righteousness, shoe-peace, shield-faith, helmet-salvation, and sword-word—each related to the attributes, deeds, or utterances of God (6:10–17).
>
> > 12.1.1   *The power of evil supernatural foes arrayed against the people of God is withstood by their divine empowerment in the form of God's armor (6:10–12).*
> >
> > 12.1.2   *Victory in spiritual warfare is achieved by the employment of God's armor: belt-truth, breastplate-righteousness, shoe-peace, shield-faith, helmet-salvation, and sword-word—each related to the attributes, deeds, or utterances of God (6:13–17).*
>
> 12.2   An essential part of the Christian's spiritual warfare is constant, alert engagement in Spirit-driven prayer for all believers, that they may be bold in their proclamation of God's grand plan for the cosmos (6:18–20).
>
> 12.3   Divine peace and love springing from faith—as manifested in the relationships between God's people—as well as grace, suffuse the lives of those who love the Lord Jesus Christ in sincerity (6:21–24).

OVERVIEW

Thus far it has all been about *walking* (Eph 4:1, 17; 5:2, 8, 15); now the focus shifts to *standing* (6:11, 13 [×2], 14).[1] What was a communal journey through life, aided by the Spirit (5:15–18), now becomes a communal resistance, also aided by the Spirit (6:17, 18). Walking leads to standing, and divine power is required if believers are to stand firm in the strife. And every victory won by believers is another triumph of God over his foes, the antagonistic denizens of the evil realm. As has been mentioned before, the lives of Christians are of tremendous significance in God's grand scheme to consummate all things in the cosmos in Christ, as the battle of the universe is won by the kingdom of light with the final defeat of the kingdom of darkness. In this grand operation, far beyond our sight and even further beyond our ability to conceive and comprehend, every seemingly small skirmish faced by the believer has significant ramifications for the vast campaign. Therefore believers are to stand, and to stand firm!

The connections with previous pericopes include: "power," 6:10–11 and 1:19–20; 3:7, 16, 20; "put on," 6:11, 14 and 4:24; "schemes," 6:11 and 4:14; "devil," 6:11; and 2:2; 4:27; evil spiritual forces, 6:12 and 1:21; 2:2; 3:10; "darkness," 6:12 and 5:8, 11; "heavenlies," 6:12 and 1:3, 20; 2:6; 3:10; "day of evil," 6:13 and 5:16; "truth," 6:14 and 1:13; 4:15, 21, 24, 25; 5:9; "righteousness," 6:15 and 4:24; 5:9; "gospel," 6:15 and 1:13; 3:6; "peace,"

---

1. Also see 1 Cor 10:12; 16:13; Phil 1:27; 1 Thess 3:8; 2 Thess 2:15, for the imagery of "standing."

6:15, 23 and 1:2; 2:14–17; 4:3; "word," 6:17 and 5:26 (also 1:13, but a different Greek word); "faith," 6:16 and 1:13, 15, 19; 2:8; 3:12, 17; 4:5, 13; salvation, 6:17 and 1:13; 2:5, 8; 5:23; "Spirit/spiritual," 6:17, 18 and 1:13, 17; 2:18, 22; 3:5, 16; 4:3, 4, 30; 5:18; "saints," 6:18 and 1:1, 15, 18; 2:19; 3:8, 18; 4:12; 5:3; prayer, 6:18–20 and 1:15–19; 3:14–20; "boldness," 6:19–20 and 3:12; imprisonment, 6:20 and 3:1; 4:1; and "mystery," 6:19 and 1:9; 3:3–4, 9; 5:32. While the recurrences of these significant themes do not necessarily indicate a conclusion or a closing summary here, this pericope is clearly recapitulating the major motifs of the letter.

> Recapitulation takes place as various concerns, themes, and terminology from earlier in the letter are taken up. It is not so much that assertions or exhortations are restated but that they recur in a different form. The same issues—believers' identity, their relation to Christ and to the resources of power in him and in God, their need both to appropriate salvation from God and to live a righteous life in the world, the cosmic opposition to God's purposes for human well-being—appear again but now under new imagery. . . . Through their recapitulation in this guise, these leading themes of the letter are magnified.[2]

But the unique feature and emphasis of this pericope is the battle metaphor.[3] This motif, with God as a warrior equipping his people with his own armor, is frequent in the OT: Ps 35:1–3; Isa 42:13; Hab 3:8, 9; etc. His surrogates and agents (his people) need his power for victory in these campaigns: Pss 19:1, 2, 32, 39; 28:7; 59:11, 16, 17; 68:35; 89:21; 118:14; Isa 52:1; etc. And so divine armor is necessary for these triumphs: Isa 11:4, 5; 52:7; 59:17. Indeed, Wis 5:17–20 (borrowing from Isa 59:17) has: "The Lord will take his zeal as his *whole armor,* and will arm all creation to repel his enemies; he will *put on righteousness* as a *breastplate,* and wear impartial justice as a helmet; he will take holiness as an invincible shield, and sharpen harsh wrath as a sword." Many of these concepts are shared with Eph 6:10–17, though not all the vocabulary is identical (common words in Greek are italicized).[4]

Reinhard notes the balance of divine provision and human responsibility with regard to each item of the divine armor:[5]

---

2. Lincoln, *Ephesians,* 433.

3. The picture of warfare was introduced in Eph 4:8, but there it was Christ battling and victoriously taking captives (also see 1:21–23). There is also the implication of a supernatural battle in 2:1–3, involving hostile forces in control of unbelievers. These forces are mentioned in 1:21–22; 3:10; and 4:27, besides here in Eph 6.

4. Battle metaphors for supernatural engagements are common in ancient writers: Tertullian, *De corona militis* 15; Epictetus, *Discourses* 3.24 (who said "human life is a warfare"); and all of 1QM, the *War Scroll.* Paul himself employed that motif often: Rom 6:13; 13:12; 2 Cor 6:7; 10:3–5; Phil 2:25; 1 Thess 5:8; Phlm 2; as also did other NT writers: 2 Tim 3:3–5; 1 Pet 4:1; and the fathers: Polycarp, *To the Philippians* 4.1; Ignatius, *To Polycarp* 6.2; Shepherd of Hermas, *Mandate* 12.2.4.

5. From Reinhard, "Ephesians 6:10–18," 525–26.

Armor	Divine Provision	Human Responsibility
Truth (6:14)	Salvation through *truth* (1:13) Fruit of light: *truth* (5:9)	Speak *truth* (4:15, 25)
Righteousness (6:14)	New person: *righteousness* (4:24) Fruit of light: *righteousness* (5:9)	Put on the new person (4:24)
Peace (6:15)	*Peace* from God and Christ (1:2) Christ and *peace* (2:14, 17)	Preserve *peace* (4:3)
Faith (6:16)	*Faith:* gift from God (2:8–9) Building up in *faith* (4:11–14)	*Believe* in Christ (1:13)
Salvation (6:17)	*Salvation* by grace (2:5, 8–9) Christ and *salvation* (5:23)	Believe in Christ: *salvation* (1:13)
Word of God (6:17)	*Word* brings salvation (1:13)	Believe the *word* (1:13) Edify with Scripture (5:18–19)

Thus there is a tension between the indicative (what God has done: divine provision) and the imperative (what believers must do: human responsibility; see table above). What God has done must be appropriated and lived out—this is what believers must do.

"The appeals for unity and maturity, for living out the life of the new humanity, for truthful and edifying talk, for honest work, for love, for purity in word and deed, and for wise and Spirit-filled living in marriage, family, and work all depend on believers appropriating the resources they have in God and Christ and resisting the forces that pull in the opposing direction," forces under the control of evil supernatural powers.[6] Therefore, to conclude the epistle with this pericope is quite appropriate. "The individual who engages in productive work or who speaks the truth or who loves his wife is successfully resisting and standing his ground in the fight against the powers."[7] Not only these activities but all that has been demanded of the believer thus far in previous pericopes calls for standing firm in battle: by recognizing divine blessing, acknowledging divine power, being grateful for salvation, practicalizing the union of all (believing) humanity, manifesting divine work in life, expressing the indwelling of the fullness of the Godhead, working for unity in the body, exercising gifts for corporate growth, avoiding sexual immorality, demonstrating the filling by the Spirit in worship and submission, maintaining proper relationships within the household, etc. All these can now be seen to be part of resisting the powers of evil and appropriating Christ's strength. "[T]he appeal is for believers to preserve and appropriate all that has been done for their salvation and their conduct by God in Christ, and to do so in the face of evil, seen from the perspective of its ultimate transcendent source."[8] In fact, part of abiding by divine demand anywhere in Scripture involves resisting evil powers and thereby furthering the kingdom of Christ and God (5:5). "The Church that lives out the ethical exhortations of the letter is the *militia Christi* that has put on the divine

---

6. Lincoln, *Ephesians*, 439.

7. Wild, "The Warrior and the Prisoner," 298.

8. Lincoln, *Ephesians*, 430.

armor and is standing its ground in the battle with evil in all its manifestations."⁹ There is thus an integral connection between what has been said in prior pericopes and what is being said in this one, for tapping into the power of God enables his people to live according to divine demand, despite the maleficent efforts of evil powers to thwart God's will.

All these considered, it is not surprising that the root for "power," δυν- (*dyn-*), occurs a number of times in this pericope: believers are "empowered" (ἐνδυναμόω, *endynamoō*, 6:10), so that they "may be able/may have power" (δύναμαι, *dynamai*, 6:11) to stand against the devil, thus "being able/having power" (δύναμαι, 6:13) to resist in the evil day, and "being able/having power" (δύναμαι, 6:16) to extinguish the evil one's missiles. All this power is absolutely necessary in this battle, because the opponents are "evil"—another word that echoes in this pericope (6:12, of hostile spiritual forces; 6:13, of the current age; and 6:16, of the devil).¹⁰ And besides, Paul wants his readers "to know that their chances of success in this battle are more than possible or even probable: victory will be a reality given their dependence upon the divine power."¹¹

In this closing pericope, then, matters are being looked at from a cosmic perspective. However, the divine demands in the prior pericopes of Ephesians (and, indeed, in every pericope of the Bible) "are not simply matters of personal preference, as many within our contemporary and postmodern world contend. On the contrary, they are essential elements in a larger struggle between the forces of good and evil." Though Christ has already triumphed over his enemies (1:21–22; 4:8), "the fruits of that victory have 'not yet' been fully realized, so Christians must be aware of the conflict and be equipped with divine power to stand against them."¹²

Pericope 12 may be divided as follows:

6:10	Introduction
6:11–12	Foes
6:13–17	Divine armor
6:18–20	Believers' operation
6:21–23	Conclusion

The first verse, 6:10, functions as an introductory statement. Then, 6:11–12 lists the foes that warrant consideration of this battle as serious: believers need serious help in this serious battle. The idea seems to be repeated in 6:13, emphasizing the gravity of the situation, but this verse serves to head the section, 6:13–17, that lists the divine armor that must be donned by believers in this campaign against evil foes. The next three verses, 6:18–20, recall the operation that believers themselves are to engage in: prayer (6:13–17,

---

9. Ibid., 459.

10. Heil, *Ephesians*, 287. Power language earlier in Ephesians is found in 1:19, 21; 3:7, 16, 20 (noun: δύναμις, *dynamis,* "power"); and in 3:4, 20; 6:11, 13, 16 (verb: δύναμαι, *dynamai,* "have power/be able"): δύναμαι is only an auxiliary verb, but the link with δύναμις is unmistakable.

11. Arnold, *Ephesians*, 107.

12. O'Brien, *Ephesians*, 457–58.

on the other hand, mostly dealt with the divine help rendered in the form of armor). Finally, the pericope closes in 6:21–23 with a few concluding remarks from Paul.

12.1 Ephesians 6:10–17

THEOLOGICAL FOCUS OF PERICOPE 12.1

12.1 Victory in warfare against supernatural foes is achieved by divine empowerment in the form of God's armor: belt-truth, breastplate-righteousness, shoe-peace, shield-faith, helmet-salvation, and sword-word—all related to the attributes, deeds, or utterances of God (6:10–17).

> 12.1.1 *The power of evil supernatural foes arrayed against the people of God is withstood by their divine empowerment in the form of God's armor (6:10–12).*

> 12.1.2 *Victory in spiritual warfare is achieved by the employment of God's armor: belt-truth, breastplate-righteousness, shoe-peace, shield-faith, helmet-salvation, and sword-word—each related to the attributes, deeds, or utterances of God (6:13–17).*

TRANSLATION 12.1

6:10 *In the remaining time, be empowered in the Lord, and in the strength of His might.*

6:11 *Put on the whole armor of God, that you may be able to stand against the schemes of the devil.*

6:12 *For our struggle is not against blood and flesh, but against the rulers, against the authorities, against the world-forces of this darkness, against the spiritual beings of evil in the heavenlies.*

6:13 *For this reason, take up the whole armor of God, so that you may be able to withstand in the evil day, and having readied everything, to stand.*

6:14 *Stand therefore, girding your waist with truth, and putting on the breastplate of righteousness,*

6:15 *and shoeing the feet with the preparation of the gospel of peace;*

6:16 *in all, taking up the shield of faith with which you will be able to extinguish all the flaming arrows of the evil one;*

6:17 *and take the helmet of salvation and the sword of the Spirit, which is the word of God.*

NOTES 12.1

There is no question that Paul sees spiritual warfare and the hostile actions of these supernatural forces as impinging upon the daily lives of believers and interfering with their ability to live according to divine demand. Those evil powers—already defeated and subject to Christ (1:21–22)—attempt to thwart the will of God and, therefore, must be resisted in a cosmic struggle of great intensity that requires divine armor, divine power.

> It is striking that a letter which in its first half depicts the peace produced by the gospel should in its second half conclude with an emphasis on war. But this only underlines that God's purposes are not yet complete and that the powers that are hostile to the well-being of believers, to the existence of the Church, and to the advance of the gospel have not yet given up their ultimately futile opposition. In this way, the readers are given a realistic perspective on Christian existence and disabused of any naïve notion that living out their calling in the world will be an effortless or trouble-free assignment.[13]

And thus, the "already, but not yet" theme sounds again.

12.1.1   *The power of evil supernatural foes arrayed against the people of God is withstood by their divine empowerment in the form of God's armor.*

What is normally translated "finally," τοῦ λοιποῦ (*tou loipou*), is likely a shortened from of τοῦ λοιποῦ χρόνου (*tou loipou chronou*) meaning "in the remaining time" or "henceforth," as in Gal 6:17; Josephus, *Jewish Antiquities* 4.187; Shepherd of Hermas, *Similitudes* 9.11.3; Herodotus, *Histories* 2.109.[14] Perhaps after mentioning rewards in the future in Eph 6:9, Paul was refocusing readers back to present time, to get them to be diligent in spiritual warfare "in the remaining time," until those final days when rewards will be obtained.

"The strength of his might" (6:10) was displayed in 1:19, in connection with the resurrection and exaltation of Jesus Christ, God's awesome demonstration of his power. Now that power is being manifested on behalf of his people. Though Paul constantly prayed that God would give readers comprehension of his great strength given to them in Christ (1:17–23), the apostle is now exhorting believers to put that power into action, in the battle against evil foes. There may also be a progression in the level of activity being exhorted: "be empowered" is a *passive* imperative (6:10); "put on" is a *middle* imperative (6:11); and finally there is "take up," an *active* imperative (6:13).[15]

With 6:11, Paul begins to explain how one can "be empowered in the Lord, and in the strength of His might" (6:10), and that is by "donning the divine panoply" (from πανοπλία, *panoplia*, "whole armor"; 6:11, 13).[16] This "putting on" (6:11, 14) is like the "putting on" of the new person in the image of God to be righteous and holy in the truth (4:24). The alliteration is powerful: "be empowered" is ἐνδυναμοῦσθε (*endynamousthe*, 6:10); "put on" is ἐνδύσασθε (*endysasthe*, 6:11). To "be empowered" then is subtly being equated to "putting on" the whole armor of God; that is how the child of God can "stand firm against the schemes of the devil" (6:11).[17] The empowerment exhorted here is "in the Lord," the sphere in which they are strengthened, for believers

13. Lincoln, *Ephesians*, 458.

14. Thielman, *Ephesians*, 417.

15. Heil, *Ephesians*, 277.

16. O'Brien, *Ephesians*, 462. Heil, *Ephesians*, 272, thinks that the emphasis on the "whole/all" (i.e., the παν- [*pan-*] in πανοπλια, *panoplia*, "whole armor"; 6:10) may allude to "all" (also πᾶν) the fullness of God that Paul prays will fill believers (3:19; also 1:23; 4:10; 5:18).

17. Some of the nefarious characters in 6:11–12 were encountered earlier: "rulers" (1:21; 2:2), and "authorities" (1:21).

are hardly able to empower themselves.[18] The "and" (καί, *kai*) is epexegetical, explaining what was said; thus: "be empowered in the Lord, *that is,* in the strength of his might" (6:10).

God is described as an armed warrior in battle in Isa 59:17; both our pericope and Wis 5:16–23 draw from that OT text (also see Isa 11:5 and 52:7 for the messianic armor alluded to in Eph 6).[19] With that source text in mind, it is clearly God's own armor that is being given to his people. In fact, truth, righteousness, peace, and salvation—elements of the armor (Eph 6:14–16)—appear to be characteristics of God himself. Snodgrass may be right: "[I]n the end all the armor language is a way to talk about identification with God and his purposes."[20] Indeed, as we will see later, many of the items of the armor are actually divine virtues.

"Schemes" are found in the NT only in 6:11 and in 4:14; while we are not told what specifically this constitutes or how it works, this is clearly a cunning and devious strategy to defeat believers as they attempt to meet divine demand and glorify God.[21] The "devil" had shown up earlier in 2:2 and 4:27 trying to do exactly that—thwart Christians and the plan of God. "Schemes" seems to imply that the primary tactic of the enemy is subterfuge and deception, looking "more like seductions than military offensives."[22] That seems to be the thrust of 6:12 as well; in a struggle that is not against "blood and flesh," one can hardly expect conventional maneuvers.[23] Darkness is the sphere of these hosts of evil, wickedness their vocabulary, the world their domain, and supernatural ("spiritual") their resources. One can expect nothing less in opposition than incredible power that calls for an even greater power—*divine* power—in order to overcome them! And that power, God amply provides his children in the form of the "whole armor of God" (6:11).

Four times the picture of "standing" is employed, in 6:11, 13 (×2), 14. This is the goal for believers engaged in spiritual warfare, to *stand* their ground, yielding nary an inch to evil. These deceitful forces are quick to gain a foothold if Christians are not firmly standing in place (see 2:2–3; 4:22, 26–27; 5:6). And such capitulation hinders God's grand plan to consummate all things in Christ (1:10). Though there is a seeming sense of being overwhelmed by the spiritual might of the evil one and his hordes, one cannot but agree that "[t]he entire passage is suffused with a spirit of confidence and hope and the reader is left, not with a feeling of despair, but with the sense that Satan can be defeated."[24] And why should that not be the case, when Christ is "far above every rule and authority and power and dominion"—hostile powers now put by God "in subjection under His [Christ's] feet" (1:21–22)? God's purposes can never be thwarted and even now, his plan to consummate all things in Christ is being triumphantly an-

18. Also see Rom 4:20; Phil 4:13; 1 Tim 1:12; 2 Tim 2:1; 4:17 for divine empowerment.

19. As also found in Rom 13:12; 2 Cor 10:3–6; 1 Thess 5:8; 1 Tim 1:18; and 2 Tim 2:3–4.

20. Snodgrass, *Ephesians*, 339.

21. See 2 Cor 4:4; 11:13–14; 2 Thess 2:9; 1 Tim 4:1–3; 1 John 4:1–3.

22. Fowl, *Ephesians*, 204.

23. In the Greek, it is literally "blood and flesh" (as the translation of 6:12 has it).

24. Page, *Powers of Evil*, 187.

nounced to those already defeated (but still active) forces of evil (3:10). The very existence of the church, the body of Christ, corroborates this inevitable outcome. Perhaps that is why believers are not commanded to win victories in the spiritual warfare they engage in; rather, they are only asked to *stand*—to stand in a victory that has already been won! After all, Paul said, believers are now seated with the victorious Christ in the heavenlies (2:6). Yet another "already-but-not-yet" situation.

"Struggle" (παλή, *palē*; 6:12) is a hapax legomenon in the Greek Bible. The fivefold repetition of the preposition πρός (*pros*, "against,") + accusative (6:12) underscores this struggle. There is the sense of a face-to-face and hand-to-hand combat, perhaps to remind readers that these struggles are fought individual by individual.[25] The last four of these prepositional phrases, all without conjunctions, describe the foes Christians are up against: rulers, authorities, world-forces of darkness, and spiritual beings of evil. They are not of flesh and blood, therefore flesh-and-blood contrivances and devices will never suffice against them.[26] Evil spiritual forces were already encountered in 1:21 and 3:10; and "darkness" in 5:8, 11 (also see 4:18). "World-forces" translates κοσμοκράτωρ (*kosmokratōr*, 6:12), another hapax legomenon, probably the first time it shows up in Greek literature.[27] These are "spiritual" beings (the word πνευματικός, *pneumatikos,* is also used of the Holy Spirit, 1:3; 5:19), likely related to the "the spirit that is now working in the sons of disobedience" (2:2). "The first-century readers of the letter, and we ourselves, need to understand the spiritual dimension of this struggle, the supernatural, evil nature of the opposition, and the necessity of putting on divine armour for the battle. If we think that the Christian life is simply a matter of human effort or exertion, then we have misread the nature of the campaign and will not be able to resist the evil one's fiery darts."[28] In other words, without divine empowerment—divine armor—there can be no victory in this supernatural battle. What exactly the divine armor comprises is listed in the next section, 6:13–17.

12.1.2   *Victory in spiritual warfare is achieved by the employment of God's armor: belt-truth, breastplate-righteousness, shoe-peace, shield-faith, helmet-salvation, and sword-word—each related to the attributes, deeds, or utterances of God.*

This section of this pericope, 6:13–17, begins with "for this reason." In other words, *because of who the foes are,* the armor of God is critical. The focus in 6:13–17—dealing with the divine armor to be donned by Christians—is more on battle preparations than with the actual battle itself. Indeed, Paul says so himself, expecting the Christian "hav-

---

25. Hoehner, *Ephesians,* 825.

26. Of course, these forces of wickedness may work through human (i.e., flesh and blood) institutions, traditions, and power structures—military, societal, judicial, or economic: for example, the involvement of such hostile powers in events of history (1 Thess 2:18), in the circumstances of life (Job 1–2), by imprisonment of saints (Rev 2:10), through the distresses of life (Rom 8:38), with disease (Matt 9:32; 12:22; Luke 9:42), by heresy (2 Cor 11:13–15; 1 Tim 4:1; 1 John 4:1; Col 2:20–21); etc. (from O'Brien, *Ephesians,* 469).

27. It is also found in *T. Sol.* 8.2; 18.2, likely dated later than the NT.

28. Ibid., 468.

ing readied everything, to stand," apparently not an active sort of skirmish (6:13).[29] Ephesians 6:13 essentially reiterates 6:11, but also gives the day of battle a label: "the evil day." The "evil day" has apocalyptic overtones and is associated with end-time events (1 Tim 4:1; 2 Tim 3:1; 4:3; 2 Pet 3:3; Jude 18). But the present age has already been referred to as evil in this letter (Eph 5:16), and the context suggests a warfare that is ongoing, not one that is yet to come. The "evil day" may therefore refer to a present reality marked by "specific times of satanic attack that come with extraordinary force and when the temptation to yield is particularly strong."[30]

In 6:14, there is an imperative, "stand," followed by four participles, "girding," "putting on," "shoeing," and "taking up" (6:14–16). This is how the believer can stand—by donning, as instructed, these items of God's armor: a belt of "truth," a "breastplate of righteousness," feet shod "with the preparation of the gospel of peace," and a "shield of faith." It is not the weapons themselves (or their specific uses in battle) that are important in this war against non-flesh and non-blood adversaries, but the significance of each item.[31] Each is dealt with briefly below.

The belt alluded to was, for a Roman soldier, a leather apron under the armor protecting the thighs. Fastening clothing around the waist indicated readiness for action (Luke 12:35, 37; 17:8); here, of course, it indicates readiness for battle. To be clad with "truth" is to be prepared with God's truth—including the gospel—practically working out in the lives of God's people (Eph 1:13; 4:15, 21, 24, 25; 5:9).

The "breastplate" was a metal piece that protected the chest. To don "righteousness" is to produce righteous fruit in life, as one lives by divine demand (4:24; 5:9 also have "truth" juxtaposed to "righteousness"). This is to put on the new person, to conform to the likeness of God in Christ (4:24).

Footwear is the only item in the panoply that is not found in the description of Yahweh's personal armor in Isa 11:4–5 or 59:17; but it is connected with the Messiah's presence in Isa 52:7. The shoes implied in Eph 6:15 are likely to be the Roman soldier's leather half-boot, open at the sides and ankles, and with metal studs on the sole for traction. "Preparation" translates ἑτοιμασία (hetoimasia), another hapax legomenon. "Of the gospel of peace" has two genitives: the first is likely one of source (preparation sourced in the gospel: "of the gospel") and the second likely one of content (gospel, the content of which is peace: "of peace").[32] "Gospel" (εὐαγγέλιον, euangelion) is always the good news in Ephesians: 1:13 and 6:19, the good news of of salvation (2:17 employs the cognate verb: Christ proclaiming [εὐαγγελίζω, euangelizō] peace); and 3:6, the good news of the unity of all (believing) humankind. In short, in its broad sense, the gospel is the good news of God's grand plan for consummating all things in Christ

29. The verb κατεργάζομαι (katergazomai) can mean to "ready"/"prepare" or "do." The former fits the context, where battle preparations are going to be described in 6:14–17. In other words, 6:13 speaks in general about such preparation; 6:14–17 provides the specifics, i.e., the items of the divine armor to be worn—the readying of everything (6:13). See, for a similar sense of the verb, 2 Cor 4:17; 5:5.

30. Ibid., 471.

31. Best, *Ephesians*, 597.

32. Hoehner, *Ephesians*, 843.

(1:10). All of this produces "peace" (also in 1:2; 2:14, 15, 17; 4:3). Thus the believer in battle is encouraged, prepared by the knowledge of the gospel—God is going to win, his purposes are never going to be thwarted, his plans to consummate all things in Christ is indubitably coming to pass! "It is the believers' 'surefootedness' in the tranquility of the mind and security of the heart in the gospel of peace that gives them readiness to stand against the devil and his angelic hosts."[33] Of course, it is rather ironic that the gospel of peace prepares the child of God for war!

The shield of the soldier was a large rectangular piece of equipment about 4 × 2.5 feet, like a door (which is θύρα, *thyra*, from which comes θυρεός, *thyreos,* "shield"), covered with skins and reinforced with metal. These when soaked with water could quench flaming arrows dipped in pitch.[34] In the OT, God himself is a "shield" (Ps 35:2 LXX). "Of faith" is a genitive of apposition: "shield which is faith" ("faith" is also found in Eph 1:13, 15, 19; 2:8; 3:12, 17; 4:5, 13). Unlike the participles in 6:14–15, the fourth participle, "taking up," dealing with the shield of faith, is preceded by "in all" (6:16). In other words, faith is a requirement for every other activity, it undergirds everything else, and is the ground upon which the believer stands firm. Therefore, "in all" the Christian is to utilize the shield, i.e., faith. And this shield is capable of extinguishing "*all* the flaming arrows of the evil one." No matter what the wile, the stratagem, or device, faith in God in *all* circumstances rescues the child of God from *all* these devastating attacks.

The next verse, 6:17, gives two more items of divine armor: a helmet and a sword, but both are associated with an explicit imperative, "take," though they are still dependent upon the verb "stand" in 6:14. Perhaps "take" indicates that the helmet-salvation and sword-word are "gifts from God and are not 'virtues' in the conventional sense," as are belt-truth, breastplate-righteousness, shoes-peace, and shield-faith.[35]

The helmet of the Roman soldier was a simple metal bowl, with brow, neck, and cheek guards extending from its margins. "Of salvation" is a genitive of apposition: thus, "helmet, which is salvation." "Salvation," seen also in 1:13, is best taken in the broad sense as encompassing justification, sanctification, and glorification—i.e., the larger purpose of God for his children. The element of salvation-past has already been secured (2:5, 8; 5:23); salvation-present is ongoing, and salvation-future is yet to come, but all these are guaranteed by the Holy Spirit, the divine pledge of future glory (1:14). Therefore, believers can be utterly confident of the long-term outcome of their place in the plan of God, i.e., "the redemption of [God's own] possession, for the praise of His glory" (1:14). What reason then to be diffident and despondent in seasons of warfare, though the enemy be strong? This confidence in God's working out of the Christian's salvation, is related, then, to the faith mentioned in 6:16. While the particular item of armor dealing with faith—the shield—dealt with faith in God's protection, this one

---

33. Ibid., 844.

34. O'Brien, *Ephesians*, 479n168, 480.

35. Wild, "The Warrior and the Prisoner," 287.

(helmet-salvation) relates to faith in this particular (and marvelous) work of God in Christ: the entire, sure, and guaranteed process of salvation of the child of God.

Much has been made of the sword as the only offensive armament in the arsenal of the Christian soldier. But without the sword, no itemization of armor would be complete, and therefore it might be best not to read too much into this offensive weapon amongst the other defensive paraphernalia.[36] In any case, "sword" is a short-handled weapon, useful in close-range combat. "Of the Spirit" is a genitive of source, i.e., "sword from the Spirit."[37] So also is "word of God": "word that comes from God." "Word" here is ῥῆμα (*rhēma*), used also in 5:26—there, it referred to the "*the* word" (with an article, unlike in 6:17) of the gospel, that sanctified and cleansed the bride of Christ. In 6:17, this sword-word could be an allusion to Isa 11:2–4 that refers to the Spirit-empowered Messiah who strikes the earth with the "word" (but here it is λογός, *logos*) of his mouth and destroys the wicked with the breath (πνεῦμα) of his lips. Isaiah 11:4 is also cited in 2 Thess 2:8, for Christ's slaying of the antichrist. Thus this implement, the sword, is an appropriate weapon against supernatural forces. But what exactly is the "word of God"? Citing Christ's own response to his temptation (Matt 4:1–11/Luke 4:1–13), Hoehner considers this to refer to Jesus' employment of Scripture in his own spiritual warfare against the devil. Indeed, in reply to the first temptation, Christ cited Deut 8:3: "Man shall not live by bread alone but by every *word* [and it is ῥῆμα here] that comes from the mouth of God" (Matt 4:4). Rather than the preaching of the gospel, the use of the sword-word is the deployment of Scripture against the attacks of the evil one— "speaking the word of God in Christ's name empowered by God's Spirit," who is, after all, the divine author of Scripture.[38]

All of these items of divine armor—belt-truth, breastplate-righteousness, shoe-peace, shield-faith, helmet-salvation, and sword-word—are the attributes (truth, righteousness), deeds (peace, faith, salvation), or utterances of God (word), underscoring the truth that without divine help in all these aspects, there can be no victory against powerful, supernatural foes. Each of these elements, in a sense, describes the natural history of the Christian life, as enabled and empowered by God: the God of *truth* and *righteousness*, accomplishes *salvation* for those who exercise *faith*, and consummates his grand and glorious plan through them, bringing *peace* to humanity and to the cosmos, triumphing over his foes by the power of his *word*. Such a comprehensive view of life, as a battle fought with divine armor, mandates the reliance of the believer upon God for everything, especially in the face of attack from the dominion of darkness.

12.2 Ephesians 6:18–20

THEOLOGICAL FOCUS OF PERICOPE 12.2

---

36. Fowl, *Ephesians*, 208.

37. The Holy Spirit in Ephesians is found in 1:13, 17; 2:18, 22; 3:5, 16; 4:3, 4, 23, 30; 5:18; 6:17, 18.

38. Hoehner, *Ephesians*, 853.

> 12.2   An essential part of the Christian's spiritual warfare is constant, alert engagement in Spirit-driven prayer for all believers, that they may be bold in their proclamation of God's grand plan for the cosmos (6:18–20).

TRANSLATION 12.2

6:18 *With all prayer and petition, praying at all times in the Spirit, and to this end, staying alert with all perseverance and petition for all the saints,*

6:19 *even for me, that word might be given to me in the opening of my mouth, to make known with boldness the mystery of the gospel*

6:20 *—for which I am an ambassador in chains—that about it I may speak boldly, as I ought to speak.*

NOTES 12.2

12.2   An essential part of the Christian's spiritual warfare is constant, alert engagement in Spirit-driven prayer for all believers, that they may be bold in their proclamation of God's grand plan for the cosmos.

While it appears that Eph 6:10–17, loaded with martial metaphors, is distinct from 6:18–20 that lacks those motifs, the whole pericope is one integrated "story": either the main verb of the 6:14–17, "stand" (in 6:14), or the last imperative, "take" (in 6:17),[39] is qualified by the two participles in 6:18, "praying" and "staying alert." "Standing" (or "taking up") and prayer and alertness belong together, partners in the same dangerous undertaking against deadly foes. Besides, "Spirit" is present in both 6:17 and in 6:18, unifying the two sections.

The previous section dealt with the items of divine armor—*God's* operation in warfare, in a sense. Here in 6:18–20, prayer is the focus—*believers'* operation in warfare. Thus, the "praying" and "staying alert," though linked to the previous section, take on an imperatival hue of their own here in 6:18. There are four references to prayer—with two words repeated: "prayer"/"praying" and "petition"[40]—and four uses of the adjective πᾶς (*pas*, "all") in 6:18, emphasizing "the all-embracing, comprehensive nature of the audience's prayer": through "all" (πάσης, *pasēs*) prayer at "all" (παντί, *panti*) times with "all" (πάσῃ, *pasē*) perseverance for "all" (πάντων, *pantōn*) the saints.[41] Prayer itself is not linked to any weapon (the "spear of prayer" would have been conceivable); it apparently needs no analogy with armor for, in fact, it supports every other implement. Perhaps another reason for its not being considered a weapon

---

39. Or even the first imperative of the pericope, "be strong," in 6:10.

40. The different words for prayer are likely to be synonymous, as are other such redundancies in this letter.

41. Heil, *Ephesians*, 291. The alliteration with words beginning with π (*p*) in 6:18 must not be missed: Διὰ πάσης προσευχῆς καὶ δεήσεως προσευχόμενοι ἐν παντὶ καιρῷ ἐν πνεύματι, καὶ εἰς αὐτὸ ἀγρυπνοῦντες ἐν πάσῃ προσκαρτερήσει καὶ δεήσει περὶ πάντων τῶν ἁγίων (*Dia pasēs proseuchēs kai deēseōs proseuchomenoi en panti kairō en pneumati, kai eis auto agrypnountes en pasē proskarterēsei kai deēsei peri pantōn tōn hagiōn*).

is that prayer is always directed towards God, and on behalf of fellow-warriors ("all the saints"), unlike the other accouterments that are not so directed. And after exhorting readers to pray for "all the saints" (6:18), Paul requests prayer for himself, "less than the least of all the saints" (3:8), that he might effectively employ the sword-word in his proclamation of the gospel.[42]

Two ἵνα- (hina-) clauses give the purpose for Paul's request for prayer for himself: that he would be given utterance (i.e., λογός, logos, "word"[43]) to make known the gospel boldly (6:19–20a); and that he would speak boldly "about it" (i.e., about the gospel) as he should (6:20b).[44] "Mystery of the gospel" is a subjective genitive: thus, "mystery announced by the gospel."[45] This is not simply the salvific good news, but the broader plan of God encompassed in *all* the phases of salvation—past, present, and future—and with a scope that spans the cosmos and extends across time: the grand plan of God to consummate all things in Christ (1:10). "If the apostle's own grasp of the mystery is due to God's grace (3:2, 7, 8), it is no less true that he needs divine assistance in its proclamation."[46]

All of this indicates that prayer is being given greater prominence in this martial context than any of the items of armor in the previous section. It is, no doubt, "foundational for the deployment of all other weapons."[47] A supernatural battle can only be waged with supernatural weapons and by tapping into a supernatural power. If Christians are to "stand" successfully in spiritual battles, the donning of God's armor and, perhaps even more, the adoption of prayer as a lifestyle of alertness, in an attitude of constant dependence upon God, is critically important.[48] Such prayer is, appropriately enough, to be conducted "in the Spirit," by his power, and through his advocacy (Rom 8:15–16; Jude 20). Perhaps there is a closer link to the "sword of the Spirit" here; the word authored by the Spirit is uttered by the believer to foes, and prayer in the Spirit is word uttered to God. Words to foes and words to God are both necessary. And in both transactions, it is the Holy Spirit who is the mediator. "Those who are united in their access to the Father through the Spirit ([Eph] 2:18), who are built into God's dwelling place in the Spirit (2:22), [to whom is revealed the plan of God in the Spirit (3:5),] and who are being filled with the Spirit (5:18) can and should pray constantly in

---

42. The conjunction, καί (kai, 6:19) is translated as bearing adjunctive force, "*even* for me." It is customary for Paul to request prayer for himself at the end of his epistles: see Rom 15:30–32; 2 Cor 1:11; Phil 1:10; Col 4:3–4; 1 Thess 5:25; 2 Thess 3:1–2.

43. Though a different Greek word, one cannot but link this with the sword-word of 6:17. To maintain the wordplay, I have translated it literally as "word," but should be taken to mean "utterance."

44. Note that Paul does not ask for prayer that he be released from prison!

45. Another option would be to see it as an epexegetical genitive: thus, "the mystery, i.e., the gospel." Here, too, "gospel" is being seen in its broader sense. "Mystery" in Ephesians was seen elsewhere in 1:9; 3:3, 4, 9; 5:32.

46. O'Brien, *Ephesians*, 486–87.

47. Arnold, *Ephesians*, 112.

48. Incessant prayer is necessary for incessant struggles. Such constant prayer is found elsewhere in Paul in Rom 1:9–10; Phil 1:4; Col 1:3; 4:12; 1 Thess 5:17; 2 Thess 1:11. Paul himself modeled this sort of unceasing intercession in Eph 1:15–23 and 3:14–21.

and through this Spirit."[49] In sum, prayer is to be unceasing in frequency, Spirit-driven in power, zealous in devotion, and ecumenical in breadth.[50]

There is irony in Paul's self-description as "an ambassador in chains" for the mystery-gospel (6:20)—the paradox of dignified status and humiliating station, a contrariness that was already encountered in Pericope 5 (3:1–13). Then again, the apostle's "chains" may be symbolic of his calling—his bondage to Christ, and his obligation to his Lord, and to the message of his God.[51] The context of a battle also gives "chains" significance: it might appear that in a given small sliver of time, supernatural and evil foes are winning. But that is simply the illusion of small sample size. In the larger, broader, ageless context of divine activity, the victory has *already* been won by "the kingdom of Christ and of God" (5:5), though the full manifestation and consummation thereof remains *not yet.*[52]

"Boldness" shows up both as a noun (παρρησία, *parrēsia,* 6:19) and as a cognate verb (6:20). Wild suggests that boldness "most properly refers to the mode of speech which befits a free human being. It is, therefore, first and foremost associated with freedom, whether this freedom be conceived of in the political, moral, or even cosmic orders." Leviticus 26:13 LXX is particularly illuminating in this regard: "I am the Lord your God who redeemed you from the land of Egypt when you were slaves of the land of Egypt and broke the fetters [or "bonds"] of your yoke and led you in freedom [μετὰ παρρησίας, *meta parrēsias*]."[53] As well, Wis 5:1 talks of the "boldness" of the righteous person in confronting persecutors. Paul's oppressors, in context, are *both* the Romans who jailed him, and the hostile cosmic powers behind every evil.

> All of this is to make it clear that the last portion of Eph 6:10–20 is not introduced merely as a bit of autobiographical embroidery. Rather, 6:19–20 presents us with a typological model of true Christian existence in the world. The cosmic and demonic powers still seek to exercise a tyranny over the Christian, and in that sense the Christian appears to be "in bonds." In actuality, however, the bonds are broken and the powers are defeated "in Christ."[54]

And, so, despite chains, shackles, fetters, bonds, or any other temporary deprivation, destitution, or disaster, the child of God persists in living a life pleasing to God (5:10), boldly standing unconquered by the dark forces of wickedness by donning divine armor and by immersion in prayer.

---

49. Lincoln, *Ephesians,* 452.

50. From Thielman, *Ephesians,* 434.

51. O'Brien, *Ephesians,* 489.

52. Temporary setbacks in skirmishes do happen, even when the larger campaign is winning. In Paul's own situation as a prisoner, 2 Tim 4:17 explains that in his appeal to the courts, although there was no one to support the apostle, "the Lord stood with me and empowered me, so that through me the proclamation of the gospel would be fulfilled . . . and I was delivered from the mouth of the lion."

53. Wild, "The Warrior and the Prisoner," 291. The translation of Lev 26:13 and the notes in parentheses are from ibid., 292.

54. Ibid., 294.

12.3 Ephesians 6:21–24

> **THEOLOGICAL FOCUS OF PERICOPE 12.3**
>
> 12.3 Divine peace and love springing from faith—as manifested in the relationships between God's people—as well as grace, suffuse the lives of those who love the Lord Jesus Christ in sincerity (6:21–24).

TRANSLATION 12.3

6:21 *But so that you also may know my circumstances, how I am doing, Tychicus, beloved brother and faithful servant in the Lord, will make everything known to you,*

6:22 *whom I have sent to you for this very purpose, so that you may know about us and that he may encourage your hearts.*

6:23 *Peace to the brethren, and love with faith, from God the Father and the Lord Jesus Christ.*

6:24 *Grace [be] with all those who love our Lord Jesus Christ in sincerity.*

NOTES 12.3

12.3 *Divine peace and love springing from faith—as manifested in the relationships between God's people—as well as grace, suffuse the lives of those who love the Lord Jesus Christ in sincerity.*

These final verses of Ephesians share a personal moment with the readers, as Paul assures his readers about sending Tychicus, likely the carrier of this epistle, to the Ephesians.[55] Yet, after this personal touch, Eph 6:23–24 has Paul wishing peace and grace upon "the brethren," a more distant and third-person address, unlike most of the personal and warm Pauline conclusions.[56] Perhaps this reveals that, writing after a seven-year absence from Ephesus, Paul did not personally know most of his readers. In any case, even for a letter with many redundancies, 6:21–22 seems to be over the top with Paul's anxiety that his readers know about his "circumstances" and "how I am doing," and "everything," and "about us"—he is sure Tychicus will inform and encourage them about Paul's goings-on. It reflects the deep concern the Ephesians likely had for this "ambassador in chains" (6:20).

And then, unusually, there are *two* benedictions, one wishing the Ephesian peace and love (6:23), and the other wishing them grace (6:24).[57] "Peace" and "grace" are found in 1:2, as well, but in reverse order. But it is that part about "love with faith" that is unclear (6:23). The Ephesians had been commended for their faith and love (1:15),

---

55. Besides Eph 6:21–22, Tychicus is mentioned in Acts 20:4; Col 4:7–9; 2 Tim 4:12; and Titus 3:12. The first two verses in this section, Eph 6:21–22, share thirty-two words with Col 4:7–8, except for "how I am doing" in Eph 6:21, and "and fellow-servant" in Col 4:7.

56. Another exception is Gal 6:16.

57. And individually, these are longer than any of the other benedictions uttered by Paul, with the exception of 2 Cor 13:14.

and Christ's indwelling of them was by faith, as they were founded in love (3:17).[58] As Paul wishes them peace amongst themselves, it is likely that he is praying for their deeper love for one another as well, a love based on faith—perhaps faith in God's own love for them in the first place, the basis for all other human loves. Their commendable "love for all the saints" (1:15), however, was not to last; and the final benediction of Paul that they may be possessed of a "love with faith" (6:23) would not bear fruit. For, many years later, another writer of Scripture, in the form of a letter to the same church in Ephesus from Jesus Christ himself, would lament the loss of their "first love," the love they had at first, in former times, perhaps in these days of Paul (Rev 2:4).

While love among believers and God's love for them have been mentioned in Ephesians, Eph 6:24 has the only mention of love *for* Christ.[59] This is a love in ἀφθαρσία (*aphtharsia*). The word usually means immortality or incorruptibility, which is taken by many translators to indicate a love not corrupted by mortality—i.e., believers' unceasing love of Christ.[60] However, Thielman notes that *Pss. Sol.* 6.6b (ca. first century BCE) has a structure similar to Eph 6:24. In both these texts there is listed, in sequence, an abstract quality that God grants humans, the recipients of that grant who love, the object of that love, and another abstract noun prefaced with the preposition ἐν (*en*, "in")[61]:

	Ephesians 6:24	**Psalms of Solomon 6:6**
Blessing		εὐλογητὸς κύριος ὁ ποιῶν (*eulogētos kyrios ho poiōn*) "Blessed be the Lord who shows"
Abstract noun God → man	ἡ χάρις (*hē charis*) "Grace"	ἔλεος (*eleos*) "mercy"
Recipients who love	μετὰ πάντων τῶν ἀγαπώντων (*meta pantōn tōn agapōntōn*) "[be] with all who love"	τοῖς ἀγαπῶσίν (*tois agapōsin*) "to those who love"
Object of that love	τὸν κύριον ἡμῶν Ἰησοῦν Χριστὸν (*ton kyrion hēmōn Iēsoun Christon*) "our Lord Jesus Christ"	αὐτὸν (*auton*) "Him"
Abstract noun + preposition	ἐν ἀφθαρσίᾳ (*en aphtharsia*) "in immortality/incorruptibility"	ἐν ἀληθείᾳ (*en alētheia*) "in truth/sincerity"

58. Love and faith show up together in Ephesians also in 1:15; 2:4 and 2:8; 3:17; 4:2 and 4:13.

59. Love of believers, one for another, was mentioned in 1:15; 4:2, 15, 16; 5:2, 25, 28, 33; the love of God for believers was seen in 1:4; 2:4; 3:17–19; 5:2, 25.

60. Hoehner, *Ephesians*, 874, 877.

61. Thielman, *Ephesians*, 447.

Perhaps this was a common template for liturgical expressions; other similar blessings appear in *Pss. Sol.* 4:25; 10:3; and 14:1. In light of this similarity, "in immortality/incorruptibility" is best understood as a virtue, as is "truth." Thus, the Ephesians love Christ "incorruptibly," or "in sincerity/integrity," quite comparable to the sense of the blessing in *Pss. Sol.* 6:6. May God's grace, Paul prays, be upon those who love the Lord Jesus Christ with a love free from any hint of corruption, who love him "simply and purely, in a way untainted by the futility, darkness, and alienation that characterized his readers' lives ([Eph] 2:1–3; 4:17–19; 5:8–12, 16; cf. 6:12) before they experienced the grace, love, and peace of God through their faith in the gospel."[62] Amen!

SERMON FOCUS AND OUTLINES

THEOLOGICAL FOCUS OF PERICOPE 12

12 Victory against supernatural foes is achieved by divine empowerment in the form of God's armor (commitment and dependence upon God) and by Spirit-driven prayer (6:10–24).

The final pericope of Ephesians is a fitting conclusion to the book, tying in several of the notes sounded earlier. But most importantly, it provides the means of victory against the inimical powers seeking to thwart God's grand and glorious plan to consummate all things in the cosmos in Christ. And the means of victory is divine power accessed by donning the armor of God, and engaging in intercession to God. Each of the elements in the Christian's arsenal—belt-truth, breastplate-righteousness, shoe-peace, shield-faith, helmet-salvation, and sword-word—is related to God, i.e., to his attributes, deeds, or utterances. Prayer in the Spirit for all the saints at all times is essential, if believers are to withstand their formidable foes with boldness. The pericope (and the book) ends with a benediction of peace, and love, and grace to all who love the Lord Jesus Christ sincerely.

The part of the pericope dealing with divine armor is yet another list, creating its own problems for preaching if one seeks to expound the list item by item. A better way is to focus more generally on the importance of divine empowerment for the Christian. Prayer, of course, is a significant facet of the believer's successful encounter with spiritual enemies.

Possible Preaching Outlines for Pericope 12

I. The Attack
      The foes (6:11b–13, 16)
      "Already" defeated, but "not yet" (recap: 1:20–22; 3:10; 4:8)
      The power of these evil foes (recap: 2:2–3; 4:22, 26–27; 5:6)
      Move-to-relevance: How these forces of darkness affect the church
II. The Arms
      The call to arms (6:10, 11, 13a, 14a)
      Divine armor (6:14b–17): characteristics of God
      The call to arms as a call for total dependence upon/commitment to God
      Move-to-relevance: Why we depend on ourselves instead

62. Ibid., 447–48.

II. The Action
    All sorts of prayer, at all times, for all saints (6:18a)
    Prayer in the Spirit and with alertness and perseverance (6:18b)
    Prayer for boldness to discharge one's responsibilities in God's grand plan (6:19–20)
    Peace in a time of war (and love and grace) (6:21–24)
    Move-to-relevance: Why our prayer lives are not rigorous or intensive
III. *Commit to and communicate with the Commander!*
    Specifics on a life of commitment and dependence upon God
    Specifics on improving battle communications with God

With a slight variation, the outline above can be transformed into a standard Problem-Solution-Application structure:

I. PROBLEM: The Campaign
    The foes (6:11b–13, 16)
    "Already" defeated but "not yet" (recap: 1:20–22; 3:10; 4:8)
    The power of these evil foes (a recap: 2:2–3; 4:22, 26–27; 5:6)
    Move-to-relevance: How these forces of darkness affect the church
II. SOLUTION: The Covering
    Divine armor (6:10, 11, 14–17): characteristics of God
    All sorts of prayer, at all times, for all saints (6:18)
    Prayer for boldness to discharge one's responsibilities in God's grand plan (6:19–20)
    Resulting peace in a time of war (and love and grace) (6:21–24)
    Move-to-relevance: Why we depend on ourselves instead
    Move-to-relevance: Why our prayer lives are not rigorous or intensive
III. APPLICATION: *Commit to and communicate with the Commander!*
    Specifics on a life of commitment and dependence upon God
    Specifics on improving battle communications with God

CONCLUSION

*"In the remaining time, be empowered in the Lord,
and in the strength of His might."*

Ephesians 6:10

Those who labor in pulpits on a weekly basis deal with the "the astonishing supposition that texts which are between possibly 3,000 and almost 2,000 years old can offer orientation for the discovery of truth in the third millennium."[1] It is, indeed, a remarkable predication that from these ancient texts may be discerned and preached, not just truth that informs, but truth that transforms—that is applicable and that changes lives for the glory of God. Yet the lot of the homiletician is not easy, neither is the responsibility of such a one minimal: each week, the preacher has to negotiate this formidable passage from ancient text to modern audience to expound, with authority and relevance, a specific biblical pericope for the faithful. But how may this august responsibility be discharged?

> [C]onscientious biblical preachers have long shared the little secret that the classical text-to-sermon exegetical methods produce far more chaff than wheat. If one has the time and patience to stay at the chores of exegesis, theoretically one can find out a great deal of background information about virtually every passage in the Bible, much of it unfortunately quite remote from any conceivable use in a sermon. The preacher's desk can quickly be covered with Ugaritic parallels and details about syncretistic religion in the Phrygian region of Asia Minor. It is hard to find fault here; every scrap of data is potentially valuable, and it is impossible to know in advance which piece of information is to be prized. So, we brace ourselves for the next round of exegesis by saying that it is necessary to pan a lot of earth to find a little gold, and that is true, of course. However, preachers have the nagging suspicion that there is a good deal of wasted energy in the traditional model of exegesis or, worse, that the real business of exegesis is excavation and earth-moving and that any homiletical gold stumbled over along the way is largely coincidental.[2]

1. Schwöbel, "The Preacher's Art," 7.
2. Long, "The Use of Scripture," 343–44.

Unfortunately, commentaries, generally written by biblical scholars not particularly acquainted with preaching, have tended towards with what I call "a hermeneutic of excavation"—the exegetical turning over of tons of earth, debris, rock, boulder, and gravel: a style of interpretation that yields an overload of biblical and Bible-related information, most of it unfortunately not of any particular use for one seeking to preach a relevant message from a specific text.[3] Karl Barth's indictment is appropriate:

> My complaint is that recent commentators confine themselves to an interpretation of the text which seems to me to be no commentary at all, but merely the first step toward a commentary. Recent commentaries contain no more than a reconstruction of the text, a rendering of the Greek words and phrases by their precise equivalents, a number of additional notes in which archaeological and philological material is gathered together, and a more or less plausible arrangement of the subject matter in such a manner that it may be made historically and psychologically intelligible from the standpoint of pure pragmatism.[4]

I have listened to Long and given heed to Barth, and attempted to go beyond random excavation and the "first step toward a commentary," to deliver not so much what the author was *saying* in comprehensible fashion, but also the nuggets—clues from the text as to what the author was *doing* with what he was saying. With an avid interest in preaching, I come to this task of commentary writing with the hope of providing preachers what they can use profitably to create sermons.[5] In other words, *Ephesians: A Theological Commentary for Preachers* is one small attempt in a larger endeavor to help the preacher move safely, accurately, and effectively across the gulf between text and application. Thereby, this intrepid soul, aided by the Holy Spirit, becomes the pastoral agent of the life-transforming truths of Scripture.

Ephesians, like any other book of the Bible, is designed to "seduce" its readers to change their lives in thought, in feeling, and in action, to comply with the precepts, priorities, and practices of God's world (i.e., the theology of the pericope) that is displayed in, with, and through the inspired writing. All this to move God's people to dwell in God's world, aligned to God's values. Or, to put it another way, so that pericope by pericope, God's people would be moved towards Christlikeness—a *christiconic* mode of interpreting Scripture.[6]

That is to say—again!—that the author of Ephesians is *doing* something with what he is saying. The theological agenda of the writer mandates that interpreters, particularly those who interpret for preaching purposes, attend not only to what is being said, but also to what is being *done* with what is being said. In aiding the preacher,

---

3. See Kuruvilla, *A Vision for Preaching.*

4. Barth, "Preface to the Second Edition," 6.

5. It bears repeating that the commentaries in this current series are only "theological" commentaries, not "preaching" commentaries. They take the preacher only part of the way to a sermon, from text to theology (the hermeneutical step). It remains the preacher's burden to complete the crossing by moving from theology to application, i.e., making concrete application that is specific for the particular audience, and presenting all of this in a sermon that is powerful and persuasive (the rhetorical step).

6. See Kuruvilla, *Privilege the Text!* 238–69.

this commentary has approached Ephesians in a unique fashion, undertaking a form of exegesis geared towards discerning the theology of the pericope—the author's *doing-with-his-saying*.[7]

It is a foundational conviction of this work that valid application of a pericope of Scripture may be arrived at only via this critical intermediary between text and praxis, pericopal theology.[8] The hermeneutical philosophy behind this commentary also holds that such valid application to change lives for the glory of God is the appropriate goal of every sermon. As Miroslav Volf put it, "at the heart of every good theology lies not simply a plausible intellectual vision but more importantly a compelling account of a way of life."[9] And the task of the preacher with a pastoral heart ought to include the proffering of specific ways in which the theological focus of the pericope may be translated into the real life of real people.

Here again is the broad theological focus of the entire letter to the Ephesians: *A blessed God blesses his people graciously and lovingly in his beloved Son, redeeming them as his own possession to undertake divinely empowered good works, so that they may manifest his power and glory as a united body of all (believing) humanity, exercising grace-gifts for edification to Christlikeness, with selfless love abandoning all activities not conducive to community, adopting a wise and worshipful lifestyle pleasing to God—filled by the Spirit with the divine fullness of God in Christ, submitting to one another, modeling marital relationships after the Christ-church relationship, maintaining household structures in accordance with God's plan—and gaining victory over supernatural foes by divine empowerment—all of this an integral part of God's grand and glorious plan to consummate all things in the cosmos in Christ.*

As is obvious from this statement, and as has hopefully been evident in the commentary, the larger thrust of Ephesians concerns God's plan to consummate all things in the cosmos in Christ. Indeed, if one desired key verses for the Epistle, it would be Eph 1:8b–10:

1:8b *with all wisdom and insight*

1:9 *He made known to us the mystery of His will, according to His good pleasure that He purposed in Him*

1:10 *for the administration of the fullness of times, the consummation of all things in Christ—the things in the heavens and the things on the earth in Him;*

It is this larger theme that drives the rest of the book, with each pericope of Ephesians contributing a slice or a quantum of theology to this broad theological focus: the God who has blessed his people, including them in this grand and glorious venture, is himself worthy of blessing (Pericope 1; Eph 1:1–14); this grand undertaking is a demonstration of God's incomparable power (Pericope 2; Eph 1:15–23); it all began with

---

7. See Introduction in this work, and Kuruvilla, *Privilege the Text!* 33–65; *Text to Praxis*, 142–90; and "Pericopal Theology," 265–83, for details on this hermeneutical entity, pericopal theology, and its value for the homiletical process.

8. In the commentary, a crystallization of pericopal theology shows up as the "Theological Focus."

9. Volf, *Captive to the Word of God*, 43 (italics removed).

God's saving of believers, by grace through faith, that they may, in service of God's grand plan, demonstrate him to the universe (Pericope 3; Eph 2:1–10), as all (believing) humanity is united in one body in Christ and is becoming the dwelling of God in the Spirit (Pericope 4; Eph 2:11–22); the revelation of God to the cosmos by believers is modeled for them by Paul, "the least of the saints" (Pericope 5; Eph 3:1–10), and takes place as they are conformed to Christ and comprehend Christ's love, thus being filled to the fullness of God, glorifying him (Pericope 6; 3:14–21); specifically, believers selflessly love one another and exercise Christ's grace-gifts toward one another to grow the body into the stature of Christ (Pericope 7; Eph 4:1–16), they eschew licentious living, instead being renewed by God into his likeness (Pericope 8; Eph 4:17–32), they imitate God and please him by being filled by the Spirit, living worshipfully (Pericope 9; Eph 5:1–20), and submissively to one another, especially in spousal relationships that model the Christ-church relationship (Pericope 10; Eph 5:21–33), as well as in child-parent, and employee-employer relationships, thus gaining eternal rewards (Pericope 11; Eph 6:1–9)—all key facets of God's glorious program of consummating all things in Christ, that is clinched by believers' victory over every supernatural anti-God foe as they don divine armor and engage in Spirit-driven prayer (Pericope 12; Eph 6:10–24).

Each pericope of Ephesians thus makes an integral theological contribution to the larger picture. In preaching the book of Ephesians, then, week by week and pericope by pericope, preachers are called to fulfill the solemn responsibility, with divine aid from the Holy Spirit, to align themselves and their listeners closer to the grand and glorious divine program of consummating all things in Christ. Inasmuch as the application propounded by homileticians in each sermon is faithfully assimilated into listeners' lives, creating Christian dispositions and forming Christlike character, the people of God will have aligned themselves to the will of God for the glory of God—the goal of preaching. Text will have become praxis, the people of God will have experienced and enjoyed divine blessings, and Christlikeness will have been inculcated in God's children, for each pericope depicts a facet of Christlikeness. Then one can say, not that the kingdom of God is near, but that, when all things are consummated in Christ, it is actually *here*!

BIBLIOGRAPHY

Arnold, Clinton E. *Ephesians: Power and Magic: The Concept of Power in Ephesians in Light of Its Historical Setting*. Grand Rapids: Baker, 1992.

Bales, William. "The Descent of Christ in Ephesians 4:9." *Catholic Bible Quarterly* 72 (2010) 84–100.

Barth, Karl. "Preface to the Second Edition." In *The Epistle to the Romans*, edited by Karl Barth and translated by Edwyn C. Hoskyns, 2–15. 6th edition. London: Oxford University Press, 1933.

Barth, Markus. *Ephesians: Introduction, Translation, and Commentary on Chapters 1–3*. Anchor Bible 34. New York: Doubleday, 1974.

Bauckham, Richard J. "Pseudo-Apostolic Letters." *Journal of Biblical Literature* 107 (1988) 469–94.

Best, Ernest. *A Critical and Exegetical Commentary on Ephesians*. International Critical Commentary. Edinburgh: T. &. T. Clark, 1998.

———. "The Reading and Writing of Commentaries." *Expository Times* 107 (1996) 358–62.

Bruce, F. F. *The Epistles to the Colossians, to Philemon, and to the Ephesians*. New International Commentary on the New Testament. Grand Rapids: Eerdmans, 1984.

———. "St. Paul in Rome. 4. The Epistle to the Ephesians." *Bulletin of the John Rylands Library* 49 (1967) 303–22.

Caragounis, Chrys C. *The Ephesian* Mysterion: *Meaning and Context*. Lund: CWK Gleerup, 1977.

Coleridge, Samuel Taylor. *Specimens of the Table*. London: John Murray, 1858.

Cranfield, C. E. B. *The Epistle to the Romans*. International Critical Commentary. 2 vols. Edinburgh: T. & T. Clark, 1979.

Dahood, Mitchell. *Psalms II: 51–100*. Anchor Bible 17. Garden City, NY: Doubleday, 1968.

Dawes, Gregory W. *The Body in Question: Metaphor and Meaning in the Interpretation of Ephesians 5:21–33*. Leiden: Brill, 1998.

Dillard, Annie. *Teaching a Stone to Talk: Expeditions and Encounters*. New York: Harper & Row, 1982.

Fee, Gordon D. *Paul, the Spirit, and the People of God*. Peabody, MA: Hendrickson, 1999.

Feynman, Richard P. "Appendix I: Interview with Richard P. Feynman for 'Viewpoint.'" In *Perfectly Reasonable Deviations (From the Beaten Track): The Letters of Richard P. Feynman*, edited by Michelle Feynman, 419–30. New York: Basic Books, 2006.

Foster, Robert L. "'A Temple in the Lord Filled to the Fullness of God': Context and Intertextuality (Eph. 3:19)." *Novum Testamentum* 49 (2007) 86–96.

Fowl, Stephen E. *Ephesians: A Commentary*. New Testament Literature. Louisville: Westminster John Knox, 2012.

Fowler, R. L. "Aristotle on the Period (*Rhet.* 3.9)." *Classical Quarterly* 32 (1982) 89–99.

Girard, Marc. "Love as Subjection, the Christian Ideal for Husbands and Wives: A Structuralist Study of Ephesians 5:21–33." In *Women Also Journeyed with Him: Feminist Perspectives on the Bible*, translated by Madeleine Beaumont, 125–52. Collegeville, MN: Liturgical, 2000.

Gombis, Timothy G. "Being the Fullness of God in Christ by the Spirit: Ephesians 5:18 in its Epistolary Setting." *Tyndale Bulletin* 53.2 (2002) 259–72.

———. "Cosmic Lordship and Divine Gift-Giving: Psalm 68 in Ephesians 4:8." *Novum Testamentum* 47 (2005) 367–80.

———. *The Drama of Ephesians: Participating in the Triumph of God*. Downers Grove, IL: InterVarsity, 2010.

———. "Ephesians 2 as a Narrative of Divine Warfare." *Journal for the Study of the New Testament* 26 (2004) 405–8.

———. "Ephesians 3:2–13: Pointless Digression, or Epitome of the Triumph of God in Christ?" *Westminster Theological Journal* 66 (2004) 313–23.

Grudem, Wayne. "Does Κεφαλή ('Head') Mean 'Source' or 'Authority Over' in Greek Literature? A Survey of 2,336 Examples." *Trinity Journal* 6 (1985) 38–59.

Harris, W. Hall, III. "The Ascent and Descent of Christ in Ephesians 4:9–10." *Bibliotheca Sacra* 151 (1994) 198–214.

Heil, John Paul. *Ephesians: Empowerment to Walk in Love for the Unity of All in Christ.* Studies in Biblical Literature 13. Atlanta: SBL, 2007.

Hoehner, Harold W. *Ephesians: An Exegetical Commentary.* Grand Rapids: Baker, 2002.

Knight, George W., III. "Husbands and Wives as Analogues of Christ and the Church: Ephesians 5:21–33 and Colossians 3:18–19." In *Recovering Biblical Manhood and Womanhood*, edited by John Piper and Wayne Grudem, 165–98. Wheaton: Crossway, 1991.

Köstenberger, Andreas J. "What Does it Mean to be Filled with the Spirit? A Biblical Investigation." *Journal of the Evangelical Theological Society* 40 (1997) 229–40.

Kuhn, Karl Georg. "The Epistle to the Ephesians in the Light of the Qumran Texts." In *Paul and Qumran: Studies in New Testament Exegesis,* edited by Jerome Murphy-O'Connor, 115–31. Chicago: Priory Press, 1968.

Kuruvilla, Abraham. *A Vision for Preaching: Understanding the Heart of Pastoral Ministry.* Grand Rapids: Baker, forthcoming.

———. *Genesis: A Theological Commentary for Preachers.* Eugene, OR: Resource, 2014.

———. "Pericopal Theology: An Intermediary between Text and Application." *Trinity Journal* 31 (2010) 265–83.

———. *Privilege the Text! A Theological Hermeneutic for Preaching.* Chicago: Moody, 2013.

———. *Text to Praxis: Hermeneutics and Homiletics in Dialogue.* Library of New Testament Studies 393. London: T. & T. Clark, 2009.

Lee-Barnewall, Michelle. "Turning Κεφαλή on its Head: Paul's Argumentative Strategy in Eph. 5:21–33." In *Christian Origins and Greco-Roman Culture: Social and Literary Contexts for the New Testament*, edited by Stanley E. Porter and Andrew W. Pitts, 599–614. Early Christianity in Its Hellenistic Context 1. Texts and Editions for New Testament Study 9. Leiden: Brill, 2013.

Lincoln, Andrew T. *Ephesians.* WBC 42. Nashville: Thomas Nelson, 1990.

Long, Thomas G. "The Use of Scripture in Contemporary Preaching." *Interpretation* 44 (1990) 341–52.

Lunde, Jonathan M., and John Anthony Dunne. "Paul's Creative and Contextual Use of Psalm 68 in Ephesians 4:8." *Westminster Theological Journal* 74 (2012) 99–117.

Metzger, Bruce M. "St. Paul and the Magicians." *Princeton Seminary Bulletin* 38 (1944) 27–30.

Norden, Eduard. *Agnostos Theos: Untersuchungen zur Formengeschichte religiöser Rede.* Leipzig: B. G. Teubner, 1913.

O'Brien, Peter T. *The Letter to the Ephesians.* Pillar New Testament Commentary. Grand Rapids: Eerdmans, 1999.

Page, Sydney H. T. *Powers of Evil: A Biblical Study of Satan and Demons.* Grand Rapids: Baker, 1994.

———. "Whose Ministry? A Re-appraisal of Ephesians 4:12." *Novum Testamentum* 47 (2005) 26–47.

Reinhard, Donna R. "Ephesians 6:10–18: A Call to Personal Piety or Another Way of Describing Union with Christ?" *Journal of the Evangelical Theological Society* 48 (2005) 521–32.

Schwöbel, Christoph. "The Preacher's Art: Preaching Theologically." In *Theology Through Preaching*, edited by Colin Gunton, 1–20. Edinburgh: T. & T. Clark, 2001.

Second Council of Nicaea. *Sacred Councils: Book 8.* Edited by Philip Labbe. Revised by Sebastian Colet. Venice: Sebastianum Coleti et Jo. Baptistam Albrizzi, 1729.

Smith, Gary V. "Paul's Use of Psalm 68:18 in Ephesians 4:8." *Journal of the Evangelical Theological Society* 18 (1975) 181–89.

Smith, James K. A. *Desiring the Kingdom: Worship, Worldview, and Cultural Formation.* Cultural Liturgies 1. Grand Rapids: Baker Academic, 2009.

———. *Imagining the Kingdom: How Worship Works.* Cultural Liturgies 2. Grand Rapids: Baker Academic, 2013

Snodgrass, Klyne. *Ephesians.* New International Version Application Commentary. Grand Rapids: Zondervan, 1996.

Temple, William. *Nature, Man, and God.* Edinburgh: T. & T. Clark, 1940.

Thielman, Frank. *Ephesians.* Baker Exegetical Commentary on the New Testament. Grand Rapids: Baker, 2010.

Volf, Miroslav. *Captive to the Word of God: Engaging the Scriptures for Contemporary Theological Reflection.* Grand Rapids: Eerdmans, 2010.

Wallace, Daniel B. *Greek Grammar Beyond the Basics: An Exegetical Syntax of the New Testament.* Grand Rapids: Zondervan, 1996.

Wild, Robert A. "The Warrior and the Prisoner: Some Reflections on Ephesians 6:10–20." *Catholic Bible Quarterly* 46 (1984) 284–98.

Witherington, Ben. *The Letters to Philemon, the Colossians, and the Ephesians: A Socio-Rhetorical Commentary on the Captivity Epistles.* Grand Rapids: Eerdmans, 2006.

INDEX OF ANCIENT SOURCES

GRECO-ROMAN WRITINGS

INDEX OF MODERN AUTHORS

INDEX OF SCRIPTURE

Made in the USA
Monee, IL
26 September 2020